PSYCHOEDUCATIONAL ASSESSMENT

PSYCHOEDUCATIONAL ASSESSMENT
Integrating Concepts and Techniques

George B. Helton, Ph.D.
Associate Professor
Department of Psychology
University of Tennessee at Chattanooga
Chattanooga, Tennessee

Edward A. Workman, Ed.D.
Assistant Professor
Department of Psychology
University of Tennessee at Chattanooga
Chattanooga, Tennessee

Paula A. Matuszek, Ph.D.
Assistant Professor
Department of Educational and Counseling Psychology
University of Tennessee at Knoxville
Knoxville, Tennessee

Grune & Stratton
A Subsidiary of Harcourt Brace Jovanovich, Publishers
New York   London
Paris   San Diego   San Francisco   São Paulo
Sydney   Tokyo   Toronto

Library of Congress Cataloging in Publication Data

Helton, George B.
  Psychoeducational assessment.

  Bibliography.
  Includes index.
  1. Ability—Testing. 2. Educational tests and
measurements. I. Workman, Edward, 1952– .
II. Matuszek, Paula A. III. Title.
LB1131.H38567 1982   371.2'6   82-11775
ISBN 0-8089-1482-0

Grune & Stratton, Inc.
111 Fifth Avenue
New York, New York 10003

Distributed in the United Kingdom by
Academic Press Inc. (London) Ltd.
24/28 Oval Road, London NW 1

Library of Congress Catalog Number 82-11775
International Standard Book Number 0-8089-1482-0
Printed in the United States of America

To our families

Contents

Acknowledgments

We WOULD LIKE to express our appreciation to a number of people who contributed to the preparation of this book. Editorial assistance was provided by Debbie Edgemon, Linda Helton, Jennifer Mason, Deborah Monroe, and Jenny Partin. Joseph Ballard, Eugene Bartoo, George Fincher, Louise Helton Miller, Larry Roberts, Marty Roberts, Barbara Thomas, and Barry Torrence provided helpful information and/or reactions. Louise Helton Miller and Ted Miller furnished initial encouragement. Our spouses—Linda Helton, Brooks Workman, and David Matuszek—gave the support and understanding necessary for the book's completion. Debbie Edgemon and Karen Mayes typed the manuscript in a timely and skillful fashion. The staff of Grune & Stratton assisted patiently in the book's development. All of these people deserve our sincere thanks.

In addition, appreciation is extended to the authors and publishers who gave us permission to quote from their works. Since material from some works appears throughout the book, we gratefully acknowledge these sources and permissions below:

American Psychological Association. Ethical principles for psychologists. *American Psychologist*, 1981, *36*, 633–638. Copyright 1981 by the American Psychological Association. Reprinted by permission of the publisher and author.

Bersoff, D., & Miller, T. Ethical and legal issues in behavioral assessment. In D. Sabatino & T. Miller (Eds.), *Describing learner characteristics of handicapped children and youth*. New York: Grune & Stratton, 1979. With permission.

Davis, W. *Educator's resource guide to special education*. Boston: Allyn and Bacon, 1980. With permission.

Helton, G., & Workman, E. Considerations in assessing the mildly handicapped. In T. Miller & E. Davis (Eds.), *The mildly handicapped student*. New York: Grune & Stratton, 1982. With permission.

Martin, R. *Educating handicapped children: The legal mandate*. Champaign, Ill: Research Press, 1979. With permission.

Miller, T. A review of the psychometric approach to measurement. In D. Sabatino & T. Miller (Eds.), *Describing learner characteristics of handicapped children and youth.* New York: Grune & Stratton, 1979. With permission.

National Association of School Psychologists. Principles for professional ethics. *Membership Directory.* Washington, D.C.: National Association of School Psychologists, 1978. With permission.

Reschly, D. Nonbiased assessment. In G. Phye & D. Reschly (Eds.), *School psychology: Perspectives and issues.* New York: Academic Press, 1979. With permission.

Preface

W E STRONGLY BELIEVE that the ultimate purpose of psychoeducational assessment is to promote the welfare of children who are assessed, and we hope that this book will be helpful in achieving this goal in terms of current assessment conditions. Such conditions include the need for assessment to serve both classification and programming functions. Limited resources for assessment require that these functions be served as efficiently as possible, without compromising legal and ethical requirements in the promotion of children's welfare—a difficult challenge.

While we believe that careful attention must be given to the classification function of assessment, we also believe that assessment must serve its programming function more effectively than it has in the past. We suggest that programming efforts are best served by behavioral-ecological approaches to assessment and recommend such approaches, whenever appropriate, throughout the book. We also comment from time to time on what we see as needed improvements in both assessment techniques and the legal and situational contexts in which assessment is conducted.

In a more general sense, we also believe that assessment must involve an integration of a variety of factors. In assessing an individual child, the assessment practitioner must be aware of the purposes to be served by the assessment, the available assessment models, the domains in which assessment is conducted, the technical adequacy of various assessment techniques, legal considerations, ethical considerations, and situational constraints. Many practitioners experience difficulty in successfully integrating these factors in assessment practice. The difficulty can usually be traced to a lack of understanding of one or more of the factors or to the lack of a system that includes them all. Hence, another of our goals in writing this book is to provide a basic understanding of each of the factors and a system for integrating them in assessment practice.

The book is divided into three sections. Chapter 1 provides an overview of the major factors involved in assessment and of our system for integrating these factors. Part I (Chapters 2 through 4) covers legal and ethical considerations in assessment. Part II (Chapters 5 through 11) describes representative techniques associated with the major domains in which assessment is conducted. In this section, separate chapters are devoted to the assessment of health factors, general intellectual functioning, modality skills, academic functioning, social/emotional functioning, adaptive behavior, and environmental influences on school coping. Within each of these chapters, the techniques are discussed in terms of their usefulness for classification and programming, their relationship to assessment models, their technical adequacy, and their practicality. Part III provides a more detailed explication (including case examples) of our integrative system for assessment practice.

The contents of the book emphasize certain topics that we see as important in assessment practice but that appear to be under-represented in many general assessment books—topics such as legal and ethical considerations in assessment and assessing environmental influences on school coping. We hope to provide a better understanding of these topics without sacrificing adequate coverage of more traditional topics in assessment, such as techniques used in various assessment domains and the technical adequacy of assessment techniques. Where the latter is considered, the book will be most helpful to persons with prior or concurrent instruction in measurement and statistics.

Space limitations preclude an exhaustive review of all assessment techniques that can be used in the various assessment domains. Instead, we discuss representative individually administered assessment techniques within each domain. Some techniques were chosen for discussion because of their frequent use, while others were chosen because we believe them to be particularly valuable. Some attention is given to use of these techniques with lower-incidence handicapped populations, but the major focus is on their use with higher-incidence handicapped populations.

We also lack space to present detailed discussions of the steps involved in integrating data on individual children and in report writing. However, the final chapter provides a description of the steps involved in integrating the basic factors of assessment into general assessment practice, and the case report illustrations in this chapter can serve as models for data analysis and report writing on individual children.

We hope that this book will be helpful to both students in child

assessment disciplines and persons currently engaged in psychoeducational assessment practice. We particularly hope that the reader
will react thoughtfully to our presentations, and we shall be satisfied
if these reactions are incorporated into and enhance the reader's own
approach to psychoeducational assessment.

Factors Involved in Psychoeducational Assessment

WE VIEW psychoeducational assessment as a complex endeavor requiring knowledge of a number of topics (such as child development and principles of measurement), many specific skills (such as test administration and interpretation, report writing, and consultation), and a good understanding of the social contexts in which assessment occurs. The breadth of knowledge and skills needed for effective assessment practice is not always understood by persons new to the field, who often anticipate that assessment primarily involves learning how to give, score, and interpret a number of specific tests. While these skills are, in fact, crucial to effective assessment practice, further assessment experience typically leads to an understanding that assessment involves a number of factors, all of which must be integrated in practice. This understanding is also accompanied by a perception that the integration of relevant factors in assessment practice is a difficult task and that each assessment practitioner must develop his or her own approaches to this task.

This book presents our approach to this challenging task and is designed both for students in child assessment disciplines and persons currently engaged in psychoeducational assessment practice. Thoughtful reactions to the book's contents by readers in both groups should enhance their personal conceptions of effective assessment practice.

With this in mind, we believe that assessment requires an integration of seven key factors. They are (1) the purposes to be served by assessment; (2) assessment models; (3) the domains in which assessment is conducted; (4) the technical adequacy of various assessment techniques; (5) legal considerations; (6) ethical considerations; and finally (7) situational constraints. While intellectual understanding of these factors and of the need to integrate them in practice cannot guarantee appropriate assessment, a clear understanding of each factor can help the assessment practitioner determine the needs of the children he or she wishes to serve. To be effective, the practitioner must also stay abreast of fairly rapid changes in both the techniques of assessment and the contexts in which these techniques are used.

This latter point is well illustrated by the Reagan administration's proposed changes in the legal, financial, and administrative contexts of psychoeducational assessment practice. These proposed changes involve efforts to (1) abolish the U.S. Department of Education; (2) shift federal responsibilities in special education from categorical to block grant programs; (3) reduce federal funds for the education of handicapped persons; and (4) deregulate major federal laws that affect education for handicapped persons (Public Law 94-142 and Section 504 of Public Law 93-112). While this book describes context factors in psychoeducational assessment as they currently exist, readers should attempt to determine the outcomes of the efforts mentioned above. To aid this process, we provide discussions of these efforts at the end of this chapter and elsewhere in the book. In addition, we provide footnotes in this chapter and Chapter 2 that describe sections of federal regulations identified as "targets of opportunity for deregulation" in a briefing paper developed by the Office of Special Education and Rehabilitative Services, U.S. Department of Education (Note 1). The Reagan administration views these sections as exceeding statutory requirements.

We now turn to a discussion of the purposes of psychoeducational assessment. Our discussion includes both current emphases and possible future emphases in the purposes of assessment.

PURPOSES OF ASSESSMENT

Individual psychoeducational assessments are typically conducted to serve two purposes. These purposes have been described by Coulter and Morrow (1978) as involving, first, the classification of children as handicapped and, second, the design of programs to meet their needs. Initially, these two purposes seem quite straightforward and complementary. Unfortunately, such is not the case, since there are a number of problems in achieving each purpose and a good integration of the two purposes. In addition, fulfilling and integrating these two purposes should advance the ethical goal of promoting the welfare of children who are assessed.

Classification

It must be recognized from the outset that any system for classifying people experiencing problems is intended to serve multiple purposes. These purposes typically include conducting research on the etiology and remediation of problems, organizing public and private service agencies, planning services, funding services, and accounting for funds expended for service provision (Hobbs, 1980). To be maximally effective, any classification system (or combination of systems) must serve all of these purposes reasonably well. Unfortunately, the current classification system used in the identification of handicapped children serves only some of them well (Bardon & Bennett, 1974; Duffey, Salvia, Tucker, & Ysseldyke, 1981; Helton & Workman, 1982; Hobbs, 1975, 1980). This situation raises a number of difficult issues for psychoeducational assessment practitioners.

For most psychoeducational assessment practitioners, classification involves deciding whether or not each child assessed is eligible for one or more of the handicapping-condition labels found in the regulations implementing Public Law (PL) 94-142, the Education for All Handicapped Children Act of 1975 (*Federal Register*, August 23, 1977). Children so labeled on the basis of assessment results are eligible for special education services and related services as required by this law. Specifically, the regulations implementing PL 94-142 provide for special education services for children classified as

> mentally retarded, hard of hearing, deaf, speech impaired, visually handicapped, seriously emotionally disturbed, orthopedically impaired, other health impaired, deaf-blind, multi-handicapped, or as having specific learning disabilities, who because of these impairments need special education and related services. (*Federal Register*, August 23, 1977, p. 42478)

PL 94-142 has been described as a mechanism "for a historic break-through in providing educational services to all handicapped children" (Cruickshank, 1979, p. xiii). This law mandates a free and appropriate public education for handicapped children, guarantees due process rights to handicapped children and their parents, requires a written individualized educational program (IEP) for each handicapped child, and stipulates that handicapped children should be educated in the least restrictive environment possible (Davis, 1980, p. 239).* We view these provisions of the law as laudatory. However, the classification system embodied in PL 94-142 has a number of serious shortcomings. As a result, the classification system serves only some of its intended purposes well.

Those purposes well served by the classification system embodied in PL 94-142 include the provision of a conceptual framework "for writing legislation, organizing government bureaus, channeling the flow of funds, mobilizing advocacy groups, and defining professional territories and agency domains" (Hobbs, 1980, p. 286). In other words, this system provides workable mechanisms for funding and administering special education services. However, the system is seriously flawed in relation to the pupose of meeting the needs of children with problems. Some of these flaws involve imprecision in the handicapping-condition labels (Bardon & Bennett, 1974; Duffey et al., 1981); a lack of relationship between the labels and the instructional needs of those labeled (Bardon & Bennett, 1974; Hallahan & Kauffman, 1976); and the fact that numerous children can "fall between the cracks" of current service-delivery systems and fail to receive needed help (Hobbs, 1980).

In relation to the latter point, psychoeducational assessment practitioners are acutely aware that children experiencing school problems will usually not be eligible for special education services unless they are assigned one of the handicapping-condition labels found in PL 94-142. Since there are numerous reasons for children to experience school problems, many children referred for assessment will not be so labeled. It should be noted that individual states can permit more children to be eligible for special education services by expanding the list of handicapping conditions found in PL 94-142. This step involves adding handicapping conditions not covered by the federal law to state laws. However, expanding the number of children served by adding handicapping conditions to state laws may be very difficult in the context of a tight economy. Therefore, many children referred for school problems will not be provided special education services.

---

*Sections of the regulations implementing the free and appropriate education, due process, IEP, and least restrictive environment provisions of PL 94-142 have been identified as "targets of opportunity for deregulation" according to a briefing paper developed by the Office of Special Education and Rehabilitative Services (Note 1). A discussion of deregulation efforts is presented at the end of this chapter and additional "opportunities for deregulation" are discussed in footnotes appearing in this chapter and Chapter 2.

Some of these children found ineligible for special education services are eligible for other remedial services. For example, numerous children receive such assistance through Title I (now Chapter 1 of the Educational Consolidation and Improvement Act) programs for economically disadvantaged, underachieving children. Nevertheless, many children with problems cannot be classified either as handicapped or as economically disadvantaged, and in most cases, they remain the exclusive responsibilities of their regular classroom teachers. Such children may, in that sense, "fall between the cracks" of the schools' service-delivery systems.

Assessment practitioners react in various ways to the possibility of referred children's failing to receive services. Some practitioners see their primary responsibility as enabling the maximum number of children to be labeled as handicapped so that they can receive special education services. These practitioners often fear that the children's regular classroom teachers are unable or unwilling to respond effectively to the problems that led to referral. They are also aware that state and federal funds for special education services are often allocated on the basis of the number of children within the school district identified as handicapped. Classifying most of the children referred as handicapped is therefore seen as beneficial both to the children and to their school districts.

Other practitioners are more concerned about protecting children from handicapping-condition labels. Such practitioners often describe these labels as stigmatizing to the children who receive them, and they also tend to focus on legal and ethical problems involved in assigning labels to children who may not deserve them. Assigning labels is usually not problematic with severely handicapped children. However, most children in special education programs are mildly handicapped, and since the criteria defining the milder handicapping conditions tend to be vaguely stated in the law (Bardon & Bennett, 1974; Duffey et al., 1981), decisions about labeling such children are often difficult. To complicate matters further, these practitioners are often aware of equivocal research findings on the benefits associated with special class placements of mildly handicapped children. Such findings are discussed in sources such as MacMillan and Meyers (1980) and Carlberg and Kavale (1980).

Many graduate students and some practitioners in child assessment disciplines react to the issues involved in labeling by calling for the elimination of all labels as prerequisites for special education services. We recognize the good intentions underlying this call but view it as impractical. We instead concur with Hobbs's (1975) argument that some type of classification system will probably always be needed if children are to receive the special education services they need. If Hobbs is correct, then the most appropriate task before us is developing and implementing classification systems less problematic than those found in PL 94-142.

One approach to this task is to move away from classification systems that categorize children in terms of handicapping-condition labels. In this vein, Hobbs (1975, 1980) proposes that an ecologically oriented, service-based classification system for children needing special services be adopted. He suggests that such a noncategorical classification system will improve the effectiveness of services to children experiencing school difficulties by focusing on the specific services they require in order to function more successfully. Presumably this system would also result in fewer children failing to receive services.

Other authors (Hallahan & Kauffman, 1976; Duffey et al., 1981; Helton & Workman, 1982) join Hobbs in calling for noncategorical classification systems. To illustrate, Duffey et al. urge the abandonment of "such imprecise diagnostic classifications as 'mental retardation,' 'emotional disturbance,' and 'learning disabilities' " in favor of "classification systems based on purely educational criteria" (p. 433). They argue that classification in terms of levels of development of educational skills would result in assessment being "based on the actual service provided by the schools: the teaching of a curriculum" (p. 433). As previously noted, Bardon and Bennett (1974) and Hallahan and Kauffman (1976) suggest that handicapping-condition labels are largely irrelevant to the teaching of a curriculum, since they provide little specific guidance in developing IEPs for those labeled.

We frankly agree that a need exists for noncategorical classification systems such as those proposed by Hobbs (1975, 1980) and by Duffey et al. (1981). To represent an overall improvement, however, such systems must not only solve the problems embedded in the current classification system but must also provide workable mechanisms for funding and administering special education services. Hobbs (1980) believes that noncategorical classification systems can serve most important purposes reasonably well and points with hope to recent implementations of such systems in Massachusetts and Connecticut.

We hope that these experiments with noncategorical classification systems will prove successful and thereby stimulate similar developments on both state and national levels. However, replacing the categorical classification system found in PL 94-142 represents only one of the two options appropriate to the resolution of labeling issues. The second option is to improve the quality of the assessments that lead to classifications of children as handicapped under the current system (Duffey et al., 1981).

In spite of our philosophical commitment to noncategorical classification systems, this book is directed primarily toward the second option. Most psychoeducational assessment practitioners must currently classify children under the requirements of PL 94-142, and it is too early to tell whether noncategorical classification systems will come to be widely adopted. Hence, this book's primary concern with improving assessment under the current classification system appears to us to be its most currently practical focus.

Programming

Psychoeducational assessment must identify a child's specific problems in educational functioning and must also yield information useful in planning a program to remediate those problems. Again, these tasks appear initially to be quite straightforward, but a number of difficult decisions are involved in assessment for programming. Legal mandates concerning classification and programming services, divergent assessment and programming models, and situational constraints all affect programming decisions and increase the difficulty of making such decisions. Since these decisions will be discussed in greater detail elsewhere in this and other chapters, they will be only briefly introduced here.

We indicated previously that PL 94-142 requires a written IEP for each child identified as handicapped. The intent of this requirement of the law is to provide for each child's appropriate development. This intent will be realized only to the degree that each IEP is well constructed and well implemented. Hence, the adequacy of IEPs is an important consideration in providing special education programs of high quality. Legally, an adequate IEP is defined as one that includes

(a) A statement of the child's present levels of educational performance; (b) a statement of annual goals, including short-term educational objectives; (c) a statement of the specific special education and related services to be provided to the child, and the extent to which the child will be able to participate in regular educational programs; (d) the projected dates for initiation of services; and (e) appropriate objective criteria and evaluation procedures and schedules for determining, on at least an annual basis, whether the short-term instructional objectives are being achieved. (*Federal Register*, August 23, 1977, p. 42491)*

It should be noted that section *c* refers to "related services." The regulations implementing PL 94-142 define *related services* as including

transportation and such developmental, corrective, and other supportive services as are required to assist a handicapped child to benefit from special education and includes speech pathology and audiology, psychological services, physical and occupational therapy, recreation, early identification and assessment of disabilities in children, counseling services, and medical services for diagnostic or evaluation purposes. The term also includes school health services, social work services in schools, and parent counseling and training. (*Federal Register*, August 23, 1977, p. 42479)†

As the above passages make clear, assessment for programming must involve specifications of a child's educational performance levels and subsequent judgments about reasonable progress goals, criteria by which to judge progress, special educational and related services needed by the child for progress to occur, and the degree to which the child should participate in school activities with nonhandicapped peers. The regulations implementing PL 94-142 require that these judgments be made by a specified group of people. This group must include a representative of the public agency qualified to provide or supervise special education, the child's teacher, personnel knowledgeable about assessment procedures, one or both of the child's parents, the child (if appropriate), and other persons at the discretion of the parents or the school.‡

If the IEP content and group participation requirements have been met, the resulting IEP is legally adequate. Unfortunately, however, a legally adequate IEP may be ineffective in promoting a child's appropriate development. In order to do so, the IEP must incorporate

---

*While sections of the regulations implementing the IEP provision of PL 94-142 have been identified as "targets of opportunity for deregulation," the wording of this particular section is very close to statutory language.

†Most of the related services in the regulations and listed above are also mentioned in PL 94-142. However, the related services of parent counseling and training, school health services, and social work services in schools are not.

‡PL 94-142 does not mention participation of other persons in the IEP meeting at the discretion of the parents or the school. Hence, this option for participation in IEP meetings represents an "opportunity for deregulation."

reasonable judgments about the child's programming needs. Such judgments require knowledgeable choice between divergent assessment and programming models.

Two models relevant to assessment and to programming judgments are the psychoeducational process model and the task analysis model, as described by Mercer and Ysseldyke (1977). These models differ in important ways in their assumptions about what factors are most relevant for programming purposes. In essence, the professional debate between proponents of these two models involves different views about what types of deficits in children should be addressed in efforts to remediate their learning problems.

The *psychoeducational process model* assumes that children experience learning difficulties as a result of deficits in processing skills, such as visual perception, auditory perception, and short-term memory. Since it is assumed that adequate processing skills are a prerequisite to academic success, it then becomes important to identify and remediate each child's processing skills deficits.

The *task analysis model*, on the other hand, assumes that children have difficulty learning because of past failures to master prerequisite academic skills incorporated in a hierarchy of skills. An example of such an assumption is that children must learn to discriminate the letters of the alphabet from one another before learning the sounds associated with each letter. From this perspective, it is crucial to identify the lower-level skills that have not been mastered and to help children master such skills. "It is assumed that the acquisition of academic skills in a sequential fashion will best facilitate academic success and that remediation of processing skills deficits is less clearly relevant to improving students' academic performances" (Helton & Workman, 1982).

It should be evident that one's choice of assessment techniques and approaches will be governed to some extent by a primary allegiance to either the psychoeducational process model or the task analysis model. We believe that a primary allegiance to either should represent an informed choice, and we present both models in greater detail in the next section. In later chapters, we describe how psychoeducational processing skills may be conceptualized and assessed as "entering behaviors" in the context of our primary allegiance to the task analysis model.

Before we proceed to a more detailed discussion of assessment and programming models, it should be noted that situational constraints can affect assessment for programming through two interacting factors. First, PL 94-142 requires that assessment serve both classification and programming purposes. This dual requirement would present few practical problems were it not for the second factor of limited resources for psychoeducational assessment Time, in particular, is often limited, and assessment practitioners must frequently try to serve both classification and programming purposes in the shortest time possible.

Time pressures are exacerbated by the fact that most assessment instruments and approaches have been designed primarily for either classification or programming purposes (Coulter, 1980a). Thus, an instrument or approach designed for one of these purposes may be of little or no value for the other.

We advocate a "branching" assessment system (described in more detail at the end of this chapter) as the most appropriate response to the need for psychoeducational assessment to serve both classification and programming purposes in the context of limited time for assessment. This system incorporates a series of steps to be followed in conducting an assessment and permits practitioners to choose techniques and approaches appropriate to both classification and programming purposes. In addition, it permits individualization of assessment techniques and approaches in terms of the unique characteristics of each child assessed. It also permits the use of both psychoeducational process models and task analysis models as needed to address the dual purposes of assessment and the unique characteristics of the child. Finally, it results in time-efficient assessment, since only assessment techniques and approaches clearly relevant to the referring problem are used. It should be noted that this system does not, in our opinion, represent a particularly innovative organizational procedure. It is instead, a distillation of what we regard as the best practices already in use.

ASSESSMENT MODELS

We have described the psychoeducational process model and the task analysis model as the models most relevant to the programming function of psychoeducational assessment. Three other models are especially relevant to the classification function of psychoeducational assessment: the medical model, the social-system model, and the pluralistic model. A detailed discussion of these five models follows.

Programming Models

To be used effectively for programming purposes, both the psychoeducational process model and the task analysis model should satisfy the evidential requirements of four assumptions (Ysseldyke, 1979): (1) the deficits in children emphasized by the model cause academic problems; (2) the deficits emphasized by the model can be reliably and validly assessed; (3) the deficits emphasized by the model can be remediated; and (4) remediation of the deficits emphasized by the model leads to improved academic performance.

Ysseldyke asserts that the task analysis model is more successful than the psychoeducational process model in satisfying the evidential requirements of these assumptions. The importance of this issue requires that we examine the bases of his assertion.

Ysseldyke notes that there is correlational evidence linking psychoeducational processing skill levels to levels of academic performance. While this evidence suggests that processing skill deficits in children cause them to experience academic problems, it does not prove it, he argues. Proof for this first assumption of the psychoeducational process model requires experimental, rather than correlational, evidence, and such evidence has not yet been found. Given this situation, Ysseldyke concludes that the psychoeducational process model does not currently satisfy the evidential requirements for its first assumption. In contrast, the task analysis model currently satisfies the evidential requirements; numerous experimental studies support the notion that failure to master prerequisite academic skills leads to later academic problems (Hallahan & Kauffman, 1976).

Ysseldyke also reports that many of the instruments used to assess children's psychoeducational processing skills lack adequate reliability and validity. Instruments with limited reliability and validity should be used very cautiously, if at all. Under these circumstances, the psychoeducational process model appears to be somewhat deficient relative to the evidential requirements for its second assumption of reliable and valid assessment of psychoeducational processing skills. Within the task analysis model, however, "procedures with demonstrated reliability are used to assess skill development strengths and weaknesses" (Ysseldyke, p. 104). Hence, the task analysis model satisfies the evidential requirements of the second assumption.

Remedial efforts within the psychoeducational process model usually focus on psycholinguistic or perceptual-motor deficits. There has been considerable professional debate on the question of whether psychoeducational processing skill deficits are remediable and, if so, whether such remediation leads to improved academic performance. In reference to psycholinguistic training, Lund, Foster, and McCall-Perez (1978) and Minskoff (1975) have judged the research evidence favorably, while Hammill and Larsen (1974, 1978) have presented pessimistic judgments. Kavale (1981) has concluded that deficits in psycholinguistic processing skills are remediable but presents no conclusions on whether such remedial efforts lead to improved academic performance. In a similar vein, Hallahan and Cruickshank (1973) concluded that efficacy studies of perceptual-motor training have failed to yield clear-cut results. Thus, the psychoeducational process model does not clearly satisfy the evidential requirements for the third and fourth assumptions. On the other hand, many studies indicate the possibility and efficacy of remediating gaps in prerequisite academic skills as a method of improving academic performance (Hallahan & Kauffman, 1976). Hence, the task analysis model does satisfy the evidential requirements for the third and fourth assumptions.

In commenting on the research base underpinning the programming uses of the two models, Ysseldyke concludes that we should focus our efforts on implementing assessment and programming activities compatible with the task analysis model. That is also our view: we feel that the task analysis model is the most appropriate model for programming purposes. Yet, as discussed at the end of this section, federal regulations imply the use of assessment and programming procedures compatible with the psychoeducational process model, thus creating a serious dilemma for the assessment practitioner.

Classification Models

The models most relevant to the classification function of psychoeducational assessment are the medical, social-system, and pluralistic models, as described by Mercer and Ysseldyke (1977). Failure to understand models relevant to classification may lead to classification errors. Such errors occur when children are either classified as handicapped when they are not (false positives) or not classified as handicapped when they are (false negatives). Essentially, judgments about the existence or nonexistence of a handicapping condition in a child are based on data relative to the nature and degree of that child's abnormality. Each of the three classification models involves a different perspective from which to evaluate the nature and degree of a child's abnormality. Again, failure to use the correct model (or models) or confusing the models may lead to classification errors. As discussed in Chapters 2 and 3, such errors violate at least the spirit of PL 94-142, and some of them have led to a number of successful legal challenges to disproportionate representation of ethnic minority students in special education programs (Reschly, 1979).

The medical model of assessment assumes that students are abnormal when they exhibit biological symptoms of physical impairment (such as deficient hearing). Consequently, measurement techniques within this model are designed to detect such biological symptoms. When the medical model is used, data that suggest, but do not prove, a biological abnormality should be initially regarded as indicating biological abnormality until the absence of such an abnormality can be conclusively demonstrated. This decision rule is quite important and prevents us from ignoring and failing to treat problems in children that are responsive to medical intervention.

The social-system model of assessment, on the other hand, assumes that students are abnormal when their behaviors do not conform to the expectations of the social systems in which they function. In the public school setting, failure to make passing grades would be construed as abnormal behavior (since most students pass). Measurement techniques within the social-system model are designed to detect deviation from social-system norms. Social-system model data that indicate only moderate deviation from norms should be regarded as evidence of acceptable normality. Abnormality is defined only in terms of gross deviations from social norms. This decision rule prevents us from assigning categorical handicapping-condition labels to children and placing them in special education programs in the absence of compelling reasons to do so.

The pluralistic model of assessment assumes that children are abnormal when their behaviors are deviant from the behavioral norms for their particular subcultural groups. From this perspective, black dialect would not be considered abnormal when used by a black child living in an urban ghetto. Measurement techniques within this model are designed to detect deviation from subcultural norms. Pluralistic-model data that indicate only moderate deviation from subcultural norms should be regarded as evidence of acceptable normality. Abnormality is defined only in terms of gross deviations from subcultural norms. This decision rule prevents us from assigning categorical handicapping-condition labels to children and placing them in special education programs when their behaviors are deviant from those of "mainstream culture peers," but not from those of subcultural peers.

Models: A Sample Case

Now let us place the models described above into a more unified framework. Our branching assessment system is designed to allow adequate attention to both classification and programming and therefore it ought to incorporate models appropriate to both purposes.

Let us consider the hypothetical case of a black child of lower socioeconomic status referred for assessment by his elementary school teacher because of poor academic progress. The teacher reports that the child is not a behavior problem and suggests that the child's academic difficulties may be the result of mental retardation. In the context of the branching assessment system, the child should be evaluated from the perspective of all three classification models. First, assessment techniques under the medical model should be used to rule out the possibility that medically treatable conditions (such as poor vision) are causing the academic problems. If no biological problems are found, the child should be assessed with techniques appropriate to the social-system model. For instance, he might be given the Wechsler Intelligence Scale for Children—Revised (Wechsler, 1974). If his IQ scores fall within the mentally retarded range (below 70), he would be considered abnormal from the social-system perspective. Before seeking data on his performances at home and in his neighborhood, we could consider his IQ scores from the perspective of the pluralistic model. If pluralistic-model norms appropriate to the child are available, we might find that his IQ scores are not grossly deviant from those of other black children of similar sociocultural backgrounds. This child would be considered mentally retarded in terms of the social-system model but not the pluralistic model. Since his IQ scores are roughly comparable to the scores of other children of similar acculturation, we would, in keeping with the decision rule of the pluralistic model, be hesitant to classify him as mentally retarded.

This child might be considered for placement in a Chapter 1 program for economically disadvantaged, underachieving children. Alternatively, it might be appropriate to request special education services for him on the basis of a handicapping condition other than mental retardation. For instance, data at this point might suggest that he has a learning disability. To classify him as a learning disabled child, psychoeducational processing measures are implied, but probably not required, by the federal guidelines to PL 94-142 implying that a learning disabled child is one whose academic problems are the result of deficits in psychoeducational processing skills (*Federal Register*, December 29, 1977, p. 65083). Of course, any scores for psychoeducational processing measures that have low reliability or questionable validity should be cautiously interpreted. In addition, a case would have to be made that this child does not achieve at a level commensurate with his age and ability and that his poor achievement is not primarily the result of another handicapping condition or environmental disadvantage. Only then could he be classified as a learning disabled child.

Even if this child is ultimately classified as learning disabled, we must still pay close attention to his programming needs in planning his IEP. Since we concur with Ysseldyke's conclusion that there is a greater evidential basis for the task analysis model than for the psychoeducational process model, we would next use assessment techniques compatible with the former as aids to planning his educational program.

ASSESSMENT DOMAINS

In the course of this book, we give considerable attention to the domains in which assessment is conducted (health factors; intellectual functioning; modality skills; academic functioning; social/emotional functioning; adaptive behavior; and environmental influences on school coping). Our extensive attention to such domains is at least partially predicated on the regulations implementing PL 94-142. We have already seen that the IEPs mandated by this law require specifications of handicapped children's educational performance levels and determinations of their needs for educational and related services. As an aid in making such judgments, assessment must be conducted "in all areas related to the suspected disability, including, where appropriate, health, vision, hearing, social and emotional status, general intelligence, academic performance, communicative status, and motor abilities" (*Federal Register*, August 23, 1977, p. 42497). While assessment of all of these areas will not be necessary for each child assessed, "no single procedure is used as the sole criterion for determining an appropriate educational program" (*Federal Register,* August 23, 1977, p. 42497). In interpreting data from the domains and sources appropriate to the case, assessment practitioners are not to draw inferences about limited aptitude or achievement in children when test scores actually reflect impaired sensory, manual, or speaking skills.*

It is clear that the regulations implementing PL 94-142 require careful and comprehensive assessment of handicapped children. Our branching assessment system allows for the incorporation of data from the assessment domains appropriate to the consideration of each case. This system encourages the use of only those measures in the assessment domains actually relevant to the case, in the interest of making assessment as time-efficient as possible. We illustrate this strategy in Chapter 12.

TECHNICAL ADEQUACY OF ASSESSMENT TECHNIQUES

Technical adequacy is a complex topic. In this section, we present a general introduction to methods by which the technical adequacy of assessment techniques can be judged, leaving detailed discussion of the adequacy of particular techniques for later chapters. Throughout, we assume our readers' familiarity with measurement techniques and statistical methods.

Technical adequacy involves more than the question of the quality of individual tests: the purpose for which a test is to be used must be considered. In relation to the two usual purposes of assessment— classification and programming—some assessment techniques are far better suited to one of these purposes than to the other. In particular, most assessment techniques fall into two broad categories: norm-referenced measures and criterion-referenced measures. *Norm-referenced measures* "rank student performances compared with a normative population, utilize standard scores, and provide information useful in making placement decisions" (Mercer, 1979a, p. 90). *Criterion-referenced measures* "focus on specific academic areas, com-

---

*While PL 94-142 requires that no single assessment procedure be used as the sole criterion for determining a child's educational program, it does not specifically require assessment in all the domains mentioned above or caution that inferences about limited aptitude or achievement should be avoided when a child's test scores actually reflect other problems.

pare the student's performance with criteria linked to a particular curriculum, utilize raw scores, and provide information useful in planning educational programs" (Mercer, 1979a, p. 90). As Mercer indicates, norm-referenced measures are especially helpful for the purpose of classification, while criterion-referenced measures are particularly helpful for the purpose of programming.

In essence, norm-referenced measures help us to judge the nature and degree of a child's abnormality, which, as we have said, is at the crux of classification decisions. For the purpose of classification norm-referenced measures can, in turn, be interpreted in terms of the three classification models—the medical model, the social-system model, or the pluralistic model (or some combination thereof). Criterion-referenced measures help us judge the specific gaps in the child's learning that are impeding his or her progress in a particular curriculum. Such determinations are quite helpful, at least from the perspective of the task analysis model, for the purpose of programming.

In addition to these considerations concerning the appropriateness of norm-referenced and criterion-referenced measures to the dual purposes of assessment, the question of the technical adequacy of particular measures involves the degrees to which they may be judged as having reliability and validity. Well-established procedures are available for determining whether norm-referenced measures are reliable and valid. As we shall see, however, there is less agreement on how the technical adequacy of criterion-referenced measures should be judged. Some procedures for judging the reliability and validity of norm-referenced measures may be applied to judgments about criterion-referenced measures. These procedures may need some modification when applied to criterion-referenced measures, and additional procedures for evaluating the technical adequacy of criterion-referenced measures are in developmental stages. Given this situation, we provide a general introduction to the concept of reliability and then provide separate discussions of procedures used to judge the reliability of norm-referenced measures and criterion-referenced measures. The same arrangement is used to present the concept of validity and ways of judging the validity of norm-referenced and criterion-referenced measures.

Reliability

Reliability basically "refers to the consistency of a measure" (T. Miller, 1979, p. 84). Since no assessment technique measures with perfect consistency, all psychoeducational assessments involve some degree of measurement error. However, evidence bearing on the reliability of an assessment technique allows us some knowledge of the amount of error present in the measurement.

Norm-Referenced Measures

Reliability evidence for norm-referenced measures is expressed in terms of correlation coefficients, with higher coefficients indicating greater reliability. Four approaches to evaluating the reliability of norm-referenced measures are in common use (T. Miller, 1979).

Split-Half Reliability. In this procedure, "items on a single test are dichotomized in some manner (first–second half or, more usually, odd–even) and correlated to provide an index of reliability" (T. Miller, p. 85). The results provide an indication of the assessment technique's internal consistency. High split-half reliability coefficients indicate that the assessment technique is measuring something consistently from the first to the last item of the test.

Item Analysis. Under this procedure, scores on each item of the test are correlated with total scores. An overall index of internal consistency "is usually accomplished by means of the *coefficient alpha* technique or the older and more limited *Kuder-Richardson 20* formula" (T. Miller, p. 84).

Alternate Forms Reliability. In this procedure, two forms of the same test are given to a group of people and the scores on the two forms are correlated. If the resulting reliability coefficient is high, one may assume that the two forms of the test are measuring essentially the same content or skill and therefore may be used interchangeably.

Test-Retest Reliability. Under this procedure, a number of people take a test and then retake that same test at a later date. Scores on the two tests are correlated, and the resulting correlation coefficient is an index of the test score's stability over time. There are as many test-retest reliabilities as there are intervals between initial testing and subsequent testing (Anastasi, 1976).

T. Miller notes that each of these four approaches to evaluating the reliability of norm-referenced measures has its strengths and weaknesses. He advocates that in evaluating a test, assessment practitioners determine the adequacy of the procedures used to establish the reliability of the test and compare the reliability coefficients produced for the test by the various reliability procedures.

The use of assessment techniques of low reliability can lead to errors in classification and programming. Salvia and Ysseldyke (1978) therefore recommend that wherever possible only measures with reliability coefficients of 0.90 and above be used in making classification decisions. As we shall see in Chapters 5 through 11, this is a rigorous standard that many assessment techniques fail to meet. In view of this problem, Ysseldyke (1979) proposes a second (and less restrictive) approach. He recommends "computing estimated true scores for all obtained scores, constructing confidence intervals around estimated true scores, and interpreting assessment information in light of these considerations" (p. 109). Since this method requires us to use our knowledge of the amount of error present in a measurement, we advocate it throughout this book.

The estimated true score represents the score the child should receive under ideal assessment conditions. Nunnally (1967, p. 220) provides the following formula for computing the estimated true score:

$$X' = \overline{X} + (r)(X - \overline{X})$$

where X' = the estimated true score, r = the test's reliability coefficient, X = the obtained test score, and $\overline{X}$ = the test's mean.

After computing the estimated true score, one must then utilize the standard error of measurement in constructing a confidence interval around the estimated true score. The standard error of measurement is defined as

$$Sem = SD \sqrt{1 - r}$$

where Sem = standard error of measurement, SD = standard deviation of scores on the test, r = the test's reliability coefficient, and 1 = a constant. "Most test manuals report the Sem directly although caution should be taken to select an appropriate value for an individual case because the Sem will vary across age ranges" (T. Miller, p. 89).

Finally, one can be about 68 percent certain that the child's true score falls within a range of scores extending from one standard error of measurement below the estimated true score to one standard error of measurement above the estimated true score. About 95 percent certainty on the location of the true score may be obtained by extending the confidence interval two standard errors of measurement above and below the estimated true score. A certainty of 95 percent should suffice for most purposes.

Criterion-Referenced Measures

Salvia and Ysseldyke (1978) report that reliability information is often unavailable on many criterion-referenced measures. They attribute this paucity of information to the belief of test authors that reliability is less important in criterion-referenced than in norm-referenced measurement. Anastasi (1976) notes that reliability procedures appropriate to norm-referenced measures may not be appropriate to criterion-referenced measures. She further indicates that statistical indices of reliability more appropriate for criterion-referenced measures have not yet been fully developed.

Nevertheless, Anastasi, and Salvia and Ysseldyke, view reliability as an important consideration in criterion-referenced assessment and propose some procedures for making judgments in this area. Essentially, Salvia and Ysseldyke focus on the reliability of scores on criterion-referenced measures, while Anastasi focuses on the reliability of decisions based on criterion-referenced measures.

Salvia and Ysseldyke express some concern with the limited number of items typically devoted to each specific skill area in criterion-referenced measures. When a test is constructed in this way, it is especially important that each item contribute reliable information about the development of the skill being tested. Hence, Salvia and Ysseldyke indicate that "test authors *can* and should report test-retest reliabilities for each item" (p. 195). These authors also advocate that alternate-form reliabilities be reported when alternate forms of a criterion-referenced measure are available.

Anastasi also expresses concern with the limited numbers of items in each skill area. However, she approaches this issue by trying to determine how many items are required to reliably measure a skill. She also focuses on the question of what proportion of items in a skill area must be passed in order for mastery of that skill to be assumed. Anastasi proposes that decisions about mastery of skills be assessed in the light of subsequent experience. Specifically, she suggests that if persons assumed to have mastered lower-level skills have difficulty mastering higher-level skills, then the assessment of the lower-level skills has been unreliable. When such situations occur, the number of items measuring lower-level skills can be increased, or the proportion of items passed required for an assumption of mastery can be increased. Either procedure should raise the reliability of the decisions made concerning mastery or nonmastery of skills. If alternate forms of criterion-referenced measures are available, Anastasi recommends that the two forms be administered to the same persons. Then the percentage of persons on whom the same decision (mastery or nonmastery) is reached on both forms should be computed.

Validity

"The validity of a test generally refers to how well the test measures what it purports to measure" (T. Miller, 1979, p. 80). A number of procedures can be used to provide evidence bearing on the validity of a test. Before briefly reviewing these, however, we call the reader's attention to two facts. First, a test's title may not accurately convey what the test in fact measures. Instead, "most test names provide short, convenient labels for identification purposes. They are far too broad and vague to furnish meaningful clues to the behavior area covered" (Anastasi, 1976, p. 134). Second a test cannot be valid unless it is reliable. Put another way, reliability is a necessary but insufficient condition of validity.

Essentially, validity evidence comes from procedures designed to address questions of content validity, criterion-related validity, and construct validity. Procedures appropriate to each of the three types of validity questions are presented below.

Norm-Referenced Measures

Content Validity. Procedures for assessing the validity of a test's content address the question of whether the content includes a representative sample of the knowledge or skills one wishes to measure. Content validity is usually achieved by writing test items to meet test specifications that show the content areas to be covered, the skills to be assessed, and the relative importance of each content area and skill. Content validity may be checked empirically by comparing scores for each item and total scores of persons judged to be at differing levels of knowledge and skill (Anastasi, 1976). For instance, sixth graders should perform better on arithmetical computation problems than third graders. Content validity is the most important type of validity for an achievement test, regardless of whether the achievement test is a norm-referenced or criterion-referenced measure.

Criterion-Related Validity. Procedures for evaluating criterion-related validity involve relating scores on some measurement device to another indicator of performance. One type of criterion-related validity is *concurrent validity*. Concurrent validity procedures involve correlating test scores with another indicator of current status. For example, a developer of a new intelligence test might test a group of people with the new test and with an existing intelligence test with demonstrated technical adequacy. If the correlation between the scores on the two tests is high, this is evidence for the concurrent validity of the new test.

A second type of criterion-related validity is *predictive validity*. Predictive validity involves correlating test scores with indicators of future status. For instance, one might wish to use performance on a test to predict later success in a particular occupation. In this situation, one would administer the test to persons entering that occupation and later determine whether the scores are related to indicators of occupational performance. If there is a reasonably good relationship between test scores and later occupational performance, this is evidence for the predictive validity of the test for this specific occupation. It should be noted that tests may show evidence of predictive validity relative to some future performances but not to others.

Construct Validity. This procedure evaluates "the extent to which a test measures a theoretical construct or trait that is presumed to be an underlying determinant of behavior" (T. Miller, 1979, p. 82). Although construct validity is a complex concept, Anastasi (1976) and Messick (1980) argue that it is the most comprehensive approach to validity and, as such, incorporates but goes beyond evidence bearing on content- and criterion-related validity. Anastasi describes six major types of evidence useful in demonstrating a test's construct validity: (1) test scores that reflect expected changes in a person's performance over time; (2) scores that have moderate correlations with scores on tests thought to measure the same construct, accompanied by low correlations with tests seen as irrelevant to the construct; (3) factor-analytic studies indicating that the major factors determining scores on the test are appropriate to the construct it purports to measure; (4) test construction and evaluation procedures relevant to the test's internal consistency; (5) demonstrations that test scores change as a result of training or other interventions; and (6) significant correlations between test scores and variables appropriate to the construct, accompanied by nonsignificant correlations between test scores and with variables unrelated to the construct.

Criterion-Referenced Measures

Of the various approaches to validity, "content validity is particularly appropriate for . . . criterion-referenced tests" (Anastasi, 1976, p. 138). This is because criterion-referenced measures are used to determine where a person stands relative to the acquisition of well-defined areas of knowledge or skill. Hence, accurate judgments of the person's status depend on measures appropriate to the knowledge or skills being assessed. As with norm-referenced tests, the content validity of criterion-referenced tests is achieved by writing test items that correspond to specifications describing needed coverage of knowledge or skill areas.

In addition, criterion-referenced measures represent attempts to place knowledge or skill items into a hierarchical arrangement. Such an arrangement assumes that mastery of basic knowledge or skill areas is prerequisite to mastery of more advanced knowledge or skill areas. Hence, the content validity of a criterion-referenced measure is also related to the adequacy of the hierarchical arrangement of items within the measure. If the items are inappropriately arranged, then we may make inappropriate decisions about where to begin instruction in a knowledge or skill area. Anastasi (1976) warns that criterion-referenced measures are most appropriate to basic school subjects in which there is at least some consensus on the hierarchical progression of knowledge or skill acquisition. In contrast, norm-referenced measures may be more appropriate in advanced subjects in which learning hierarchies are more flexible.

Anastasi also suggests that at least some construct-validity procedures are appropriate to judgments about the validity of criterion-referenced measures. One such procedure involves evidence that learning in a particular knowledge or skill area does, in fact, proceed in terms of a fixed sequence of mastery of knowledge or skills. A second procedure involves ascertaining that scores on criterion-referenced measures do improve as a result of specific instructional activities.

The concurrent validity of a criterion-referenced measure might be judged in terms of the degree to which its estimations of mastery coincide with those of another criterion-referenced measure of the same knowledge or skill areas. This could be done by calculating the percentage of identical decisions of mastery or nonmastery in each area for persons administered both measures.

Criterion-referenced measures are not designed to assist us in making predictions about future performances in any long-range sense. Hence, the concept of predictive validity is irrelevant to criterion-referenced measures, at least as this concept is typically used. However, we expect that a person judged to have mastered lower-level skills in a hierarchy of learning tasks will be able to master the skills at the next level in a reasonable amount of time. If this expectation proves to be false, then our predictive assumption was incorrect. In such situations, we need to modify the measure in ways that correct this problem. As indicated earlier, we may need to increase the number of items at the lower level or raise the score required for a judgment of mastery at that level. We might, alternatively, reexamine the respective positioning of the levels within the measure, since it is possible that the lower-level skill was not actually prerequisite to the skill placed above it.

Norms

It will be recalled that criterion-referenced measures compare a person's performance to a level of proficiency judged to represent mastery of a particular knowledge or skill area. The person's performance is *not* judged in relation to the performances of others on that same measure. Thus, it would be illogical to discuss norms in relation to criterion-referenced measures.

On the other hand, norms, by definition, constitute an essential component of norm-referenced measures. It is imperative that such measures include norms derived from representative samples of the populations for which they are designed. Salvia and Ysseldyke (1978) suggest that the representativeness of any norm group be judged in terms of the following factors: age, sex, acculturation, geographic region, race, and intelligence level. In addition, they note that test norms should be updated periodically in order to reflect changes in the population over time. Further, the normative population must of course include a sufficient number of people to make the group representative of the population.

Salvia and Ysseldyke (1978) also indicate that test users must ascertain the relevance of test norms for both the persons being assessed and the uses to which the test is to be put. Let us reconsider briefly the hypothetical case of the black child of lower socioeconomic status referred because of suspected mental retardation. His social-system IQ scores on the Wechsler Intelligence Scale for Children — Revised (1974) are in the mentally retarded range. These scores represent a fair and appropriate comparison of the child's current status on the test in relation to a nationally representative group of his age peers. However, his social-system IQ scores are suspect if used for the purpose of classifying him as mentally retarded, since use of such norms requires an assumption that the child's acculturation has been comparable to that of most persons in the norm group. A classification of mental retardation would be more appropriate for this child if his scores also fell in the mentally retarded range when pluralistic norms were used, since pluralistic norms rank the child's performance in relation to the performances of children of similar acculturation. Pluralistic norms actually appropriate to this child may not be available, however. We will look into this problem in more detail in subsequent chapters.

Technical Adequacy: Conclusions

Technical adequacy considerations are vitally important in psychoeducational assessment. Our survey of the subject here has necessarily been brief. Readers interested in exploring the subject in more depth are urged to consult sources such as Anastasi (1976). In addition, all readers are urged to become familiar with, or review, guidelines presented in *Standards for Educational and Psychological Tests* (APA, 1974). Some other treatments of technical adequacy issues are listed in the Suggested Readings section at the back of the book.

Our discussion has been limited to a review of methods of determining the adequacy of norm-referenced and criterion-referenced measures. A third type of assessment technique, involving observational recordings of children's behaviors is also important in psychoeducational assessment. Methods of determining the technical adequacy of procedures of this type will be discussed as appropriate in later chapters.

Even if all proper precautions have been taken to ensure the use of technically adequate assessment techniques, tests can yield misleading information if administered under inappropriate conditions. Hence, "the examiner must insure the comfort of the examinee and the elimination of distractions, . . . be certain that all materials are available and in readily usable condition, and . . . assure that no obvious procedures or circumstances that could invalidate the test appear" (T. Miller, 1979, p. 91). In addition, interpretative errors will occur when assessment practitioners are inadequately trained or are insensitive to sociocultural differences between themselves and the children they assess (Bersoff & Miller, 1979).

LEGAL CONSIDERATIONS

Earlier in this chapter we described several features of PL 94-142 that bear on the practice of psychoeducational assessment. These include the need for assessment to serve classification and programming functions; the formulation of IEPs designating needed educational and related services; the involvement of specified groups of people in the forumlation of IEPs; and assessments being conducted in domains relevant to the suspected handicapping conditions.

Although we have so far devoted exclusive attention to PL 94-142, it should be noted that the legal framework for psychoeducational assessment extends far beyond this single federal law. For example, PL 93-380 (Education Amendments of 1974) and PL 93-112

(Rehabilitation Act of 1974) as amended by PL 93-516 (Rehabilitation Act Amendments of 1974) also relate to assessment practice (Bersoff & Miller). In addition, a number of federal court rulings have affected assessment as practiced within the jurisdictions of those courts. Hence there are numerous sources of law regulating assessment and other services to handicapped children (Martin, 1979).

At this point it is appropriate to establish only some general understanding of these sources of law. First, a number of successful court challenges to special education assessment, classification, and programming practices during the 1960s and the early 1970s contributed to the enactment of the federal laws noted above. Some of the principles and procedures built into those laws were based on these cases. In this sense, legislation has tended to follow litigation (Bersoff, Note 2).

The cases addressed at least two major issues pertinent to our concerns. The first issue involved the exclusion of some handicapped children (especially those with severe handicaps) from public school programs. One basis for their exclusion was a narrow definition of education as "the teaching of 'normal' subjects to 'normal' children" (Martin, 1979, p. 12). Severely handicapped children were seen as unable to benefit from education defined in this way, and psychoeducational assessment practitioners were called upon to determine whether or not some handicapped children were educable. Court challenges to the exclusion of severely handicapped children, however, resulted in a broadened definition of education as "any kind of training that a child might need" (Bersoff & Miller, 1979, p. 135). Clearly, even the most severely handicapped child can benefit from education as it is currently defined. Hence, assessment practitioners are no longer called upon to determine a child's educability. Instead, the regulations implementing PL 94-142 require a free, appropriate education for any handicapped person between the ages of 3 and 21. Special education services to children 3 through 5 years of age and students 18 through 21 years of age, however, are not required if prohibited by state law or court order.

Although assessment practitioners no longer make determinations about whether a child can profit from education, they are increasingly being asked to guard against unwarranted classifications of children as handicapped. As indicated previously, there have been a number of successful legal challenges to the disproportionate representation of ethnic minority children in special education programs (Reschly, 1979). Ross, De Young, and Cohen (1971) suggest that plaintiffs in these cases have tended to raise concerns in the following areas: the use of inappropriate tests in making classification decisions; incompetent administration of tests and inappropriate interpretation of test results; lack of parental involvement in assessment and decision making; the provision of inadequate special education programs; and the stigma resulting from unwarranted classification and special education placement. In responding to successful litigation, legislators have attempted to incorporate corrective measures in federal legislation that emphasize both the use of appropriate assessment methods and the use of more responsive decision-making procedures in approximating a goal of nondiscriminatory assessment.

We have already noted that the regulations implementing PL 94-142 require assessment in all areas related to the suspected handicapping condition, use of more than one assessment procedure in determining an appropriate educational program, decision making by a specified group, and avoidance of conclusions about limited aptitude or achievement when test results actually reflect impaired sensory, manual, or speaking skills. Additional corrective measures found in the regulations implementing PL 94-142 require that tests and other evaluative measures be administered in the child's native language (unless this is clearly not feasible), the use of tests that have been validated for the specific uses to which they are put, and the use of tests by qualified personnel in accordance with the instructions of the tests' producers (*Federal Register*, August 23, 1977, p. 42496). Other sections of these regulations also require that each IEP be reviewed and, if necessary, modified at least once a year. In addition, each child receiving special education services must be reassessed at least once every three years, with reassessments meeting the same standards required of initial assessments (*Federal Register*, August, 23, 1977, pp. 42490, 42497).* "Such review and reassessment requirements are for the purpose of determining which students continue to be eligible for and require special education services" (Helton & Workman, 1982). Again, one of the purposes of the steps mentioned in this paragraph is to promote assessment and placement practices that are racially and culturally nondiscriminatory.

Regulations such as these do not, by themselves, put an end to inappropriate practices. Practitioners must actually be able to use classification and programming practices in accordance with the regulations. While our branching assessment system permits this, it re-

---

*PL 94-142 does not specifically require that tests be validated for the purposes for which they are used; that tests be used by qualified personnel according to instructions of the tests' producers; or that children be reassessed at least every three years.

mains a difficult task. Problems arise owing to vagueness in the regulations, the lack of technically adequate assessment techniques, and situational constraints.

First, key provisions of the regulations (such as those dealing with nondiscriminatory assessment) are vague in meaning and therefore open to conflicting interpretations (Bersoff & Miller, 1979, p. 156). Meeting such requirements in specific and agreed-upon ways is difficult. Second, many of the assessment techniques traditionally used have not been validated for the purposes for which they are now being used (Bersoff & Miller, pp. 155–156). Certainly, lack of technical adequacy would cause an assessment technique to be suspect in terms of validity for a particular purpose. Also, the previously noted confusion about what constitutes nondiscriminatory assessment includes questions about what is required in validating tests for specific purposes. Hence, the practitioner must collect data for classification and programming purposes without being certain whether the means of data collection have been sufficiently validated. Third, decisions about appropriate assessment practices are often made under pressure of time. Such pressure can lead to ill-considered or expedient judgments and thereby increase the chances of violating the letter or the spirit of federal regulations. In addition, Weatherly and Lipsky (1977) suggest that assessment practice is easily corrupted by the needs of teachers or school systems and deflected from its intended functions. Examples of such corruption have included "scheduling of assessments in favor of children who were behavior problems, who were not likely to cost the system money, or who met the needs of school personnel seeking to practice their individual specialties" (p. 194). Preferential scheduling of this type may result in failure to deliver services to eligible children.

In view of these problems, it should not be surprising that assessment practitioners sometimes experience difficulty in their attempts to comply with federal regulations. One promising approach to compliance is presented by Reschly (1979). He proposes that we "cut through" some of the confusion surrounding assessment practices by focusing on their social consequences for individuals. From this perspective, assessment practices are appropriate to the degree that they promote more effective interventions for the children assessed. Assessment practices leading to more effective interventions are likely to be those that address the concerns expressed by plaintiffs in special education litigation. Specifically, such practices are likely to require parental involvement, competent assessment personnel, and the use of technically adequate measures. Further, classification of children as handicapped is less likely to be perceived as stigmatizing if that classification leads to effective programming for them.

ETHICAL CONSIDERATIONS

Many assessment practitioners belong to professional organizations that have developed codes of ethics. These ethical codes are intended to guide the professional behaviors of organizational members. Since we believe that these codes of ethics provide a good introduction to the ethical issues involved in assessment practice, we will refer to them frequently. Examples are the Ethical Principles for Psychologists of the American Psychological Association (APA, 1981) and the Principles for Professional Ethics of the National Association of School Psychologists (NASP, 1978).

Both the APA and NASP ethical codes state that professional competence is a necessary condition of ethical practice. Principle 2e of the APA's Ethical Principles indicates that competent assessment practice requires adequate understanding of measurement principles, test validation problems, and other areas of assessment research. Principle II,b of the NASP's Principles for Professional Ethics requires that only assessment techniques appropriate to the individual child be utilized; sufficient competence in assessment is obviously required to abide by such provisions. In addition to technical knowledge, we believe that assessment practitioners must develop detailed conceptions of their areas of personal competence and incompetence. Such self-knowledge is required if practitioners are to honor their ethical responsibilities to use only those assessment techniques that they are personally competent to use. Children needing services that exceed the expertise of a particular practitioner must, ethically, be referred to another practitioner possessing the necessary expertise.

The APA and NASP ethical codes also require that assessment data be presented objectively and that reservations about the accuracy of test results be clearly stated. In addition, both codes require that psychologists take steps to ensure that their assessment results are not misused by other professionals. Further, both codes indicate an obligation to honor client privacy, to inform clients of the nature and purpose of assessment activities, and to explain assessment findings and subsequent recommendations in understandable terms. Finally, the APA's code stipulates that psychologists are responsible, as individuals, for upholding the highest standards of the profession.

This responsibility includes a requirement to attempt to correct ethical misconduct on the part of colleagues in psychology.

Just as it is difficult for assessment practitioners to comply in all ways with federal regulations, so it is also difficult for them to fully apply the ethical codes of such professional organizations in assessment practice. In saying this, we do not mean in any sense to condone inappropriate practice, but simply to point out the real difficulties involved.

One problem presented by ethical codes involves their ambiguity in reference to specific situations (Bersoff, 1975). Ethical codes must be written in rather general terms, since there are myriad ethically problematic situations that might arise in practice. In order to make an ethically appropriate response to a particular situation, the practitioner often must attempt to interpret the most relevant provisions of an ethical code (or codes) and decide how these provisions apply in a given case. When interpretation proves difficult, practitioners should consult with colleagues or the ethics committees of their respective organizations.

Another problem faced by assessment practitioners is that compliance with ethical codes does not, by itself, guarantee that all aspects of practice will meet all legal requirements of practice. Bersoff (1975) illustrates this point by describing how ethical responses to five situations might represent legal violations. He urges psychologists to become familiar with both legal and ethical requirements pertinent to their duties and points out that some situations may require a choice between legal and ethical obligations.

A third problem involves the long-standing but important issue of clientage (Fagan, 1980). Resolution of this issue requires that the practitioner determine which of the parties involved in a situation is to be regarded as the client and, as such, the recipient of the practitioner's primary allegiance. One possible way of deciding this issue is to define the client as the party paying for the practitioner's services. We, however, cannot recommend this decision rule in the case of psychoeducational assessment. Instead, we recommend that the child being assessed be defined as the client, in accordance with our conviction that the ultimate purpose of assessment is to benefit the child. This decision rule is compatible with numerous provisions of both the APA and NASP codes, provisions that essentially urge psychologists to be alert to, and try to correct, organizational practices detrimental to those served by the organization. At the same time, both ethical codes indicate that psychologists should respect the rights and prerogatives of their employing organizations. In the case of client–organization conflicts, psychologists are further urged to clarify their loyalties to all parties and to attempt to work out solutions that respect the needs of those parties.

Efforts to respect the needs of both clients and employing organizations often involve difficult challenges for assessment practitioners. While we believe that such efforts are usually successful, this is not invariably the case. Illustrative of this point are the due process hearings being held around the nation. Such hearings are provided for by PL 94-142 to deal with situations in which parents and school officials cannot agree on matters of classification, programming, or procedure. An impartial hearing officer is employed to decide the matters under dispute in each case. This mechanism for resolving disputes is described in detail in Chapter 2.

Another example of clientage problems faced by practitioners may be found in the case of *Forrest* v. *Ambach* (Prasse, 1981b). The plaintiff in this case, Muriel Forrest, charged that she was dismissed from her position as a school psychologist because she refused to comply with what she perceived to be illegal and unethical directives from school administrators. Compliance with these directives, in her opinion, would have resulted in unacceptable services to children and parents. School officials, on the other hand, maintained that she was dismissed because of unsatisfactory work and refusal to follow orders directing her to change. When the state commissioner of education upheld Forrest's dismissal, she sought a judgment from the supreme court of the state of New York (Albany County). The court found in part for Forrest by ordering the commissioner to review and reconsider her dismissal. The court held that the commissioner should have considered Forrest's allegations in arriving at his initial judgment. In his description of this case, Prasse quotes from the court's ruling as follows:

> While a school board is in the position of an employer, those professionals employed by a school board do have a level of professional competence and standards which must be recognized and respected, not only for the profession itself, but for the purpose of rendering the best services to the school board and ultimately to the students they service. The ethical standards of any professional employed by a school board cannot be cavalierly dismissed as irrelevant to the employer-employee relationship, and may indeed become quite relevant in certain circumstances. If, in fact, petitioner was dismissed solely due to her own professional standards as a psychologist, then her dismissal by said school board would be arbitrary, capricious, and unconstitutional. (p. 3)

As this case suggests, the issue of clientage can indeed be a problematic one for assessment practitioners, particularly in view of the fact that the commissioner, on reconsideration, again upheld Forrest's dismissal. Believing that the commissioner did not respond appropriately to the court's directive, Forrest plans to continue her legal challenge to her dismissal (Ramage & Johnston, Note 3). Regardless of the ultimate outcome of this case, Shaffer (1981) reports that Donald Bersoff (attorney for the American Psychological Association) believes that the initial court ruling established a precedent that ethical standards can be considered legitimate aspects of legal deliberations. In this vein, Frith (1981) suggests that clientage issues are becoming problematic for all professionals working with handicapped children. He describes numerous situations in which the needs of these children are perceived as conflicting with the administrative, financial, and logistical needs of school districts. He then recommends that all professionals involved in special education carefully consider their responses to such conflicts. He also reports that the Council for Exceptional Children is considering the development of a formalized code of ethics for its members.

A response to Frith's article indicates that the Council for Exceptional Children believes that the role of the professional as an employee should not conflict with the professional's role as a child advocate (Editor, 1981). "If what is perceived as good for exceptional children is bad for the professionals who serve them, then the benefit to children is nullified. In the same way, improvements in the professional's position must never be at the expense of an individual child" (Editor, p. 492). The Council for Exceptional Children is exploring ways in which it might work to enhance the conditions under which professionals work with exceptional children (Editor). Similar concerns are illustrated by the Guidelines to Work Conditions for School Psychologists formulated by division 16 of the American Psychological Association (APA, undated).

We would like to summarize our own position on the matter of ethics (a more detailed discussion is presented in Chapter 4). First, we believe that in spite of the difficulties involved, psychoeducational assessment practitioners should strive vigorously to comply with the provisions of the APA and NASP ethical codes. They should not acquiesce to pressures to alter test scores or classification judgments. Further, we feel that "imprecision in the handicapping condition labels themselves does not justify assigning them to students in imprecise ways" (Helton & Workman, 1982). In making classification judgments, the models relevant to such judgments (the medical, social-system, and pluralistic models) should be utilized. In addition, the social consequences of classification should be carefully considered. This caution is seen as compatible with our definition of the child being assessed as the client and our conviction that classification leading to effective intervention is less likely to involve unacceptable stigmatization.

It follows that psychologists and other assessment specialists who embrace our reasoning may sometimes be in conflict with their employing organizations. Such conflicts, however, represent opportunities to focus organizational attention on better ways of serving client needs. As such, they should be entered into (albeit constructively and tactfully) rather than avoided. (Helton & Workman, 1982)

SITUATIONAL CONSTRAINTS

Classification and programming can lead to beneficial social consequences for children, but only if they are done carefully, systematically, and with children's best interests at heart. Obviously, careful and systematic work incorporating thoughtful judgments requires time. Excessive time pressure tends to result in ill-considered or expedient judgments. Hence excessive time pressure should not be placed on psychoeducational assessment personnel in the performance of their duties, particularly since assessment is easily corrupted in the first place.

Excessive time pressure and other situational constraints on psychoeducational assessment practice result from a number of interacting forces. School administrators, under the law, are now required to provide extensive assessment and programming services to previously unserved groups of children and to ensure that all services meet at least the letter of federal regulations and litigative precedents. At the same time, their efforts to increase and improve services are occurring "in the context of . . . reductions in funding, material, and personnel. Many of the policies and procedures generated in this context transgress professional ethics, abort professional safeguards of practice, ignore the law, and destroy adequate and necessary service to students" (APA, undated, p. 1). As previously noted, failures to provide appropriate services are leading to due process hearings, cases such as *Forrest* v. *Ambach*, and clientage dilemmas for professionals associated with special education.

In the development of strategies for coping with time pressures and other constraints on assessment practice, it is important to appreciate the difficulties that many school administrators find themselves in as they attempt to comply with federal regulations and litigative precedents. Administrators do have a right to expect dedicated effort and time-efficient assessment from assessment practitioners. They do not, in our judgment, have a right to sacrifice standards of service for savings in time and money. Drawing the line between appropriate and efficient services, as opposed to inappropriate but efficient services, requires thoughtful consideration and tactful communication on the part of all parties involved. It also requires consensus on the conclusion that inappropriate services can only be efficient on a short-range basis (as we shall see in the next section).

One necessary strategy in coping with time constraints involves the recognition that school administrators and others may not understand the amount of time required by appropriate assessment practices. They may be surprised to learn that an initial assessment of a child (including report writing) often requires a full workday (and sometimes more). Part of this lack of understanding stems from the "quickie" testing that used to be done with children being considered for special education services. Such assessment will no longer meet legal standards (and never has met professional standards). Assessment practitioners should take time to work constructively with school administrators in efforts to promote better understanding of the time requirements of assessment.

One time-efficient approach to providing appropriate and efficient assessment services involves a team approach in which school psychologists, school counselors, school social workers, school nurses, regular teachers, special education teachers, and others share the assessment load. This interdisciplinary approach ensures that assessment responsibilities do not fall exclusively on an individual practitioner and is also compatible with both the letter and the spirit of the regulations implementing PL 94-142. However, a team approach must ethically utilize professionals representing different specialties in ways that are appropriate to their respective areas of competence. "Such an approach must also involve a spirit of cooperation among team members rather than competitiveness within the team, a situation which does not automatically occur" (Helton & Workman, 1982).

Although a team approach may advance the goal of appropriate and efficient assessment, no single strategy will overcome all problems. For instance, it is not uncommon for members of assessment teams to complain that they are so caught up in assessment that they have too little time for other activities appropriate to their roles. One corrective approach to this situation is to incorporate other services of assessment team members in IEPs. A hypothetical IEP constructed in this manner might include parent training on the part of the school counselor and consultation with the child's regular teacher on the part of the school psychologist. Such related services are required by the law if the child needs them in order to benefit from special education. Inclusion of such related services in IEPs not only represents compliance with the regulations implementing PL 94-142 but also allows assessment team members to provide other role-appropriate services.

In some instances, even creative approaches to appropriate and efficient assessment may not prove successful. Such failures are likely to be the result of inadequate numbers of assessment personnel. If this is the case, assessment practitioners need to request that school administrators employ more staff. This request is likely to cause many problems for administrators confronted with declining revenues with which to operate school districts. Nevertheless, decisions not to employ additional staff may lead to legally and ethically inappropriate services.

THE BRANCHING ASSESSMENT SYSTEM

At this point, we should reiterate what has already been said about our branching assessment system. We have noted that the system allows for the choice of assessment techniques useful in addressing the dual functions of assessment; the use of techniques appropriate to the unique characteristics of the child being assessed; the use of techniques compatible with both the psychoeducational process and task analysis models of assessment and programming; and the practice of appropriate and efficient assessment (in the sense that only assessment techniques actually relevant to the referral problem are used). We have also illustrated the system's ability to incorporate the medical, social-system, pluralistic, psychoeducational process, and task analysis models with the hypothetical case of the black male child referred for suspected mental retardation. Finally, we have described the system as a distillation of practices already in use, rather than as a radically innovative approach. The remainder of this section describes some additional features of the system in order to set the stage for the detailed description of the system presented in Chapter 12.

Our branching assessment system is presented as a means of promoting appropriate and efficient assessment. To clarify what we mean by efficient assessment, let us contrast the branching assessment system with a fixed assessment battery. Some assessment practitioners utilize a relatively fixed battery, partially as a strategy to keep assessment time to a minimum. Our experience suggests that fixed batteries are often oriented almost exclusively to the classification function of assessment. The use of fixed batteries for classification purposes may result in failure to use assessment techniques appropriate to the children being assessed or to collect data in all areas relevant to their suspected handicapping conditions. Even if these failures are avoided, assessment for programming may be neglected. Such assessment might be efficient in terms of time spent per child, but could (and should, if inadequate) lead to more time-consuming activities, such as due process hearings. Hence fixed batteries used mostly for classification purposes are likely to result in short-range efficiency at the expense of more costly, long-range inefficiency. We advocate that efficiency be judged in terms of long-range considerations.

This pragmatic approach to efficiency also incorporates our belief that assessment should not be prolonged unnecessarily. We view practitioners who collect more data than are necessary for classification and programming purposes as using limited assessment resources inefficiently. Hence, our branching assessment system should not be used for either the over- or the under-collection of data. From a more philosophical perspective, we also judge efficiency in terms of value per unit of assessment time spent. Each unit is valuable to the extent that accurate and relevant data leading to improved programming for the child are collected.

Our branching assessment system always incorporates health screening and an interview with the person who has referred the child for assessment. The health screening involves the use of medical model measures and is intended to detect any sensory or health problems contributing to the child's difficulties. The referral-source interview allows the assessment practitioner to conceptualize the referral problem as an academic behavior problem or as a social/emotional behavior problem, or, in some cases, both. Detailed instructions for conducting referral-source interviews may be found in Bergan (1977).

If the child is experiencing sensory or health problems, the assessment should be delayed until these problems have been remediated or until it has been determined that the problems cannot be remediated. Next, an initial conceptualization of the case based on the referral-source interview allows the practitioner to enter a particular branch or branches within the system. The hypothetical case of the black male child referred for academic problems and suspected of being mentally retarded illustrates this process. Since this child was free of sensory or health problems and presented no classroom behavior problems, the practitioner entered a branch designed to check the possibility that mental retardation was, as the teacher suspected, the source of the child's academic problems. Social-system norms for the Wechsler Intelligence Scale for Children—Revised supported mental retardation as a possible cause of his difficulties. Pluralistic norms, however, indicated that the child was not grossly deficient in general intellectual functioning relative to age peers of similar acculturation. This finding caused the practitioner to leave the branch appropriate to a determination of mental retardation and to enter a second branch.

This second branch was one permitting a judgment about whether or not the child might be classified as learning disabled. As previously indicated, this branch requires the use of norm-referenced measures of academic achievement and might include the use of measures of psychoeducational processing skills. If our hypothetical child's academic achievement was below expectancies based on his age and ability levels, such data would support further data collection within this branch. Such data would necessarily include observations of the child's classroom behavior, as required by federal regulations governing the assessment of learning disabled children (*Federal Register*, December 29, 1977, pp. 65082 – 65085).* If the observational data suggested the presence of social/emotional problems, the practitioner should also enter a third branch appropriate to a determination of emotional disturbance. Ultimately, a classification of the child as learning disabled would require a judgment that his learning problems are not primarily the result of another handicapping condition (such as emotional disturbance) or environmental disadvantage. Assessment for programming within the learning disabilities branch would incorporate the classroom observational data already collected, as well as criterion-referenced measures of academic skills.

This hypothetical case sets the stage for several points to be made about the branching assessment system. First, each branch permits a classification judgment to be made in regard to the appropriateness of the handicapping-condition label being considered for the child. Each branch is followed until data contraindicate that label. Second, each branch permits the collection of data appropriate for programming, as well as classification purposes. Third, initial conceptualizations of a case sometimes prove erroneous, and when that occurs, practitioners shift to other branches of the system. Fourth, some children are ultimately not classifiable as handicapped, and the system is not used for the purpose of finding labels for such children. Fifth, the system guides assessment by delineating sequential steps in the assessment process. The specific assessment techniques used within each branch are chosen at the discretion of the practitioner.

---

*PL 94-142 does not require classroom observations of children suspected of being learning disabled.

Efficient use of the system is predicated on initial efforts to enter the correct branch or branches and on the sequential use of only those assessment techniques appropriate to the branch or branches judged to be relevant to the case. Such use of the system is illustrated with actual cases in Chapter 12.

CONCLUSIONS

We opened this chapter by stating that psychoeducational assessment is a complex endeavor requiring much background knowledge, many specific skills, and a good understanding of the social contexts in which assessment occurs. We hope that we have not discouraged readers from thinking that quality assessments are possible under current conditions. We must acknowledge, however, that assessment practitioners often function under difficult conditions. One serious problem they often face is that they have little control over their own standards of performance (Meyers, Sundstrom, & Yoshida, 1974). Contributing to this problem is the fact that "all . . . assessments involve complex socio-political and economic issues and are not always resolved in the best interest of the child" (Meyers et al., 1974, p. 31). Again, at a minimum, practitioners should attempt to work constructively with school administrators to establish the use of appropriate and efficient assessment procedures. Failure to gain the cooperation of administrators may result in a deterioration in the practitioners' own work conditions and in services to children.

We also advocate that psychoeducational assessment practitioners be involved in the larger political arena. Many of the Reagan administration's proposals for changes in the legal, financial, and administrative contexts of assessment and special education services have provoked heated controversy. These proposals include efforts to abolish the U.S. Department of Education, shift federal responsibilities in special education from categorical to block grants, reduce federal funding of special education, and deregulate major federal laws that affect special education. These proposals and some of the reactions to them are discussed below.

White (1982b) indicates that the Reagan administration is seeking congressional approval to reduce the Department of Education to a sub-Cabinet-level agency to be called the Foundation for Educational Assistance. She further reports that this change could involve the transfer of 31 federal education programs to other federal agencies and the elimination of 23 other federal education programs. Ramage (1982) reports that over 150 interest groups (including the National Association of School Psychologists and the Council for Exceptional Children) are attempting to convince Congress to retain a Cabinet-level Department of Education. Advocates for the retention of the Department of Education generally express concerns about a diminished federal commitment to education as a national priority, while groups favoring the abolition of the Department of Education express concerns about excessive federal control of state and local school system operations. While an extensive discussion of the issues involved in this debate are beyond the scope of this book, interested readers can find references on such issues in the Suggested Readings section at the back of the book.

In addition to efforts to replace the Department of Education with a Foundation for Educational Assistance, the Reagan administration's budget for fiscal 1983 "requests Congress to change existing law by creating two education-of-the-handicapped block grants" ("Reagan Again Proposes," 1982, p. 1). If enacted by Congress, these block grants would be administered by the Foundation. An apparent rationale of the special education block grant proposal is the reduction of federal restrictions and regulations in the operation of state and local special education programs ("Reagan Again Proposes," 1982). Some observers, however, fear that these proposed changes in federal special education law "would be tantamount to repeal of the substantive protections and quality assurances contained in Public Law 94–142" ("Reagan Again Proposes," 1982, p. 1).

White (1982a) reports that the Reagan administration's budget for fiscal 1983 includes a 33 percent reduction in funds for the Department of Education as compared to fiscal 1982. This decrease will be even greater if Congress approves the abolition of the Department of Education in favor of a Foundation for Educational Assistance (White, 1982b). More specifically, the administration's budget reflects a 38 percent decrease in Chapter 1 funds from fiscal 1981 to fiscal 1983 and a 17 percent decrease in special education funds from fiscal 1981 to fiscal 1983 ("The 1983 Education Budget," 1982). Proponents of Chapter 1 programs are lobbying against such cuts (Title I Coalition, 1982) as are proponents of special education programs ("Reagan again Proposes," 1982). An article in *Update*, published by the Council for Exceptional Children, indicates that Congress in 1981 "summarily rejected" Reagan administration recommendations for large special education budget cuts and a repeal of PL 94-142. More recently, congressional leaders

> went on record in opposition to drastic setbacks in the federal special education commitment. Prior to the President's official transmission of his (fiscal 1983) budget to Congress, over one-half of the members of

Congress wrote to him asking that he reconsider Department of Education Secretary Bell's request to seriously cut and block-grant special education programs.*

As indicated, deregulation efforts are also underway. The *Federal Register* of January 13, 1982 indicates that portions of the regulations implementing Section 504 of PL 93-112 as amended by PL 93-516 (Rehabilitation Act Amendments of 1974) have been targeted for deregulation (pp. 1858–1859) as have portions of the regulations implementing PL 94-142 (pp. 1861–1862). As previously noted in this chapter, deregulation efforts are directed toward those sections of federal regulations seen as exceeding requirements contained in federal laws. More specifically, the regulations implementing both Section 504 and PL 94-142 have been designated for regulatory review by President Reagan's Task Force on Regulatory Relief. According to the January 13, 1982 edition of the *Federal Register*, the goal of regulatory review and deregulation is to

> amend the regulations in order to reduce regulatory burdens and costs while continuing to comply with the authorizing statute. If costs imposed by the regulations can be reduced, more money will be available for educating handicapped children. (p. 1862)

This edition also indicates that proposed amendments to the regulations implementing PL 94-142 will appear in an April, 1982, edition of the *Federal Register*. Proposed amendments to the regulations implementing Section 504 are scheduled to appear in June, 1982. Public comment periods are to follow, and public hearings on the proposed amendments to the PL 94-142 regulations are to be held in six cities across the country. Dates for the publication of final amended regulations to these laws have, to our knowledge, yet to be determined.

While the substantive changes to these two sets of regulations are unknown at this writing, a briefing paper from the Office of Special Education and Rehabilitative Services (Note 1) outlines the steps involved in the regulatory review–deregulation process for PL 94-142. Some of the steps indicated in the briefing paper (Note 1) are as follows:

> Analyzing and comparing statutory and regulatory provisions to determine if portions of the regulations are not mandated by specific statutory provisions.
>
> Researching the legislative history of the Act and judicial precedent

---

*From "Reagan again proposes cutting special education." *Update*, 1982, *13*(6), 1 – 5. Published by the Council for Exceptional Children. With permission.

to determine the legal support for regulatory provisions that contain requirements not specified in the Act.

Summarizing and analyzing comments on regulatory provisions submitted by numerous public and private organizations and agencies, parents of handicapped children, educators, and interested citizens.

Identifying regulatory provisions which may be overly prescriptive (in relation to statutory provisions), ineffective because they are unclear to those who are affected by these rules, or unnecessary for fiscal accountability and program evaluation. . . .

Developing and critically examining regulatory alternatives that will be consistent with statutory purposes and requirements while:

— relieving educational agencies of fiscal, paperwork, compliance and other burdens;
— protecting the rights of handicapped children to equal educational opportunity;
— liberating public educational agencies from unnecessary Federal direction and control;
— decreasing the number and impact of regulatory requirements; . . .

Recommending adoptions of the regulatory options that best achieve the above objectives.

Developing and publishing proposed amendments of current regulations for public comment. . . .

Preparing and publishing final rules following the review and consideration of written comments and recommendations received through . . . public participation efforts. (pp. 6 – 7)

The briefing paper (Note 1) further indicates 4 general areas and 16 sets of regulatory sections as initial "targets of opportunity for deregulation." These are listed below.

Area 1   Definitions
— Handicapped Children (including "specific learning disabilities")
— Special Education and Related Services
Area 2   Grants Administration
— State Plans, Local Educational Agency Applications
— State Advisory Panels
— Allocation of Funds; Reports
Area 3   Services
— Free Appropriate Public Education
— Extended School Year Program
— Suspension and Expulsion
— Out-of-State Placement of Handicapped Children
— Individualized Education Programs
— Services Provided to Children Placed in Private Schools by Their Parents
— Comprehensive System of Personnel Development

Area 4   Procedural Safeguards
          —Due Process Procedures
          —Nondiscrimination in Evaluation Procedures
          —Least Restrictive Environment
          —Confidentiality of Information. (p. 2)

It should be emphasized that outcomes relative to the Department of Education, special education block grants, cuts in federal funds for education, and deregulation of federal laws impacting special education are as yet unknown. Since the contents of this book are partially predicated on existing federal regulations, we feel an obligation to provide additional footnotes on "opportunities for deregulation" in Chapter 2 and to continue commenting on the contexts for psychoeducational assessment throughout the book. In essence, we feel a responsibility to assist readers in both understanding current contexts and in anticipating possible changes in these contexts.

Part I

LEGAL AND ETHICAL CONSIDERATIONS

The Impact of Federal Legislation

PREVIOUS DISCUSSIONS have shown how greatly psychoeducational assessment practice is affected by the numerous requirements of the regulations implementing Public Law (PL) 94-142, as well as by other federal laws and federal court decisions. In this chapter, we will take a closer look at these federal laws and their attendant regulations, and their effect upon assessment practice.

The legal framework for psychoeducational assessment is continually changing, as described in the previous chapter. Changes in laws and implementing regulations are noted in the *Federal Register*, and practitioners should periodically review this source in order to keep up to date. In addition, publications such as the *Monitor* of the American Psychological Association (APA) and the *Communique* of the National Association of School Psychologists (NASP) contain frequent reviews of legal developments bearing on assessment practice.

Practitioners must also keep themselves informed about changes in legislation or implementing regulations in their respective states. For example, the Tennessee law governing services to handicapped children was recently amended to delete references to "socially maladjusted," "functionally retarded," and pregnant students. As a result of this amendment, such students are no longer eligible for special education services (although some pregnant students might be considered "other health impaired" and therefore receive the services of home and hospital teachers). "Intellectually gifted" students, however, are still included in the Tennessee special education law, even though services for such students are not required by PL 94-142. Current Tennessee law illustrates the point made earlier that states can add handicapping conditions to those listed by PL 94-142. As we shall see, states may add to the list of handicapping conditions covered by PL 94-142 but may not delete from the list unless they are willing to risk loss of federal funds.

While the legal framework for psychoeducational assessment practice continually changes, an understanding of federal legislation as it currently exists is a prerequisite to legally appropriate practice. Let us look more closely at these federal laws.

FEDERAL LAWS

Public Law 94-142

Davis (1980) reviews a number of pieces of federal legislation related to the education of handicapped persons. PL 94-142 is, in his words, "the most comprehensive and significant piece of legislation regarding the education of handicapped children" (p. 239). A major reason for its importance is that this law provides for the allocation of federal funds for assessment, educational, and related services. Under the law, federal funds may be provided for up to 40 percent of the excess costs involved in providing the services required by the law. This level of funding, however, is not automatic and has never been actually allocated by Congress.

Whatever the level of funding allocated by Congress for a given year, funds are distributed to state departments of education and passed through to local school districts with the provision that they comply with the requirements of the law and its implementing regulations. In order to receive funds allocated under PL 94-142, state departments of education must file acceptable plans for complying with the law's requirements. These plans are submitted for review to the U.S. Department of Education. If a state plan is judged to be acceptable, federal funds are provided to that state department of education. The state department of education, in turn, passes through portions of the state allotment to those local school districts that have filed acceptable compliance plans with the state department.

At this point, it should be noted that state departments of education and local school districts are exempt from the requirements of PL 94-142 if they decline funds provided under that law. However, as we shall see, Section 504 of PL 93-112 (Rehabilitation Act of 1973) provides for loss of any federal funds provided to organizations found to be engaged in practices that discriminate against handicapped persons. As we shall also see, the regulations implementing this section of PL 93-112 (*Federal Register*, May 4, 1977, pp. 22676–22702) contain many of the same requirements found in the regulations implementing PL 94-142. Hence, state departments of education and local school districts are expected to comply with most of the regulations implementing PL 94-142 unless they accept no federal funds at all (Bersoff, Note 2).

In this context, PL 94-142 requires the provision of a free, appropriate public education to all persons 3 through 21 years of age judged to suffer from one of the handicapping conditions listed in the law, unless a state law or court order precludes services to persons 3 through 5 and/or 18 through 21. In addition, school districts must implement procedures designed to locate persons who are or will be eligible for special education services. Such "child find" procedures must be provided for persons from birth through 21 years of age. The age range for child find activities should enable school districts to plan for services for young children (when they become old enough to receive special education services) as well as to provide initial special education services to students currently in school. The child find procedures required by the regulations implementing PL 94-142 are consistent with that law's emphasis on local school districts' assuming responsibility for the education of all handicapped children within their jurisdictions. Local school districts may meet this responsibility by providing their own programs or by contracting for services from another district or agency. Finally, school districts must also implement procedures by which handicapped children and their parents are afforded procedural safeguards. The procedural safeguards requirements of the regulations implementing PL 94-142 are described in a later section.

Section 504 of Public Law 93-112

Section 504 of PL 93-112 is regarded as the first federal civil rights law for handicapped persons (Davis, 1980, p. 237). Although Section 504 originally was restricted to the employment of handicapped persons, Section III,a of PL 93-516 (Rehabilitation Act Amendments of 1974) extended these rights to educational settings. Essentially, the regulations implementing Section 504 state that failure to provide handicapped persons services equal to those received by nonhandicapped persons constitutes a violation of handicapped persons' civil rights. As noted, such civil rights violations on the part of an educational agency could result in a cutoff of all federal funds.

We have also noted that the regulations implementing Section 504 of PL 93-112 are similar to the implementing regulations of PL

94-142. Both sets of regulations require child find activities; the provision of a free, appropriate education in the least restrictive environment; procedural safeguards; nondiscriminatory assessment; and periodic reevaluation. In addition, the regulations implementing Section 504 describe IEPs as viable means of establishing appropriate educational programs.

The regulations implementing Section 504 of PL 93-112 also require the provision of "non-academic and extra-curricular services and activities in such manner as is necessary to afford handicapped students an equal opportunity for participation in such services and activities" (*Federal Register*, May 4, 1977, pp. 22683). These services and activities may include counseling, recreation, athletics, transportation, health services, special-interest clubs, referrals to other agencies, and employment. In relation to assessment, it is clear that assessment for the purposes of vocational guidance and education must be available to handicapped students if provided by the school district to nonhandicapped students. Vocational counseling of handicapped persons must avoid steering them toward a restricted range of occupations (*Federal Register*, May 4, 1977, p. 22683).*

Public Law 93-380

PL 93-380 (Education Amendments of 1974) "provided the basic framework for Public Law 94-142" (Davis, 1980, p. 238). It also contained the Family Rights and Privacy Act (Title V, Sections 513 and 514), which is often referred to as the Buckley Amendment. The Buckley Amendment gives parents (and students 18 years of age and over) the right to inspect, correct, and control access to a student's educational record. Failure on the part of a school district to comply with the regulations implementing the Buckley Amendment (*Federal Register*, June 17, 1976, pp. 24670–24675) could result in loss of all federal funds.

The regulations implementing the Buckley Amendment "are reiterated in the regulations under Public Law 94-142 and Section 504" (Martin, 1979, p. 121). These three sets of regulations preclude school officials' denying parents access to their child's educational record. Reports of assessment findings are usually considered part of a child's educational record. Completed test-record forms might also be considered part of the child's educational record, and assessment

---

*Recall from Chapter 1 that the regulations implementing Section 504 represent "targets of opportunities for deregulation." Some of the services indicated above may no longer be required when the deregulation process is completed.

practitioners may be concerned about compromising test security by showing record blanks to parents. Suggestions for responding to parental requests to review record forms may be found in "Test Protocols in Relation to Sole Possession Records" (APA, updated). Under the Buckley Amendment, parents also have the right to request that school officials amend statements in their child's record that are, in the parents' judgment, inaccurate or misleading. If such requests are denied, parents may insert their written objections into the record, and these objections must be retained in and transmitted with the record. Further, parents' consent must be obtained for the release of information on their child to parties outside the school system. Their consent must be in reference to specific documents and must indicate specific persons or agencies to receive them.

Other Federal Laws

PL 92-424 (Economic Opportunity Amendments of 1972) stipulates that not less than 10 percent of the enrollment opportunities in the country's Head Start programs are to be made available to handicapped children. This law also requires that appropriate services to meet their special needs be provided (Davis, 1980, p. 237).

In a similar vein, PL 94-482 (Vocational Education Act Amendments of 1976) "requires that 10 percent of federal funds allocated to states for vocational education be *set aside* to be spent on the cost of special programs, services, and activities for the handicapped" (Davis, 1980, p. 240, emphasis in the original). Local school districts applying to states for funds allocated under this act must agree to comply with the regulations implementing PL 94-142. Thus "Public Law 94-482, in conjunction with Public Law 94-142 and Section 504 of Public Law 93-112, provides comprehensive program opportunities and procedural safeguards for handicapped individuals" (Davis, p. 240). However, PL 94-482 is now under consideration for reauthorization by the Congress ("Will Reauthorization Jeopardize," 1982, p. 5).

Assessment practitioners should also be familiar with three pieces of federal legislation outlining the rights of developmentally disabled persons. PL 91-517 (Developmental Disabilities Services and Construction Act of 1970) made federal funds available for programs designed to assist developmentally disabled persons (defined then as those suffering from mental retardation, cerebral palsy, and epilepsy) (Davis, p. 237).

PL 94-103 (Developmental Disabilities Assistance and Bill of Rights Act of 1975) expanded the list of conditions subsumed under the term *developmental disabilities*. It also cited several services that are necessary to assist developmentally disabled persons to realize their full potentials and indicated that these services should be available to them as a matter of basic rights. "Such services include developmental programs, residential services, employment services, identification services, facilitating services, treatment services, transportation, and leisure and recreation" (Davis, p. 239). PL 94-103 further required that each state develop a system to protect and advocate the rights of developmentally disabled persons. Each state system is to be functionally independent of any state agency providing services to developmentally disabled persons and is empowered to pursue legal or administrative remedies in the course of its protection and advocacy activities (Martin, 1979, p. 25).

PL 95-602 (Rehabilitation, Comprehensive Services, and Developmental Disabilities Act of 1978) amended previous definitions of developmental disabilitites. The current legal definition incorporates any severe disability occurring before age 22 that results in substantial functional limitation in specified areas of life requiring lifelong services (Davis, p. 240).

Assessment practitioners should be aware of the federal protections afforded developmentally disabled persons. Many of these people are eligible for special education services under PL 94-142 and should be provided with services required by that law and the laws specific to the developmentally disabled. Practitioners should be prepared to deal with advocacy groups for the developmentally disabled organized in accordance with PL 94-103. Such groups are "limited to pursuing issues involving the developmentally disabled, but the remedies they achieve will establish precedents for all handicapped children" (Martin, 1979, p. 25).

Before concluding this section, we should note that assessment practitioners in some states (such as Tennessee) are required to provide assessment services to gifted students. As indicated previously, services for such students are not required by PL 94-142 but are required by some state laws.

With this overview of relevant federal laws and their implementing regulations behind us, we now turn to an analysis of the effects of these laws in a number of key assessment areas.

HANDICAPPING CONDITIONS AND ELIGIBILITY CRITERIA FOR SPECIAL EDUCATION SERVICES

As previously noted, PL 94-142 requires that special education and "related services" be provided children 3 through 21 years of age judged to suffer from 1 or more of the 11 handicapping conditions listed in that law (mentally retarded, hard of hearing, deaf, speech impaired, visually handicapped, seriously emotionally disturbed, orthopedically impaired, other health impaired, deaf-blind, multi-handicapped, or having specific learning disabilities).

Readers should bear in mind that "all assessments involve complex socio-political and economic issues" (Meyers, Sundstrom, & Yoshida, 1974, p. 31). The Reagan administration's desire to reduce federal funds for special education and to amend the regulations governing the provision of special education services probably represents, at least in part, a perceived need to reduce the costs involved in special education programming. Concerns over such costs demonstrate that political and economic considerations weigh heavily in determinations of which children are to be served and to what degree. As previously noted, we support classification systems such as those advocated by Hobbs (1975, 1980) and Duffey, Salvia, Tucker, and Ysseldyke (1981), which should decrease the number of children "falling between the cracks" of our current classification and programming systems. Whether or not our society is willing to pay for appropriate services, however, is a determination to be made largely in the political arena.

Regardless of future political decisions, assessment practitioners must at present make classification decisions in reference to the handicapping conditions listed in PL 94-142. Failure to identify children suffering from any of these conditions would constitute noncompliance with this law and possibly result in loss of federal funds. In addition, some of the children classified as handicapped may also be regarded as developmentally disabled and should be treated in accordance with federal legislation pertinent to those conditions.

Definitions of Handicapping Conditions

The regulations implementing PL 94-142 provide definitions for each of the 11 handicapping conditions. Each state department of education receiving funds allocated under this law must develop eligibility criteria that, at a minimum, include the definitions of handicapping conditions found in the regulations (Martin, 1979, p. 30). The definitions are as follows.

(1) "Deaf" means a hearing impairment which is so severe that the child is impaired in processing linguistic information through hearing, with or without amplification, which adversely affects educational performance.

(2) "Deaf-blind" means concomitant hearing and visual impairments, the combination of which causes such severe communication and other developmental and educational problems that they cannot

be accommodated in special education programs solely for deaf or blind children.

(3) "Hard of hearing" means a hearing impairment, whether permanent or fluctuating, which adversely affects a child's educational performance but which is not included under the definition of "deaf" in this section.

(4) "Mentally retarded" means significantly subaverage general intellectual functioning existing concurrently with deficits in adaptive behavior and manifested during the developmental period which adversely affects a child's educational performance.

(5) "Multihandicapped" means concomitant impairments (such as mentally retarded–blind, mentally retarded–orthopedically impaired, etc.), the combination of which causes such severe educational problems that they cannot be accommodated in special education programs solely for one of the impairments. The term does not include deaf-blind children.

(6) "Orthopedically impaired" means a severe orthopedic impairment which adversely affects a child's educational performance. The term includes impairments caused by congenital anomaly (e.g. clubfoot, absence of some member, etc.), impairments caused by disease (e.g. poliomyelitis, bone tuberculosis, etc.), and impairments from other causes (e.g. cerebral palsy, amputations, and fractures or burns which cause contractures).

(7) "Other health impaired" means limited strength, vitality or alertness, due to chronic or acute health problems such as a heart condition, tuberculosis, rheumatic fever, nephritis, asthma, sickle cell anemia, hemophilia, epilepsy, lead poisoning, leukemia, or diabetes, which adversely affects a child's educational performance.

(8) "Seriously emotionally disturbed" is defined as follows:

(i) The term means a condition exhibiting one or more of the following characteristics over a long period of time and to a marked degree, which adversely affects educational performance:

(A) An inability to learn which cannot be explained by intellectual, sensory, or health factors;

(B) An inability to build or maintain satisfactory interpersonal relationships with peers and teachers;

(C) Inappropriate types of behavior or feelings under normal circumstances;

(D) A general pervasive mood of unhappiness or depression; or

(E) A tendency to develop physical symptoms or fears associated with personal or school problems.

(ii) The term includes children who are schizophrenic or autistic. The term does not include children who are socially maladjusted, unless it is determined that they are seriously emotionally disturbed.

(9) "Specific learning disability" means a disorder in one or more of the basic psychological processes involved in understanding or in using language, spoken or written, which may manifest itself in an

imperfect ability to listen, think, speak, read, write, spell, or to do mathematical calculations. The term includes such conditions as perceptual handicaps, brain injury, minimal brain dysfunction, dyslexia, and developmental aphasia. The term does not include children who have learning problems which are primarily the result of visual, hearing, or motor handicaps, of mental retardation, or of environmental, cultural, or economic disadvantage.

(10) "Speech impaired" means a communication disorder, such as stuttering, impaired articulation, a language impairment, or a voice impairment, which adversely affects a child's educational performance.

(11) "Visually handicapped" means a visual impairment which, even with correction, adversely affects a child's educational performance. The term includes both partially seeing and blind children. (*Federal Register*, August 23, 1977, pp. 42478 – 42479)*

The amended regulations implementing PL 94-142 given in the *Federal Register* of January 16, 1981, indicated that autistic children are no longer to be classified as seriously emotionally disturbed. Instead, they are now to be classified as other health impaired. These amended regulations contain a statement indicating that the amendment reflects expanded knowledge of the nature of autism (p. 3865).

As we have indicated, these definitions of handicapping conditions have been criticized as imprecise (Bardon & Bennett, 1974; Duffey et al., 1981), as failing to guide instruction (Bardon & Bennett; Hallahan & Kauffman, 1976), and as resulting in failure to serve some children experiencing school problems (Hobbs, 1980).

In addition, careful reading of the definitions reveals that a classification of a child as handicapped requires a conclusion that the child not only suffers from a handicap but that the handicap adversely affects his educational performance.† Some children suffering from demonstrable handicaps may not have their educational performances adversely affected. Such children are, therefore, ineligible for special education services. In the case of a preschooler, classification is, of course, contingent on a prediction that the handicap will adversly affect educational performance.

The definitions also require that the sources of educational prob-

---

*PL 94-142 provides only a definition of specific learning disability and does not incorporate the terms *deaf-blind* or *multihandicapped*. Hence, the definitions of handicapping conditions found in the regulations implementing PL 94-142 represent "targets of opportunity for deregulation."

†The term *adversely affects educational performance* has been criticized as lacking sufficient clarity to guide classification decisions. The Office of Special Education and Rehabilitative Services (Note 1) is considering steps to provide greater clarity.

lems experienced by children lie primarily within the children. In order to receive special education and related services, children must perform poorly in school because they are mentally retarded, learning disabled, or otherwise handicapped. Children who experience school problems primarily as a result of conditions external to themselves (economic disadvantage, frequent changes in schools, poor instruction, and so forth) are ineligible for special education services and may "fall between the cracks."

Psychoeducational assessment practitioners are most often called upon to assist in the classification of children as mentally retarded, seriously emotionally disturbed, or suffering from a specific learning disability. One of the reasons for this is that such practitioners are usually not trained to determine the presence and severity of handicapping conditions such as deafness and orthopedic impairments. Another reason is that mental retardation, emotional disturbance, and learning disabilities occur with greater frequency than do all but one of the other handicapping conditions. Speech impairments represent the exception to this rule, and children with such impairments are best assessed by persons trained in speech pathology.

It will be recalled from the previous chapter that mental retardation, emotional disturbance, and learning disability have been particularly singled out as "imprecise diagnostic classifications" (Duffey et al., 1981, p. 433). It will also be recalled that most children suffering from one of these three handicapping conditions are mildly handicapped. Since classification decisions essentially involve judgments about the nature and severity of problems, it is understandable that classification decisions involving children thought to be mentally retarded, emotionally disturbed, or learning disabled are particularly problematic. The frequency with which assessment practitioners encounter children being considered for one of these three labels and the problems involved in their assignment warrant more detailed attention to these definitions.

Mental Retardation

Children are classified as mentally retarded partially on the basis of evidence of "significantly subaverage general intellectual functioning," according to the definition just quoted. There are several problems with this portion of the definition. One problem involves the term *significantly subaverage*. State departments of education are required to clarify this term in their eligiblity criteria for special education services. In Tennessee, the term means

Approximately one-half to three-fourths the normal rate of functioning in development and/or ability (educable mentally retarded). Approximately one-fourth to one-half the normal rate of functioning in development and/or ability (trainable mentally retarded). Approximately less than one-fourth of the normal rate of functioning in development and/or ability (profoundly mentally retarded). (Tennessee State Board of Education, 1979, p. 74)

Evidence for such significantly subaverage general intellectual functioning usually takes the form of scores on intelligence tests. In Tennessee, IQ scores ranging from 50 to 75 are considered appropriate for a classification of a child as educably mentally retarded. Many practitioners, however, will not so classify a child unless his or her IQ score is below 70. Even with a score below 70, several cautions are in order. Did the test have adequate technical adequacy? Was a confidence interval of two standard errors of measurement above and below an estimated true score established? If so, did the upper end of that confidence interval extend above an IQ of 70 or 75? Was the test an adequate sample of what could be considered intelligent behaviors? Did testing conditions facilitate the child's best efforts? Did the child appear to exert his or her best effort? Was the test normed adequately? Can it be assumed that the child is comparable in acculturation to most of the children in the norm group? If not, are pluralistic norms available? Is the child free of physical or sensory problems that might account for the low score?

Evaluating the meaning of a low IQ score obviously requires much professional knowledge and good judgment. Essentially, a practitioner must decide that the low IQ score is an accurate and fair reflection of the child's current functioning before accepting an as yet tentative conclusion that the child is mentally retarded. If this tentative conclusion still seems viable after intelligence testing, the practitioner must investigate whether or not the child's significanly subaverage intellectual functioning is accompanied by deficits in adaptive behavior.

Judging the nature and severity of deficits in adaptive behavior is also difficult. There is some disagreement as to what is meant by the term *adaptive behavior* (see Chapter 10). Some techniques for measuring adaptive behavior focus only on the child's performance of nonacademic tasks in the school setting. We feel, however, that the term "most appropriately refers to a student's level of social functioning in home and neighborhood environments" (Helton & Workman, 1982). We believe that by assessing a child's home and neighborhood performance, as well as his or her school performance, we can achieve a more complete picture of the child's functioning across settings to be used in making a classification decision. We also are concerned about overlooking evidence of intellectual potential reflected in children's successful coping behaviors in home and neighborhood settings.

Much controversy surrounds the assessment of adaptive behavior (Oakland & Goldwater, 1979). Not only is there debate about the settings in which adaptive behavior is to be assessed; there is also debate about how severe the deficit in adaptive behavior must be for the child to warrant a classification of mentally retarded. The federal definition of mental retardation speaks to neither of these issues. In Tennessee, the eligibility criteria for mental retardation are also silent on these matters. Hence, judgments about a child's adaptive behavior may be essentially at the practitioner's discretion. Again, the practitioner may be torn between a desire to classify (or not classify) accurately and a recognition of the child's need for special assistance.

> Perhaps as many as 75% of the EMR [educably mentally retarded] population would be declassified if we insisted upon below average performance on both IQ and adaptive behavior measures. This would serve to severely decrease the number of children mislabeled, but it might also deny to them special resources available through this classification.*

Ultimately at issue in the classification of a child as mentally retarded is the nature of mental retardation itself. Reschly (1980) indicates that classification of children as mentally retarded on the basis of deficits in both intellectual functioning and adaptive behavior reflects a conception of mental retardation as a condition that is biological or constitutional in origin, evident across all settings, and permanent. He suggests that this is an accurate conception of severe mental retardation but not of mild mental retardation. He further suggests that failure to classify as mentally retarded children with IQ scores indicating mild retardation but average adaptive behavior scores not only reflects a misunderstanding of the nature of mild mental retardation but also fails to address these children's educational problems. He proposes that changes be made in the classification system for such children and notes that such changes must address several questions. Reschly suggests that we ask "what sort of classification will be acceptable yet effective in generating sufficient special monies for needed services; what sort of educational programs are most effective (and acceptable); and are these children and

---

*From Oakland, T., & Goldwater, D. Assessment and interventions for mildly retarded and learning disabled children. In G. Phye & D. Reschly (Eds.), *School psychology: Perspectives and issues.* New York: Academic Press, 1979. With permission.

programs within the purview of special education" (Reschly, 1980, pp. 131 – 132).

We are sympathetic to the concern about lack of special education services to children with IQ scores indicating mild retardation but generally average adaptive behavior scores, and we concur with Reschly's call for changes in the classification system that will reflect the important differences between such children and severely retarded children. However, at the present time, we advocate that such children not be classified as mentally retarded, since we are fearful that such children will be viewed (incorrectly) as biologically and permanently impaired and programmed for on this basis. Instead, we urge assessment practitioners to seek other special services (such as Chapter 1 programs) for such children and to assist their regular classroom teachers in meeting their programming needs.

Emotional Disturbance

Several features of the definition of "seriously emotionally disturbed" require attention. To be classified as such, a child must exhibit "one or more" of the listed characteristics. Further, the child must exhibit one or more of these characteristics "over a long period of time and to a marked degree." In addition, one or more of these characteristics must adversely affect the child's educational performance.

Several issues are immediately apparent. What constitutes a long period of time? What is meant by "to a marked degree"? While the definition does not address these issues, it is clear that the intent is to exclude from this classification children who are experiencing short-term, situational problems. It is also clear that children experiencing academic problems are not to be classified as emotionally disturbed if their academic problems result primarily from intellectual, sensory, or health impairments.

Several other issues are more subtle. Our experience suggests that many practitioners are reluctant to classify children under this category because it is termed *"seriously* emotionally disturbed." Where is the line between "mild" and "serious" disturbance? Notice also that children who are socially maladjusted are not included in the category unless there is evidence that they are "seriously emotionally disturbed." Hence predelinquent and delinquent children are apparently not to be so classified unless a case can be made that their antisocial behaviors result from emotional disturbance.

An important issue in the classification of children as seriously emotionally disturbed involves the types of data considered in assigning this label. Notice that evidence must be collected demonstrating that the child exhibits one or more of five characteristics. These five characteristics represent a mixture of observable behaviors and unobservable feelings, such as "a general pervasive mood of unhappiness or depression." Traditionally, children suspected to be emotionally disturbed have been assessed through the use of projective techniques. Such techniques require children to react to ambiguous test materials, such as inkblots or pictures of social situations, and their reactions have been considered indicative of unobservable, perhaps even unconscious, feelings. Children whose reactions have been judged to reflect unusual and problematic feelings sometimes are classified as seriously emotionally disturbed.

We are frankly uncomfortable with the use of projective techniques for this purpose. Interpretation of children's responses to such techniques requires great professional skill and experience. In addition, projective techniques have been found to have very limited technical adequacy (Bardon & Bennett, 1974; O'Leary, 1972). Further, we do not see results of projective testing as particularly useful for programming purposes.

In Chapter 9, we discuss projective techniques in more detail but propose alternative strategies for assessing social/emotional problems in children, strategies incorporating both norm-referenced behavior checklists and criterion-referenced observation systems. While these strategies do not eliminate problems inherent in the vague definition of emotional disturbance, we believe that they represent the best available method for classifying and programming for emotionally disturbed children.

Learning Disability

"One of the amendments that Public Law 94-142 made to prior legislation was the addition of children with specific learning disabilities to the definition of handicapped persons" (Bersoff & Miller, 1979, p. 153). In an apparent attempt to limit the number of children classified as learning disabled and to establish some uniformity in their assessment, Congress mandated that regulations and eligibility criteria specific to this category be published at a later date (Bersoff & Miller, pp. 153–154). After a year of study, the following conclusions relative to this category were published in the *Federal Register* of November 29, 1976 (Bersoff & Miller, p. 154).

1. It is not possible to specify all the components of each specific learning disability, except to say that there is a major discrepancy between expected achievement and ability.

2. Several theories exist as to the cause of learning disabilities.
3. There is no universally accepted explanation as to how and why such children learn or do not learn.
4. It is not possible to list specific diagnostic instruments appropriate for these children nor are there any generally accepted instruments helpful in this regard. (Bersoff & Miller, p. 154)

These conclusions were followed by the regulations implementing PL 94-142 published in the *Federal Register* on August 23, 1977. These regulations include the definition of a "specific learning disability" presented earlier (see pp. 52– 53). This definition was amended slightly in regulations concerning learning disabilities published in the *Federal Register* of December 29, 1977 (pp. 65082 – 65085). The amended definition added emotional disturbance to the list of conditions that, if present and seen as a major source of a child's problem, would not permit that child to be classified as learning disabled.

As indicated previously, this definition of a "specific learning disability" implies that the child's learning problems are caused by a deficit (or deficits) in psychoeducational processing skills: in other words, it is based on the psychoeducational processing model discussed in Chapter 1. This implication has resulted in many practitioners' including formal psychoeducational process measures in assessment batteries used with children suspected of being learning disabled. Such measures (discussed in Chapter 7) may be used in the context of our branching assessment system. However, we do not view them as being absolutely requisite for classification purposes or as particularly useful for programming purposes.

Our position on this matter represents a synthesis of several lines of reasoning. First, we are not convinced that deficits in psychoeducational processing skills cause academic problems, that such deficits can be reliably and validly assessed, and that remediation of such deficits leads to improved academic functioning. As indicated in Chapter 1, for programming our primary allegiance is to the task analysis model.

Second, the regulations concerning the assessment of children suspected of being learning disabled published in the *Federal Register* of December 29, 1977, do not contain direct reference to the use of formal psychoeducational processing skill measures. The "criteria for determining the existence of a specific learning disability" read as follows:

(a) A team may determine that a child has a specific learning disability if:
(1) The child does not achieve commensurate with his or her age and ability levels in one or more of the areas listed in paragraph (a) (2)

of this section, when provided with learning experiences appropriate for the child's age and ability levels; and

(2) The team finds that a child has a severe discrepancy between
achievement and intellectual ability in one or more of the following areas:

 (i) Oral expression;
 (ii) Listening comprehension;
(iii) Written expression;
(iv) Basic reading skill;
 (v) Reading comprehension;
(vi) Mathematics calculation; or
(vii) Mathematics reasoning.

(b) The team may not identify a child as having a specific learning
disability if the severe discrepancy between ability and achievement is primarily the result of:

(1) A visual, hearing, or motor handicap;
(2) Mental retardation;
(3) Emotional disturbance; or
(4) Environmental, cultural or economic disadvantage. (*Federal Register*, December 29, 1977, p. 65083)

What these regulations do require is evidence documenting a severe discrepancy between expected and actual achievement in one or
more of seven areas. While the regulations are silent on what constitutes a "severe" discrepancy, evidence of such a discrepancy usually
comes from intelligence and achievement testing. Typically, expected achievement levels are established on the basis of IQ scores (with
all the problems that entails), while actual achievement levels reflect
scores on norm-referenced achievement tests.

These regulations also require judgments that the severe discrepancy between expected and actual achievement is not the result of (1)
lack of appropriate learning experiences, (2) the presence of another
handicapping condition, or (3) disadvantaged acculturation. Other
sections of these regulations further require evaluation by a multidisciplinary team, including observation of the child in the regular
classroom setting. This observation is to be made by someone other
than the child's regular classroom teacher. Following the evaluation,
the team must prepare a written report of the results of the evaluation. The report must include statements of

(1) Whether the child has a specific learning disability;
(2) The basis for making the determination;
(3) The relevant behavior noted during the observation of the child;
(4) The relationship of that behavior to the child's academic functioning;
(5) The educationally relevant medical findings, if any;

(6) Whether there is a severe discrepancy between achievement and ability which is not correctable without special education and related services; and

(7) The determination of the team concerning the effects of environmental, cultural, or economic disadvantage. (Federal Register, December 29, 1977, p. 65083)

In addition,

Each team member shall certify in writing whether the report reflects his or her conclusion. If it does not reflect his or her conclusion, the team member must submit a separate statement presenting his or her conclusions. (*Federal Register*, December 29, 1977, p. 65083)*

Conclusions

We have sought to illustrate here the difficult judgments required of assessment practitioners in classifying children as mentally retarded, emotionally disturbed, or learning disabled. We will elaborate our views concerning the assessment of such children in subsequent chapters and illustrate them in the final chapter. For now, however, we turn to some additional key areas of assessment affected by federal legislation.

RELATED SERVICES

In the first chapter, we indicated that each IEP must list any related services seen as necessary for a handicapped child to benefit from special education, and we listed the 13 related services described in the regulations implementing PL 94-142. We now present the definitions of these related services found in those regulations.

(1) "Audiology" includes:
(i) Identification of children with hearing loss;
(ii) Determination of the range, nature, and degree of hearing loss, including referral for medical or other professional attention for the habilitation of hearing;

---

*While 94-142 defines a specific learning disability, the law does not outline procedures for determining whether a child does or does not exhibit this handicapping condition. Hence, the criteria for making this determination, the involvement of a multidisciplinary evaluation team in assessing children suspected of being learning disabled, the required classroom observation, and the team report represent "opportunities for deregulation."

   (iii) Provision of habilitative activities, such as language habilitation, auditory training, speech reading (lip-reading), hearing evaluation, and speech conservation;

   (iv) Creation and administration of programs for prevention of hearing loss;

   (v) Counseling and guidance of pupils, parents, and teachers regarding hearing loss; and

   (vi) Determination of the child's need for group and individual amplification, selecting and fitting an appropriate aid, and evaluating the effectiveness of amplification.

   (2) "Counseling services" means services provided by qualified social workers, psychologists, guidance counselors, or other qualified personnel.

   (3) "Early identification" means the implementation of a formal plan for identifying a disability as early as possible in a child's life.

   (4) "Medical services" means services provided by a licensed physician to determine a child's medically related handicapping condition which results in the child's need for special education and related services.

   (5) "Occupational therapy" includes:

   (i) Improving, developing or restoring functions impaired or lost through illness, injury, or deprivation;

   (ii) Improving ability to perform tasks for independent functioning when functions are impaired or lost; and

   (iii) Preventing, through early intervention, initial or further impairment or loss of function.

   (6) "Parent counseling and training" means assisting parents in understanding the special needs of their child and providing parents with information about child development.

   (7) "Physical therapy" means services provided by a qualified physical therapist.

   (8) "Psychological services" include:

   (i) Administering psychological and educational tests, and other assessment procedures;

   (ii) Interpreting assessment results;

   (iii) Obtaining, integrating, and interpreting information about child behavior and conditions relating to learning;

   (iv) Consulting with other staff members in planning school programs to meet the special needs of children as indicated by psychological tests, interviews, and behavioral evaluations; and

   (v) Planning and managing a program of psychological services, including psychological counseling for children and parents.

   (9) "Recreation" includes:

   (i) Assessment of leisure function;

   (ii) Therapeutic recreation services;

   (iii) Recreation programs in school and community agencies; and

   (iv) Leisure education.

(10) "School health services" means services provided by a qualified school nurse or other qualified person.

(11) "Social work services in schools" include:

(i) Preparing a social or developmental history on a handicapped child;

(ii) Group and individual counseling with the child and family;

(iii) Working with those problems in a child's living situation (home, school, and community) that affect the child's adjustment in school; and

(iv) Mobilizing school and community resources to enable the child to receive maximum benefit from his or her educational program.

(12) "Speech pathology" includes:

(i) Identification of children with speech or language disorders;

(ii) Diagnosis and appraisal of specific speech or language disorders;

(iii) Referral for medical or other professional attention necessary for the habilitaton of speech or language disorders;

(iv) Provisions of speech and language services for the habilitation or prevention of communicative disorders; and

(v) Counseling and guidance of parents, children, and teachers regarding speech and language disorders.

(13) "Transportation" includes:

(i) Travel to and from school and between schools;

(ii) Travel in and around school buildings; and

(iii) Specialized equipment (such as special or adapted buses, lifts, and ramps), if required to provide special transportation for a handicapped child. (*Federal Register*, August 23, 1977, pp. 42479 – 42480)*

While these definitions include a wide range of related services, the regulations make it clear that services not included in the definitons are required if needed by a handicapped child (p. 42480). The regulations also note, however, that not all handicapped children will require a related service (p. 42480). When necessary, related services are to be provided a handicapped child or that child's parents (parent counseling and training) without cost (p. 42478).

A determination that a handicapped child or that child's parents need related services in order for the child to benefit from special education sometimes involves a difficult prediction. Essentially, the prediction involves a judgment about whether or not the child will benefit from special education without the related service. Such pre-

---

*Recall from Chapter 1 that the related services of parent counseling and training, school health services, and social work services in schools are not mentioned in PL 94-142. In addition, PL 94-142 does not define any of the related services listed above. Hence, there are "opportunities for deregualtion" in terms of both inclusion of certain related services and definitions of all related services.

dictions require careful consideration and the application of the best professional judgment available.

Assessment practitioners sometimes experience pressure from school administrators not to recommend related services, since such services are sometimes quite expensive to school districts. Practitioners faced with these pressures must be prepared to defend recommendations for related services. In our view, however, they must also be prepared to stick to their guns when they view related services as necessary for any handicapped child.

REQUIRED ASSESSMENT DOMAINS

As we have seen, the regulations implementing PL 94-142 require that an assessment be conducted in all areas related to the suspected disability and that no single procedure be used as the sole criterion for determining an appropriate educational program. We have also stated that it is possible to fulfill the law and to make an assessment of each child that is sufficiently comprehensive to ensure appropriate classification and programming decisions without taking inordinate amounts of scarce assessment time. We have further indicated that we advocate individualized assessment of each child within the context of our branching assessment system.

Several clarifications and elaborations of these general points are needed at this time. We advocate that each child assessed be screened for sensory, motor, and health problems that might interfere with educational performance. After such screening and an interview with the referral source, other techniques within the assessment domains seen as relevant to the case should be used. Some children will require assessment across a greater number of assessment domains than other children. For instance, the referral-source interview may indicate that the only problem experienced by the child is an articulation disorder. This child can be classified as speech impaired on the basis of a health screening, the referral-source interview, a standardized articulation test, and an observation of articulation behavior in conversational speech. Such assessment would also probably suffice for programming purposes. This assessment might involve only the child's regular classroom teacher, a school nurse, and a speech pathologist.

In contrast, the child suspected to be suffering from a "specific learning disability" must be assessed across a wider range of domains. These would include (at a minimum) health factors (through the health screening), intelligence, academic achievement, and class-room behavior (assessed through the referral-source interview and classroom observation). The child's psychoeducational processing skills might also be assessed. In addition, data would have to be collected to rule out emotional disturbance or disadvantaged accultura-tion as primary causes of the child's academic difficulties. This more comprehensive assessment of the learning disabled child would require both more time and more personnel than would the assessment of the speech impaired child. Specifically, the assessment of the learning disabled child would probably require the assembly of a team including the child's regular classroom teacher, a school nurse, a school psychologist, a special education teacher, and perhaps others.

It should also be remembered that assessment for purposes of vocational education and guidance must be provided as needed to handicapped students if such assessment is available to nonhandi-capped students. Such assessment services are particularly appropri-ate for handicapped students of secondary school age and are de-scribed for interested readers in sources such as S. Miller (1979), Patton (1981), and Stodden and Ianacone (1981).

REQUIRED CHARACTERISTICS OF ASSESSMENT TECHNIQUES

We have already seen that the regulations implementing PL 94-142 require that tests and other evaluation techniques be validated for the specific purposes for which they are used.* We have noted that this requirement has not always been honored and that currently much confusion exists as to what is required to validate a test for a particular purpose. At this point, we reiterate some points previously made about evaluating the use of assessment techniques for par-ticular purposes and also present some additional information on this topic.

One consideration in evaluating the use of an assessment tech-nique for a particular purpose involves the type of decision to be made. Ysseldyke (1979) describes five types of decisions that incorpo-rate data from assessment techniques.

---

*Recall from Chapter 1 that PL 94-142 does not require that tests be validated for specific purposes for which they are used. Hence, this portion of the regulations imple-menting PL 94-142 represents an "opportunity for deregulation."

Screening and Identification Decisions.   The purpose of screening and identification is to determine whether or not a particular child appears sufficiently different in some characteristic from other children to warrant further assessment. We have stated that we believe that all children referred for psychoeducational assessment should be screened for sensory, motor, and health problems that might inhibit educational performance. Assessment techniques appropriate to this task are described in Chapter 6. Screening data that suggest such problems should constitute a basis for referrals for further assessment and treatment of the suspected problems. Screening techniques should have reasonable reliability and validity, but since only tentative judgments are involved in screening, such techniques may permissibly have less technical adequacy that do techniques used for classification and placement purposes.

Classification and Placement Decisions.   Techniques appropriate to decisions concerning classification and placement yield data useful in determining whether or not children can be judged as suffering from handicapping conditons. Such data should address the nature and severity of the handicapping conditions so that a correct classification can be made. Techniques used for classification purposes should be highly reliable and valid, since important and conclusive determinations are involved in classification decisions. We have suggested that assessment data relevant to such decisions should be considered in terms of confidence intervals constructed around estimated true scores (see p. 19).

Instructional Planning Decisions.   Techniques appropriate to instructional planning decisions yield data useful for programming purposes. Such decisions involve determinations of what to teach children (content) and how to teach it (methodology). While programmming decisions require reliable and valid information, incorrect decisions can usually be recognized and corrected more quickly than is the case with incorrect classification decisions, since the success or failure of the remediation can quickly be seen. IEPs that are not judged to be effectively promoting children's progress should be modified as soon as such judgments are made.

Pupil Evaluation Decisions.   Techniques appropriate to pupil evaluation decisions yield data useful for determinations about whether or not children are progressing adequately in their current educational placements. Decisions that children are not making adequate progress in their regular classrooms may lead to their initial referral for psychoeducational assessment. Such decisions about children already participating in special education programs should lead to modifications in their IEPs. In the latter cases, further assessment involving possible reclassifications of handicapping conditions are usually not necessary.

Program Evaluation Decisions.   Techniques appropriate to program evaluation decisions yield data useful for determing whether or not specific educational programs are benefitting participating children. While data are collected on individual children participating in the programs, these data are analyzed with reference to the group, rather than the individual child. It should be noted that data from many assessment techniques (such as academic achievement measures) may be analyzed from either an individual or a group perspective.

Although all five decisions require assessment data of reasonable reliability and validity, it is especially important that assessment techniques used for classification purposes be technically adequate. Again, classification decisions have the most potential for stigmatizing individual children and are usually reconsidered less frequently than are programming and pupil evaluation decisions. Further, screening decisions are, by definition, tentative, and program evaluation decisions do not focus on individual children.

Even if an assessment technique is seen as generally appropriate for a particular type of decision, that technique may not be appropriate for a particular child. For instance, the technique may not be appropriate for the child's age or ability level. Or, the technique may have been normed on children quite different in acculturation from the individual child. Further, the technique may not reflect academic content similar to the content to which the child has been, or will be, exposed. Finally, the technique may require sensory or physical skills that the child does not possess.

Unless assessment techniques have been chosen in terms of the considerations presented above, it is unlikely that they will be valid for the purposes for which they are used. Choosing assessment techniques appropriate to various types of decisions and individual children is a complex task requiring good professional judgment.

Screening, classification, and programming decisions for children who are (or are suspected to be) mentally retarded, emotionally disturbed, and learning disabled are particularly difficult. Psychoeducational assessment practitioners play key roles in the assessment of such children, but should bring in other specialists as needed for assistance in specific cases. Similarly, psychoeducational assessment practitioners should be brought in to consult as needed in the evaluation of handicapped children for whom other assessment practitioners (physicians, nurses, optometrists, audiologists, and speech pathologists) play key roles. Such children (with the exception of speech impaired children) are likely to suffer from one or more infrequently encountered (or low-incidence) handicaps. Psychoeducational assessment practitioners lacking sufficient expertise to assist in the evaluation of any child with a handicap of low incidence must, ethically, refer that child to a colleague possessing the necessary expertise. Readers interested in learning more about assessment techniques appropriate to such children should consult sources such as Gerken (1979).

ASSESSMENT PERSONNEL

We have already alluded to the regulations implementing PL 94-142 requiring that tests and other evaluation materials be "administered by trained personnel in conformance with the instructions provided by their producer" (*Federal Register,* August 23, 1977, p. 42496). *Trained personnel* is defined as those who are deemed qualified by state departments of education to perform specific tasks. Each state department of education, then, must determine which types of personnel are allowed to perform various assessment activities.

Since the regulations implementing PL 94-142 require that a child be assessed in all areas related to the suspected disability, some children will require the assessment services of a number of different practitioners.* Legally, each practitioner should not utilize assessment techniques or draw conclusions about a child that fall outside the recognized boundaries of the professional discipline he or she represents. Ethically, each practitioner must also be aware of the limits of his or her personal expertise in using the techniques he or she may be legally entitled to use, in order to avoid the provision of legally acceptable but ethically inadequate services.

The regulations implementing PL 94-142 also require that, when feasible, children be assessed in their native languages or other preferred modes of communication. While assessment practitioners would obviously want to avoid classification errors such as labeling

---

*Recall from Chapter 1 that the requirements that tests be administered by trained personnel and that the child be assessed in all areas related to the suspected disability are not found in PL 94-142. Again, these requirements represent "opportunities for deregulation."

monolingual Spanish-speaking children as mentally retarded partially on the basis of intelligence tests administered in English, these practitioners should also be aware of problems involved in translating intelligence and achievement tests. Items in such tests may not have the same meanings or levels of difficulty when translated into another language. Hence, norms established only on English-speaking populations may be of questionable value in judging the performances of children tested in another language. While it has been suggested that translators be used in the administration of intelligence and achievement tests, this should probably be done only with tests that have norms specific to translated versions. If such norms are unavailable, "perhaps the wisest course of action is to simply avoid the use of norm-referenced standardized tests of achievement and ability" (Reschly, 1979, p. 239). Part of the rationale for avoiding the use of such tests with monolingual, non-English-speaking children involves the recognition that many of these children will probably be better served in educational programs designed especially for non-English-speaking children than in special education programs. When inferences about the intellectual functioning of such children must be made and norms based on translation are unavailable, it may be preferable to use nonverbal measures of intelligence, rather than translated verbal tests (Gerken, 1978).

While we believe that these cautions about the translation of intelligence and achievement tests and about educational programming for monolingual non-English-speaking children are also appropriate for bilingual children whose primary language is not English, we do see translators as appropriately involved in other assessment domains. Specifically, we see no major problems in using translators in the assessment of sensory and health factors, some modality skills, adaptive behavior, and social/emotional functioning.

The use of translators (interpreters) may also be appropriate in the assessment of deaf and hearing impaired children who possess limited speech reading and speaking skills. While it is preferable that the assessment of such children be conducted by assessment practitioners familiar with finger spelling and sign language, such practitioners are often unavailable (Gerken, 1979). When interpreters are used in the assessment of children, they should, ideally, be familiar with testing procedures and the psychology of deafness (Levine, 1976). Again, intelligence and achievement tests used with such children are most appropriately used in the context of norms for administration *through* finger spelling and sign language.

Parents (and, when appropriate, children) should be considered active partners in the assessment process. Their active participation enhances the quantity and quality of assessment data, and hence should result in more appropriate classification and programming judgments. Their active participation is also encouraged by the APA and NASP codes of ethics and, as we have mentioned, is now mandated by federal law.

Before concluding this section, we should note our concurrence with Helton and Kicklighter's (Note 4) argument that efforts to reform assessment practice have tended to pay too little attention to the competencies required of assessment personnel. While efforts to improve assessment techniques and use existing techniques appropriately are warranted, upgrading the competencies required of assessment practitioners represents an important part of the solution to inappropriate assessment practices. Such efforts will require involvement on the part of federal and state government, training programs, professional associations, and individual practitioners. Concern about this topic may be growing, as evidenced by articles by Cegelka (1978) and Gerken (1979). These articles outline the knowledge and skills seen as necessary to the assessment of mentally retarded persons (Cegelka) and hearing, vision, and orthopedically impaired persons (Gerken).

PARTICIPANTS IN MEETINGS

A team approach is one of the best ways to ensure comprehensive and adequate classification and programming decisions. The team should include practitioners representing different specialties as dictated by the needs of each individual child and by legal and ethical considerations. Parents and, when appropriate, children should be considered active partners in activities leading to both classification and programming decisions. These suggestions represent what we believe to be "best practice" recommendations for assessment work. At this point, it is appropriate to contrast these "best practice" recommendations with practices required by federal legislation and implementing regulations.

As previously noted, the regulations implementing PL 94-142 require that each IEP be formulated by a specified group. The group is essentially responsible for making programming decisions reflecting the perceived needs of the handicapped child. The group must consist of the child's regular classroom teacher, special education personnel, "personnel knowledgeable of assessment," and one or both of the child's parents (unless parents refuse to participate). The regulations therefore do not specifically mandate the inclusion of a psychoeducational assessment practitioner. In addition, the child may participate in the team, as may others, at the discretion of the school or the parents.

The regulations governing participation in meetings to develop IEPs have been interpreted in some school districts as not requiring the presence of psychoeducational assessment practitioners who assisted in assessing the child, as long as someone in the group is judged to be "knowledgeable of assessment." In such school districts, psychoeducational assessment practitioners are sometimes encouraged not to attend IEP meetings, partially because their attendance might delay their assessment work with other children. While we recognize the need for such practitioners to assess children as efficiently as possible, we believe that their encouraged absence from such meetings is problematic.

This practice may involve an assumption that psychoeducational assessment practitioners are knowledgeable about classification, but not about programming. Our experience suggests that this is usually incorrect. Such practitioners often have much to offer in regard to clarifications of children's current levels of educational functioning and decisions involving needed educational and related services, provision of services in the least restrictive alternative, and criteria and procedures for evaluating children's progress. Failure to utilize their expertise may result in IEPs that are legally acceptable but less effective than they might be in promoting children's development.

This practice also raises ethical questions. Both the APA and the NASP ethical codes require that psychologists take steps to ensure that their assessment results are not misused by others. In addition, both ethical codes require that assessment results be presented objectively and clearly to clients and that reservations about the accuracy of assessment data be communicated. We believe that compliance with these ethical requirements is best assured by assessment practitioners' active participation in IEP meetings. Their absence from such meetings, in our judgment, is justified only when psychoeducational assessment practitioners make careful determinations that meeting participants will make appropriate programming decisions and honor ethical requirements in their absence. This is not to suggest that psychoeducational assessment practitioners are more expert or ethical than other school personnel. Instead, it reflects our belief that psychoeducational assessment practitioners usually have specialized areas of expertise and unique perspectives that are often beneficial to the children for when IEPs are developed. Their participation in the development of IEPs would also help ensure continuity across assessment and programming activities.

It is true that assessment practitioners' routine attendance at IEP meetings may delay their assessment work with other children. We agree that efficient assessment is important, but efficiency should not take precedence over good programming decisions or professional ethics. When efficiency considerations threaten more important considerations, school officials should recognize that additional assessment personnel may be needed. The costs involved in hiring additional personnel to address these more important considerations are justified from the perspective of children as clients. Assessment personnel, for their part, must be willing to work not only diligently but also collaboratively within the school system in efforts to assist children.

THE INDIVIDUALIZED EDUCATIONAL PROGRAM

In the previous chapter, we noted that each IEP must contain statements of the child's current levels of educational performance and a listing of the specific special education services and related services to be provided the child. In addition, the IEP must indicate the degree to which the child will participate in regular educational programs, dates for initiation of services and their anticipated duration, and criteria and procedures for evaluating the child's progress. We also noted that the IEP must be reviewed and, if needed, modified at least once a year. We suggested that an IEP be reviewed more often if the child does not seem to be making appropriate progress.

We have also implied that the IEP is an important document, since a well-formulated and well-implemented IEP will contribute to the child's optimal progress. Unfortunately, as we have stated, a poorly formulated IEP may be legally acceptable but may not make much of a contribution to the child's progress. The IEP should be carefully formulated by a multidisciplinary team consisting of all the persons who can make valuable contributions to it. This can be a time-consuming but worthwhile endeavor. We have also suggested that effective programming compensates to a degree for any stigmatization resulting from the labeling of the child.

It should be remembered that the regulations implementing PL 94-142 require that handicapped children be provided a free, *appropriate* public education. The special education services and related services specified in the IEP must be appropriate to the child's needs and not simply the services that the school district is already providing to other handicapped children (Martin, 1979, p. 82). Formulating IEPs that are truly individualized requires that school districts provide a continuum of services for their handicapped children. As previously noted, school districts may contract with other school districts, agencies, or individual practitioners for some of these services. Nevertheless, school districts must make available a range of educational placements, including regular classes, special classes, special schools, home instruction, and instruction in hospitals and institutions. In addition, school districts must provide resource room or itinerant instruction in conjunction with regular class placements (*Federal Register*, August 23, 1977, p. 42497).

The regulations implementing PL 94-142 also require that all educational placements of handicapped children be in the "least restrictive" environment. Careful professional judgment on the part of assessment practitioners and others is required to determine what constitutes the least restrictive environment possible for each handicapped child. While no handicapped child should be placed in educational or other settings in which he or she cannot make adequate progress, each child must be educated with nonhandicapped children to the maximum extent possible. The regulations implementing PL 94-142 provide some guidance in making decisions about what constitutes the least restrictive environment for a handicapped child. Specifically, a handicapped child may be removed from the regular educational environment "only when the nature and severity of the handicap is such that education in regular classes with the use of supplementary aids and services cannot be achieved satisfactorily" (*Federal Register*, August 23, 1977, p. 42497). Further, "unless a handicapped child's individualized education program requires some other arrangement, the child is educated in the school which he or she would attend if not handicapped" (*Federal Register*, August 23, 1977, p. 42497). Finally, "in providing or arranging for the provision of nonacademic and extracurricular services and activities . . . each public agency shall insure that each handicapped child participates with nonhandicapped children in those services and activities to the maximum extent appropriate to the needs of that child" (*Federal Register*, August 23, 1977, p. 42497).*

In addition, a well-formulated IEP will contain progress goals that the child can be reasonably expected to attain. Suggested proce-

---

*PL 94-142 does not specifically require that school districts make a range of educational placements available to handicapped students; that such students should be educated in the schools they would attend if not handicapped; or that handicapped students participate in nonacademic and extracurricular services with nonhandicapped students. Hence, these particular regulatory requirements represent "opportunities for deregulation."

dures for formulating such goals may be found in sources such as *Functions of the Placement Committee in Special Education* (NASDSE, 1976) and Tymitz-Wolf (1982). These progress goals must be stated in measurable terms to allow for later determination of whether or not the child has attained the goals.

According to the regulations, the progress goals included in an IEP represent judgments about expected progress, rather than guarantees that the progress goals will be met. However, this qualification "does not relieve agencies and teachers from making good faith efforts to assist the child in achieving the objectives and goals listed in the individualized education program" (*Federal Register*, August 23, 1977, p. 42491).

The regulations implementing PL 94-142 not only dictate IEP content but also require that IEPs be provided for children in various settings within specified time limits. Specifically, IEPs must be formulated and implemented for handicapped children receiving special education services in public schools and also for handicapped children placed in private schools and other agencies by public schools. Regardless of the participating handicapped child's placement, a meeting to develop an IEP must be held within 30 days of the determination of eligibility for services. Implementation of the IEP must occur without undue delay (*Federal Register*, August 23, 1977, p. 42490).*

Before this section is concluded, it should be noted that IEPs may not be formulated so as to deny handicapped children equal opportunities to participate in any of the school's subject matter offerings or nonacademic services. Further, IEPs may not preclude handicapped children's participation in the school's regular physical education program unless specially designed physical education programs are provided when needed. The nature of these specially designed physical education programs should be described in the IEPs of the handicapped children needing them (*Federal Register*, August 23, 1977, p. 42489).†

One final note: School personnel (including assessment practi-

---

*PL 94-142 does not specifically require formulation of an IEP within 30 days of determination of eligibility for services or implementation of an IEP without undue delay. Hence, these particular sections of the regulations represent "opportunities for deregulation."

†While PL 94-142 does require that handicapped children receive instruction in physical education, it does not specifically require that such instruction be in the school's regular physical education program (when appropriate) or that specially designed physical education programs be described in IEPs. Hence, these particular sections represent "opportunities for deregulation."

tioners) will sometimes experience pressure to limit the special education services and related services specified in IEPs to those that are already available or inexpensive to provide. In such situations, it is important to remember that all services actually appropriate to the needs of the child should be included in the IEP. However, while these services must be "appropriate," they are not required to be as good as or clearly superior to similar services provided elsewhere (Martin, 1979, p. 52).

PERIODIC REASSESSMENT

We have previously noted that the regulations implementing PL 94-142 require that handicapped children be reassessed at least every three years.* Individual handicapped children must be reassessed more often than every three years "if conditions warrant or if the child's parent or teacher requests an evaluation" (*Federal Register*, August 23, 1977, p. 42497). Such reassessments are partially for the purpose of determining which handicapped children continue to be eligible for and in need of special education and related services. Reassessments thus help prevent children from continuing in special education programs when it is no longer appropriate for them to do so.

Reassessments of handicapped children must meet the same standards required of initial assessments under the regulations. Thus assessment must be conducted in all areas related to the suspected disability; no single procedure may be used as the sole criterion for determining an appropriate educational program; inferences about limited aptitude or achievement are not to be drawn when assessment results actually reflect impaired sensory or motor skills; assessment techniques must be validated for the specific purposes for which they are used; they must, when feasible, be administered in the child's native language or preferred mode of communication; and they must be administered by trained personnel in conformance with instructions provided by the producers of the techniques.

While we agree with the need for reassessments to be conducted at least every three years, it should be acknowledged that reassessments further strain the limited time resources available for psychoeducational assessment. Given this fact, assessment practitioners

---

*Recall from Chapter 1 that PL 94-142 does not specifically require periodic reassessment of handicapped children. Again, this requirement represents an "opportunity for deregulation."

are sometimes tempted to cut corners in performing reassessments of children believed to be "known quantities." These temptations should be resisted.

PROCEDURAL SAFEGUARDS

The regulations implementing PL 94-142 require extensive procedural safeguards in assessment-related activities. We have already described parental rights under the Buckley Amendment (part of PL 93-380) relative to inspection, modification, and release of educational records in general. In addition, sections of the regulations implementing PL 94-142 deal with parental rights to receive prior notice of certain actions, to consent to certain actions, to appeal decisions, and to receive an independent evaluation of their child (*Federal Register*, August 23, 1977, pp. 42494–42496).

The regulations implementing PL 94-142 require that a child's parent (or parents) give written, informed consent for their child's initial assessment for special education services. Although this requirement seems rather straightforward, Bersoff (Note 2) suggests that such parental consent should meet the legal requirements of knowledge, voluntariness, and capacity. This means that consent should involve adequate knowledge of the action to be taken, freedom from coercive pressure, and parental ability to make a considered decision. In relation to this, the regulations implementing PL 94-142 require that information be conveyed to parents in their native languages or other preferred modes of communication. Further, parents may revoke their previously given consent at any time. These regulations also stipulate that consent must be obtained from a parent surrogate when a legal guardian cannot be located or when the child is a ward of the state.

Written, informed parental consent is also required for the initial placement of a child in a special education program of any sort. If parents fail to consent to an initial assessment or initial special education placement, the school district must proceed in terms of state law governing such situations. For instance, state law may require a court order before a school district can proceed without parental consent. If there is no state law specific to such situations, the school district may seek a due process hearing (described later in this section) for the purpose of receiving sanction to proceed without parental consent (Martin, 1979, p. 104).*

---

*PL 94-142 does not specifically require parental consent for initial assessment of initial placement. Hence, these particular sections of the regulations implementing PL 94-142 represent "opportunities for deregulation."

As implied above, the regulations include procedures for resolving disputes between parents and schools. Both parents and schools have the right to call for due process hearings. A due process hearing must be held in a timely manner, must be presided over by a hearing officer who is not employed by the school district involved in the dispute, and must be followed by a timely decision on the part of the hearing officer. If either party to the dispute believes that the hearing officer has erred in his decision, that party may appeal the decision to the court system.

The regulations implementing PL 94-142 allow both parties to the due process hearing to be represented by legal counsel, to present evidence, to call and cross-examine witnesses, to prohibit the introduction of any evidence not revealed to the other party five days in advance of the hearing, to obtain a written record of the hearing, and to receive the written decision of the hearing officer. Prior to the hearing officer's decision, the affected child must be permitted to begin school or to stay in her or his present educational placement unless both parties agree to waive this requirement.

One possible basis for parent–school disputes leading to due process hearings may be parents' disagreement with assessment data and findings produced by school personnel. In such instances, parents may request an independent assessment from a private practitioner or other community agency, and this independent assessment is to be paid for by the school. The school, in turn, may request a due process hearing if it sees no need for an independent evaluation at public expense. Whether or not the school pays for the independent evaluation, the results of that evaluation must be considered by school officials in making decisions about the child.

The regulations also require that written notice be provided parents prior to the school's initiating or changing the identification, evaluation, or educational placement of the child or the provision of a free, appropriate public education to the child. Notice must also be given if the school refuses a parental request to undertake any of these activities. The prior notice requirement is designed to give parents adequate time and information to agree to or contest school actions. Parents could contest actions by requesting a due process hearing.

Any prior notice to parents must meet certain standards. In addition to the notice's being in the parents' native language or preferred mode of communication, it must include

(1) A full explanation of all of the procedural safeguards available to the parents;
(2) A description of the action proposed or refused by the agency, an explanation of why the agency proposes or refused to take the

action, and a description of any options the agency considered and the reasons why those options were rejected;

(3) A description of each evaluation procedure, test, record, or report the agency uses as a basis for the proposal or refusal; and

(4) A description of any other factors which are relevant to the agency's proposal or refusal. (*Federal Register*, August 23, 1977, p. 42495)*

Finally, we have indicated that parents must be included in IEP meetings unless they refuse to participate. Parent participation in IEP meetings is governed by the following regulations.

(a) Each public agency shall take steps to insure that one or both of the parents of the handicapped child are present at each meeting or are afforded the opportunity to participate, including:

(1) Notifying parents of the meeting early enough to insure that they will have an opportunity to attend; and

(2) Scheduling the meeting at a mutually agreed on time and place.

(b) The notice under paragraph (a) (1) of this section must indicate the purpose, time, and location of the meeting, and who will be in attendance.

(c) If neither parent can attend, the public agency shall use other methods to insure parent participation, including individual or conference telephone calls.

(d) A meeting may be conducted without a parent in attendance if the public agency is unable to convince the parents that they should attend. In this case the public agency must have a record of its attempts to arrange a mutually agreed on time and place such as:

(1) Detailed records of telephone calls made or attempted and the results of those calls.

(2) Copies of correspondence sent to the parents and any responses received, and

(3) Detailed records of visits made to the parent's home or place of employment and the results of those visits.

(e) The public agency shall take whatever action is necessary to insure that the parent understands the proceedings at a meeting, including arranging for an interpreter for parents who are deaf or whose native language is other than English.

(f) The public agency shall give the parent, on request, a copy of the individualized education program. (*Federal Register*, August 23, 1977, pp. 42490–42491)†

---

*These detailed regulations for parental notice are more specific than required by PL 94-142, and this specificity makes them "targets of opportunity for deregulation."

†These detailed regulations relative to parental participation in IEP meetings are more specific than required to PL 94-142, which makes them "targets of opportunity for deregulation."

CONCLUSIONS

While we have attempted to describe the major features of the federal mandates that affect psychoeducational assessment practice and have quoted in full crucial provisions of the regulations, we have not presented an exhaustive view of federal legislation and implementing regulations. Assessment practitioners are urged to review these primary sources themselves and to monitor changes at both the federal and state level in the legal framework for psychoeducational assessment.

In the next chapter, we will look at some of the litigative precedents for the federal laws discussed in this chapter and will also examine the interpretation of these laws in various federal court decisions.

3

The Impact of Federal Litigation

IN PREVIOUS CHAPTERS, we have stated that federal legislation in the area of special education has been, in part, a response to successful legal challenges to inappropriate assessment, placement, and programming practices. We have noted that suits involving allegations of exclusion of handicapped children from educational programs and of misplacement of children in special education programs have been particularly important in shaping those sections of federal laws dealing with assessment practice and that litigation involving allegations of improper assessment and placement procedures have also shaped those sections of the laws toward improved methods of making decisions about children.

In this chapter, we examine suits that have set precedents later incorporated into federal laws and their implementing regulations and, in the process, trace some of the origins of particular sections of these laws and regulations. Particular emphasis is given to the litigative origins of the IEP, least restrictive environment, nondiscriminatory assessment, periodic reassessment, "child find," appropriate education, and procedural safeguards requirements. We also examine some suits decided subsequent to the effective dates of these laws and regulations. Such suits have been argued partially or exclusively on the basis of the requirements of federal laws and regulations and hence shed light on how courts interpret these requirements. While our analysis of suits is far from exhaustive, it highlights those representative of the concerns of this book.

Before undertaking these analyses, some comments, taken largely from Bersoff and Miller (1979), on the nature of the judicial process are in order. First, judicial decisions in civil cases originate in disputes. These disputes can be over a party's obligations to another party under statutory law, under a state's constitution, or under the Constitution of the United States. Court rulings represent legal judgments about whether alleged obligations exist, the circumstances (if any) under which the obligations exist, and legally acceptable means of fulfilling the obligations.

Second, the ruling of a court is binding only within the jurisdiction of that court. If a ruling on a case is appealed to a higher court, the appellate court's ruling is similarly binding only within its jurisdiction. The only court whose jurisdiction encompasses the entire country is the U.S. Supreme Court. Hence only decisions rendered by the Supreme Court are binding on the nation as a whole. While few cases relevant to psychoeducational assessment practice have reached the Supreme Court, decisions rendered by federal district courts and by federal appeals courts often establish legal precedents that can be argued successfully in other federal courts, including the Supreme Court. Thus, court decisions in cases considered important are eagerly awaited as indications of how other courts might rule.

Third, in ruling on statutory and constitutional obligations, courts are sometimes required to address inconsistencies across levels of government. For example, a state law or policy may be found to be inconsistent with a federal law. Under most circumstances, the court must base its decision on the federal law, since federal law generally takes precedence over state law. When a court rules that a federal law supercedes a state law, the ruling usually has the effect of negating the state law and causing it to be either amended to conform to the requirements of the federal law or repealed. Similarly, a court may find that either a state law or a federal law is inconsistent with the U.S. Constitution. In such circumstances, the Constitution takes precedence, and the law must either be amended to conform to the requirements of the Constitution or repealed. To summarize, the Constitution takes precedence over both state and federal law, with federal law usually taking precedence over state law. Courts must follow this hierarchy of precedence in order to resolve inconsistencies across levels of government.

The preceding comments illustrate the point made earlier that multiple sources of law affect psychoeducational assessment practice. State law, state regulations, federal law, federal regulations, court decisions, and the Constitution may singly or in combination be relevant to an issue in assessment. Assessment practitioners therefore need to have a working knowledge of these sources of law, not only to facilitate legally appropriate assessment but also to place a single source of law into a more comprehensive framework. Put in another way, "examining all sources of law can help one better understand each individual source" (Martin, 1979, p. 11).

Such understanding is important, since the past 15 years or so has seen "an explosion of litigation and legislation" (Bersoff, 1980, p. 112) relevant to psychoeducational assessment. Further, this litigation and legislation has had important effects on assessment practice (Monroe, 1979, p. 39). Nevertheless, the role of courts in ruling on assessment issues has been (and probably will continue to be) controversial. One reason for controversy involves the technical nature of some assessment issues. Many judges have expressed discomfort about hearing cases involving such technical issues, since these subjects lie outside their areas of expert knowledge (Bersoff & Miller, 1979, p. 156). Nevertheless, the judges have concluded that the statutory and constitutional questions presented by assessment and special education cases have left them little choice but to make decisions.

In some situations, two courts have rendered conflicting decisions in what appear to be similar cases. When this occurs, assessment practitioners in the jurisdiction of the first court are obligated to behave differently from practitioners in the jurisdiction of the second court. Even Supreme Court cases are decided with reference to the particulars of cases decided previously by lower courts. Similar cases heard at later dates by the Supreme Court may be decided differently, since the particulars of the later cases may differ in legally important ways from those of the previous cases. In addition, Supreme Court cases argued partially or exclusively on constitutional grounds are decided on the basis of what the Constitution requires in light of current societal conditions. In essence, constitutional interpretations undergo some changes as our society itself changes (Roberts, Note 5). These comments illustrate the general point that case law (precedents established by court decisions), like statutory law (laws enacted by legislative bodies), is continually changing and hence must be continually monitored.

The fact that some important assessment cases have been settled by consent decrees (Oakland & Laosa, 1977) has also been a source of controversy. Since consent decrees represent out-of-court settlements approved by courts, they are less instructive on legal questions than are cases actually heard by courts (because such cases are not argued in detail in court).

A fourth source of controversy about courts' roles in influencing assessment practice involves fundamental differences between the primary concerns of courts and those of scientific or professional disciplines. Courts are basically concerned with questions of justice under the law, while scientific and professional disciplines are more concerned with questions of scientific truth. While many of the issues in assessment suits cannot be judged conclusively on scientific grounds, courts must rule in absolute legal terms on the issues in dispute (Reschly, 1979, p. 222).

Court decisions (and consent decrees) are also limited in their effects by social and economic factors. Court decisions, consent decrees, and legislation can satisfy the claims of handicapped children and their parents only to the extent that educational personnel are adequately trained to meet their obligations under law and that legislative bodies allocate sufficient monies to allow actual compliance with these obligations (Turnbull, 1978).

In spite of the controversial role of courts in influencing assessment practice, litigative influences on assessment are likely to continue. A number of the requirements of the regulations implementing PL 94-142 and other federal laws are sufficiently vague so that they will probably spark disputes that will end up in litigation (Bersoff & Miller, 1979, p. 156). A second factor that contributes to continued litigation is the professional inertia of psychoeducational assessment practitioners, who have sometimes failed in the past to take actions that would make litigative challenges to assessment practices unnecessary (Coulter, 1979). Practitioners are certainly not totally to blame for such litigation, however, since they often have limited control over their own standards of performance (Meyers, Sundstrom, & Yoshida, 1974, p. 31). Nevertheless, at least one author wonders whether litigative challenges to assessment and special education practices would have been so frequent if professionals had worked harder to provide for due process rights, placement in the least restrictive environment, comprehensive assessment, and more effective special education programs (Reschly, 1979, p. 246).

LITIGATION PRECEDING PUBLIC LAW 94-142

A tradition of educational practices and court rulings forms the historical backdrop for recent litigation concerning special education and assessment. Bersoff and Miller (1979) report that public school programs for handicapped children were not begun until around the turn of the century. Previously, handicapped children (and adults) were typically provided services as residents of institutions. Courts at that time tended to approve the practice of excluding handicapped children from public school programs. With the passage of time, however, greater numbers of public school systems began to offer special education programs. While this arrangement enabled some handicapped children to receive services in settings less isolated than institutions, special education classes tended to be self-contained, thereby somewhat isolating their students from contact with non-handicapped peers. As the number of handicapped children served by public schools increased, so did the need to develop eligibility criteria and utilize selection devices related to those criteria. Psychometric testing rather quickly became an important part of the process of determining eligibility. "It was this need to assess for placement purposes that closely linked special education, testing, and, eventually, the law" (Bersoff & Miller, 1979, p. 132).

These practices represent the historical backdrop for recent litigation in assessment and special education. Some cases in this litigation have been argued partially or exclusively on constitutional grounds. Oakland and Laosa (1977) indicate that rights established by the U.S. Constitution have an indirect influence on assessment practice. Specifically, the Fifth and the Fourteenth Amendments to the Constitution contain due process provisions requiring that any law be reasonable and include sufficient safeguards to ensure its fair application. The Fourteenth Amendment also guarantees equal protection under the law, including the right to be free from unjustifiable discrimination. While these constitutional requirements have been subject to differing interpretations over time and in various cases, they have figured importantly in recent litigation.

Denial of Educational Services to Handicapped Children

Although public schools have, since the turn of the century, dramatically increased their services to handicapped children, two landmark cases in the early 1970s challenged the continued exclusion of severely handicapped children from public school programs. As noted earlier, psychoeducational assessment practitioners, not too long ago, were required to help determine whether children were capable of benefitting from public education at all. It will be recalled that such judgements were linked to a conception of education as "the teaching of 'normal' subjects to 'normal' children" (Martin, 1979, p. 12). It will also be recalled that recent litigation has resulted in a broadened conception of education as "any kind of training that a child might need" (Bersoff & Miller, 1979, p. 135).

One of the landmark cases leading to this broadened conception of education was *PARC* [Pennsylvania Association for Retarded Children] v. *Commonwealth of Pennsylvania* (1972). In this case, the federal district court "ruled that all mentally retarded children were capable of benefitting from training and ordered the state to provide them a free educational program" (Bersoff & Miller, p. 135). The state, in turn, voluntarily agreed to stop classifying children as uneducable. The right to an education established for severely mentally retarded children in this case was soon after extended to all children regardless of handicap in *Mills* v. *D.C. Board of Education* (1972). In this case, the federal district court ordered the Washington, D.C., school system to provide educational programs to handicapped children previously excluded from services. Although the defendants in this case pleaded lack of sufficient financial resources to provide such services, the court ruled that exclusion of children from services was a violation of both the due process and equal protection requirements of the Constitution. These two decisions were followed quickly by many other right to education suits filed on behalf of excluded handicapped children (Martin, 1979, p. 15).

While these two decisions prompted a flurry of similar suits, they also suggested that handicapped children enjoy constitutional rights to equality of educational opportunity. Courts have recently defined equality of educational opportunity for handicapped children as meaning both a free public education and an education to which they can respond. Providing such an education to handicapped children is more expensive than providing similar opportunities to non-handicapped children. Recognizing this fact, Congress provided for federal funding of some of the costs of special education when it passes PL 94-142 and other federal laws. However, the level of funding allocated by Congress under these laws has typically accounted for only about 9 percent of the total costs involved in delivering special education services (Zigler & Muenchow, 1980, p. 242). If the cuts in federal allocations recommended by the Reagan administration are approved, it is likely that school administrators will find it increasingly difficult to satisfy the requirements of the law and its implementing regulations. These problems may lead, in turn, to pressures on Congress to amend PL 94-142 in ways which will make its requirements less costly to satisfy, and handicapped children and their parents are likely to experience a reduction in the rights currently afforded them by statute. Such a development might ultimately prompt them to file suits contending that these rights are protected by the Constitution.

Regardless of future developments in legislation and litigation, assessment practitioners should be aware of how courts have ruled to date on questions of equal educational opportunity for handicapped children. Several cases are instructive in this regard.

One such case is *Lau* v. *Nichols* (1974). This case began when a suit was filed against the San Francisco Public Schools for failure to provide Chinese-speaking students with any instruction in their native language. The U.S. Supreme Court ruled that providing such students instruction only in English foreclosed their opportunities for any meaningful education. In essence, the court ruled that these students must be provided an education to which they could respond (Martin, 1979, pp. 59–60). While these students were not handicapped students, cases involving handicapped children have had similar outcomes.

In *Fialkowski* v. *Shapp* (1975), the plaintiffs contended that the placement of severely mentally retarded children in programs emphasizing academic skills resulted in no opportunity for them to receive a meaningful education. The defendant school system argued that under the Supreme Court's ruling in *San Antonio Independent School District* v. *Rodriquez* (1973), children were not legally entitled to an appropriate education. The *Fialkowski* court, however, found that the *Rodriquez* ruling did establish the consitutional right to at least a minimal level of education. In addition, the *Fialkowski* court also found that the *Rodriquez* ruling called attention to the need for schools to honor the constitutional rights of persons considered members of a "suspect class." Members of a "suspect class" were defined by the *Rodriquez* ruling as those persons who suffered from disabilities or who had been the victims of prior discrimination. The *Fialkowski* court found its handicapped children plaintiffs to be members of such a class and ordered the defendent school system to provide an appropriate program (Martin, 1979, pp. 57–60).

In *Frederick L.* v. *Thomas* (1976), plaintiffs contended that the defendant school system failed to provide educational programs appropriate to their learning disabilities. The court ruled that the plaintiffs must be provided with educational programs that were as well suited to their needs as were the programs provided nonhandicapped students (Martin, 1979, pp. 60–61).

It should be recognized that court decisions upholding the rights of handicapped plaintiffs to an education to which they can respond are based on two assumptions. One is that those children's individual differences are identifiable. The second is that an education to which they can respond (that is, an appropriate education) requires the matching of educational responses to their individual differences (Bersoff & Miller, 1979, p. 135). We have contended thus far that assessment for classification purposes involves deciding whether or not a child's difficulties are of a nature and severity sufficient for her or him to be classified as handicapped. Assessment for programming, we have argued, involves deciding what the child's specific problems in educational functioning are and what strategies might assist in remediating these problems. If appropriate education consists of matching educational strategies to a handicapped child's unique characteristics, then assessment for programming is the key to appropriate education. It also follows that if programming does not assist a child in overcoming her or his remediable problems, then classification of children cannot be supported (Bersoff & Miller, 1979, p. 137). In this sense, assessment for classification and assessment for programming are intertwined in the process of meeting legal obligations to provide appropriate education for handicapped children.

Martin (1979) summarizes the implications of court decisions on questions of equal and appropriate education for handicapped children. He concludes that special education programs for handicapped children will not be considered legally appropriate unless they (1) are designed according to the results of proper assessments; (2) are designed for individual children (that is, are individualized Educational Programs [IEPs]); (3) actually correspond to the written IEPs; (4) incorporate the results of periodic reassessments; (5) offer children chances to benefit; (6) are as suitable to the needs of handicapped children as regular educational programs are to the needs of nonhandicapped students; and (7) incorporate procedural safeguards.

We have mentioned that one way in which assessment practice can be corrupted is when a school district fails to assess children who might add to the district's special education costs (Weatherly & Lipsky, 1977). Such failures have resulted in litigation. The defendant school system in the *Frederick L.* v. *Thomas* case argued that it had no responsibility to identify children eligible for special education services. The court, however, ruled that school districts have an affirmative duty to identify such children (Martin, 1979, p. 34). A similar ruling characterized another court's decision in *Pierce* v. *Board of Education* (1976) (Martin, pp. 29–30).

Discriminatory Assessment and Placement Practices

In a number of suits, plaintiffs have sought relief from what they believe to be discriminatory special education classification and programming practices. Such plaintiffs tend to be ethnic minority children who may have been misidentified as handicapped and subsequently exposed to special education programs inappropriate to their needs. Their lawyers often cite the Supreme Court's ruling in the landmark desegregation case, *Brown* v. *Board of Education* (1954), that children have a constitutional right to participate in regular and nonsegregated educational programs unless school systems have legitimate interests in treating them differently. In essence, such plaintiffs contend that they have not been afforded due process and equal protection of law and, consequently, have been unfairly classified as handicapped and programmed for inappropriately. As we have indicated, courts have ruled that school systems must not only identify handicapped children but must also take steps to prevent children from being classified as handicapped when they are not. It follows that "if the referral for evaluation is wrongly motivated or if the assessment is flawed, then the mistake is one of constitutional dimensions" (Martin, 1979, p. 28).

As we have noted, plaintiffs alleging discriminatory assessment and special education placement tend to express concerns in the following areas: the use of inappropriate tests in making classification decisions; incompetent administration of tests and inappropriate interpretation of test results; lack of parental involvement in assessment and decision making; the provision of inadequate special education programs; and unwarranted stigmatization of misclassified children (Ross, DeYoung, & Cohen, 1971). Several of these concerns are illustrated in various combinations in the cases discussed below.

Plaintiffs in a California case, *Diana* v. *State Board of Education* (1970), alleged that nine Mexican-American children were misclassified as mildly retarded and placed in special education classes on the basis of inappropriate intelligence tests (the Stanford-Binet Intelligence Scale and the Wechsler Intelligence Scale for Children) administered in English. Plaintiffs indicated that several of the children achieved IQ scores above the retarded range when later given intelligence tests in Spanish and that other plaintiff children were misclassified because of the tests' unfair emphases on verbal facility and middle class information (Oakland & Laosa, 1977). Plaintiffs also supported their claim of misclassification by noting that Spanish-surnamed children comprised 33.3 percent of the enrollment in the school district's classes for the mildly retarded but only 18.5 percent of the district's total enrollment. Finally, plaintiffs argued that the special education classes for the mildly retarded did not provide instruction appropriate to the needs of the misclassified (that is, nonretarded) children (Reschly, 1979, pp. 218–219).

The *Diana* suit was settled by a consent decree resulting from negotiations between the plaintiffs, representatives of the Monterey County school district, and representatives from the California State Department of Education. This consent decree required the following:

1. Assessment of primary language competence prior to administration of other assessment procedures. If the child's primary language competence was determined to be Spanish, subsequent assessment procedures had to be administered in Spanish.
2. Unfair portions of current tests such as knowledge of English word

meanings were to be deleted, and greater emphasis was to be placed on the results of nonverbal or performance measures.
3. All bilingual children currently enrolled in special classes for the mildly retarded were to be reevaluated within a short time period using procedures consistent with points 1 and 2 above.
4. School districts and the State Department of Education were required to develop services to assist those children who were returned from special education to regular classes as a result of the reevaluation.
5. The California State Department of Education was required to adopt and standardize a more appropriate test for Latino youth. (Author's note: Apparently this project was never initiated.)
6. Finally, the consent decree included a rather strongly worded warning to districts that disproportionate numbers of any ethnic or racial group placed in special education programs must be explained and justified. (Reschly, 1979, p. 219)

Several points should be made about the consent decree in the *Diana* case. First, the decree was binding on all school districts in California and led to the return of several thousand children originally classified as having some degree of retardation and placed in special education classes to regular classes. Yoshida, MacMillan, and Meyers (1976) report that the children returned to regular classes performed generally at below-average levels socially and academically but nevertheless made better adjustments than expected. Reschly (1979, p. 219) suggests that their better-than-expected adjustments to regular classes illustrate the importance of periodic reviews of special education placements. Second, the consent decree may have been interpreted as acknowledging that individual intelligence tests are biased against ethnic minority children (MacMillan & Meyers, 1980, p. 137). As we shall see, the issue of test bias is very complex and may never be resolved to the satisfaction of all parties (Reschly, 1979, p. 217).

Another important suit alleging discriminatory assessment and special education placement was *Guadalupe* v. *Tempe Elementary District* (1972), heard by an Arizona federal district court. This suit involved issues very similar to those raised in the *Diana* suit and was also settled by a consent decree. The consent decree in the *Guadalupe* suit included all of the requirements found in the *Diana* consent decree plus several others. These additional requirements were as follows: no child was to be placed in a program for the mildly retarded without IQ scores at least two or more standard deviations below the mean; IQ scores were not to be used as the exclusive or primary basis for a child's classification as mentally retarded; classification decisions for children with a primary language other than English were to be based on nonverbal or performance tests; and no child was to be classified as mentally retarded without an assessment of adaptive behavior conducted through an interview with the child's parents held in the child's home (Reschly, 1979, p. 220).

Both the *Diana* and *Guadalupe* suits were brought largely on behalf of Mexican-American children and were settled by consent decrees. Two other noteworthy suits (*Larry P. v. Riles* and *PASE* [Parents in Action on Special Education] v. *Hannon*) have also charged discriminatory assessment and special education placement practices. While these suits also alleged that biased intelligence tests were being used to misclassify ethnic minority children as mentally retarded, these latter suits were brought on behalf of black children and were settled by court decisions. The arguments and decisions in the *Larry P.* and *PASE* cases reflect the complexity and controversy involved in questions of discriminatory assessment and placement practices and hence merit discussion. It should also be noted that the decisions in the two cases appear to contradict one another and that both decisions are likely to be appealed to higher courts (Prasse, 1980a, 1980b). It is possible that these appeals will ultimately reach the Supreme Court.

Larry P. v. Riles was originally filed in 1971. The suit charged that black children were overrepresented in classes for the mildly retarded in the San Francisco Public Schools as a result of the middle class biases of the intelligence tests used in the classification process. The plaintiffs further alleged that such classes were ineffective in promoting the educational development of misclassified children, that the classification of mental retardation was stigmatizing to such children, and that the overrepresentation of black children in these classes violated the constitutional guarantee of equal protection of law (Reschly, 1979, p. 221). The Federal District Court for Northern California issued a preliminary injunction in 1972 against the continued use of intelligence tests for the purpose of classifying black children as mentally retarded if the consequence was racial imbalance in classes for the mentally retarded. In 1974, an appellate tribunal affirmed the lower court's injunction. The court then ordered that the ban be extended to the entire state of California. In 1975, the State of California Department of Education issued a memorandum prohibiting the use of intelligence tests for the purpose of classifying any child (regardless of race) as mentally retarded (Bersoff, 1980, p. 115). It should be noted that these actions permitted the continued use of intelligence tests in California for purposes other than that of classifying children as mentally retarded (Reschly, 1979, p. 221).

A trial to determine whether the preliminary injunction should become permanent was begun in October of 1977, with testimony stretching into mid-1978. In October of 1979, the federal district court published its ruling that the preliminary injunction issued in 1972 would become permanent (Bersoff, 1980, p. 115).

In issuing a permanent injunction, the court ruled for the plaintiffs on both constitutional and statutory grounds. The court concluded that the state of California had intentionally failed to provide equal protection by adopting practices that it knew disproportionately assigned black children to classes for the mildly retarded. Such practices had not, in the court's opinion, been carefully evaluated against alternative practices that might have prevented disproportionate assignments. The court characterized classes for the mildly retarded as designed for children unable to profit from regular classes (even with remedial instruction) and, as such, unlikely to return children to regular educational programs. On the basis of this finding, the court determined that the classification of children as mentally retarded involves serious consequences for them, consequences that are unacceptable if such classifications are inaccurate (Bersoff, 1980).

In continuing the injunction against the use of intelligence tests for the purpose of classifying black children as mentally retarded, the court found intelligence tests deficient on several grounds. First, the court found no persuasive evidence in the state's testimony that there is a higher incidence of mild mental retardation among black children than among children of other ethnic or racial groups. Hence, the disproportionate assignment of black children to classes for the mildly retarded was judged to reflect bias in the content of intelligence tests against such children. Therefore, the court rejected testimony that intelligence test scores predict achievement test scores as accurately for black children as they do for other children. Viewing intelligence and achievement tests as measuring highly overlapping characteristics, the court instead required evidence that intelligence test scores accurately predict the school grades of black children. Since such evidence was not presented in the trial, the court held that intelligence tests must show evidence of ability to predict which black children would be unable to profit from regular classes with remedial instruction (Bersoff, 1980). In essence, the court required (but did not find) evidence that intelligence tests accurately identify black children whose low IQ scores reflect biological and permanent impairments evident across all settings.

The *Larry P.* case was initiated prior to the enactment of PL 94-142 but was concluded after its enactment. As previously suggested, the court found that the plaintiffs had been denied constitutional guarantees of equal protection. The court also found that intelligence tests had not been validated for the purpose for which they were being used, as required by the regulations implementing PL 94-142. Specifically, the court required (but did not find) evidence that intelligence tests accurately identify black children who are "truly" (and therefore permanently) mentally retarded. This ruling on what constitutes validation of a test for a particular purpose (as required by the PL 94-142 regulations) represents a strong challenge to the continued use of intelligence tests in classifying children as mentally retarded. As we shall see, however, the court in *PASE* v. *Hannon* adopted a different (and less stringent) stance on what is required for an intelligence test to be validated for this purpose.

Although the *PASE* v. *Hannon* suit was filed after the enactment of PL 94-142, we include it here for purposes of comparison. Like *Larry P.* v. *Riles*, *PASE* v. *Hannon* also alleged misclassification of black children as mentally retarded, this time by the Chicago Public Schools. The plaintiffs charged that the alleged misclassifications were a function of content bias in intelligence tests and that the misclassifications constituted denial of equal protection guarantees and violations of PL 94-142 and Section 504 of PL 93-112. In a finding radically different from that in the *Larry P.* case, the *PASE* federal court found little content bias in the intelligence tests in question and failed to issue an injunction against their use. In arriving at this decision, the *PASE* court called the conflicting testimony on test bias "a draw" and undertook a detailed but subjective review of the items included in the Stanford-Binet Intelligence Scale, the Wechsler Intelligence Scale for Children, and the Wechsler Intelligence Scale for Children — Revised. The court found only nine items in the three tests to be racially biased against black children and concluded that so few biased items would be unlikely to result in misclassifications. The *PASE* court also noted that data in addition to IQ scores are required for a classification of mental retardation and stated that the regulations implementing PL 94-142 do not require a single test to be completely bias-free. In essence, then, the *PASE* court, in finding for the defendant, did not agree with the *Larry P.* court's finding that intelligence tests lack validity for the purpose of classifying black children as mentally retarded (Coulter, 1980b; Prasse, 1980b).

At least three of these suits (*Diana*, *Guadalupe*, and *Larry P.*) called attention to the disproportionate representation of ethnic minority children in classes for the mildly retarded. Further, results of retesting of the allegedly misclassified children were used to bolster the plaintiffs' arguments in at least three of the suits (*Diana*, *Larry P.*, and *PASE*). The groundwork for the *Diana* suit involved retesting in Spanish. Similar groundwork for the *Larry P.* suit involved the rephrasing of test questions and the accepting of answers considered representative of the experiences of black, urban youth. One of the sources of impetus for the *PASE* suit was the reclassification of two black children as learning disabled following earlier classifications of these children as mildly retarded.

One important issue raised by these four cases is the question of whether disproportionate representation of ethnic minority children in classes for mildly retarded children necessarily signifies discriminatory assessment and placement practices. Our opinion is that such situations at least suggest discriminatory practices, if mild mental retardation is conceptualized as biological in origin, as permanent, and as evident across all settings. Such a conceptualization seems to be imbedded in both the definition of mental retardation found in the regulations implementing PL 94-142 and in the four suits described above. While we agree with Reschly's (1980) contention that this is an erroneous conceptualization of mild mental retardation, we advocate procedures that give children the benefit of the doubt by precluding their classification as mentally retarded in the absence of assessment data strongly supporting this action.

Our rationale is twofold. First, the important differences between children with IQ scores suggesting mild retardation and those with IQ scores suggesting severe retardation do not seem to be widely or well understood, which could result in inappropriate educational programs for many in the former group. Second, since regular class instruction may also not be totally appropriate to the needs of children with IQ scores indicating mild retardation, we suggest that many children—those who evidence home and neighborhood adaptive behavior skills above the retarded range—receive supplemental services such as those provided by compensatory education programs. We suggest the same programming for children whose IQ scores show mild retardation from the perspective of regular (or social-system) norms but not from the perspective of pluralistic norms. Some of these children might legitimately warrant a special education classification other than mental retardation. Others, at a minimum, would probably benefit if consultation about special materials or programming were provided to their regular classroom teachers.

It should be noted that pluralistic norms are available for the Wechsler Intelligence Scale for Children—Revised (WISC-R). Such norms are provided in Mercer's (1979b) System of Multicultural Pluralistic Assessment (SOMPA). As previously noted, the use of these pluralistic norms allows one to compare a child's WISC-R performance to those of children of comparable sociocultural status and ethnic origin (black, white, Hispanic). In contrast, use of the regular WISC-R norms compares the child's WISC-R performance to those of children in general. While ethnic minority or economically disadvantaged children, as a group, are more likely than other groups of children to obtain WISC-R IQ scores indicating mild retardation when regular norms are used, they are not more likely than other groups of children to receive such scores when pluralistic norms are used. The use of pluralistic norms would prevent the overrepresentation of ethnic minority children or economically disadvantaged children in classifications of children as mentally retarded on the basis of IQ scores. Mercer (1979b) recommends the use of pluralistic norms in such classifications but urges that pluralistic norms be developed for local use (since the pluralistic norms found in SOMPA were developed only for black, white, and Hispanic children in California).

While we agree that pluralistic norms can be helpful in classification decisions, we are not comfortable with translating intelligence tests into languages other than English unless there are norms for such translations. Instead, we prefer (when necessary) the use of nonverbal intelligence tests with children lacking primary English-language skills or the use of pluralistic IQ norms with children whose English is adequate but who do not come from middle class backgrounds. The latter strategy is superior to the practice of rephrasing intelligence test questions in subcultural English and then interpreting test performances in terms of norms based on standardized testing procedures.

In the final analysis, it may prove impossible to achieve consensus on what constitutes test bias or what is required to validate a test for the purpose of classifying children as mentally retarded (Reschly, 1980). Nevertheless, both statutory and case law indicate that mentally retarded and other handicapped children must be identified, and require that classification be made only after careful and comprehensive assessments. When classifications decisions are made, the regulations implementing PL 94-142 require that multidisciplinary teams consider all data relevant to such decisions and also require written parental consent for both the initial assessment and the special education placement of a child. While these regulations attempt to ensure nondiscriminatory assessment and special education placement practices through an emphasis on data collection, review, and consent procedures, the use of assessment systems designed to improve classification decisions (such as the SOMPA) should also be considered. Whatever assessment techniques are ultimately used, each should have adequate technical adequacy and be appropriate to both the decision to be made and to the child. Assessment practitioners should, in addition, consider carefully the likely consequences of classification for each child assessed. The consequences are likely to be no better than neutral (and perhaps preponderantly negative) unless assessment for programming leads to an appropriate IEP, reasonable judgments about the child's least restrictive placement, and means by which the effectiveness of the IEP can be judged. Finally, the child being assessed should be regarded as the appropriate client of assessment practitioners. Clientage issues arising from this stance should be faced directly and considered as opportunities to improve organizational responses to client needs.

Procedural Issues

Several of the suits discussed earlier as involving allegations of denials of educational services or discriminatory assessment and placement practices also sought procedural changes in the ways school officials made decisions about children. For instance, the *Diana* consent decree, in addition to the requirements listed earlier, also required that parents be fully notified of any psychological testing before it was done; that they agree in writing to the placement of their child in special education, and that a conference be held with parents informing them of all assessment results and actions planned for their child (Cohen & DeYoung, 1973). Similarly, the *Guadalupe* consent decree required that parents provide informed consent for both assessment and placement, that handicapped children be placed in the least restrictive environments, and that the school district furnish data on the effectiveness of its special educaton programs (Reschly, 1979, p. 220).

While the *Diana* and the *Guadalupe* consent decrees included requirements for notice, for consent, and for placement in the least restrictive environment, the *PARC* and *Mills* decisions included requirements for due process hearings and independent assessments at school district expense. Specifically, these decisions required that parents be given notice (in advance of the due process hearing) of the basis for the child's special education classification; be permitted to submit evidence at the hearing; be allowed to cross-examine witnesses; be permitted to be represented at the hearing by a lawyer; be given chances for disputes to be settled by an independent hearing officer; be given the details of the school's position; and be provided an independent assessment at school district expense if there were questions about the adequacy of the school's assessment (Buss, 1975, p. 302).

These requirements are compatible with our belief that assessment and programming decisions will be enhanced by active involvement of parents and, when appropriate, children. However, Martin

(1979) indicates that both statutory and case law are unclear in relation to situations in which parents consent to a child's special education placement over the child's objection. In a related case involving commitment for treatment of mental illness—*Parham* v. *J. L. and J. R.* (1979)—the Supreme Court ruled that a hearing of the adversary type before an impartial tribunal was not required prior to the placement of minors in state mental institutions as long as the parents (or surrogate parents) consented to the placement and the admissions procedures of the institution adequately protected children from arbitrary admissions decisions (Prasse, 1979, pp. 3, 5). A case involving special education placement with parental consent but over the objections of the child has not, to our knowledge, yet reached the courts. Nevertheless, we shall have more to say about the ethical issues involved in situations pitting the conflicting interests of the state, parents, and children against one another, in the next chapter.

Procedural issues relative to handicapped children's expulsion from school have recently come before the courts. In *Davis* v. *Wynne* (1977), a mildly retarded boy challenged his expulsion from school for disruptive behavior. He claimed that his disruptive behavior was caused by the school's failing to provide an appropriate placement. A consent decree barring his expulsion and requiring a proper placement resulted from this suit (Martin, 1979, p. 67). Other expulsion cases have been argued at least partially on the basis of the requirements of the regulations implementing PL 94-142 and will be discussed in the next section.

In summarizing his remarks on procedural safeguards, Reschly (1979, p. 235) notes that professional ethics and best-practice standards have always emphasized parental involvement in assessment and decision making.

> A good guideline for most professionals to use in evaluating their performance in carrying out the spirit of informed consent and due process is, "Would you be satisfied that your rights and interests were respected and considered by the communications used if the child under consideration were your own?" (Reschly, 1979, p. 235)

LITIGATION SUBSEQUENT TO PUBLIC LAW 94-142 AND OTHER FEDERAL LAWS

A number of suits involving assessment and special education placement have been filed alleging violations of PL 94-142 and other federal laws. The consent decrees and decisions in such cases shed light on how courts interpret various provisions of these laws.

One of the most comprehensive of these suits was that of *Mattie*

T. et al. v. *Holladay et al.* This suit was filed in 1975 as a class action on behalf of all handicapped children in Mississippi. The suit challenged the alleged denial of educational services to some handicapped children, the segregation of some handicapped children in overly restrictive placements, racially discriminatory assessment and placement practices, and the absence of procedural safeguards for handicapped children and their parents. All of these charges were seen as contrary to the requirements of Section 504 of PL 93-112.

In 1977, the federal district court granted the plaintiffs' motion for a summary judgment, and in 1979 the court issued a consent decree. The consent decree required the state department of education to make further efforts to identify unserved handicapped children; provide clear notice of rights to parents; make further efforts to place handicapped children in least restrictive environments; make greater efforts to end discriminatory assessment and placement practices; expand the monitoring of local special education practices; establish a statewide procedure for receiving special education complaints; and provide opportunities for children no longer classified as mentally retarded to receive educational assistance permitting them to become fully functioning adults. In addition, the consent decree required that racial imbalances in classes for mildly retarded and learning disabled children be eliminated by 1981 (Hildman, 1979).

Another case argued in terms of alleged violations of Section 504 of PL 93-112 was *Hairston* v. *Drosick* (1976). In this case, the plaintiff child had a spine impairment that caused her to walk with a limp and to experience incontinence of the bowels. The court ruled that the school district could not make her regular classroom placement contingent on her mother's coming to school periodically to attend to her physical needs. In essence, the federal district court in West Virginia held that requiring the mother's periodic presence as a condition of a regular class placement violated the requirement of Section 504 that children remain in the regular school program whenever possible (Martin, 1979, pp. 89–90).

A third case bearing on Section 504 of PL 93-112 is *Kruse* v. *Campbell* (1977). In this case, the school district decided that the plaintiff (a learning disabled child) could not be placed in a school-district-operated program. The district provided the parents a tuition grant to be used to defer the cost of a private school placement. The tuition grant, however, did not provide the full cost of the private school tuition, and the suit charged that this situation discriminated against the child and his parents. A federal district court found for the plaintiff, but, on appeal, the Supreme Court vacated the judgment and ordered that the case be reconsidered by the district court in terms of the requirements of Section 504. Martin (1979, p. 49) suggests that the district court is likely to rule again in the plaintiff's favor. In this context, Leonard (1981) reports that courts have ordered school districts to pay the full costs of residential treatment of handicapped children in *North* v. *D.C. Board of Education* (1979) and *Mahoney* v. *Administrative School District No. 1* (1979).

As indicated previously, several cases involving the expulsion of handicapped students from school have been argued at least partially on the basis of the regulations implementing PL 94-142. In *Stuart* v. *Nappi* (1978), a federal district court in Connecticut enjoined school officials from holding a disciplinary hearing to consider expulsion of the plaintiff, a learning disabled child. The court held that expulsion constituted a change in educational placement and that such changes, under PL 94-142 and Section 504 of PL 93-112, must be considered only by a team meeting for the purpose of devising an alternative IEP and affording parents required precedural safeguards. The court further ordered that the plaintiff child be allowed to stay in her current placement until an alternative IEP had been formulated. The decision indicated that school officials may be able to suspend, but not expel, handicapped students, since expulsion would violate the child's right to education in the least restrictive environment (Martin, 1979, p. 71).

Another court, a federal district in New Hampshire, in *Stanley* v. *School Administrative Unit No. 40*, held that special education students may be suspended for nonemergency reasons for up to 10 days (Flygare, 1981). A third court, the U.S. Fifth Circuit Court of Appeals, in *S-1* v. *Turlington*, held that special education students could be expelled but only under certain conditions. One of these conditions involves prior utilization of the procedural safeguards embodied in the regulations implementing PL 94-142 and Section 504 of PL 93-112. Another condition involves the provision of some form of educational services (such as homebound teaching) to the expelled student (Flygare, 1981). These conditions were left intact by the Supreme Court's recent refusal to hear an appeal of *S-1* v. *Turlington* ("High Court Refuses," 1982, p. 368). In commenting on these cases, Flygare suggests that schools are probably on safe legal ground in using emergency suspensions not to exceed three days in dealing with handicapped children judged to be dangerous to themselves or others. He also suggests that longer suspension (or expulsion) decisions should proceed in terms of all procedural safeguards found in federal law, that such actions not be taken if the child's poor conduct is believed to be a manifestation of his or her handicap, and that any expulsions should be accompanied by home-based educational services. He concludes by stating, "School officials must constantly balance the rights of individual students against the interests of the larger school community. Special education laws present an opportunity to do such balancing with wisdom and compassion" (p. 671).

Armstrong v. *Kline* (1980) was also argued at least partially in terms of the regulations implementing PL 94-142. In this case, the plaintiffs were three severely handicapped children who challenged state policies restricting the instructional year for handicapped students to a maximum of 180 days. The plaintiffs argued that these policies precluded them from receiving the free, appropriate education required by the regulations implementing PL 94-142. Specifically, they indicated that their handicaps were severe enough so that regression would occur in the absence of year-round instruction. Such regression, they argued, was incompatible with the goal of appropriate education. The federal district court ruled for the plaintiffs. The decision was appealed to the U.S. Third Circuit Court of Appeals, which also ruled in favor of the plaintiffs. In striking down the 180-day rule, the circuit court noted that states generally have the authority to establish educational goals and the means by which to reach them. The court also noted, however, that states receiving federal monies under PL 94-142 are obligated to provide handicapped students appropriate educational programs as established in IEPs. Since IEPs must incorporate services appropriate to the unique needs of each child, the court found the 180-day rule to be too rigid to allow for such individualized program planning (Prasse, 1981a, p. 3). The Supreme Court refused to hear this case (subsequently known as *Battle* v. *Scanlon*) on appeal, and thus the Circuit Court's decision is binding ("Supreme Court Refuses," 1981, p. 5). In this context, Stotland and Mancuso (1981) suggest that any inflexible rule governing the provision of educational and related services will be found to be incompatible with PL 94-142.

CONCLUSIONS

We have not attempted an exhaustive review of all suits involving assessment and special education placement but have selected cases relevant to the concerns of this book. Since assessment practitioners are often consulted about a wide variety of legal issues in assessment and special education, they will need to become familiar with many other legal precedents and issues that could not be included here. Some of these are discussed in the literature listed in the Suggested Readings section at the back of the book.

We should note that not all cases involving assessment and special education are settled to the satisfaction of advocates for the handicapped. The *Parham* v. *J. L. and J. R.* case described earlier illustrates this point, as does another Supreme Court decision in *Pennhurst* v. *Halderman*. In the latter case, the court held that PL 94-103 (Developmental Disabilities Assistance and Bill of Rights Act of 1975) does not require that states provide services to the retarded in the least restrictive environment, in spite of language to that effect in the law. Specifically, the court held that Congress had failed to allocate sufficient monies under that law to hold the states to the law's requirements. The court, however, did not address the question of whether the retarded have a constitutional right to treatment in the least restrictive environment and sent the case back to the appeals court for a ruling on that question ("Rights of Retarded," 1981, p. 13).

Looking to the future, we see continued litigation involving assessment and special education placement, as well as continued efforts to amend existing laws. We are concerned that such legislative and litigative efforts may propel us in the direction of reduced services and rights for handicapped children. We note increasing public opposition to both the extra expenses involved in educating the handicapped (particularly in the context of a tight economy) and to federal control over local educational practices. President Ford threatened to veto PL 94-142, suggesting that this law has never enjoyed universal popularity (Thomason, 1981). Recently, five states joined the state of New Mexico in an appeal of a court's decision in *New Mexico Association for Retarded Citizens et al.* v. *the State of New Mexico et al.* In this case, a federal district court found the state to be in violation of Section 504 of PL 93-112 and its own state rules for educating the handicapped ("CEC Joins," 1981, p. 5). Further, the Reagan administration's efforts to abolish the Department of Education, cut funds for special education, block grant special education, and deregulate the PL 94-142 and Section 504 regulations are also cause for concern.

A balanced presentation requires, however, that we acknowledge the difficulties faced by school officials in implementing present federal laws under present conditions of a troubled economy and shrinking appropriations. Zigler and Muenchow (1980) suggest that "no public system, such as the schools, should be expected to absorb the full cost of handicaps, a problem whose prevention and amelioration properly rests with us all" (p. 247). Similarly, Makuch (1981) indicates that PL 94-142 may not be the proper vehicle for providing the full range of services needed by handicapped children. He proposes legislation requiring all human service agencies to combine their resources to provide a free appropriate education and related services to these children. Finding appropriate legal and social solutions to the complex problem of assisting such children will require vigorous and innovative efforts by many in our society.

4

Ethical Considerations

WE STATED at the beginning of this book our belief that the ultimate purpose of assessment practice is to promote the welfare of the
children who are assessed. A commitment to the welfare of the client
is, in our opinion, the key value that should guide the ethical decisions of the assessment practitioner. This is also the key value expressed in the ethical codes of the American Psychological Association (APA) and of the National Association of School Psychologists
(NASP), portions of which have been referred to previously. (Some
readers may also wish to review the ethical codes of other professional organizations such as the American Personnel and Guidance Association.) Since the APA and NASP codes explore in some detail many
of the ethical issues that are important in assessment practice, we
find them a useful guide to the subject. Our goal in this chapter is to
effect a more integrated and comprehensive understanding of the
ethical issues involved in assessment than we have thus far presented.

All professionals are happy to gain success and status within
their professions, and there is no necessary conflict between such at-
tainment and the goals of ethical practice. Power and influence may,
in fact, be used very effectively for ethical purposes if the individual
professional uses them to help effect social changes that promote the
welfare of clients. Where such power and influence are sought for the
purpose of self-aggrandizement, however, the ethical purpose of professional activity is corrupted. We believe that psychoeducational as-

sessment practitioners will function ethically only to the degree that they bear in mind that the true purpose of their professional activity is to promote, not their own advancement, but the well-being of the school children they serve.

Situations sometimes arise in assessment practice, however, that are difficult to judge in terms of ethical values or the requirements of a code. When this occurs, practitioners can seek advice from colleagues or from the ethics committees of professional organizations to which they belong (while making sure to maintain confidentiality of information about clients). Viewing the child as client also may sometimes put practitioners at odds with their employers. Such conflicts should be approached directly but tactfully and viewed as opportunities to improve the quality of organizational responses to client needs.

Both the APA and NASP ethical codes indicate that the professional is individually accountable to the highest standards of the profession and impose sanctions to punish unethical conduct. A practitioner found guilty of violating requirements of an ethical code may be expelled from membership in the professional organization that developed the code. Such expulsion occurs occasionally, but probably not frequently enough. In addition, ethical misconduct sometimes results in other punitive measures, such as loss of license to practice. In commenting on individual accountability for ethical practice, Martin (1981) notes that such accountability sometimes poses dilemmas, particularly for salaried practitioners. He reports that many of the situations referred to the ethics committee of APA's division of school psychology involved employer demands that, if honored, might have conflicted with the requirements of the APA ethical code. He also reports that the complexity of the issues involved in many of these situations and the fact that it is difficult for an employee to disobey his or her employer has led to suggestions that such issues be treated by the organizations as problems of professional standards, rather than as problems of professional ethics. This solution "would be aimed at relieving the individual psychologist of ethical responsibility for individual actions where required by an employing body" (Martin, 1981, p. 3). Martin, however, argues against this policy, and we agree. We think that practitioners are individually accountable for ethical practice and that if they are placed in such a position of conflict, they should attempt to modify the organizational pressures and practices that conflict with the requirements of ethical codes. As a last resort they should leave their employers rather than cooperate in the use of unethical assessment practices.

GENERAL REQUIREMENTS OF ETHICAL PRACTICE

Several sections of the APA ethical code refer generally to practitioners' responsibilities to promote client welfare and specify activities that practitioners should pursue as well as those that they should avoid or try to prevent. These sections are as follows:

> Psychologists respect the dignity and worth of the individual and strive for the preservation and protection of fundamental human rights. . . . They make every effort to protect the welfare of those who seek their services. . . . They accept responsibility for the consequences of their acts and make every effort to insure that their services are used appropriately. . . . They are alert to personal, social, organizational, financial, or political situations and pressures that might lead to misuse of their influence. . . . As employees or employers, psychologists do not engage in or condone practices that are inhumane or that result in illegal or unjustifiable actions. Such practices include, but are not limited to, those based on considerations of race, handicap, age, gender, sexual preference, religion, or national origin in hiring, promotion, or training. . . . In their professional roles, psychologists avoid any action that will violate or diminish the legal and civil rights of others who may be affected by their actions. (APA, 1981, pp. 633 – 634)

> Psychologists understand the areas of competence of related professions. They make full use of all the professional, technical, and administrative resources that serve the best interests of consumers. The absence of formal relationships with other professional workers does not relieve psychologists of the responsibility of securing for their clients the best possible professional service, nor does it relieve them of the obligation to exercise foresight, diligence, and tact in obtaining the complementary or alternative assistance needed by clients. (p. 636).

Like the APA code, the NASP ethical code also addresses some general ethical requirements of practice.

> The school psychologist is committed to the application of professional expertise for promoting improvement in the quality of life available to each person. This objective is pursued in ways that protect the dignity and rights of persons served. Professional skills, position, and influence are applied only for purposes which are consistent with those values. (NASP, 1978a, p. 109)

These sections of the APA and NASP ethical codes stress the professional's commitment to client welfare. The codes also state that the professional has a responsibility to see that clients receive competent service. Referrals to other professionals are required when individual practitioners lack the knowledge or skills necessary to serve particular clients. We support these provisions, and we believe that practitioners should evaluate their own services by asking whether or not they would be satisfied with the services provided if the child served was their own. This perspective should also be applied to organizational responses to client needs when an assessment practitioner is one of several staff members providing services. Our rationale for this position and some of its attendant dilemmas are presented in subsequent sections.

ENFORCEMENT OF ETHICAL GUIDELINES

Both the APA and the NASP have committees and procedures for the purpose of investigating complaints of ethical misconduct and, if necessary, recommending expulsion of persons from the organizations. The NASP document entitled "Procedures for Handling Complaints of Alleged Violations of Ethical Principles" (NASP, 1978b) illustrates in a general way how such mechanisms tend to function.

The committees and procedures are typically designed to address complaints of ethical misconduct directed against individual members, rather than against agencies employing psychologists. When a NASP member suspects a psychological colleague of ethical misconduct, the NASP code of ethics suggests that the professional organization be consulted first to determine the appropriate next steps (NASP, 1978a, p. 111). The APA code of ethics is more explicit about the initial steps in addressing the problem. Specifically,

> When psychologists know of an ethical violation by another psychologist, and it seems appropriate, they informally attempt to resolve the issue by bringing the behavior to the attention of the psychologist. If the misconduct is of a minor nature and/or appears to be due to a lack of sensitivity, knowledge, or experience, such an informal solution is usually appropriate. Such informal corrective efforts are made with sensitivity to any rights to confidentiality involved. If the violation does not seem amenable to an informal solution, or is of a more serious nature, psychologists bring it to the attention of the appropriate local, state, and/or national committee on professional ethics and conduct. (APA, 1981, p. 637).

We favor this procedure and view it as compatible with the spirit of the NASP code of ethics as well.

While both APA and NASP members are subject to expulsion for ethical misconduct, they may, alternatively, be disciplined with official reprimands. Again, such reprimands are probably not administered as frequently as they should be. Reprimand and expulsion represent the only direct disciplinary measures that these professional organizations can take against their members. However, the organizations can also report ethically errant members to units of state governments that issue licenses to practice. Such reports might lead to suspensions or revocations of licenses to practice.

While we favor disciplinary actions against individual practitioners judged to be practicing unethically, we also recognize that it is often difficult to resist employers' pressures to engage in unethical practice. It is usually easier to threaten to resign a professional position than to actually do so. We suggest that practitioners placed in ethical dilemmas by their employers try, individually or collectively, to negotiate more acceptable practices with the employers. If such efforts fail, practitioners should approach their professional organizations for assistance in such negotiations. Should further negotiations prove impossible or fail, practitioners should not immediately resign from their employing organizations. Legal challenges to employer requirements may be possible and should be explored. Legal challenges should also be considered in situations in which practitioners are fired for failure to obey unethical employer dictates. The court in the *Forrest* v. *Ambach* case (see pp. 31–32) held that professional ethics "cannot be cavalierly dismissed as irrelevant to the employer–employee relationship" (Prasse, 1981b, p. 3). Further, professional organizations may assist with the expenses involved in legal challenges to unreasonable employer demands or actions.

ETHICAL PRACTICE AND LEGAL PRACTICE

Some situations in assessment practice may require a choice between ethical and legal obligations. The NASP code of ethics recognizes the possibility of such conflicts by reminding practitioners of "the ever present necessity to differentiate between legal mandate and ethical responsibility" (NASP, 1978a, p. 108). Despite this reminder, little specific advice about handling ethical—legal conflicts is found in the NASP code. The code, however, does recognize the practitioner's right to employ customary (socially accepted) procedures for bringing about social (including legal) changes. The APA code of ethics, in its latest revision (1981), indicates that

> in the ordinary course of events, psychologists adhere to relevant governmental laws and institutional regulations. When federal, state, provincial, organizational, or institutional laws, regulations or practices are in conflict with Association standards and guidelines, psychologists

make known their commitment to Association standards and guidelines and, whenever possible, work toward a resolution of the conflict.
Both practitioners and researchers are concerned with the development of such legal and quasi-legal regulations as best serve the public
interest, and they work toward changing existing regulations that are
not beneficial to the public interest. (APA, 1981, p. 634)

Essentially, then, the APA code of ethics encourages active efforts to
resolve existing ethical–legal conflicts at the local level, to help develop new laws and regulations required by the public interest, and
to work toward changing dysfunctional laws and regulations. Such
efforts obviously propel psychologists, individually and collectively,
into the legislative arena. We believe that this is appropriate as long
as psychologists who are speaking out as individuals indicate that
they are not representing the profession as a whole.

These comments may make it appear that ethical and legal requirements of practice are usually or frequently in conflict. This is
not the case. In fact, some of the recent revisions in the APA code of
ethics represent deliberate efforts to bring the code into closer congruence with statutory and case law. In addition, some of the regulations implementing Public Law (PL) 94-142 and other federal laws
provide legal sanction for many practices previously advocated on
ethical and "best practice" grounds. Further, courts are beginning to
pay closer attention to professional standards and ethical codes in
interpreting the law, as illustrated by the decision in *Forrest* v. *Ambach*. Nevertheless, conflicts certainly do occur. Practitioners must
know both ethical and legal requirements, since the two are not always in agreement. When there is a conflict, difficult choices must be
made in the short term. Long-term efforts to resolve the conflicts
must also be initiated, if the goal of offering appropriate assessment
services to children is to be attained.

APPLYING ETHICAL GUIDELINES TO
PSYCHOEDUCATIONAL ASSESSMENT
PRACTICE

Selection of Assessment Techniques

We have indicated previously that compliance with the regulations implementing PL 94-142 and other federal laws requires comprehensive assessment in all areas related to each child's suspected
disability. These regulations illustrate the point that recent legislation provides legal sanction for some practices long considered to be
ethically desirable. In this case, the law is in harmony with ethical

standards. Implementing comprehensive assessment obviously requires adequate knowledge of measurement principles, test validation research, and other research on assessment. Since assessment
techniques need to be appropriate to both the decisions to be made
and to the unique characteristics of each child assessed, knowledge of
child development and the effects of particular health problems and
environmental circumstances specific to each child is also required.

The APA and NASP ethical codes reflect and clarify the above
points. Specifically, the NASP code of ethics says that

> the school psychologist strives to maintain the highest standards of ser-
> vice by an objective collecting of appropriate data and information nec-
> essary to effectively work with the student. In conducting a psychologi-
> cal evaluation, due consideration is given to individual integrity and
> individual differences by the selection and use of appropriate proce-
> dures and assessment techniques. . . . The school psychologist insists
> upon collecting data for an evaluation in a manner that lends itself to
> maximum verification, includes relevant information, and is based on
> assessment techniques which are appropriate for the client. (NASP,
> 1978a, pp. 108–109)

The APA code provides some additional guidance on the selection and
utilization of assessment techniques.

> Psychologists recognize differences among people such as those that
> may be associated with age, sex, socioeconomic and ethnic back-
> grounds. When necessary, they obtain training, experience, or counsel
> to assure competent service or research relating to such persons. (APA,
> 1981, p. 634)
> Psychologists do not encourage or promote the use of psychological
> assessment techniques by inappropriately trained or otherwise unqual-
> ified persons through teaching, sponsorship, or supervision. (p. 637)

Competent selection and utilization of assessment techniques is an
important means by which practitioners can help to assure that assessment is beneficial to the client and therefore in accordance with
ethical standards. Again, only techniques with sufficient technical
adequacy and relevance to the decisions to be made should be utilized, and these techniques must also be appropriate to the characteristics of the child being assessed.

Decision Rules for Assessment Models

Classification Decisions

As we have briefly suggested earlier, client welfare is also dependent on the selection of appropriate assessment models for judging
performance on assessment techniques used for classification pur-

poses. The decision rules incorporated in each of these models must also be correctly applied.

It will be recalled from Chapter 1 that classification decisions may be served by the application of medical, social-system, and pluralistic models to assessment data. As we have shown earlier, these models may often be used in combination in determining whether or not a particular classification should be assigned to a child. Failure to use models relevant to a classification decision, or incorrect use of models, may lead to errors in classification, which, in turn, can lead to unwarranted stigmatization of a child and to the provision of inappropriate services.

Medical-Model Decisions.   Failure to use medical-model measures to screen for the presence of biological symptoms may result in a child's being classified as mentally retarded when his or her school problems actually reflect a problem such as hearing loss. A classfication error such as this might then lead to programming that fails to address the child's hearing problem. While such programming might contain some beneficial aspects, it obviously would not represent programming most responsive to the child's needs and therefore would not be as effective as it should be in promoting and protecting the child's welfare.

It is no overstatement to say that ethical psychoeducational assessment practice requires, at a minimum, screening for hearing and vision problems in each child assessed. It is imperative that the medical-model decision rule be followed when screening results even suggest hearing or vision problems. The decision rule for the medical model is that children suspected (after screening) of having hearing or vision problems be referred for more comprehensive medical evaluation. Further psychoeducational assessment of such children should be deferred until the results of more comprehensive medical evaluations are available. Children with known medical problems should not be assessed psychoeducationally without the benefit of current information on the status of their medical disabilities.

Social-System Model Decisions.   While medical-model data on children have occasionally been neglected in psychoeducational assessment, social-system model data are almost always collected, at least in classifying children as mentally retarded, seriously emotionally disturbed, or learning disabled. The collection of social-system model data is imperative for these classifications, since such data allow us to make judgments about the nature and severity of a child's problems. The decision rule of the social-system model, for classification decisions, is that classifications are assigned only when social-system model data indicate extreme or severe deviations from what is considered average performance. Children with mild performance deficits should be able to be adequately served in regular classrooms, perhaps with supplemental services other than those provided by special education programs.

Pluralistic Model Decisions.   Our position on the use of pluralistic-model data in classification is more complicated. We do not view the use of such data as ethically imperative in making classification decisions. However, we do view such data as potentially helpful in determining whether some children warrant classification as mentally retarded or learning disabled.

Pluralistic norms have been developed by Mercer (1979b) for the Wechsler Intelligence Scale for Children—Revised (WISC-R), an intelligence test frequently used in assessment of intellectual functioning in children. These norms were developed for black, Hispanic, and Anglo children residing in California. Mercer recommends that pluralistic norms for the WISC-R be developed for other sections of the country and for additional racial and ethnic groups. The intent of the development of pluralistic norms for the WISC-R is to obtain a better estimate of a child's intellectual capacity. In contrast, the social-system norms presented in the WISC-R manual indicate a child's current intellectual functioning in relation to a nationally representative sample of age peers. Mercer (1979a) suggests that the WISC-R social-system norms be used to judge whether a child needs remedial assistance (i.e., to make programming decisions) and that pluralistic norms for the WISC-R be used to judge whether a child warrants a special education classification (i.e., to make classification decisions). She argues that social-system norms assume equal learning opportunities on the part of all children and hence unfairly penalize culturally different or economically disadvantaged children when used for classification decisions.

Mercer appears to view a classification of mental retardation as appropriate only when a child's poor performance on an intelligence test can be assumed to reflect a permanent impairment. While we believe that IQ scores indicating mild retardation often fail to reflect permanent impairment on the part of many culturally different or economically disadvantaged children, many educators and some psychologists seem to assume that they do. If such an assumption is widespread and leads to inappropriate programming or social stigmatization, then classifying a temporarily impaired child as mentally retarded will produce negative consequences for the child. If it is important to so classify only permanently impaired children, the use of pluralistic norms for the WISC-R (and other intelligence tests) would help prevent misclassification of children as mentally retarded.

The misconception that mild mental retardation is always a permanent condition appears to be so widespread that we agree that temporarily impaired children should not be classified as mentally retarded. Nevertheless, the use of pluralistic IQ norms is, in our view, discretionary. If practitioners supplement social-system IQ data with social-system data on adaptive behavior in home and neighborhood settings, many culturally different or economically disadvantaged children will not warrant classification as mentally retarded. This will particularly be the case when the social-system model decision rule of requiring extreme deviations from the average on both measures before classifying a child as mentally retarded is followed.

In summary, we believe that client welfare will not currently be served if temporarily impaired children are classified as mentally retarded. Such children should, however, receive remedial assistance in meeting the social-system demands of the classroom, either through compensatory education programs or through special materials and consultation provided regular classroom teachers. As we shall also see, some children with low social-system—norm IQ scores might, alternatively, be eligible for special education services because of their classification as learning disabled.

It should be recalled that classifying a child as learning disabled requires, at a minimum, evidence of a severe discrepancy between expected academic achievement (usually based on an IQ score) and actual achievement (usually based on an achievement-test score). If a culturally different or economically disadvantaged child obtains a low IQ score when social-system norms are used, then his or her expected achievement will also be low. This circumstance will often make it difficult to document a significant discrepancy between expected and actual achievement. However, if the child's IQ score is higher when pluralistic norms are used, then that discrepancy may be easier to document. Nevertheless, classifying a child as learning disabled also requires a judgment that the discrepancy between expected and actual achievement is not primarily due to cultural difference or economic disadvantage. Since pluralistic norms attempt to compensate for just such factors in estimating intellectual capacity, the use of pluralistic norms will not necessarily result in the classification of culturally different or economically disadvantaged children as learning disabled. Each case must be judged on its own merits and the judgments required will be difficult to make.

Programming Decisions

The choice of assessment models used for programming has a great effect on the welfare of clients. As we emphasized in Chapter 1, we believe that research to date provides more support for assessment and programming congruent with the task analysis model than with the psychoeducational process model. Hence, we believe that client welfare will therefore be best served by an emphasis on task analytic assessment and programming. While one is certainly free to interpret the research literature as one sees it, an emphasis on either model should reflect an informed and thoughtful choice. Assessment and programming practices based mostly on tradition or hearsay will not advance the ethical goal of promotion and protection of client welfare.

Access to Information

As we have mentioned, the Buckley Amendment gives parents (and students 18 years old and above) certain rights relative to access to educational records, corrections to the records, and release of the records to parties outside the school system. We have also pointed out that the regulations implementing PL 94-142 require parental consent for initial assessment and for initial special education placement. These regulations further require that schools provide notice to parents about certain actions they plan or do not plan to take.

The APA and NASP ethical codes encourage active sharing of information and decisions with parents and, when appropriate, children. The APA code states that psychologists

> fully inform consumers as to the purpose and nature of an evaluative, treatment, educational, or training procedure, and they freely acknowledge that clients, students, or participants in research have freedom of choice with regard to participation. . . . When working with minors or other persons who are unable to give voluntary, informed consent, psychologists take special care to protect these persons' best interests. (APA, 1981, p. 636)

While the APA code of ethics suggests that children may not have the legal right to withhold consent for psychoeducational assessment, the NASP code of ethics does not seem to acknowledge this fact. The NASP code does require parental consent for assessment and the provision of information to parents on how assessment results will be communicated. In addition, however, the NASP code states that "the school psychologist . . . respects the student's right of choice to enter or to participate in services voluntarily" (NASP, 1978, p. 109). Although it is desirable to secure the child's consent for assessment, we believe that such consent is not an appropriate requirement of ethical practice. Some children will not be capable of making a reasoned choice. Also, children who are legal minors are unlikely to have legal standing to make a choice. Nevertheless, the APA code correctly requires that persons lacking capacity or legal standing to give consent be afforded "special care" to ensure that their best interests are safeguarded. This special care would, in our view, include postponing assessment of a child who is uncooperative with the assessment process. It would also include communicating reservations about whether assessment results reflect a child's best performances when the child is suspected of having exerted less than her or his best effort.

Some steps involved in providing the child special care are also suggested by the NASP code. Specifically,

> The school psychologist explains to the student who the psychologist is, what the psychologist does, and why the student is being seen. The explanation includes the uses to be made of information obtained, procedures for collecting the information, persons who will receive specific information, and any obligation the psychologist has for reporting specified information. This explanation should be in language understood by the student. . . . The school psychologist informs the student of the rationale of sharing information. The course of action proposed takes into account the rights of the student, the rights of the parent, the responsibilities of school personnel, and the expanding independence and mature status of the student. . . . The school psychologist discusses with the student all contemplated changes in status and plans which are suggested as a result of psychological study. The discussion includes positive and negative consequences and an account of alternatives available to the student. (NASP, 1978a, pp. 109–110)

Although the NASP code suggests that these explanations be provided by the school psychologist, we think they can be given by other persons competent to do so. If no one is explaining assessment to children, steps should be taken to see that someone does so. We feel that children have a right to know about the assessment process and that they will be more cooperative as a result.

Both ethical codes contain provisions concerning the sharing, interpreting, and utilizing of information collected through the assessment process. In regard to the sharing of information, the APA code of ethics states:

> Psychologists have a primary obligation to respect the confidentiality of information obtained from persons in the course of their work as psychologists. They reveal such information to others only with the consent of the person or the person's legal representative, except in those unusual circumstances in which not to do so would result in clear

danger to the person or to others. Where appropriate, psychologists inform their clients of the legal limits of confidentiality. . . . Information obtained in clinical or consulting relationships, or evaluative data concerning children, students, employees, and others, is discussed only for professional purposes and only with others clearly concerned with the case. Written and oral reports present only data germane to the purposes of the evaluation, and every effort is made to avoid undue invasion of privacy. . . . Psychologists make provisions for maintaining confidentiality in the storage and disposal of records. (APA, 1981, pp. 635 – 636)

Somewhat more generally, the NASP code of ethics states that

the school psychologist is obligated to ascertain that psychoeducational information reaches responsible and authorized persons and is adequately interpreted for their use in helping the pupil. This involves establishing practices which safeguard the personal and confidential interests of those concerned. (NASP, 1978a, p. 110)

These sections of the ethical codes essentially pertain to protecting information about clients. Another issue concerning confidentiality involves parental access to tests used with children. As we have mentioned, completed test record forms may be considered part of a child's educational records under the Buckley Amendment. Assessment practitioners are often fearful that showing completed forms to parents or allowing parents to copy completed forms may compromise test security. The APA code of ethics indicates that psychologists should use tests in ways that "respect the client's right to know the results, the interpretations made, and the bases for their conclusions and recommendations. Psychologists make every effort to maintain the security of tests and other assessment techniques within limits of legal mandate (APA, 1981, p. 637)." Detailed suggestions for responding to parental requests to see or copy completed test record forms may be found in "Test Protocols in Relation to Sole Possession Records" (APA, undated). Essentially, this document recommends that parents be allowed to see completed test forms if they request it, but that they be given only written copies of a child's responses to test questions. The document recommends that copies of test questions not be given parents in the interests of protecting test security and abiding by copyright laws.

Both the APA and NASP codes of ethics also contain provisions relative to interpretations of assessment results. The APA code states:

In using assessment techniques, psychologists respect the rights of clients to have full explanations of the nature and purpose of the techniques in language the client can understand, unless an explicit exception to this right has been agreed to in advance. When the explanations

are to be provided by others, psychologists establish procedures for ensuring the adequacy of these explanations. . . . In reporting assessment
results, psychologists indicate any reservations that exist regarding
validity or reliability because of the circumstances of the assessment or the inappropriateness of the norms for the person tested. (APA,
1981, p. 637)

The NASP code states:

When reporting data which are to be representative of the student,
the school psychologist makes certain that the information is in such
form and style as to assure that the recipient of the report will be able
to give maximum assistance to the client. The emphasis is on the interpretation and organization rather than the simple passing along of test
scores, and will include a professional appraisal of the degree of reli-
ance which can be placed on the information. . . . The school psychologist communicates findings and recommendations in language readily
understood by the school staff. These communications describe possible favorable and unfavorable consequences associated with the alternative proposals. . . . The school psychologist insures that recommendations and plans for assisting the child are discussed with the parent.
The discussion includes probabilities and alternatives associated with
each set of plans. The parents are advised as to sources of help available at school and those available in the community. (NASP, 1978a, pp.
109– 110)

Finally, the APA code of ethics addresses the utilization of assessment
results. The code states:

Psychologists have the responsibility to attempt to prevent distor-
tion, misuse or supression of psychological findings by the institution
or agency of which they are employees. (APA, 1981, p. 633)
Psychologists strive to insure that the results of assessments and
their interpretations are not misused by others. (p. 637)

Cooperation with Others and Resolution of Conflicts

The APA code of ethics makes it clear that practitioners have certain obligations to their communities and employing organizations,
as well as to their clients. Specifically, the code states:

Psychologists' moral and ethical standards of behavior are a personal
matter to the same degree as they are for any other citizen, except as
these may compromise the fulfillment of their professional responsibilities or reduce the public trust in psychology and psychologists. Regarding their own behavior, psychologists are sensitive to prevailing
community standards and to the possible impact that conformity to or
deviation from these standards may have upon the quality of their performance as psychologists. Psychologists are also aware of the possible

impact of their public behavior upon the ability of colleagues to perform their professional duties. (APA, 1981, p. 634)

Psychologists act with due regard for the needs, special competencies, and obligations of their colleagues in psychology and other professions. They respect the prerogatives and obligations of the institutions or organizations with which these other colleagues are associated. (p. 636)

The NASP code indicates that an understanding of the schools and their programs is a prerequisite to the delivery of competent psychoeducational services.

In addition to mastery of professional psychological skills, the school psychologist prepares for this special area of functioning by becoming knowledgeable of the organization, objectives, and methods of the school. This is a basic requirement for rendering competent psychological services in the school. (NASP, 1978a, p. 108)

The school psychologist recognizes that a working understanding of the goals, processes, and legal requirements of the educational system is essential for an effective relationship with the school. Familiarization with the organization, instructional materials, and teaching strategies of the school are basic for the psychologist to contribute to the common objective for fostering maximum self-development opportunities for each student. (p. 110)

We agree that psychoeducational assessment practitioners must know the schools in which they work and act with due regard for community standards and the prerogatives of their employing organizations, but we believe that conflicts between the requirements of ethical codes and organizational practices must also be recognized and appropriately addressed. Our position is stated succinctly in the NASP code: "The school psychologist maintains the skills and ethics of the profession while cooperating with other professionals" (NASP, 1978a, p. 111).

In addressing apparent conflicts between professional ethics and organizational practices, the APA code states:

When conflicts of interest arise between clients and psychologists' employing institutions, psychologists clarify the nature and direction of their loyalties and responsibilities and keep all parties informed of their commitments. . . . When the demands of an organization require psychologists to violate these Ethical Principles, psychologists clarify the nature of the conflict between the demands and these principles. They inform all parties of psychologists' ethical responsibilities and take appropriate action. (APA, 1981, p. 636)

The NASP code states that "where a situation occurs in which there are divided or conflicting interests (as parent– school– student), the school psychologist is responsible for working out a pattern of action which assures mutual benefit and protection of rights for all concerned" (NASP, 1978a, p. 109).

It is usually possible to arrive at courses of action that honor ethical requirements, client needs and legal rights, and organizational needs and prerogatives. Negotiating such solutions requires good faith efforts on the part of all parties to the conflict. The responsibility for good faith efforts may rest most heavily on assessment practitioners, since such practitioners often have specialized expertise in human behvior and human relations. Assessment practitioners should be able to appreciate that conflict can be healthy if it leads to efforts that assure mutual benefit and protection. They should also understand that their points of view will not always prevail and that this is an acceptable (perhaps desirable) fact of life, so long as they are free to make their opinions known and clients are afforded due process for redress of grievances. When such conditions are not present, legal action should be considered.

Assessment practitioners, in our view, have a special responsibility to monitor their own behaviors, those of employing organizations, and those of parents, as they affect the assessment process, to make sure that the process is working to the benefit of children. All parties to psychoeducational assessment should demonstrate strong commitments to the protection and promotion of children's legal rights and best interests. If federal and other laws are seen as requiring inappropriate services to handicapped children, then instead of finding ways to avoid the law efforts to change the laws should be undertaken. It is hypocritical for schools to teach good citizenship if they are involved in efforts to avoid or subvert the law. Practices viewed as detrimental to children's welfare should be openly discussed within the school organization and efforts to modify such practices should be undertaken. Assessment practitioners should be careful not to claim overall moral or technical superiority to administrative superiors or colleagues, many of whom have excellent contributions to make to the assessment process, but should actively utilize their specialized expertise and points of view in resolving conflicts that arise and promoting cooperative efforts.

CONCLUSIONS

While psychoeducational assessment practitioners must respond to the ethical problems unique to their practices, their attempts to resolve these problems must be placed in a more general context. This context is the challenging, yet necessary, attempt by all human-service professionals to provide adequate services to clients.

In our view, ethical assessment practice requires adequate understanding of the particular contexts in which assessment is performed, technical skills, and personal commitment. When such qualities are used in situations in which good faith is also present, useful outcomes for children are likely. Such outcomes can occur even in situations in which the perceived interests of children, parents, and schools are in conflict. Our experience is that desirable outcomes, while not inevitable, usually occur when committed efforts are made. These efforts honor the legal rights of parents and schools but also involve special care in defining and advancing the best interests of children.

Good will and good intentions are essential to assessment practice but so is knowledge. A thorough understanding of assessment techniques is an absolute prerequisite to competent psychoeducational assessment practice. In the next chapters we examine some representative assessment techniques used in each of the seven assessment domains.

Part II
ASSESSMENT DOMAINS

5

Assessment of Health Factors

ASSESSING HEALTH FACTORS may not normally be thought of as the psychoeducational assessment practitioner's role, but it is nonetheless important for the practitioner to be aware of this area. Health factors clearly must be evaluated if children who are referred for special services are to be properly assessed.

From the assessment practitioner's point of view, the primary purpose of such assessment is likely to be classification. Health factors must be assessed so that vision or hearing problems, and other difficulties, can be ruled out before a decision is made that a child should be placed in a category such as mentally retarded. While the assessment practitioner may perform screening, it is not typically the role of the assessment practitioner to certify a child as visually impaired, hearing impaired, or as belonging to one of the other health-related handicapping classifications; such certification will be done by a specialist in these fields.

The role of the assessment practitioner is therefore somewhat more difficult to define in the area of health factors assessment than in most of the areas in which the assessment practitioner works. On the one hand, other professionals, with their own training and skills, normally have the chief responsibility for assessing these health factors. On the other hand, the assessment practitioner is often the primary person in the assessment process who has a clear overview of the entire process and the responsibility for being sure it is completed correctly. Thus it may well fall to the assessment practitioner to ensure that needed evaluation of a child's health factors is carried out.

It may also be the assessment practitioner's responsibility to en-

121

sure that these results are used properly, in both classification and programming decisions. While it would not be appropriate for an assessment practitioner to determine whether a child should be classified as visually impaired, for instance, it may well be the role of this practitioner to determine whether adequate checking of vision has been carried out and whether additional handicapping conditions such as retardation are also present. Similarly, it would not normally be the assessment practitioner who would recommend specific kinds of vision training, but it may indeed be the role of the assessment practitioner to be sure that the programming set up for a child includes adequate consideration of whatever health impairments may exist.

Thus, while assessment practitioners must be careful not to exceed their training in assessing health factors, they typically do fill two roles: performing screening, and ensuring that appropriate testing of health factors is carried out and that appropriate use is made of the results.

SPECIFIC TECHNIQUES

Visual Assessment

Visual acuity refers to the overall sharpness of a person's vision. It is normally expressed as a ratio of the distance at which a person can see compared to the distance at which a person with normal vision can see. Thus, a ratio of 20/200 means that a person can see at 20 feet what a normal person can see at 200 feet. Normal vision is 20/20; 20/15 would indicate better than average visual acuity. Another factor in determining overall visual ability is the width of the visual field. A person may have vision of normal acuity in a small portion of the field but be able to see only a very restricted portion of the field, being limited either in peripheral vision or in specific areas of the field. Finally, a person's perception of color may be impaired.

The legal definition of *blindness* is visual acuity of 20/200 or less in the better eye, with correction, or central acuity of more than 20/200 if the widest diameter of the visual field subtends an angular distance of no more than 20°. The legal definition of *partially sighted* is vision between 20/70 and 20/200.

While the legal definition of blindness has many uses, many educators feel that it is misleading, since the degree of useful vision a child has is related to a number of factors besides acuity. Thus many educators prefer to consider a child's visual handicap in terms of educational implications, such as whether the child can learn to read print in some form or must be taught braille. While such a definition is less objective than the legal definitions and harder to implement, the assessment practitioner should be aware that a legally blind child may well have substantial usable vision.

Snellen Chart

The standard instrument for screening for visual acuity is the Snellen chart. This is simply the familiar wall chart with rows of letters in various standard sizes that the child is asked to read from a distance of 20 feet. Most school systems carry out routine screening with a Snellen chart at various grade levels. The assessment practitioner should have the results of this screening for all children being assessed. If the result of a recent screening is not in the child's folder, it is not difficult to ensure that the school nurse or the assessment practitioner carries it out.

The Snellen chart is used only for screening and presents a number of problems, including the fact that children may guess. In addition, making the letter discriminations may be difficult for younger children who are just learning the alphabet. The practitioner should check to see whether the child knows the alphabet before giving this test. Preschool adaptations can be used for children who do not yet know their letters. The practitioner should also check to be sure that children who have glasses are wearing them for the screening. As a screening device, the Snellen test functions well. It is simple, quick, and likely to identify major vision difficulties.

Other Techniques

If the Snellen screening suggests a visual problem, more detailed testing will typically be carried out by a vision specialist. Among the more comprehensive instruments that may be used are the Titmus Vision Tester, which checks acuity in more detail, as well as a tendency for eyes to turn in or out, and the Keystone Telebinocular Instrument. The Keystone Instrument is probably the more comprehensive; it assesses vision in each eye separately and in both together, including acuity, fusion, depth perception, and other aspects of vision. The specific details of a more comprehensive examination are likely to be relevant primarily in determining corrections; the assessment practitioner should get a clear idea from the vision specialist of what impact the findings will have on the child's ability to do seatwork and boardwork.

Warning Signs and Follow-Up

Certain problems related to visual acuity sometimes arise in school. The assessment practitioner needs to be aware of these and be ready to deal with them. One of the most common is that of the child who has glasses but does not wear them, or who has had glasses prescribed at one time but no longer has them. The assessment practitioner should be sure that follow-ups are carried through if a possible problem of acuity is identified with the Snellen screening. Typically, if a child does not pass the screening test, the school notifies the parents and expects that they will pursue the matter. For a child who is being considered for special education placement, the assessment practitioner must take more responsibility in ensuring that further testing is in fact carried out and that correction or treatment is arranged for if necessary. It is not sufficient to determine that there is probably a problem with visual acuity that is impeding a child's learning, send a note home to the parents, and assume that the child has been completely dealt with. The practitioner should also take care that needed correction is carried out before the assessment continues, so that the impact of a possible visual impairment on the assessment results is minimized.

Assessment of visual acuity with any of these methods assumes that the medical model is being followed, and consequently the assessment practitioner should be most concerned about missing children who may need help. The Snellen chart is an appropriate tool within this model; most of its difficulties are likely to result in overidentification rather than underidentification of visual problems, which is appropriate within the medical model.

Hearing Assessment

Hearing is normally measured in decibels (dB), a measure of loudness. Hearing loss is described in terms of how loud a sound must be before a person hears it. Zero dB is the level at which a person with average hearing can just detect a sound. A 40-dB hearing loss means that a sound must be at a volume of 40 dB before a person can hear it.

Assessment of hearing, however, does not consist of a single measurement of acuity. People hear sounds over a wide range of frequencies, and hearing may not be equally acute at all of these frequencies. Therefore hearing must be assessed at a number of different frequencies, typically those most used in speech. While a child's hearing loss may be given as a single value, this value is actually the average of hearing acuity at several different frequencies.

In terms of average decibel loss, it is generally considered that a loss of more than about 25 dB in either ear has definite educational implications. A loss of between approximately 27 and 40 dB is considered slight; a loss of between 40 and 55 dB is mild; a loss of between 56 and 70 dB is moderate; a loss of between 71 and 90 dB is severe; and a loss of more than 90 dB is considered profound. A child with more than a slight loss is likely to have difficulty with schoolwork and may have delayed or poor language development. A child with a moderate loss will need special help with speech development and substantial extra assistance in school. A child with a severe or profound loss is not likely to develop speech or to function in school without extensive training. Such a child may not develop comprehensible oral language even with special training.

A number of factors in hearing loss are relevant to education. One is the "shape" of the loss. *Shape* in this sense refers to the form of the curves obtained when the results of audiometric testing are plotted on a graph. A *flat* loss is one in which acuity is approximately equal at all frequencies. A *sloping* or *irregular* loss indicates greater acuity at some frequencies than at others. Given a flat loss and a sloping loss of similar degree, a flat loss is usually less handicapping educationally, because a sloping loss may involve distortions that make speech and other sound much more difficult to interpret.

Another factor relevant to educational programming for the hearing impaired is the age of onset. Children who develop language prior to the onset of hearing difficulties will have less difficulty with a regular educational setting than those whose impairment is congenital or dates from before the development of language.

The kind of hearing loss is also relevant. Sound is conveyed by the air from outside the ear through the external and middle ear. A *conductive* loss is one in which this air conduction is somehow impaired. Stimulation of the bones of the skull, however, bypasses air conduction of sound, stimulating the inner ear and neural pathways directly. An impairment somewhere within neural pathways will result in a lack of bone conduction as well as air conduction; this kind of loss is called a *sensorineural* hearing loss.

A conductive loss often has a correctable cause, such as a buildup of fluid in the middle ear owing to infection. Such a loss may be temporary, affecting the child's hearing only during a cold or infection. Such temporary losses, however, can have a substantial effect on the child's learning if they are frequent or of long duration. When such losses are frequent, they often become chronic even if the infections are eliminated medically. Thus a history of middle ear infections in a child should always be regarded as *possibly* indicative of continuing hearing problems (Miller, Note 6). Hearing impairments resulting from a conductive loss are usually slight to moderate.

A sensorineural loss is usually more severe and more permanent. Sensorineural losses occur for a variety of reasons, including congenital conditions, maternal rubella, meningitis or encephalitis, and Rh incompatibility. Although some of these can be prevented, once the impairment has occurred it can seldom be improved.

Audiometry

Typically, assessment of hearing acuity is carried out with a pure-tone audiometer, a machine that generates tones at controlled frequencies and decibels. Screening normally consists of presenting tones at several frequencies and asking the child to indicate when a tone is heard. Screening may be carried out at a single loudness, typically 20 or 25 dB, depending on the background noise in the testing situation. More detailed assessment may use the same instrument but would be carried out at more frequencies and throughout the decibel range necessary to establish the minimum threshold for each frequency. Screening typically tests only air conduction; follow-up assessment would include bone conduction measures.

The assessment practitioner is seldom responsible for screening of hearing acuity unless the practitioner has received special training. However, the assessment practitioner may well need to interpret and use the results of such testing. The results from the pure-tone audiometer are usually presented in an audiogram, or chart of the assessment results. A typical audiogram for one ear is shown in Figure 5-1. The audiogram indicates hearing level in decibels for frequencies from 125 cycles per second (Hz) to 8000 Hz. Results are indicated separately for the left ear and the right ear and separately for air conduction and bone conduction. A flat loss will look like a straight line across the audiogram; a sloping or irregular loss will have a curved or irregular shape. A conductive loss is indicated by a gap between the air conduction and bone conduction curves. The audiogram in Figure 5-1 shows an almost flat loss. There is an air conduction loss, as indicated by the gap between the air and bond conduction curves. There is also a sensorineural loss, since the bone conduction curve lies at approximately 35 dB.

In using a audiogram as part of decision making for special education, the assessment practitioner needs to be sensitive to all of the factors discussed above. The average level of hearing loss can be determined by examining the air conduction curve for each ear; this will show the degree to which the child is actually hearing spoken words, for instance. The shape of the loss can readily be observed.

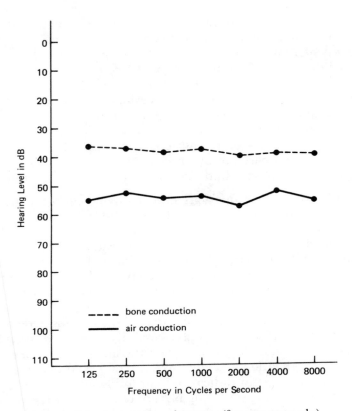

Figure 5-1   A typical audiogram (for one ear only).

Particularly important is the degree of hearing loss between 500 and 2000 Hz, because most speech sounds fall within this range. A difference between hearing in the left and right ears may also have implications in terms of classroom seating and other planning issues.

Warning Signs and Follow-Up

Every child who is referred for psychoeducational assessment should be given a hearing screening. Most schools do screen routinely at some grade levels for possible hearing difficulties. However, it may have been some time since a child was screened, and in such cases a new screening is needed. In addition, there are a number of signs that the examiner may observe that could indicate a possible hearing loss. These include

- Complaints of earache or discharge from either ear.
- Intense observation of the examiner's face; looking at the exam-

iner's face rather than his or her hands during explanations involving modeling of performance tasks.

- Frequent requests for the stimulus to be repeated; spelling a word that is similar but not identical to the word used as stimulus; frequent misunderstanding of questions.
- Verbal scores much lower than performance scores; while this discrepancy may indicate a learning disability, a hearing problem should always be ruled out first.
- Low vocabulary scores, low scores in comprehension of social situations compared to other scores.
- Poor speech for the child's age, especially after first grade.

A child who daydreams a great deal, often confuses instructions, or often seems inattentive may be having difficulty hearing instructions or following classroom discussions and interactions. A child who seems tired and cross by the end of every day may be reacting to the added strain of interpreting speech that is at the threshold of the child's hearing. While these behaviors may also be typical of children with other disabilities, the presence of any of them suggests the possibility of a hearing loss.

As in vision screening, a failure to pass the hearing screening test at some point in the past does not necessarily mean that the child has been given the needed follow-up. The assessment practitioner should watch for an indication in a child's record of a failure on a screening test with no subsequent indication that follow-up took place.

If a recent hearing screening has not been done, it is most important that screening be carried out, followed by detailed assessment if needed. Because even a mild hearing loss can have substantial educational implications, the assessment practitioner must take responsibility for being sure that any hearing impairment is fully taken into account in educational planning. This assessment again falls within the medical model, and the psychoeducational assessment practitioner is most concerned about missing a loss that may be there.

SOMPA Medical-Model Measures

The System of Multicultural Pluralistic Assessment (SOMPA), developed by Mercer (1979b), includes an assessment of various health factors. The SOMPA health-assessment measures are included within the medical-model framework. Their primary use is to ensure, before the remaining assessment is conducted, that the child being assessed is an "intact organism" (that is, free from pathological organic symptoms). Mercer's position is that if this is not the case, the standard assessment that the SOMPA incorporates cannot be interpreted in the usual way, since the child differs in some important way from the norm group (Mercer, 1979b).

The health-assessment measures in the SOMPA consist of the following scales: Physical Dexterity Scales, Bender Visual-Motor Gestalt Test, Visual Acuity, Auditory Acuity, Measures of Weight by Height, and the Health History Inventories.

Physical Dexterity Scales. Six subscales measure physical dexterity: Ambulation, Equilibrium, Placement, Fine Motor Sequencing, Finger-Tongue Dexterity, and Involuntary Movement. According to the technical manual (Mercer, 1979b), the initial tasks "were selected from the large variety of tasks commonly used by clinicians in screening for sensory-motor impairments" (p. 60). The tasks initially selected were given to the norming sample, and the results were factored to determine the scales used. In addition, relationships among the scales and reliability of administration were considered in determining the final scales.

These scales are all created and interpreted according to the medical model. They have low ceilings and are intended to distinguish possible problems from normal behavior but not normal behavior from superior performance. There is a slight relationship between the six subscales and ethnicity or socioeconomic status, but it accounts for little of the variance.

These scales are very well normed; the SOMPA norming sample is a carefully chosen random sample of approximately 1800 children, aged 5 through 11. Split-half reliabilities are acceptable. Some validity data are presented in the technical manual (Mercer, 1979b). Factor analysis indicates that the items do in fact represent six relatively separate factors. Scores improve with age, as would be expected. As noted earlier, the scores are only slightly related to ethnicity or socioeconomic status, as would be appropriate for a measure within the medical model.

However, the manual presents no data concerning the relationship of these tasks to achievement. The recommendation for interpreting them is that any child who falls more than one standard deviation below the norm should be referred for further medical testing. In addition, the likelihood that medical problems contribute to educational difficulties for this child should be considered. Whether this recommendation is reasonable in all cases remains to be determined. Nonetheless, the scales do provide a formal, normed measure of skills that may well be relevant to both classification and programming.

The Physical Dexterity Scales were given to the norming sample for the SOMPA by psychometrists. During the assessment process, however, they can be administered by the assessment practitioner, the school nurse, or other school personnel who are familiar with the scales and trained in their use. It takes approximately 20 minutes to administer the set of six tests.

Bender Visual-Motor Gestalt Test.　The Bender Test, a measure of eye-hand coordination, is included in the SOMPA measures as a med-ical-model measure. This test is discussed in more detail in Chapter 7. The Koppitz (1975b) scoring system was used. The Bender Test was administered to the SOMPA sample, and norms are provided on the basis of this sample. These are probably the best norms available for the Bender Test, since the SOMPA sample is both larger and more carefully selected than most norming samples. Small but consistent differences were found among ethnic groups in average Bender scores; although overall the measure seems to fit the medical model, it may have a sociocultural component. Norms by ethnic group are also available.

Further information on the reliability and validity of the Bender Test are presented in Chapter 7. Within the SOMPA system, the Ben-der score is interpreted similarly to the physical dexterity scores, as a possible indication of medical difficulties. Mercer also suggests that low scores may be associated with learning disabilities. As with the other medical-model scores in the SOMPA, the relationship of Bender Scores to achievement and classification is not made clear by the SOMPA materials.

Visual Acuity and Auditory Acuity Scales.　For assessing visual acuity, the SOMPA uses the Snellen screening test discussed above. Referral is recommended for any child scoring 20/40 or poorer. For assessing hearing acuity, pure-tone audiometry at 250, 500, 1000, 2000, and 4000 Hz is used, with referral recommended if a child fails the screening at 35 dB for any one frequency or 25 dB for any two frequencies in either ear.

Measure of Weight by Height.　Weight and height for the SOMPA sample were also determined by psychometrists. The measure actu-ally used in examining these data is the relationship between the two. Both overweight and underweight children are considered to be at greater risk for health problems. The manual indicates some relation-ship between this measure and the other health measures but pro-vides no indication of its relationship to educational factors. A child more than one standard deviation below or above the norm group is considered to be at risk. Separate norms are provided for girls and boys. It was found that there were few age differences in the relationship between weight and height. That is, boys who were 45 inches tall tended to weigh about the same no matter what their age was. Therefore the norms relate weight and height to each other but not to age.

Health History Inventories.   The fifth set of scales on the SOMPA is the Health History Inventories. These are designed to give a standardized, scorable history of the child's health background that may indicate a larger than usual degree of trauma or illness. The inventories are administered as part of an interview with the child's parents. The five scales included in this measure are the Prenatal/Postnatal Inventory, the Trauma Inventory, the Disease and Illness Inventory, the Vision Inventory, and the Hearing Inventory. The assumption underlying these inventories is that a child who has a large number of problems indicated in his or her medical history is more likely to have current biological dysfunctions that will in some way interfere with academic performance.

These scales are designed for administration by a psychoeducational assessment practitioner, social worker, or other nonmedical person. The numerical scoring can be carried out without special medical training. The manual recommends, however, that the results of the interview also be reviewed by medical personnel, especially if a number of problems are found.

The scales were largely derived from those used for health interviews by the U.S. Public Health Service. Item analyses, comparing the answers to trial items to other measures on the SOMPA that use the medical model, were used to select specific items. Their organization into scales is based on content, rather than any kind of factor structure, since there is no a priori reason to expect that the individual items would be related for most of the inventories. There are few overall ethnic differences for the scales; sociocultural background is related to scores, in that more pathology is found for children from lower socioeconomic levels. The differences found were not large, however, and the results on the inventories can readily be interpreted without taking family background into account.

As with the other health measures discussed above, the manual provides little direct evidence that scores on these scales are in fact related to achievement in school. Children whose scores are more than one standard deviation below the norm are considered to be at risk, and it is assumed that these children are more likely to have academic problems because of their history of health problems. Children who score at risk on the Vision or Hearing Inventory should definitely be referred for further testing.

All of the SOMPA medical scales suffer from this same weakness: the relationship between the scores and a child's actual achievement is unclear. In some cases (such as the vision screening), the existence of a relationship is easy to accept. In others, such as the height-by-weight measure, it is less clear. The primary value of these scales lies in the broad view they help give of the child being assessed. The over-all SOMPA battery provides a detailed, multifaceted picture of the child. Specific details on exactly how to interpret the results are as yet lacking. It is not clear, for instance, what effect on either classification or programming is indicated by an at-risk score on the Health History Inventories. At present, probably the best that can be said is that more routine use of these instruments would help to widen the kinds of information used in psychoeducational diagnosis; future experience may provide more evidence for the most appropriate ways to make use of the additional information. The goal of promotion of a child's welfare may be served (and cannot be hindered) by screening and referral for possible health problems.

Motor Tests

In addition to the measures given above, the assessment practitioner may at times want a measure of motor skills. While these are not, typically, directly related to academic achievement, such measures may give information that can be relevant to programming. Unless motor skills are sufficiently defective to indicate physical disability as a possible classification, they probably will not have a direct effect on classification. Optimal class placement, however, may well include consideration of whether a child has the gross motor skills to participate in games and sports with his or her classmates. Adequate fine motor skills are to some extent needed for successful classroom performance—in writing, for instance.

One measure of motor skills has already been discussed—the Physical Dexterity Scales of the SOMPA. Several other scales sometimes used by assessment practitioners are discussed below.

McCarthy Scales of Children's Abilities

The McCarthy Scales (McCarthy, 1972) are intended for administration to children aged 2½ through 8½. They include Verbal, Quantitative, Perceptual-Performance, General Cognitive, and Memory scales, as well as a Motor Scale. The Motor scale consists of measures of arm and hand coordination, leg and foot coordination, and right—left orientation. Norms for the Motor scale are provided only for the total score based on all motor items. The norm scores provided are deviation scores based on a mean of 50 and a standard deviation of 10; percentiles are also available.

The McCarthy Scales were normed on 1032 children aged 2½ through 8½. The sample was stratified according to age, sex, ethnicity, geographical region, and father's occupation. The sample was chosen to match the 1970 U.S. Census data. Only "normal" children were included in the sample; institutionalized children, children with physical impairments, and children with known brain damage were excluded, as were children with severe behavioral or emotional problems. Within these constraints, children were located by field supervisors to match the stratification set up above (McCarthy, 1972).

For the Motor Scale, the split-half reliability of the McCarthy Scales ranges from 0.60 to 0.89. The scale is more reliable at the earlier age ranges. Overall it appears to have adequate reliability. Scores on the Motor Scale correlate fairly highly with other scores on the McCarthy Scale, with correlations ranging from 0.44 to 0.79. The relationships are highest with the General Cognitive Scale and the Perceptual-Performance Scale. These correlations also lessen for older children. Since the perceptual-performance items make up one-third of the General Cognitive Scale, it is likely that this indicates primarily a relationship between motor skills and perceptual-performance skills, which could be expected for a motor test. The Motor Scale showed little relationship to either of two IQ tests also administered to a sample of children (McCarthy, 1972). This is appropriate.

The Motor scale also showed little or no relationship to an achievement test administered four months later (McCarthy, 1972). This indicates that the scale is measuring a variable other than general ability, which is appropriate for a motor scale. It also indicates yet again, however, the difficulty that the assessment practitioner may have in using motor information in the decision-making process, since its relationship to achievement is unclear.

The McCarthy Motor Scale does not fit cleanly into any of the assessment models. The characteristics it is measuring are normally assumed to be inherent in the child, and on similar tasks Mercer found few ethnic or sociocultural differences. These would normally put it into the medical model. However, the characteristics of the scale itself fit the characteristics of the social-system model better; it has a normal distribution, with a high ceiling and good ability to distinguish average from above average. In terms of decision making, the assessment practitioner who uses this test should probably follow more nearly the ethic of the social-system model and be more concerned about falsely identifying a child's performance as problematic than about missing some problems; the characteristics of the scale and the lack of a clear-cut relationship between its score and a child's achievement both suggest this more cautious approach. This motor scale does provide an additional picture of a child's overall development and as such may be useful in educational planning.

Bruininks-Oseretsky Test of Motor Proficiency

Another motor scale with which the assessment practitioner should have some familiarity is the Bruininks-Oseretsky Test of Motor Proficiency (Bruininks, 1978). This is the most recent version of a scale originally developed in Russia in the mid-1920s. It provides eight subscales of motor proficiency, including four gross motor measures, three fine motor measures, and one combined gross and fine motor measure. These eight subscales are grouped into a gross motor score, a fine motor score, and an overall score. Norms are available for children aged 4½ to 14½, including standard scores, percentile ranks, and stanines. The norms are based on a sample of 765 children, stratified by age, sex, ethnicity, community size, and geographical region, to match the 1970 U.S. Census. Reliability for the overall battery ranges from 0.86 to 0.89; for the gross motor scale and the fine motor scale it ranges from 0.68 to 0.88. Reliabilities are not as good for the individual subtests; while the reliability of the three overall scores is reasonable enough for decision making, more caution needs to be used in making use of subtest scores.

While a variety of other tests of motor skills exist, the assessment practitioner is not generally involved in assessment of this area and the tests described above are those most likely to be encountered during the assessment process.

Neuropsychological Assessment

An area of increasing interest and concern to the psychoeducational assessment practitioner is that of neuropsychological assessment. Neuropsychological assessment has developed somewhat separately from psychoeducational assessment, but for some time the ties between the two have been growing stronger. At present, with the prevalence of learning disabled children in the special education process, neuropsychological measures may be of relevance in a variety of situations.

Neuropsychology is concerned with the study of the brain and its effect on learning and performance. Many of the techniques used in neuropsychological assessment are the same as those traditionally used in psychoeducational assessment. Thus, for instance, one recent list of recommended neuropsychological procedures included the Bender Visual-Motor Gestalt Test, the Wide Range Achievement Test, the Wechsler Intelligence Scale for Children—Revised, the Peabody Picture Vocabulary Test, and Raven's Progressive Matrices (Obrzut, 1981). Other techniques are aimed at determining with as much specificity as possible the relative abilities of the subject in various sensory, perceptual, and processing modes. In all cases, however, what differentiates the neuropsychological assessment from a more typical psychoeducational assessment is the background from which results are interpreted, rather than the specific instruments used. Effective use of this approach to assessment requires a good background in physiological psychology, with "a sound understanding of the structure and functioning of the brain" (Obrzut, 1981, p. 332).

The exact relationship of neuropsychological findings to educational planning has been unclear in the past, but an increasing amount of research is being done in this area (Dean, 1981). There is still argument about the usefulness of this approach, especially for children who show only "soft signs" of brain injury—behavioral indications, but no identifiable abnormalities on a neurological examination (Sandoval & Haapanen, 1981). Nonetheless, neuropsychological assessment is becoming increasingly visible, and may eventually, as knowledge in the field progresses, become essential for any psychoeducational assessment practitioner. The extensive scientific background needed to interpret the results of neuropsychological testing is beyond the scope of this book, however, so no further discussion will be provided. Interested readers may consult Gaddes (1980), Hynd and Obrzut (1981), Lezak (1976) and Reitan and Davidson (1974).

CONCLUSIONS

The assessment of health factors can be a difficult area for the assessment practitioner to deal with. Most assessment in this domain falls clearly within another professional's expertise, and the actual assessment that the psychoeducational assessment practitioner may carry out in these areas is somewhat limited. On the other hand, some health factors have clear-cut relationships to achievement, and during the decision-making process the assessment practitioner must be aware of these factors and their possible implications. The assessment practitioner's role may range from performing a simple check to be sure hearing screening has been carried out to actually administering some medical-model instruments. The assessment practitioner's chief responsibility, however, is to ensure that decisions about other factors, such as intelligence, are made only after health factors have been taken into account.

6

Assessment of Intellectual Functioning

HISTORICAL BACKGROUND

An awareness that people differ in level of mental ability has probably been part of human culture since prehistoric times. One author writing about the history of intelligence (Peterson, 1925) traced the development of the concept through the Old Testament and Plato's works. Modern concern with individual differences in mental ability began to take strong shape in the mid-19th century. At that time, Sir Frances Galton used a variety of physical measures to study differences in response time and accuracy and sensory discrimination. These tests were expanded and used by James Cattell, who coined the term *mental test* and initiated the study of such measures in the United States. Other researchers exploring similar techniques in various settings during the last decade of the 19th century included Kraepelin, Munsterberg, Jastrow, Boas, and Gilbert (Peterson, 1925).

The measurement of reaction time and sensory discrimination does not, in fact, relate greatly to achievement in school or contribute very much to psychoeducational diagnosis. Nevertheless, these early researchers played an important role by initiating the idea that intelligence could be directly studied in the laboratory. They also laid down much of the statistical foundation for modern testing. The entire testing movement took a somewhat different turn in 1895, when Alfred Binet and Victor Henri published an article reviewing most of the work done up to that time (Binet & Henri, 1895). Their conclusions were that the tests then in use were too sensory in nature, that the functions being measured were too limited and of minor significance, and that there was little evidence regarding whether the various functions being measured were related to one another within one individual. They proposed a number of tests of "superior psychic faculties," including memory, comprehension, and others.

Binet's work resulted in the first "modern" intelligence scale when, in 1904, he was part of a committee commissioned by the minister of public instruction in Paris to find a way to distinguish children who could not benefit from the instruction given in regular classes in the public schools. The purpose of this distinction was to set up special classes for such children. This brought the entire issue fully into the realm of psychoeducational diagnosis, with the rationale for use of the instrument little different from that of today. Binet, working with Theodore Simon, developed a scale that was intended to make this distinction (Binet & Simon, 1905). In 1908 they published a revision of this scale, which grouped the items by age level and introduced the concept of mental age (Binet & Simon, 1908). Each item in the 1908 scale was assigned to the age at which half or more of all children passed it. The scale embodied most of the important ideas regarding an intelligence test that still characterize IQ tests. It had a single underlying metric along which all children could be located. It distinguished among both below normal and above normal children. It was standarized (although rather crudely), and the results were interpreted in comparison to the performance of the standardization group. The validity of the test was studied by examining the percentage of children passing items at various ages and the test scores of children nominated as superior in intelligence by their teachers. The test scores of children far behind in their academic work were also studied.

This test was rapidly and widely recognized, and by 1910 it had already been adapted for use in the United States (Goddard, 1910). In 1916, Terman, working at Stanford University, revised and standardized the Binet-Simon scales (Terman, 1916); this same instrument, the Stanford-Binet Intelligence Scale, was revised again in 1937 and 1960 and still forms one of the basic tools available for the assessment of intelligence. This scale also made the first major use of the *intelligence quotient*, or *IQ*, which was initially defined as the ratio of mental age to chronological age.

The only additional major event in the history of the development of individually administered intelligence scales was the work of David Wechsler. His initial work was with the design of a scale for adults, rather than children; as a result he moved from the concept of scaling items by age to a point-scale measurement. Rather than focusing on assessing skills at certain ages with whatever tests seemed to fit there for the norm group, Wechsler concentrated on testing with a few kinds of items, measured across an increasing range of difficulty. This also put the focus more fully on the IQ as a direct standard, rather than as a ratio of mental age to chronological age, and led to the *deviation IQ*, a standard score derived for each separate age group, normally used today.

CURRENT CONCEPTIONS AND DEFINITIONS OF INTELLIGENCE

As might be expected from the history outlined above, a variety of definitions and conceptions of intelligence still underlie the major work in this field. It is important in carrying out assessment of intelligence for the psychoeducational assessment practitioner to be aware of and sensitive to this variety. In many cases, the different rationales underlying different tests affect the interpretations of their results. Some of the most important definitions are presented below.

Binet

Binet's original conception of intelligence remains of more than historical importance because it formed the basis for the Stanford-Binet Intelligence Scale, which continues to be used extensively today. Actually, it is more accurate to speak of his conception*s* of intelligence; over the course of his career, Binet studied a variety of different aspects of intelligence. In general, however, he conceived of intelligence as reflecting higher-order mental processes—such as memory, reasoning, and judgment—the "superior psychic functions" (Peterson, 1925, p. 87), rather than the associative and sensory skills measured by many psychologists at the time. Binet also clearly considered intelligence to be composed of a variety of different abilities and recognized that a person might well be strong in some areas yet weak in others.

Binet did not necessarily equate intelligence with scholastic aptitude; indeed, he indicated that different types of tests would be needed for different purposes. However, the scales that became the basis for the Stanford-Binet test were specifically designed as measures of academic aptitude; their purpose was to assist schools in determining which children would not learn in regular classrooms. Thus the areas and items that Binet used were those that best discriminated between good and poor students. This strong emphasis on academic or scholastic aptitude continues to pervade the field of intelligence testing for children today.

Binet made another conceptual contribution to the assessment of intelligence. While the general idea of examining a child's progress by comparing it to that of other children was not new, Binet formalized it in the concept of *mental age*, which corresponds to the average score obtained by children of that chronological age (Peterson, 1925, p. 182). This in turn formed the basis for the concept of the intelligence quotient (IQ), relating mental age to chronological age, proposed by Stern (1914) and incorporated into the first version of the Stanford-Binet test by Terman (1916). Overall, most work with the assessment of children's IQ reflects Binet's view of intelligence as multifaceted and focused on higher-order process, as well as his focus on matching the assessment tool to its purpose.

Wechsler

Wechsler conceived of intelligence as a comprehensive construct, the "aggregate or global capacity of the individual to act purposefully, to think rationally, and to deal effectively with his environment" (Wechsler, 1958, p. 7). While the Wechsler scales are composed of several subtests, Wechsler did not necessarily consider these to reflect the actual factors composing intellect, and he made no attempt to order or organize them except for a verbal—performance distinction.

Spearman

While Binet and Wechsler both viewed intelligence as multifaceted, both also developed scales that yielded overall scores, suggesting a more unified view of intelligence. This viewpoint was formalized by Charles Spearman (1927), who suggested that performance on intelligence measures could be explained as consisting of two factors—a general factor (g), plus a specific factor that differed from test to test. The general factor underlying all intellectual performance accounted for the high correlations seen among most measures of intelligence, while the specific factor accounted for the obvious differences that occur in individuals' performance on different kinds of items. This concept of g, a general intelligence underlying performance on a wide variety of tasks, continues to be prevalent in IQ assessment; some tests are seen as relatively "clean" measures of g, free from a high dependence on skills that may be fairly culture-specific.

Guilford

While Spearman proposed a two-factor model of intelligence and introduced the concept of *g*, J. P. Guilford proposed a much more detailed factor-model of intelligence. He developed a model, the Structure of Intellect (SOI) (Guilford, 1967), that grouped intellectual tasks along three dimensions: the kind of mental operation performed, the content on which it is performed, and the kind of product that results. The possible kinds of mental operations proposed by the model are cognition, memory, divergent thinking (producing answers with a focus on number and variety), convergent thinking (producing answers with the focus on finding the best answer), and evaluation. The content can be figural, symbolic, semantic, or behavioral. The product may be a unit, class, relation, system, transformation, or implication. Overall, this allows for 120 different possible factors of intelligence, classified according to the above dimensions.

This model has led to some attempts to group individual items of various tests into the appropriate categories and to one test developed specifically to assess some factors of the SOI model. These will be discussed later in this chapter. Although there have been a variety of criticisms of the model (Sattler, 1974), it has broadened the general view of what some of the components of intelligence might be. In organizing the many skills assessed by different intelligence scales, Guilford's presentation of this model has also helped organize some of the thinking about intelligence.

Piaget

The theories of intelligence so far discussed all owe their origin, to a greater or lesser extent, to the assessment movement, and all have clear-cut ties to Binet's work. A very different approach is reflected in the work of Jean Piaget. While most work with intelligence has been concerned with the assessment of individual differences, Piaget's work has focused on the similarities underlying all learning. His studies have focused on the stages of development of various kinds of thought processes through which children pass. His theories regarding intelligence deal with the gradually increasing ability of the child to handle tasks, representations, and processes. He sees intelligence as an increasingly complex interaction between the organism and its environment, the "state of equilibrium toward which tend all the successive adaptations of a sensori-motor and cognitive nature, as well as all assimilatory and accommodatory interactions between the organism and the environment" (Piaget, 1950, p. 11).

Behaviorists

A recent reexamination of intelligence and its measurement has been made by the behaviorists, such as Evans and Nelson (1977). They regard intelligence test results primarily as samples of behavior, obtained under conditions that are standardized and therefore familiar to the assessment specialist. No implications are drawn from the results concerning overall intelligence or academic aptitude; rather, test results are looked at as measurements of ability to do the specific kinds of tasks given. Thus, a vocabulary test gives information about a child's ability to define words; a digit-span test gives information about her or his ability to recall numbers. Neither is assumed to be a measure of some inherent "intelligence" in the child that is more general than the specific behavior measured.

Intelligence, Deviation IQs, and Ratio IQs

To this point we have been discussing definitions of intelligence. However, the intelligence quotient, as originally incorporated into the 1916 Stanford-Binet test, is the actual measure used by assessment practitioners. Although there is some theoretical relationship between intelligence and IQ, the best-developed instruments for measuring IQ do not derive from a well-developed theory of intelligence. The remainder of this chapter will deal primarily with IQ, rather than with intelligence per se. The assessment practitioner should be aware that the intelligence quotient represents a specific expression of intelligence, but not necessarily the entire construct.

IQ was initially introduced as the ratio of mental age to chronological age. However, Wechsler, in developing his intitial adult scale pointed out a number of problems with the ratio IQ. For an adult, there is no reason to expect scores on many IQ tasks to increase with age. It is therefore not clear what justification there is for using chronological age. In addition, ratio IQs do not have a constant standard deviation. A child with a ratio IQ of 85 may be 1 standard deviation below his peers at one age, and 1½ standard deviations below at another age. To deal with both these problems, Wechsler developed the deviation IQ, a standard score derived for each separate age group, so that the mean is 100 and the standard deviation is 15. This deviation IQ approach is now used by all major IQ tests, for both children and adults.

A deviation IQ is essentially an arbitrary metric, with no inherent meaning. As a result, a number of different sets of categories have been defined for IQ scores to help interpret them. An IQ of 100 is always normal; higher scores represent higher than average ability and lower scores represent lower ability. Educators typically refer to three categories of scores: *educable mentally retarded* (approximately 50–70); *trainable mentally retarded* (approximately 30–50); and *severely retarded* (below 30). The Wechsler scale manuals suggest seven descriptive categories: *mentally deficient* (69 and below), *very superior* (130 and above), and five categories in between. The 1973 manual for the Stanford-Binet test (Terman & Merrill, 1973) presents percentages of children falling into each grouping of 10 points from between 30 to 39 and 160 to 169. The manual categorizes persons scoring below 70 as *mentally defective*, and those above 139 as *very superior*. Clearly, the actual descriptive labels and cutoffs used vary somewhat, both with the instrument being used and the use to which it is put.

Summary

In 1925 Peterson, writing about different conceptions of intelligence, identified a variety of unanswered questions, such as whether there is a general factor of intelligence or simply a series of overlapping skills and processes. Most of those questions remain unresolved today. There is some commonality visible in the different conceptions of intelligence prevalent today; most focus on higher-order skills, rather than simple perceptual measures, for instance. If intelligence is taken to be "what IQ tests measure," some additional commonality is indicated simply by the fact that most such tests correlate well with each other. There remains general disagreement, however, on such aspects as whether intelligence has a single strong overall factor underlying different kinds of skills, whether it reflects something more or less innate or within the child rather than simply current behavior, and whether it is best measured as a single overall score or as a variety of different abilities. These differences in the basic conception of intelligence lead in turn to some major issues in the use of intelligence tests.

ISSUES IN THE ASSESSMENT OF IQ

The definitions presented above represent overall views of intelligence. Some of these have led to specific techniques for assessment; others have remained general theories only. The issues most relevant to assessment practice are specifically those dealing with IQ—with intelligence turned into a score (or several scores) and used in decision making about a child.

Changes in IQ

One major issue in the use of IQ scores is the extent to which they are stable, presenting an accurate picture of a child over a prolonged period of time. Clearly, such stability is important if the scores are to be useful in making any decisions about a child's academic future. Specific information on test-retest reliabilities will be provided for individual techniques discussed below. In general, IQ tends to be fairly stable over time. Sattler (1974) summarized a variety of evidence regarding the stability of IQ. From his summary it is clear that IQ is fairly stable overall. It is more stable over shorter periods and also more stable for older than for younger children.

While overall IQ scores have good stability for most people, drastic changes in IQ scores sometimes occur for individuals. Even the standard error of measurement of most IQ tests suggests that changes of 8 points or more upon retesting, owing solely to test error, would occur for about 1 child in 20. Much greater changes have been noted when one assessment occurs under unusual circumstances or when interventions specifically aimed at increasing IQ scores or academic aptitude have taken place. The general conclusion, then, must be that while IQ, if properly measured, has sufficient stability to be useful in decision making, a single IQ score should never be considered definitive. This is especially true if the score was obtained several years ago or if the child was tested when very young. Whether intelligence is viewed as an inherent trait, not subject to change, or as a trait that may change, IQ clearly cannot be considered to be immutable.

Relationship of IQ to Socioeconomic Status and Ethnicity

Another issue raised by the use of IQ tests is the degree to which they are fair to children from a variety of backgrounds. That there are differences in mean group scores for children from different ethnic and socioeconomic statuses has been known for some time (Laosa, 1977). The issue of to what degree these differences are due to innate differences in intelligence, specific experiences, or simply bias in the tests remains unresolved and heavily debated. For the assessment practitioner, however, the question of whether groups differ in intelligence is less relevant than the issue of how IQ scores are used to make decisions about individuals within these differing groups. Several different models have been suggested for the culture-fair use of psychological tests. These models all reflect test use in a setting where the test score is being used to predict future performance of some kind, and a selection decision is being made based on this prediction. This setting is typical for the use of IQ tests in educational decision making: the tests are being used as predictors of future learning in the school setting.

The simplest culture-fair model is the "quota" model. This model states that persons will be selected in the same ratio in which they exist in the population. Thus, for instance, if the population of a school district is 25 percent black, a test would be considered fair if 25 percent of the students identified for classes for the retarded were black also. Any test can be used fairly by this model, simply by setting different cutoff scores for different groups.

The most traditional model of test fairness, often referred to as the Cleary (1968) model, examines the predictive value of the test for each group. According to this model, a test would be used fairly if the prediction equation using it was the best that could be developed for each group. Thus, for instance, if IQ were being used to predict achievement for both black and Anglo students, the test would be considered fair if it neither overpredicted nor underpredicted achievement for either group. This can most readily be ensured by developing different prediction equations for each group, using separate norm groups. The results of such equations can then be translated back into specific IQ cutoffs for each group, getting the cutoffs to yield the same predicted criterion score for each group.

Darlington (1971) has noted that the choice between these models and others that have been suggested (Oakland & Matuszek, 1977) cannot be made on technical grounds alone. Each model has somewhat different effects on specific decisions. Thus, for instance, the Cleary model results in the fewest children being misplaced overall, but the quota model results in fewer children being identified for special services inappropriately. The relative importance of different kinds of classification errors determines the kind of model to be followed. Darlington suggests addressing this issue directly by using a single prediction equation with points added or subtracted for certain groups to reflect societal decisions regarding the relative importance of these two kinds of error.

Specific suggestions for the use of IQ tests and other standardized tests have ranged all the way from a moratorium on any such use (Williams & Mitchell, 1977) to a business as usual approach that takes the stand that since the tests have not been shown to be biased in any way other than the quota sense described above, they are therefore appropriate for use without modification. Most assessment practitioners would take a stand somewhere between these two extremes, recognizing the greater likelihood that extraneous factors will distort the test performance of a minority child but recognizing also that the results of such tests still have useful predictive validity.

One compromise has been suggested by Mercer (1979b), who uses both the traditional IQ score and a modified score based on pluralistic norms to view the child's performance. Mercer's method is discussed further below, under "Specific Techniques."

Ability versus Achievement

Although IQ tests have their origins in prediction and decision making, rather than in theories about basic intellectual ability, they were for many years considered as measures of inherent ability. More recently it has been argued that most IQ tests are in fact achievement tests, that they test the degree to which the child has learned specific materials and skills. To some extent this is inevitably true; no physiological measure has ever been identified that correlates well with school achievement in the general population. Therefore our measurement of IQ still depends on current performance of tasks that reflect, to a greater or lesser degree, actual school and nonschool learning. Certainly any IQ test actually measures achievement, rather than potential, and for a relatively limited sample of behaviors.

However, this fact does not mean that IQ tests are measuring the same thing as standard achievement tests for mathematics, reading, and other subjects. IQ tests differ from achievement tests in that they typically measure a much broader range of skills and also in that some of the skills measured are not typically taught in our culture. Thus scores on IQ tests do measure more than formal education or school learning. While few professionals today would argue that IQ is a measure of inherent ability, independent of the influence of learning opportunities and performance variables, it is usually reasonable to consider IQ as a measure of current intellectual *functioning*.

FACTORS INVOLVED IN THE ASSESSMENT OF IQ

Purposes of Assessing Intellectual Functioning

The primary purpose of assessing intellectual functioning during the assessment process can be either classification or programming. Historically, however, classification has been the primary function of such assessment, with programming decisions tied only very generally to the IQ scores obtained. The usefulness of standard instruments and techniques for each of these purposes is considered under "Specific Techniques," below.

Classification

IQ tests have been the major instrument for classification within the field of special education ever since their development. From the beginning, when they were developed to identify children who could not profit from instruction in their regular classrooms, they have consistently been used to locate and identify children who would today be classified as mentally retarded. While the current definition of mental retardation involves adaptive behavior skills as well as IQ, the classification of children by IQ levels is still an essential part of most special education decision making.

The accuracy and usefulness of IQ measures as classification tools is currently a major issue. On the one hand, the best techniques available for assessment of IQ yield stable scores with excellent psychometric properties and are among the most technically adequate of all the tools available to the assessment practitioner. On the other hand, the issues raised above regarding assessment of minority groups raise doubt about the use of IQ scores for classification decisions about such children.

The problem is made more difficult by lack of agreement within the field regarding exactly what constitutes either good classification or good placement for various groups of children. Many years of research on the effects of classifying children, the effects of special class placement, and the effects of mainstreaming have failed to yield clear-cut information on any of these topics (Lambert, 1981; McMillan & Meyers, 1980).

IQ and the instruments that measure it have clear-cut ethnic and socioeconomic status relationships. The measures have high ceilings and distinguish among average, below average, and above average performance. Thus they clearly fit within the social-system framework. Therefore the assumption underlying the use of IQ tests for classification decisions is that it is preferable not to identify a child for services if there is some doubt about the appropriateness of such identification. This position is not universally accepted; many (perhaps most) professionals might be more concerned about failing to provide special services for a child who might need them (Algozinne & Ysseldyke, 1981). Nonetheless, current law clearly supports choosing not to classify when there is a doubt, and we personally recommend this stance. Our position is presented in more detail elsewhere in the book.

Programming

IQ tests were almost all developed as classification tools. Nonetheless, suggestions on using them for programming purposes have been made by many people. Vallett (1964) categorized Stanford-Binet test items into six general categories: general comprehension, visual-motor ability, arithmetic reasoning, memory and concentration, vocabulary, and verbal fluency. Sattler (1965) proposed a similar system using seven categories. Meeker (1969) developed templates for categorizing the Stanford-Binet test, the Wechsler Intelligence Scale for Children, and the Wechsler Preschool and Primary Scale of Intelligence items in terms of Guilford's Structure of Intellect model. The individual subtests of the Wechsler scales have been used separately and grouped in various ways (Kaufman, 1979; Sattler, 1974). In general the intent of such categorizations has been to provide greater detail about the child's pattern of intellectual performance, presumably in order to have better information on which to base programming.

Such approaches involve two problems, however. First, the excellent psychometric qualities of these instruments may be lost when these categorization schemes are applied. In using only a few items from any one category, as is often the case for post hoc divisions of items, the resulting scores may have little reliability. Especially for the Stanford-Binet test, which is designed to yield only a total score, specific areas may be represented poorly or not at all in the specific items administered to a child. While the subtests of the Wechsler scales were designed to yield separate scores as well as a total IQ score, the reliability of the subtest scores is necessarily poorer, and fairly large differences among subtest scores are needed to indicate differences that are clearly beyond the chance level.

Possibly even more important, although such categorizations may provide additional information, even accurate categorizations may not advance the goal of appropriate programming. Such categorizations fall far below the standards that we have proposed in Chapter 1 for programming techniques; they are not hierarchical, and they are not clearly associated with actual teaching activities. While the assessment practitioner may use such categorizations in addition to total IQ scores in overall decision making about a child, such use is based on the clinical judgment of the practitioner, and not on the properties of the scales themselves. Hence caution in their use is indicated.

A separate issue regarding programming is related to classification. IQ scores traditionally form one major distinction between three categories of mildly handicapped children: the educable mentally retarded (who obtain IQs below 70); the learning disabled (who obtain IQs substantially higher than their achievement in at least some areas); and the mildly emotionally handicapped (who may have both IQ and achievement within the average range). However, it has recently been suggested (Hallahan & Kauffman, 1978) that children within these three classifications are not, in fact, very different. Children in all three tend to show behavioral problems and underachievement; the distinction on the basis of an IQ score greater than or less than 70 may at times be very artificial. More important, programming for children in these three classifications often does not differ very much. Thus noncategorical grouping for instructional purposes, at least for the mildly handicapped, might provide as much information for programming purposes as the current classifications based on IQ. It is at present hard to tell whether the similarity in programming for children in these three classifications reflects a lack of real differences in the children or a lack of truly effective programming to meet three different sets of needs. IQ itself, however, does not appear to lead to useful programming decisions for mildly handicapped children.

Situational Factors

Administration Conditions

There are some basic situational factors underlying the administration of IQ tests. An IQ test is a maximum-performance instrument; it is assumed that the child is doing his or her best. The examiner needs to ensure that children do in fact have the opportunity to do their best. Among the favorable conditions for test administration that the assessment practitioner must provide are the following:

Adequate lighting, noise background, and seating. The child should be able to see the materials clearly, reach anything he or she needs to work with, be able to hear and be heard clearly, and be comfortably seated.

Adequate physical skills for the test. The child must have the required physical skills to perform the tasks that are given. This includes adequate hearing, vision, and motor skills. Aids such as glasses or a hearing aid should be used if they have been prescribed. It is the practitioner's responsibility to be sure that the child's hearing and vision are in fact adequate by discontinuing the assessment and referring the child for screening if necessary.

Adequate rapport with the assessment practitioner. If children do not feel at ease with the examiner, they may hesitate to respond, especially when they are unsure of their answers. This factor is especially important when testing young children, who are less accustomed to the entire process of academic performance on demand.

Test Fairness

Among the factors that must always be taken into account in an assessment is the fairness of using a specific test with a specific child. As already indicated, this is a complex issue, since even the meaning of "fairness" has not been clearly agreed upon by professionals. The more the child differs from the norm group of the test, however, the greater the care that should be exercised in using the results. The assessment practitioner should actively consider and make a decision about the appropriateness of the technique he or she is using for each child assessed.

Time

Ideally, it should be possible for the assessment practitioner to get a very detailed picture of each child's current intellectual performance, with great precision and in great detail. Unfortunately, the practitioner is often constrained by shortness of time, both his or her own and the child's. Therefore one consideration that enters into the assessment of IQ is the length of time that will be required for the testing, especially compared to the length of time the child can be expected to attend and perform at maximum capacity.

Legal Constraints

Because IQ measurements have been developed and used for a very long time, there are many more legal constraints and concerns about their use than for some newer measures, where the flaws have not become as obvious. The practitioner should be aware of all of the legal and ethical factors regarding decision making that have been discussed in earlier chapters.

SPECIFIC TECHNIQUES

The Wechsler Scales

David Wechsler developed IQ scales for three age groups: preschoolers, school-aged children, and adults (Wechsler, 1967, 1974, 1981). The Wechsler Preschool and Primary Scale of Intelligence (WPPSI) is normed for children aged 4 to 6½. The Wechsler Intelligence Scale for Children — Revised (WISC-R) is normed for children aged 6 through 16. The Wechsler Adult Intelligence Scale — Revised (WAIS-R) is normed for ages 16 through 74. This discussion will focus primarily on the WISC-R, since that is the instrument that covers the age range with which most assessment practitioners work.

WISC-R

The WISC-R is an individually administered IQ test consisting of 10 regular and 2 alternate subtests. These 12 subtests are divided into verbal subtests, which depend on language for both instructions and responses, and performance subtests, which have little or no overt verbal response. The five regular verbal subtests are Information, Similarities, Arithmetic, Vocabulary, and Comprehension. The alternate verbal subtest is Digit Span. The five regular performance subtests are Picture Completion, Picture Arrangement, Block Design, Object Assembly, and Coding. The alternate test is Mazes. A child is administered one subtest at a time, alternating verbal and performance subtests; a child completes all items on one subtest before another is begun. Each subtest begins with easy items and continues until the child has missed several. This gives the administration a repeating pattern, moving from easy to hard. The correct administration of the WISC-R requires extensive training and practice. It usually takes about an hour to administer the WISC-R to a child.

The verbal subtests all consist of questions to be answered by the child. They require extensive receptive and expressive language but little visual or motor skill. The performance tests consist of various kinds of materials to manipulate — puzzle pieces to be assembled into an object, for instance. They require good visual and motor skills. In addition, the directions to the performance tests are given verbally and are fairly detailed; thus, there is some requirement for receptive language. These requirements should be borne in mind in evaluating the appropriateness of the WISC-R for an individual child.

Standardization. The WISC-R was normed on a stratified sample of 2200 children. The stratification variables used were age, sex, ethnicity, (white–nonwhite), geographical region, occupation of head of household, and urban–rural residence. The sample was specified to match the 1970 U.S. Census data. Only "normal" children were included. This included possibly retarded children if they lived at home but not institutionalized retardates or children with severe emotional problems. Spanish-speaking children and other children whose native language was not English were included only if they spoke and understood English.

The scores available from the WISC-R are standard scores, presented for age intervals of three months. Scaled scores with a mean of 10 and a standard deviation of 3 are provided for each individual subtest. IQ scores with a mean of 100 and a standard deviation of 15 are provided for verbal, performance, and total composite scores. The IQ scores provided are, therefore, deviation scores.

Reliability.   The WISC-R manual provides reliabilities for each subtest by age group (Wechsler, 1974, p. 28). The individual subtests have split-half reliabilities ranging from 0.67 to 0.91, with averages across ages of 0.77 or above for verbal subtests and 0.70 or above for performance subtests. The Information, Similarities, Vocabulary, and Block Design subtests are the most reliable.

For the verbal, performance, and total IQ scores the split-half reliability is excellent, above 0.90 for almost all age groups. The verbal-scale IQ score is somewhat more reliable than the performance-scale IQ score. The total test score is the most reliable, with an coefficient of 0.95 or 0.96 for every age group.

The manual also presents test-retest reliabilities for three groups of children who were tested twice (Wechsler, 1974, pp. 32–33). The test-retest reliabilities for verbal, performance, and total IQ scores are also above 0.90. Standard errors for scaled scores and IQ scores are also provided (p. 30). These are helpful in interpreting the scores obtained. In general, the standard errors of measurement for the individual subtests are 1 to 1½ points (on a scale where the mean equals 10); the standard errors averaged across age for the three IQ scores are verbal, 3.60; performance, 4.66; and total, 3.19.

Other useful technical information provided in the manual includes intercorrelations among subtests, size of difference in scores between two subtests for a significant difference at various confidence levels, and correlations between WISC-R and WPPSI scores and between WISC-R and WAIS scores where the instruments overlap in age.

Validity.   The validity of the WISC-R has been explored in a variety of ways. Sattler (1982) summarizes a variety of studies that have examined the concurrent validity of the WISC-R with other intelligence and achievement measures. He reports median correlations for the full scale IQ in the range of 0.61 to 0.82 with other intelligence measures, 0.58 to 0.65 with various achievement tests, and 0.39 with school grades. In general, WISC-R scores are comparable to IQ scores from the Stanford-Binet test. WISC-R scores tend to be several points lower than scores on the original WISC, which was replaced by the revised version in 1974. Small differences between WISC-R IQ scores and group IQ test scores are typically found, but not in a consistent direction.

A number of factor analyses of the WISC-R have been carried out. Kaufman (1975) found that the variation of WISC-R scores could be explained by three factors, which he named Verbal Comprehension, Perceptual Organization, and Freedom from Distractability. The subtests grouped under Verbal Comprehension are Information, Similarities, Vocabulary, and Comprehension. The Perceptual Organization subtests are Picture Completion, Picture Arrangement, Block Design, Object Assembly, and Mazes. Freedom from Distractability subtests include Arithmetic, Digit Span, and Coding. Kaufman (1979) summarizes a number of other studies that found similar factor structures in the WISC-R scores for mentally retarded and learning disabled children and for adolescent psychiatric patients. A similar structure has also been found for the WISC-R scores of Mexican-Americans (Dean, 1980); there was a high degree of similarity between the structure for Mexican-Americans and that for a group of Anglos studied at the same time. Other studies reviewed by Kaufman found consistent Verbal Comprehension and Perceptual Organization factors in the WISC-R but sometimes failed to find a Freedom from Distractability factor.

A study by Reschly and Reschly (1979) examined the predictive validity of these three factors for four ethnic groups: blacks, Anglos, Mexican-Americans, and Native Americans. In predicting achievement, measured by teacher ratings and a group achievement test, scores on the Verbal Comprehension factor were found to be the best predictor for all four groups; scores on Freedom from Distractability were generally intermediate in predictive ability; and scores on Perceptual Organization were substantially less effective. The predictive validity of the factors is similar for the four groups studied, although it tended to be lower throughout for the Native American group.

Overall, then, research indicates that there are three factors underlying WISC-R performance, two of which correspond closely to the verbal–performance division of the test. Research also indicates that this factor structure tends to be the same for various groups of children. These findings lend confidence to the use of the verbal and performance WISC-R IQ scores.

Use. The WISC-R IQ score falls within the social-system model. There is a clear-cut relationship between scores on the WISC-R and such variables as socioeconomic status (Sattler, 1982). The definition of intelligence and the desirability of the behaviors assessed by the WISC-R vary from culture to culture. IQ is interpreted only with reference to a norm group, and "normal" has no meaning outside this norm comparison. The WISC-R test also fits the characteristics of a social-system measure. It measures both high and low performance across a normal distribution. Since it does not have norms that differ by ethnicity or social class, it does not fall into the pluralistic model.

Within the social-system model, the WISC-R meets the major requirements for validity; its predictive validity and reliability are excellent, and a variety of evidence indicates that it is measuring fairly comparable constructs in different ethnic groups.

In accordance with the social-system model, WISC-R scores must be considered as measuring current performance within the particular Anglo culture characteristic of our public schools. The scores should not be interpreted as a measure of innate ability, nor will they necessarily predict performance in settings very different from the standard school culture.

In accordance with the social-system model, the assessment practitioner should be more concerned to avoid using WISC-R scores to classify as needing special services a child who actually does not need them than about failing to classify a child who does. In practice, this usually means that the assessment practitioner should take great care not to misclassify a child as mentally retarded.

Within these constraints, the WISC-R is an excellent tool for decision making in educational settings. Its technical adequacy is very high. The WISC-R (and its predecessor the WISC) have been used effectively in educational settings for over 30 years and have been demonstrated to be useful for a wide variety of populations. The WISC-R should never be used as the only assessment tool for classifying a child; measures of achievement, adaptive behavior, and other abilities are needed also, and the assessment practitioner should take into account all of these data sources. If proper attention is given to these other data sources, to hearing and vision screening, and to proper test administration, the WISC-R can normally be used with reasonable confidence.

WPPSI

The Wechsler Preschool and Primary Scale of Intelligence was the third scale developed by Wechsler and is the only one currently still available in unrevised form. It is a complete scale, separate from the WISC-R but in many ways similar to it. The WPPSI has 11 subtests: Information, Vocabulary, Arithmetic, Similarities, Comprehension, Sentences, Animal House, Picture Completion, Mazes, Geometric Designs, and Block Design. The eight subtests that correspond to WISC-R subtests are downward extensions of the same tests, often including some of the same items. Animal House is a somewhat different form of Coding: the child is asked to place colored pegs below different animals, rather than write symbols for different digits or shapes. Sentences is a sentence-repetition task and is an alternative to Digit Span for the measurement of auditory memory. Geometric Design is a design-copying task and has no counterpart in the WISC-R.

The WPPSI was standardized on 1200 children, aged 4 to 6½. The sample was stratified by sex, age, ethnicity (white–nonwhite) and geographical region to match the 1960 U.S. Census. Scores provided are similar to those available for the WISC-R: standard scores with a mean of 10 and a standard deviation of 3 for the subtests, and deviation IQ scores with a mean of 100 and a standard deviation of 15 for verbal, performance, and full scale IQ scores.

The reliability of the WPPSI is excellent; average split-half reliability coefficients for the subtests range from 0.77 to 0.87, and reliabilities for the three IQ scores are all above 0.90 (Wechsler, 1967). Sattler (1982) summarizes a number of studies of its validity; in general, the WPPSI correlates adequately with other IQ measures at the same age range. The relationship between WPPSI scores and later school achievement is not as good as it is for the WISC-R, and its predictive validity is more variable with minority or disadvantaged children than with Anglo children. Factor studies of the WPPSI have found the same verbal and performance factors as for the WISC-R but have failed to find a Freedom from Distractability factor. Sattler (1982) hypothesizes that for this age range (4 – 6½) distractability enters into all test performance strongly and therefore does not emerge as a separate factor.

Overall, the WPPSI has good technical adequacy; its use would be comparable to the use of the WISC-R. However, additional caution is called for whenever very young children are being tested; IQ scores at the age range covered by the WPPSI are not as stable as for older children, and the predictive validity of the WPPSI is not as high as for the WISC-R. If a child too young for the WISC-R must be assessed, however, it is a useful test.

WAIS-R

The current (revised) version of the Wechsler Adult Intelligence Scale was published in 1981. It has 11 subtests, of which 6 are verbal and 5 performance tests. The subtests are the same as those on the WISC-R, with the exception of Mazes, which has no corresponding WAIS-R subtest; on the WAIS-R the Coding subtest is named Digit Symbol. The subtests are arranged in alternating order of verbal and performance subtests, as for the WISC-R, but the actual arrangement is somewhat different. The same scores are available as for the WISC-R and WPPSI.

The manual (Wechsler, 1981) presents split-half reliability coefficients for all subtests except Digit Span and Digit Symbol; test-retest coefficients are presented for these two subtests. Average reliability coefficients range from 0.68 to 0.96 for the subtests, and from 0.93 to

0.97 for the three scale IQ scores. Standard errors of measurement, intercorrelations among subtests, and differences between subtest scores needed for significance are also presented.

Because it is newly published, little evidence regarding the validity of the WAIS-R is available. In one study reported in the manual, correlations between WAIS scores and WAIS-R scores ranged from 0.79 to 0.91. The correlation between the verbal IQ scores was 0.91, that between the performance scores 0.79, and that between the full scale IQ scores 0.88. The manual indicates that a variety of studies on the WAIS found good correlations between the WAIS and other IQ tests. Factor analyses of the WAIS have found factors similar to the three discussed above for the WISC-R. Additional research to establish whether these findings are also true of the WAIS-R will no doubt be forthcoming.

SOMPA

While overall the WISC-R seems to have adequate validity for use in decision making within a social-system model, it would often be useful to have information about a child's performance from a different perspective. SOMPA, The System of Multicultural Pluralistic Assessment, was developed by Mercer (1979b) in an attempt to provide better assessment, in part by taking into account the background of the child being assessed. The entire system is built around three assessment models, and incorporates a variety of measures. The models themselves are presented in Chapter 1 of this book. Other assessment techniques used within the SOMPA are presented in relevant chapters (on health factors, adaptive behavior, and modality skills). The part of the SOMPA relevant to the assessment of IQ is the Estimated Learning Potential (ELP).

The ELP is based on two sets of scores: IQ, as determined from the WISC-R, and scores on the SOMPA sociocultural scales. These latter scales measure the extent to which a child's background reflects the standard Anglo "core culture." Regression equations are then used to predict the average WISC-R IQ score for a child from the same ethnic group and type of sociocultural background. The child's actual score is interpreted with reference to this average score, rather than with reference to the WISC-R norm group. The result of this procedure is to provide pluralistic norms for the WISC-R and thus move its use into the pluralistic model. Norms are provided for Anglo, black, and Mexican-American children, on the basis of a California sample.

Mercer (1979a) considers the ELP to be the best available measure of the actual innate learning potential of the child, an answer to the question, How intelligent is the child? This question may at times be relevant to assessment — in considering whether to classify a child with a borderline IQ as learning disabled, for instance. If an estimate of the child's actual potential is needed, the ELP probably offers a more justifiable indication than the WISC-R scores for children from minority or disadvantaged backgrounds. The ELP's predictive validity for school achievement as measured by achievement tests, however, has been shown to be less adequate, for both Anglo and minority group children, than the usual WISC-R scores (Oakland, 1979, 1980). Thus when making assessment-based educational decisions, the assessment practitioner should consider whether ELP scores or the usual WISC-R IQ scores are more relevant to each decision required.

Another concern that has been expressed regarding ELP is its dependence on California norms. The SOMPA standardization sample was very carefully selected, but it was selected to be representative of California. Studies have shown that regression equations calculated on local data from Texas and Arizona yield ELP scores that differ substantially from those using the California data (Oakland, 1980; Reschly, Note 7). If the ELP is to receive widespread use, additional norm groups need to be developed for other regions of the country.

In spite of these concerns, the ELP is a creative attempt to deal, in a psychometrically adequate way, with the issue of test fairness. It follows the quota model described above; it is assumed that there are not differences in innate ability between ethnic or social class groups, although there are such differences within groups. Further research will show the extent to which this assumption, the regression equations used in the SOMPA, and the usefulness of pluralistic norms can be supported in educational decision making and planning. In the meantime the assessment practitioner should be aware of this approach and may find ELP results valuable as one piece of information to consider in the decision-making process.

Stanford-Binet Intelligence Scale

The Stanford-Binet test was originally developed in 1916; revised editions were issued in 1939 and 1960, and a new set of norms, with minor revisions, was issued in 1973 (Terman & Merrill, 1973). This test, based on Binet's original work, is designed to yield a single overall IQ score. The test is normed for children aged 2 through 18. Items in the test are arranged by age level, rather than by type. At most age levels, there are six items, plus an alternate. A wide variety of skills are tested, but there is not a consistent pattern of assigning items, so that a child will be given different kinds of items at different ages. While Stanford-Binet IQ scores are intended to represent a stable measure, the specific abilities being assessed vary throughout the test.

The Stanford-Binet test is somewhat more difficult to administer than the WISC-R, since a variety of materials must be mastered, and the examiner alternates among those materials. At all but the earliest ages the Stanford-Binet test requires a higher proportion of verbal skills than the WISC-R. The age range and ability range covered are wider than in the WISC-R, however, making it useful in some situations where the WISC-R is inappropriate. Scores available include a total deviation IQ score with a mean of 100 and a standard deviation of 16, and a mental age score. The IQ score is not generally comparable to the ratio IQ score that would be obtained by dividing the mental age directly by the chronological age, since the Stanford-Binet scores are deviation scores.

Standardization.   The 1972 standardization involved 2100 children drawn from seven cities across the country. These students were children and siblings of children involved in a much larger norming project for the Cognitive Abilities Test (a group IQ test). The larger sample was stratified according to community size, geographical region, and economic status. The sample for the Stanford-Binet test was drawn from this larger sample at random, with age as a stratification variable. Although no formal stratification was carried out regarding sex, ethnicity, or socioeconomic status, students should have been represented in the sample in approximately the same frequency as they were in the population.

Reliability.   The Stanford-Binet manual discusses reliability primarily in terms of internal consistency. The average biserial correlation for items with the total score is 0.66. Little additional information is available in the literature concerning the reliability of the measure. Sattler (1974) summarizes the standard error of measurement for the IQ score on the basis of reliabilities from the 1939 edition, but the differences between that version and the current one are sufficient to make the generalizability of the data questionable. Waddell, in a 1980 summary of the data available on the 1972 restandardization, noted that "A search of the literature did not produce any reliability studies. . . . A definite need exists for new reliability studies" (Waddell, 1980, p. 206).

Validity.   Most of the validity information for the Stanford-Binet test is from the 1960 version or earlier. The test shows construct validity in that the initial constructs used to design the test, such as the assumption that increasing numbers of children would pass the items at higher age levels, continue to be found. The Stanford-Binet test is often used as the criterion against which other IQ tests are validated; Sattler gives correlations ranging from the mid-.50s to the 0.90s for the relationship between this measure and a variety of other tests. The correlation with the WISC-R total IQ score is fairly high, in the 0.80 to 0.85 range. Again, many of these figures are not for the 1972 norming, however. One recent study looking at the correlation between the Stanford-Binet test and achievement for Anglo and black students showed correlations of 0.41 to 0.59 for Anglos, but 0.26 to 0.48 for blacks, (Sewell, 1979). This indicates that there may be reason for concern regarding the predictive validity of the test; further studies are certainly needed.

Factor studies have failed to show a clear-cut factor structure that carries throughout the test. Most of the factor weight seems to fall in a single general factor (as would be expected from the rationale behind the test's development) (Sattler, 1982). A variety of categorization schemes for Stanford-Binet items have been proposed, as described above, but there is minimal research to support the validity of these schemes.

Overall the lack of adequate technical data on a scale as widely used as the Stanford-Binet test is disappointing. Most of the data provided by the authors in the manual and elsewhere is very old, based on the 1939 edition or at best the 1960 edition. The literature contains relatively little research regarding this measure's technical adequacy; most of the studies that can be found use the Stanford-Binet test as a criterion for another test, rather than studying the test itself. At present the widespread use and acceptance of the Stanford-Binet test seem to owe more to its historical importance than the adequacy of current data.

Use.   Like most IQ tests, the Stanford-Binet test falls into the social-system model. The 1972 norms include nonwhite, non–middle class children, but no separate norms are available for the different groups, so its use in terms of a pluralistic model is not feasible. For decision making in educational settings, the Stanford-Binet test has long been an accepted tool. However, technical data available are not very current. Because at many levels the test is highly verbal, and because the verbal score cannot be separated from the performance score, it may be especially inappropriate for children who come from a language background other than standard English. On the other hand, the range of scores for the test is wider than for the WISC-R, and that may make it more useful in some situations.

In general, the Stanford-Binet IQ score can be used with reasonable confidence in the same kinds of situations as the WISC-R score. That is, the assessment practitioner should be aware that the Stanford-Binet IQ score indicates current intellectual functioning within middle class Anglo school culture, not innate ability; the practitioner should also take care to use a variety of other information sources, especially in considering a child for classification as mentally retarded. In addition, a number of categorization schemes have been proposed for interpreting performance on Stanford-Binet items for programming purposes (Meeker, 1969; Sattler, 1982). However, the scale was designed to be a measure of a single general factor of intelligence, and there is little research to justify its use in other ways.

In summary, then, in spite of the lack of current technical data, the Stanford-Binet test is a useful classification tool. Although it cannot now be considered to have the technical excellence of the WISC-R, it is useful in some situations where the WISC-R is not. Its use as an instrument for programming cannot be justified at this time.

Other IQ Measures

Besides the Wechsler scales and the Stanford-Binet Intelligence Scale, there are a variety of other individually administered IQ tests, most of them designed for a more specialized population or purpose. A number of the more commonly used tests will be reviewed here.

Slosson Intelligence Test

The Slosson Test (Slosson, 1963) is a brief IQ test developed for ages 6 months through 27 years. It consists of items arranged in age groupings and yields a ratio IQ. Items at the low end of the scale are developmental; the test becomes increasingly verbal with increasing age, and after age 4 almost all items are verbally administered. Many of the items are adapted from the Stanford-Binet test. The Slosson Test takes about 10 to 30 minutes to administer. It is relatively easy to administer with minimal training, and scoring is relatively objective.

The standardization sample of the Slosson Test is poorly described; the degree to which it is representative of the U.S. population is unclear. Reliability is generally good, with split-half and test-retest coefficients in the 0.90s. Concurrent validity with other IQ tests is fair; scores correlate well with scores from the Stanford-Binet test (0.90s) and fairly well with WISC-R scores (0.50s to 0.80s) (Sattler, 1974).

Overall, the Slosson Test is useful as a screening technique. However, it cannot be considered as an adequate substitute for the Wechsler scales or the Stanford-Binet test for assessing a child's overall IQ and should not be used for classification purposes.

Peabody Picture Vocabulary Test – Revised (PPVT-R)

The PPVT-R (Dunn & Dunn, 1981) is a measure of receptive vocabulary, designed for ages 2½ through adult. It is a revision of an earlier test published in 1959. Items consist of a vocabulary word and four drawings, one of which represents the word. The subject indicates which drawing corresponds to the word. The format of the test allows for very flexible responses; any way of indicating the subjects's choice is acceptable. Testing time is between 10 and 15 minutes, and administration and scoring are simple. It yields a standard score with a mean of 100 and a standard deviation of 15. There are two forms.

The standardization sample for the PPVT-R included 4200 children and 828 adults, stratified by age, sex, geographical region, occupation of major wage earner, ethnicity, and community size to match the 1970 U.S. Census. Median split-half reliabilities are between 0.80 and 0.85 for various ages; alternate-form reliabilities have a median of 0.81. There are few validity studies for the 1981 edition, since it is new. However, studies for the previous edition indicated moderate correlations with IQ test scores (median in the 0.60s) and smaller correlations with achievement scores (median in the 0.40s) (Sattler, 1982).

The PPVT-R is not directly an IQ measure. It is a well-designed instrument with good technical characteristics, however, and because vocabulary correlates well with overall IQ, this test can sometimes be used to get an estimate of IQ with a variety of handicapped children for whom the response requirements of other tests are inappropriate. It is also useful as a screening device. Finally, it can be useful for checking against the expressive vocabulary required by the Stanford-Binet test and the WISC-R to determine whether a child who scores low on one of those subtests has generally poor language skills or only poor expressive language.

Raven's Coloured Progressive Matrices Test

Raven's Test (Raven, 1965) is a nonverbal IQ test that can be administered individually or in small groups. Each item presents a drawing of a figure with a portion missing and six choices for the missing portion. The child indicates her or his choice among the responses in any reasonable way. As in the PPVT-R, the response requirements are very flexible. Further, the instructions can also be given in pantomime. The test typically takes about 20 minutes to administer. Scores are available as percentiles.

The standardization sample for Raven's Test consisted of 627 British children, aged 5 to 10½. Little additional information is available regarding the sample. Reliability is generally adequate; test-retest coefficients are in the 0.7 to 0.9 range. Reliability is lowest for young children. A number of studies summarized by Sattler (1982) indicate that Raven's scores correlate moderately well with other IQ test scores for a variety of populations (0.55 to 0.86 with the Stanford-Binet test and the WISC-R).

Raven's Test is limited to a single modality of assessment and may therefore penalize children with good overall intellectual skills but poor visual processing skills. It is somewhat less reliable and valid than the Stanford-Binet test or the WISC-R. The norms are also poor, especially for use in the United States. Thus, it cannot be substituted for a major IQ test for the assessment practitioner's use. However, like the PPVT-R, it can be given to a variety of children who cannot make the responses required by the Stanford-Binet test or WISC-R; if it is used with the PPVT-R, a fair estimate of IQ can sometimes be made for such children. In addition, Raven's Test can be useful for obtaining additional information regarding IQ for children who have a specific language deficit, bilingual children, and any other children for whom language itself is a barrier to valid testing. As a screening instrument is it probably better to employ a test with better U.S. norms and a wider variety of items for most populations.

Columbia Mental Maturity Scale (CMMS)

The CMMS (Burgemeister, Blum, & Lorge, 1972) is a nonverbal individually administered IQ test for children aged 3½ to 10. Each item consists of several pictures; the child selects the one that is different from the others. For the easiest items, it is a simple matching task, with all except one picture identical. For more difficult items, the way in which the pictures differ becomes increasingly complex. The instructions are basically to "point to the one which does not belong"; the whole concept of "does not belong" is difficult for some young children to grasp, but otherwise the test is simple to give. The test yields an age deviation score, with a mean of 100 and a standard deviation of 16, and also a "maturity index," which is similar to mental age.

The standardization sample of the CMMS is good. It consists of

2600 children stratified according to age, sex, geographical region, ethnicity, and parental occupation, to match the 1960 U.S. Census. Reliabilities are generally in the upper 0.80s for both test-retest and split-half correlations. Correlations with other IQ test scores are generally moderate, in the 0.50s range.

Like Raven's Test, the CMMS is useful for a nonverbal estimate of IQ with children who have difficulty responding to the WISC-R or the Stanford-Binet Test and with children who have language difficulties. Its norms are better than those of Raven's Test. It is a good tool to use for screening or for obtaining additional information. Because it measures IQ through a single modality, however, it is inappropriate for use as the primary tool for classification purposes.

Other Methods of Assessing Intellectual Functioning

While IQ tests of various kinds have formed the bulk of the methods used for assessing intellectual functioning, more recently a number of attempts have been made to derive other methods. These are generally based on a theory of cognitive development or on learning theory. Elkind (1969) and DeAvila and Havassy (1975) have advocated measuring intellectual development from a Piagetian perspective. Meeker (1969, 1973) has also developed several procedures for tying standard IQ tests to Guilford's Structure of Intellect (SOI) model (Guilford, 1967). She has developed the Structure of Intellect Learning Abilities Test (Meeker & Meeker, 1979). This test measures specific cells within the SOI model; there are also materials linked directly to the same cells for programming and remediation (for example, Meeker, 1979). Others have used a technique called Learning Potential Assessment involving testing a child, training the child on the task, and testing again (Budoff & Friedman, 1964; Feuerstein, 1979). Speed of paired-associate learning has also been used (Davidson, 1964; Kratochwill, 1977).

All of these methods have some possible advantages over the traditional IQ test. Methods based on a well-developed theory such as Guilford's or Piaget's, have much better long-term potential for providing programming and remediation information. Methods such as Learning Potential Assessment, based directly on observing a child's learning within the testing setting, have potential for greater accuracy and less bias than the traditional IQ testing, since fewer assumptions need to be made about the child's previous background or exposure to the material being tested. However, the predictive validity and programming usefulness of such techniques has not yet been extensively examined.

Additional information on reliability, validity, and norms is needed before these alternate forms of assessment can be considered to be routinely useful for classification decisions. Additional information on both the effectiveness of remediation of difficulties identified and the effect of such remediation on academic performance is needed before they can be used extensively for programming. The assessment practitioner should be aware of these new approaches, however, and may find it useful to pursue some of them as part of the assessment process.

CONCLUSIONS

Assessment of intellectual functioning currently still owes its primary focus to the approach taken by Binet at the beginning of the 20th century. Most assessment is focused on a single measure of general intelligence, developed primarily to have predictive validity for school achievement. While IQ is not necessarily synonymous with intellectual functioning, IQ is the construct usually used in a decision-making framework in educational settings. Recent attempts have been made to expand the assessment of intellectual functioning beyond IQ scores, but the value of such methods remains to be determined.

A number of concerns about the use of IQ for classification decisions exist; the most critical of these have to do with test fairness and test bias for minority and disadvantaged children. These concerns have brought increasing attention to the need for caution in classifying a child as mentally retarded on the basis of a single test score alone. The assessment practitioner needs to be aware of these concerns and should follow guidelines such as the use of adaptive behavior measures or pluralistic norms, in addition to the standard IQ score, in assessing a child. Within such constraints, IQ is a useful measure for decision making.

Of the techniques currently in use, the Wechsler scales probably have the best overall technical adequacy. The Stanford-Binet test also has good reliability and validity, although there is a disappointingly small amount of technical information about the 1972 norming. Other instruments, such as the Slosson Test, the PPVT-R, and Raven's Test are available for use for screening, obtaining additional information, or meeting special circumstances. For classification decisions, however, the practitioner should normally use the Wechsler scales or the Stanford-Binet test. Overall the Wechsler scales offer somewhat better technical characteristics, more even coverage of several different modalities of response, and far more technical data about the scales. The Stanford-Binet test offers a wider range of items, in terms of both the age levels and the IQ range covered. Either should provide a stable measure of current intellectual performance, with good predictive validity, for most children.

7

Assessment of Modality Skills

IN THE PREVIOUS CHAPTER, we saw that some theorists view intelligence as a unitary factor that can express itself in various skills, while others regard it as an interactive process involving several types of cognitive skills. Regardless of which point of view is taken, the usual purpose of intellectual assessment is to obtain a description of a child's global intellectual functioning. In other words, strengths and weaknesses in various skills usually take a back seat to the global measure provided by the IQ score.

In this chapter, we explore the assessment of modality (or psychoeducational processing) skills. Modality skills, for our purposes, refer to those specific skill areas that are assumed to be of importance in learning. In contrast to the assessment of intelligence, the assessment of modality skills focuses heavily on an attempt to determine a child's strengths and weaknesses in highly specific areas of functioning. Our discussion in this chapter focuses on traditional methods of asessing these skills. Alternative methods, which we prefer, are discussed in Chapter 8.

Although literally dozens of techniques have been developed for assessing modality skills, our examination will focus on those that have been most widely used by assessment practitioners. We first ex-

---

George Fincher, a licensed psychological examiner in private practice, served as editorial consultant for this chapter.

amine the assessment of *visual processing skills*—that is, those skills involving the processing of information received through the visual channel. In this section we will examine, in some detail, the use of the Bender Visual-Motor Gestalt Test and the Frostig Developmental Test of Visual Perception. These two techniques represent commonly used methods of assessing "visual perception" processes. We also examine several methods by which visual perception processes have been assessed informally. That is, we briefly explore the use of methods that are tailored to the individual being assessed.

Following our discussion of visual processing assessment methods, we will examine several methods for assessing auditory processing—that is, we will discuss several methods for assessing "auditory perception" skills. Our discussion focuses on two of the most commonly used tests of auditory perception: the Wepman Auditory Discrimination Test and the Goldman-Fristoe-Woodcock Auditory Skills Test Battery. We will also examine an informal method of assessing auditory processing skills.

The final group of assessment methods we will discuss involves "multimodality" assessment techniques. Included in this category are those tests that purport to measure a wide range of "information processing" or "perceptual" skills. Techniques we discuss, in detail, include the Illinois Test of Psycholinguistic Abilities, the Visual-Aural Digit Span Test, and the McCarthy Scales of Children's Abilities.

PURPOSES OF ASSESSING MODALITY SKILLS

The assessment of modality skills may be useful for both classification and programming. The reader will recall that the definition of learning disability found in the regulations implementing Public Law 94-142 states that a child who is classified as learning disabled exhibits a deficit in a basic psychological process. This definition has led many assessment practitioners to attempt to measure these processes as an aid to classification.

One way of defining basic psychological process is to assume that the concept can be expressed in terms of test scores that measure (or purport to measure) critical information processing variables. If a test measures an information processing factor (that is, a modality skill) that is related to educational performance, then a deficit in that factor might be appropriately termed a "deficit in a basic psychological process." We say *might* because the nature of the relationship between the information processing factor and educational performance is crucial.

If test scores exhibit an empirically observable association with relevant educational performance (as shown in correlation coefficients), then this provides one level of evidence that the factor measured by the test represents a basic psychological process relevant to learning. For example, suppose that test x purports to measure a child's overall skill in visual perception (for example, discriminating between visually presented symbols). Furthermore, suppose that scores on test x are correlated with scores on a test of reading skill. This, very simply, suggests that visual perception, as measured by test x, is related to reading and that visual perception might be a basic psychological process that is important in acquiring reading skills. The correlation between visual perception scores and reading scores, however, does not conclusively indicate that the two factors are causally related.

The most rigorous evidence that a test measures a basic psychological process exists when data indicate that the factor measured by the test and some specific educational performance are causally or functionally related. For instance, suppose that following visual perception training students with reading deficits show improvement in both visual perception (as measured by test x above) and reading skill. Students not receiving perceptual training show no such improvement. Assuming that this hypothetical study provided sufficient controls for extraneous variables and that the changes in student scores were statistically significant, this result would indicate that visual perception skills are functionally (that is, causally) related to reading. This would represent rather clear evidence that visual perception is a basic psychological process that is causally related to reading skills. Furthermore, this would provide rigorous justification for the use of test x in classifying children on the basis of their having a deficit in a basic psychological process.

So far, we have discussed only the first purpose of psychoeducational assessment—that of classifying children. Assessment of modality skills can be useful in identifying children to be classified as learning disabled to the extent that the assessment methods can be empirically demonstrated to measure basic psychological processes causally related to academics.

The programming function of modality assessment data can take two forms. First, these data can be used to describe the child's learning style. Secondly, they can be used to specify those deficits that must be remediated in order for a child to function at his or her expected age level.

Modality assessment data are probably most widely accepted as methods for describing a child's learning style. Quite clearly, most children exhibit relative strengths and weaknesses in various modalities (Hallahan & Kauffman, 1976). At the grossest level, we frequently find children who appear to be more skilled at processing visual information than auditory information or vice versa. Some theorists contend that remedial programs should capitalize on a child's strongest areas by focusing learning experiences upon those areas (Hallahan & Kauffman, 1976). For example, suppose that a child is stronger in visual than in auditory information processing. This might suggest that the child's remedial teacher should present as much material visually as is possible while minimizing auditory presentations. The rationale behind such an approach is the idea that learning can be maximized by focusing the presentation of information on the child's strongest "learning channel." Wallace and Larsen (1978) found that this approach is widely used in planning educational programs for children, and Reynolds (1981) cites evidence that this approach is effective in facilitating children's academic development.

Modality assessment data can also serve to the extent that the instruments used to specify deficits that require remediation assess factors that are truly important from the standpoint of educational performance. For example, suppose that test y is a measure of short-term auditory memory. Further suppose that a child is found to have a deficit in auditory memory as measured by test y. If it is assumed that auditory memory skills (of a level higher than that which characterizes this child) are necessary for appropriate academic functioning, then it could be argued that the child's memory deficit requires remediation. In other words, it is assumed that the child's memory skills must be strengthened in order for maximal learning to occur.

The primary problem inherent in the use of modality data for programming of this sort involves the question we have mentioned of whether improvement in a modality skill leads to improved academic performance. In other words, such data provide educationally useful information only if they point toward ways of improving educational functioning. If, for example, the remediation of auditory memory deficits results in improved performance in reading (or mathematics, or writing) then pinpointing an auditory memory deficit has practical value. It tells the assessment specialist that a deficit area exists, the remediation of which will result in improved school performance. If, however, there is no empirical evidence that improvement in auditory memory results in academic improvement (or, at least, facilitation of the acquisition of academic skills), then what value is there in remediating auditory memory deficits? Practically speaking, improvements in a modality area that do not result in consequences of measurable academic significance are meaningless.

The value of modality assessment must be judged by the extent to which it yields data that are both related to relevant educational performance (either through association or causation) and educationally significant. Again, the educational significance of modality assessment data can be demonstrated in two ways. The data can either provide descriptions of children's learning styles that can guide demonstrably effective instruction, or it can yield information about modality deficits that, when remediated, result in improved academic performance. The remainder of this chapter is devoted to describing various modality assessment techniques and examining them in terms of reliability, validity, and educational usefulness. Our discussion does not attempt to provide an exhaustive review of the research on each technique. It does, however, attempt to provide a representative view of each assessment technique in terms of both technical adequacy and educational usefulness.

ASSESSMENT OF VISUAL MODALITY SKILLS

Visual modality skills refer to those abilities we frequently place under the general rubric of "visual perception." That is, these skills are generally defined in terms of a child's ability to accurately perceive or interpret visual environmental stimuli. The basic rationale for assessing visual modality skills is the assumption that these skills are important in the development of academic skills such as reading. It is frequently assumed that deficits in visual modality skills can negatively affect a child's ability to read (Hallahan & Kauffman, 1976).

Although numerous tests of visual perception have been developed during recent decades, we confine our discussion to three of the most commonly used techniques. These include the Bender Visual-Motor Gestalt Test, the Frostig Developmental Test of Visual Perception, and informal methods of assessing visual modality skills.

Bender Visual-Motor Gestalt Test (BGT)

This test (Bender, 1938) is probably the oldest measure of visual perception in use today. The test itself consists of nine drawings that children are asked to reproduce. These drawings are shown in Figure 7-1. Each of the nine drawings is presented to the child in card format. The child is typically asked to look at the drawing and simply copy it. Therefore, the BGT cannot be viewed as a "pure" measure of visual perception. Rather, it appears to represent a measure of visual

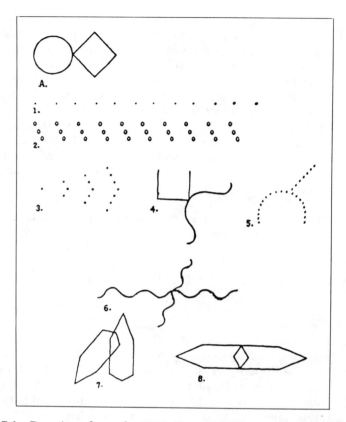

Figure 7-1   Drawings from the BGT. (from Bender, L. *The Visual Motor Gestalt Test and its clinical use.* Research Monographs of the American Orthopsychiatric Association, 1938, 3. With permission.)

perception and fine motor coordination. In other words, the BGT is best conceptualized as a measure of eye-hand coordination, which, of course, involves visual perception.

After the child has completed all nine BGT drawings, the drawings are scored in terms of number of errors. While several BGT scoring systems have been developed (Hutt, 1977; Koppitz, 1975b), we confine our discussion to the Koppitz scoring system since it appears to be the system most frequently used. Since the BGT is a negatively scored test, high scores represent relatively poor performance and low scores represent relatively adequate performance. In order to determine whether an error has been made on a given drawing, the examiner compares a child's responses to examples of errors found in Koppitz's scoring manual (1975b). Although an attempt is made in this manual to clearly describe types of scorable errors, BGT error analysis is not completely free from subjective judgment factors. The examiner must, after all, use her or his own visual perception skills to compare a child's drawing with those in the manual.

For test interpretation purposes, a child's error scores are compared to age norms found in the Koppitz manual (1975b). Norms are provided for children aged 5 years to 10 years, 11 months. Recently, Grow (1980) has provided BGT norms for students of junior high school age.

Reliability

In our opinion, one of the most crucial forms of reliability for the BGT is test-retest reliability. That is, there must exist evidence indicating that children's performances on the BGT do not vary greatly from one testing to another over reasonable periods of time. In other words, there must be evidence that BGT scores are stable over time, or temporally consistent.

Koppitz (1975b) reported the results of 10 studies of the test-retest reliability of the BGT. These studies utilized retest intervals ranging from one day to eight months. The children tested in the studies were in kindergarten through sixth grade. The average reliability coefficient was +0.71. In those investigations utilizing one- and two-week retest intervals, the average reliability was 0.74. Although these data do suggest that BGT scores exhibit some temporal stability, they also suggest that the BGT is far from a highly reliable instrument.

Inter-rater reliability is also of crucial importance for the BGT because of the subjective aspect of BGT scoring. Koppitz (1975b) reported 23 studies of the inter-rater reliability of the BGT. The range of obtained reliabilities was from 0.79 to 0.99, with an average of approximately 0.91. On the basis of these data, it can be concluded that according to almost any criterion of reliability the BGT has acceptable inter-rater reliability.

Validity

In the first section of this chapter we discussed the concept of validity in terms of whether test results are related to educational performance, either by association or causation. What we are really talking about here is one specific type of validity—*predictive validity*. If a test's scores predict specific educational problems, either current or future, it can be argued that the test has validity for the purpose of predicting specific educational problems.

A number of studies have investigated the association between

BGT scores and academic performance variables. Koppitz (1975b) reported over 50 such studies focusing on children in kindergarten through sixth grade. When BGT scores obtained during early elementary years were used to predict reading achievement in the mid- and late elementary years, significant correlations ranged from -0.24 to -0.57, with an average of approximately -0.35. This suggests a rather weak to moderately negative relationship between BGT scores and later reading achievement. In other words, high scores on the BGT are merely somewhat predictive of future reading difficulties.

Koppitz (1975b) also reports a number of studies investigating the relationship between BGT scores and mathematical performance in higher grades. Reported correlations range from -0.37 to -0.51, with an average of approximately -0.45. This indicates that BGT scores have moderate predictive validity for future mathematical skills, with high scores on the BGT suggesting the possibility of future difficulties in mathematics.

Educational Usefulness

The ultimate way of judging the educational usefulness of a modality assessment measure involves a demonstrated causal or functional relation between test scores and academic skill variables. For the BGT, this might entail a demonstration that improved BGT scores directly result in improved academic performance.

There currently exists no conclusive evidence that treatment-based changes in BGT scores result in changes in academic skills. However, it is possible to examine the effects of various related perceptual training programs to determine whether such training affects children's academic performance. Since the BGT is purported to represent a measure of "perceptual-motor skill" (Koppitz, 1975b), its educational usefulness may be evaluated in relation to the effectiveness of programs that attempt to enhance children's perceptual-motor skills. Further research should, of course, be done to assess the value of training programs based specifically on BGT results.

Several investigations (Goodman & Hammill, 1973; Hammill, 1972) have addressed the questions of whether perceptual-motor skills can be trained and, if so, what the effects of this training on academic skills are. Hammill (1972), after reviewing the published literature on perceptual training, has seriously questioned the efficacy of such training. He reports that in 10 out of 13 studies reviewed, extensive perceptual training had no significant effect on perceptual-motor skill. Studies published since Hammill's review have obtained similar results: no significant improvement in perceptual-motor skills following perceptual-motor training (Church, 1974; Sabatino, Ysseldyke, & Woolston, 1973).

Goodman and Hammill (1973) examined studies of the effects of perceptual training on academic performance. Out of 16 methodologically sound studies reviewed, none found perceptual training to be effective in improving academic performance.

It appears that perceptual-motor training has not been demonstrated to be functional in improving academic skills. It could be argued, therefore, that since the BGT is a test of perceptual-motor skills, its results have little, if any, programming value. However, predictive validity studies on the BGT suggest that it has potential as a screening instrument. In other words, BGT results might be used to target those children in need of more extensive diagnostic assessment on educationally relevant dimensions of behavior. Poor BGT scores might also contraindicate programming approaches that emphasize eye-hand coordination skills.

Frostig Developmental Test of Visual Perception

The Frostig Test purports to measure a wide array of educationally important visual perception skills in children aged 4 through 8 (Frostig, LeFever, & Whittlesey, 1966; Frostig, Maslow, LeFever, & Whittlesey, 1964). Its five subtests include

- Eye-Hand Coordination: testing the ability to integrate hand-movements with visual tracking
- Figure Ground Relations: testing the ability to discriminate between forms and their background
- Form Constancy: testing the ability to perceive similarities between apparently different forms
- Position in Space: testing the ability to perceive changes in the rotation of figures
- Spatial Relationships: testing the ability to draw figures by connecting dots.

Several Frostig Test stimulus items are shown in Figure 7-2.

Raw scores on the Frostig Test are converted to perceptual age scores. (Perceptual age scores are scores that represent the child's test performance vis-à-vis other children of a given age. For example, an age score of 5.7 would indicate that a child performed on par with the average child aged 5 years, 7 months.) These perceptual age scores are compared to the child's chronological age to determine whether the child is deficient in any of the five perceptual skill areas. Although an overall perceptual quotient can be computed, Frostig, LeFever, and Whittlesey (1966) contend that it is extremely important (for remediation purposes) to pinpoint the specific perceptual skills in

Figure 7-2 Frostig Test stimulus items (position in space). (From Frostig, M., LeFever, W., & Whittlesey, J. *Frostig Development Test of Visual Perception.* Palo Alto, Calif.: Consulting Psychologists Press, 1966. Copyright 1961. With permission.)

which a child is deficient. In other words, one of the major purported functions of the Frostig Test is the differential diagnosis of perceptual problems that are presumed to cause or at least be related to learning problems.

Reliability

Frostig, Maslow, LeFever, and Whittlesey (1964) reported test-retest reliabilities for both overall perceptual quotients and scores on individual subtests. The reliabilities for the overall scores ranged from 0.69 to 0.98. However, reliability for scores on individual sub-tests ranged from a low of 0.29 (on Eye-Hand Coordination) to a high of 0.80 (on Form Constancy). These data suggest that the Frostig Test may have sufficient reliability for use as a gross screening instrument, when only the global perceptual quotient is used. However, the low subtest reliabilities call into serious question the usefulness of the Frostig Test for the differential diagnosis of specific perceptual problem areas.

Validity

Frostig et al. (1964, 1966) have reported several studies of the predictive validity of the Frostig Test. In one of their studies, scores on the Frostig Test were correlated with reading achievement scores. Among first-grade children, the obtained correlations ranged from 0.40 to 0.50. This suggests a moderate relation between perceptual skills as measured by the Frostig Test and reading skill. However, this relation held only for first-grade children. Correlations between Frostig scores and reading among second and third graders were so low as to be meaningless.

In another study, Frostig et al. (1964) compared the Frostig scores of young children (aged 4½ to 6½) with reading difficulties with those of young children without reading difficulties. The results suggested that Frostig scores can be used to differentiate between young children with and without reading problems.

Although the above studies suggest moderate predictive validity for the Frostig Test, the purported differential diagnostic usefulness of the test requires an additional type of validity evidence. In order to be used in the differential diagnosis of specific perceptual problems, there must exist evidence that (1) the Frostig Test does, in fact, measure five separate perceptual functions and (2) each of these functions is related to academic ahievement. Of course, the latter is meaningful only if the former has been demonstrated.

Recently, several investigations have addressed the factorial validity of the Frostig Test (Becker & Sabatino, 1971; Boyd & Randle, 1970; Englehardt, 1975). Using factor analytic techniques, the authors of these studies attempted to determine whether the Frostig Test does, in fact, measure five separate and distinct factors. Overall, the results are rather discouraging. Englehardt isolated two factors measured by the test, while Boyd and Randle found only one. Becker and Sabatino isolated three factors, including visual-motor skill, figure-ground perception, and overall visual discrimination. Quite clearly, the factorial validity of the Frostig Test is yet to be established. Therefore, the use of the test in differential diagnosis is questionable at this time.

Educational Usefulness

Like the BGT, the Frostig Test measures perceptual-motor skill. Our previous discussion of the educational usefulness of the BGT is therefore equally relevant here. As Goodman and Hammill (1973) point out, perceptual-motor training, in general, appears to have little or no effect on either academic skills or, for that matter, perceptual-motor skills themselves. This makes the use of perceptual-motor tests rather meaningless, at least for programming that attempts to strengthen deficit skills.

Ross (1977) reported the results of a study involving Frostig's own perceptual training program with groups of learning disabled children. Following 16 weeks of daily perceptual training (based on results of the Frostig Test), the reading skills of "trained" children were not significantly different from those of children receiving no training at all. These data not only prompt serious questions regarding the general usefulness of visual-motor training, they specifically call into question the usefulness of training deficits identified through use of the Frostig Test.

As was the case with the BGT, the Frostig Test can only be recommended as a gross screening instrument for identifying children who might be in need of further, more precise, evaluation. Its use as a

		Yes	No
1.	Does the child complain about headaches, dizziness or nausea associated with use of the eyes?		
2.	Does the child complain about an inability to work accurately at blackboard or with books?		
3.	Does the child complain about hurting, itching, or "tiredness" of the eyes?		
4.	Does the child complain about blurred or double vision?		
5.	Does the child shut or cover one eye?		
6.	Does the child tilt or thrust head forward?		
7.	Does the child rub eyes frequently?		
8.	Does the child scowl, squint, frown, or give other facial contortions when reading or doing close work?		
9.	Does the child blink more than usual?		
10.	Does the child appear to be irritable, restless, or nervous when called upon to use the eyes for close work?		
11.	Does the child have temper tantrums, fatigue, or listlessness after doing close work?		
12.	Does the child stumble or trip frequently?		
13.	Does the child have poor eye-hand coordination?		
14.	Does the child hold a book too near or too far away?		
15.	Does the child write with face too close to paper?		

Figure 7-3 An informal checklist of symptoms indicative of potential perception difficulties. (From *Fundamentals of educational assessment* by Cregg F. Ingram. Copyright © 1980 by Litton Educational Publishing, Inc. Reprinted by permission of Wadsworth Publishing Company, Belmont, California 94002.)

major tool in either classification or programming is unwarranted at this time, except perhaps for identifying children unlikely to profit from instructional programs that emphasize adequate visual perceptual skills.

Informal Assessment of Visual Perception

Ingram (1980) has presented several methods whereby classroom teachers can informally assess the visual perception skills of their students. These methods involve observing children's classroom performance to ascertain the presence of traits such as clumsiness at motor tasks, disorganization, distractability, carelessness, and number or letter distortions.

Two of Ingram's informal checklists are seen in Figures 7-3 and 7-4.

	Yes	No
1. Does the child appear to lack prerequisite skills of visual-motor perception, such as ability to identify sizes, shapes, colors, and differences or similarities in letters?	___	___
2. Does the child have difficulty classifying or categorizing objects or pictures?	___	___
3. Does the child appear to observe objects within the visual field?	___	___
4. Does the child attach meaning to visual symbols, such as signs and gestures?	___	___
5. Does the child care for picture books, and is able to identify pictures of objects rapidly?	___	___
6. Does the child fail to use context clues from pictures or book illustrations in reading?	___	___
7. Does the child find absurdities in pictures?	___	___
8. Does the child have difficulty in grasping content of a story from a series of pictures?	___	___
9. Does the child have difficulty in putting series of pictures in proper or logical sequence?	___	___
10. Does the child respond better to spoken words than to visual aids?	___	___
11. Does the child fail to understand what is said?	___	___

Figure 7-4 A checklist for use in screening for children's potential visual perceptual problems. (From *Fundamentals of educational assessment* by Cregg F. Ingram. Copyright © 1980 by Litton Educational Publishing Inc. Reprinted by permission of Wadsworth Company, Belmont, California 94002.)

Since no data are presented on the reliability, validity, and educational usefulness of these informal methods, their use should be restricted to that of auxillary screening tools. Even though these instruments cannot currently be evaluated, they may prove useful as ways of systematizing interpretations of the results of more formal screening methods such as the Frostig Test or the BGT.

ASSESSMENT OF AUDITORY MODALITY SKILLS

Auditory modality skills involve the perception of verbal stimuli; that is, they are the abilities related to the processing of spoken language. On the basis of the assumption that there is a strong relationship between such skills and the development of academic language skills, a number of auditory assessment instruments have been developed. In this section we will review three of them, the Goldman-Fristoe-Woodcock Auditory Skills Test Battery, the Auditory Discrimination Test, and an informal instrument, the Test of Auditory Analysis Skills.

Goldman-Fristoe-Woodcock Auditory Skills Test Battery (GFW)

The GFW (Woodcock, 1976) is a multitest battery purporting to measure a wide range of auditory skills in persons aged 3 years to adulthood. The GFW Battery consists of four basic tests, including the following:

- Auditory Selective Attention Test
- Diagnostic Auditory Discrimination Test
- Auditory Memory Test
- Sound-Symbol Test

The Auditory Memory Test consists of three subtests, and the Sound-Symbol Test consists of seven subtests. Raw scores on all tests and subtests can be converted into age-equivalent scores and percentiles.

Reliability

The GFW manual (Woodcock, 1976) reported the results of a split-half reliability study on the tests within the battery. Reliabilities for a normal "nonclinic" sample ranged from 0.89 to 0.98. For a sample of individuals with speech and learning problems, reliabilities ranged from 0.74 to 0.98 with a mean of 0.86. These data, although based on subjects of widely varying age, do suggest that the internal consistency of the GFW is adequate. However, we would like to see future research address the issue of temporal stability through test-retest studies.

Validity and Educational Usefulness

The GFW manual (Woodcock, 1976) presents several studies assessing the validity of the battery. The most impressive validity data presented involve the comparison of the GFW scores of normal and clinical samples. The data clearly demonstrate that all GFW tests and subtests can differentiate between these two samples. No evidence is presented, however, demonstrating that subtests can reliably differentiate persons with different types of speech and learning problems.

A second line of validity evidence involves a study in which GFW scores are correlated with age. The obtained correlations are generally quite high at ages 3 through 8 and then decrease after age 9. This pattern would be expected for a test purporting to measure skills related to basic language development.

Although a formal factorial validity study was not described in the manual, correlations between tests and subtests are reported. These correlations, when age is partialled out, are generally low to moderate, suggesting that the GFW may be measuring a number of different factors.

Reliability and validity data suggest that the GFW is psychometrically adequate, although further research is needed on temporal stability and construct and criterion validity. As such, it could be used carefully as a classification tool — that is, it could possibly be used as a measure of basic psychological processes that have an impact on language learning. However, the programming usefulness of the GFW has not yet been evaluated. Future research is needed to assess the extent to which remediation of problems pinpointed by the GFW is possible and whether such remediation results in increments in educational performance.

Auditory Discrimination Test (ADT)

This measure (Wepman, 1973) is designed to assess children's abilities to differentiate various sounds, Although the normative base of the ADT is not described, it was developed for use with children between the ages of 5 and 8.

In administering the ADT, the examiner reads 40 pairs of words and asks the child to indicate whether the words are the same or different. The pairs of words are designed to isolate sounds that the child may not be able to discriminate. Raw scores are based on the number of word pairs correctly discriminated and are converted to a five-level scale. The scale appears to be based on percentile-like rankings, but the absence of normative data makes it impossible to determine the true meanings of these rankings.

Reliability

The ADT manual (Wepman, 1973) reports several studies of the reliability of the instrument. Although these studies are described in limited detail, reported test-retest and alternate-form coefficients are in the range of 0.90 to 0.93. This is suggestive of adequate reliability for purposes of practical use.

Validity and Educational Usefulness

Several studies, briefly described in the ADT manual, suggest that ADT scores can differentiate students with achievement and articulation problems from those without such problems. No studies have assessed the extent to which improvements in ADT scores result in achievement gains. Clearly, a great deal of research on the ADT is needed before it can be considered for any use other than gross screening.

Test of Auditory Analysis Skills (TAAS)

This measure (Rosner, 1975) is an informal instrument designed to determine the child's ability to perceive and articulate various sounds within words. Although no technical manual is provided for the TAAS, an accompanying remediation text is available (Rosner).

In administering the TAAS, the examiner asks the child to verbalize 13 words and then verbalize parts of each word, keeping certain sounds silent. Scoring is based on the number of correct responses, which is converted into a grade-level equivalent score. In the description of the test and its rationale, no normative data are provided. This precludes a meaningful analysis of the TAAS scoring system.

No data on reliability or validity are provided for the TAAS. In light of Rosner's claim that teaching correct responses to the TAAS results in improvements in reading and spelling, such data are sorely needed. In the absence of psychometric data, we consider the TAAS to be useful only as a very gross, teacher-administered instrument for assessing the possible need for a referral. We certainly cannot recommend the programming use of the test as recommended by its developer.

MULTIPLE MODALITY ASSESSMENT INSTRUMENTS

In this section, we examine several commonly used instruments that assess skills in both auditory and visual processing areas. These multiple modality assessment techniques include the Visual-Aural Digit Span Test, the Illinois Test of Psycholinguistic Abilities, and the McCarthy Scales of Children's Abilities.

Visual-Aural Digit Span Test (VADST)

This test was developed by Elizabeth Koppitz (1977) and is used to assess the memory processing skills of children aged 6 through 12. The normative sample consisted of 810 "normal" public school children ranging in age from 5 to 12. The VADST utilizes a "digit-span" test format (as found in the Wechsler scales and the Stanford-Binet test) and assesses short-term memory on a "cross-modality" basis.

The basic subtests of the VADST include the following:

- Aural-Oral: The examiner verbalizes digits and the child repeats them.
- Visual-Oral: The examiner presents digits on cards, removes them, and the child then verbalizes the digits.
- Aural-Written: The examiner verbalizes digits and the child writes them.
- Visual-Written: The examiner presents digits on a card, removes them, and the child then writes the digits.

In addition to the four basic subtest scores, seven other combination scores can be derived from the VADST. These include

- Total Score: the sum of all four basic subtest scores, purportedly reflecting global skill in "perceptual-motor integration, sequencing, and recall"
- Aural Input: the sum of the Aural-Oral and Aural-Written subtest scores, purportedly reflecting overall auditory processing skill
- Visual Input: the sum of the Visual-Oral and Visual-Written scores, purportedly reflecting overall visual processing skill
- Oral Expression: the sum of the Aural-Oral and Visual-Oral subtest scores, purportedly measuring skill in verbally expressing processed information
- Written Expression: the sum of the Aural-Written and Visual-Written subtest scores, purportedly measuring skill in expressing processed information in writing
- Intrasensory Integration: the sum of the Aural-Oral and Visual-Written subtest scores, purportedly measuring the ability to in-

tegrate "input" and "output" modalities within the same sensory channel (that is, the auditory channel for the Aural-Oral subtest and the visual channel for the Visual-Written subtest)

- Intersensory Integration: the sum of the Visual-Oral and Aural-Written subtest scores, purportedly measuring the ability to integrate input and output modalities from two different sensory channels (Koppitz, 1977)

It is quite clear that the VADST yields a great deal of information from one testing. Its efficiency is further increased by the fact that it takes only 10 to 20 minutes to administer the test.

Reliability

Koppitz (1977) reports only one study of the reliability of this measure. The retest interval for this study ranged from one week to four months. For students aged 6 to 10, she obtained test-retest correlations ranging from 0.74 (Visual-Oral) to 0.84 (Aural-Oral) for the basic subtests. The retest correlation for Aural Input was 0.85, while that for Visual Input was 0.90. The retest correlation for the total VADST score was 0.92. For students aged 11 and 12, test-retest correlations ranged from 0.72 (Aural-Written) to 0.85 (Aural-Oral). Correlations for Aural and Visual input were 0.87 and 0.88, respectively. The correlation for the total VADST score was 0.90.

This study indicates that some subtests (Aural-Oral for ages 6 through 10; Aural-Oral and Visual-Oral for ages 11 and 12) exhibit adequate test-retest reliability. However, further research on the reliability of the VADST is needed. Such research should investigate the internal consistency of the instrument, as well as provide further exploration of its temporal consistency.

Validity

In a study of the predictive validity of the VADST, Koppitz (1977) tested 100 preschool children with the measure and examined their achievement test scores three years later. She then compared the achievement levels of students above and below the 25th percentile on all 11 VADST scores. All VADST scores, with the exception of those for Written Expression, were found to predict later reading achievement. All VADST scores predicted language achievement, and all but the Aural-Written and Written Expression scores predicted mathematics achievement. The strongest VADST predictions were found for language skills.

In a set of studies correlating the four VADST basic subtest scores with current achievement, Shumar (1976) and Thompson

(1976) obtained strong correlations between several VADST scores and reading achievement. Reading recognition was significantly correlated with all VADST subtests for children in grades two, three, and four. Reading comprehension was significantly correlated with only two subtests — Aural-Written and Visual-Written.

So far, we have examined studies showing predictive or concurrent relationships between VADST scores and achievement variables. Several validity studies also compare the VADST scores of "normal" children to those of children with learning disabilities.

Koppitz (1975c) compared the VADST subtest scores of average students with those of children with behavior and learning problems. The students were matched by both age and sex. Significant differences were found between the two groups on all basic subtests except Aural-Oral.

Koppitz (1975a) also compared the VADST scores of average students with those of students with severe learning disabilities. These students were matched by age, sex and WISC IQ scores. The scores of these two groups differed at a highly significant level on all four basic VADST subtests.

Carter, Spero, and Walsh (1978) compared the VADST scores of low and average achievers in various mathematical and reading skill areas. Using an analysis of covariance (with IQ as the covariate), these researchers found that Visual-Oral and Visual-Written scores differentiated low and average achievers in vocabulary (reading recognition), and Visual-Oral, Aural-Written, and Visual-Written scores differentiated low and average achievers in the area of mathematical concepts.

Clearly, the VADST measures factors that are related to basic academic skills. It could be argued, therefore, that low scores on the VADST are suggestive of deficits in basic psychological processes. The VADST therefore appears to be potentially useful for the screening and classification of children. However, more research is needed before a conclusive analysis is possible.

Educational Usefulness

Recently, Farb and Thorne (1978) conducted a study on the "trainability" of various short-term memory or mnemonic skills. The results of this study clearly indicate that such skills can be enhanced through standard behavior modification procedures. Since the memory tasks used by Farb and Thorne were almost identical to the test tasks of the VADST, the study provides indirect evidence that some of the skills measured by the VADST might be trainable.

If they are, the next logical question is whether training

in VADST skills can improve educational performance. Although on-going research by two of the present authors and a coworker is addressing this question, there is currently no conclusive empirical evidence that improvements in memory processing skills result in enhanced academic achievement. Such evidence is needed to evaluate the usefulness of the VADST in programming. Clearly, an analysis of the programming value of the VADST requires future research.

Illinois Test of Psycholinguistic Abilities (ITPA)

This test was developed as a measure of the diverse skills involved in communication (Kirk, McCarthy, and Kirk, 1968). More specifically, it was developed as a tool for specifying those skills that require remediation in special education programs.

ITPA norms are based on an original sample of 962 children ranging in age from 2 through 10. The test consists of 10 basic and 2 supplementary subtests. The 10 basic subtests are listed below, along with the factors they purport to measure.

- Auditory Reception: the ability to accurately receive and understand verbal communications
- Visual Reception: the ability to accurately receive and understand pictorial communications
- Auditory Association: the ability to perceive analogical relationships between verbally presented concepts
- Visual Association: the ability to perceive analogical relationships among concepts presented pictorially
- Verbal Expression: the ability to verbally describe common objects
- Manual Expression: the ability to manually demonstrate the use of common objects
- Auditory Sequential Memory: the ability to remember the correct order of digits presented verbally
- Visual Sequential Memory: the ability to remember the correct order of unfamiliar symbols presented pictorially
- Grammatic Closure: the ability to verbalize correct grammatical forms of words
- Visual Closure: the ability to recognize familiar objects when only parts are presented pictorially

The ITPA profile sheet is shown in Figure 7-5.

Summary Sheet

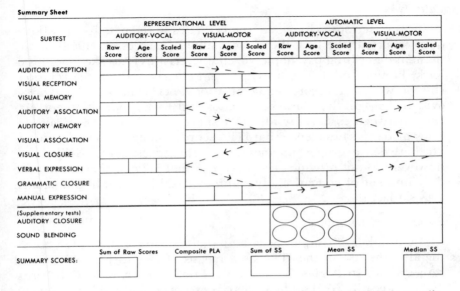

SUBTEST	REPRESENTATIONAL LEVEL						AUTOMATIC LEVEL					
	AUDITORY-VOCAL			VISUAL-MOTOR			AUDITORY-VOCAL			VISUAL-MOTOR		
	Raw Score	Age Score	Scaled Score	Raw Score	Age Score	Scaled Score	Raw Score	Age Score	Scaled Score	Raw Score	Age Score	Scaled Score
AUDITORY RECEPTION												
VISUAL RECEPTION												
VISUAL MEMORY												
AUDITORY ASSOCIATION												
AUDITORY MEMORY												
VISUAL ASSOCIATION												
VISUAL CLOSURE												
VERBAL EXPRESSION												
GRAMMATIC CLOSURE												
MANUAL EXPRESSION												
(Supplementary tests) AUDITORY CLOSURE												
SOUND BLENDING												
SUMMARY SCORES:	Sum of Raw Scores		Composite PLA			Sum of SS			Mean SS			Median SS

Figure 7-5 ITPA profile sheet. (From Kirk, S., McCarthy, J., & Kirk, W. *Illinois Test of Psycholinguistic Abilities*. Urbana: University of Illinois Press, 1968. Copyright 1968 by University of Illinois Press. With permission.)

A child's raw score on each subtest can be converted to a standard score and to a "psycholinguistic age" score. These scores allow a comparison between the child's performance on each subtest and the performance expected on the basis of his or her chronological age. An overall score, the "composite psycholinguistic age," can also be obtained.

Reliability

The ITPA manual (Kirk, McCarthy, & Kirk, 1968) contains extensive information on the reliability of the test. Coefficients of internal consistency (Kudor-Richardson 20) range from 0.51 to 0.96. The most internally consistent subtests (that is, those with reliabilities above 0.90) include Visual Sequential Memory, Auditory Sequential Memory, and Auditory Reception. The least internally consistent subtests are Grammatic Closure and Visual Closure.

The ITPA manual also describes the results of several test-retest reliability studies. Reliability coefficients range from 0.12 to 0.86. Only one subtest — Auditory Sequential Memory — has a reliability in excess of 0.80. All other subtests consistently fall short of most standards of temporal stability for purposes of practical application.

Validity

A very serious criticism of the ITPA lies in the paucity of validity data reported in either the basic manual (Kirk et al., 1968) or the manual describing psychometric characteristics (Paraskevopoulos & Kirk, 1969). No data are provided that clearly address the relationship between ITPA scores and educational performance. However, as evidence of validity, Paraskevopoulos and Kirk report high correlations between essentially all ITPA subtests and chronological age. They also report evidence that ITPA scores can accurately differentiate between average and mentally retarded students. Such data, however, do not provide clear evidence that ITPA scores predict the development of educationally significant skills, including language arts skills.

Educational Usefulness

A number of researchers and theorists have strongly recommended the use of the ITPA as a means of generating educational remediation strategies (for example, Lund, Foster, & McCall-Perez, 1978; Minskoff, 1975). In fact, there is evidence that the ITPA is widely used for this purpose (Vance, 1976).

In light of the widespread use of the ITPA as a programming instrument, one might expect clear evidence that ITPA subtest skills can be trained and that improvements on ITPA skills result in improvements in educational performance. However, in a review of 38 studies, Hamill and Larsen (1974) concluded that there is no evidence that training in ITPA subtest skills results in change of any kind, either in ITPA scores or in academic achievement.

In a recent reanalysis of the studies reviewed by Hammill and Larsen (1974), Kavale (1981) concluded that ITPA skills can, in fact, be trained. In other words, Kavale's reanalysis suggests that training in ITPA skills results in improved ITPA performance. Regardless of whether such training does improve ITPA scores, there is heated debate on whether ITPA training improves academic performance. Lund, Foster, and McCall-Perez (1978) suggest that Hammill and Larsen (1974) have been overly pessimistic on this question. Until this debate is conclusively resolved, the programming value of the ITPA will remain in question.

McCarthy Scales of Children's Abilities (MSCA)

The McCarthy Scales is a broad measure of several factors considered important in school learning (McCarthy, 1972). The test was standardized on 100 children at each of 10 age levels ranging from 2½ to 8½ years. As such, it is used with preschool-aged and early-elementary-aged children.

The MSCA consists of 18 subtests that make up six basic scales. These six scales are listed below, along with the abilities tapped by each.

- Verbal: pictorial and verbal memory, word knowledge, verbal fluency, and analogical reasoning
- Perceptual-Performance: block building, puzzle solving, drawing, and concept grouping
- Quantitative: counting, sorting, numerical memory, and answering questions about numbers
- General Cognitive: a combination of abilities from the verbal, perceptual-performance, and quantitative subtests
- Memory: pictorial, verbal, and numerical memory, and sequencing skill
- Motor: limb coordination, motoric imitation, and drawing

In addition to a general cognitive score, the MSCA provides scaled scores for each of the five other scales. The general cognitive score has a mean of 100 and a standard deviation of 16. The other scales have a mean of 50 and a standard deviation of 10. These scaled scores can be transformed into percentiles and estimated mental age scores.

Reliability

The MSCA manual (McCarthy, 1972) primarily provides split-half (internal consistency) reliability coefficients. The reliability coefficients for three of the scales across essentially all ages are fairly high. These include the Verbal, Perceptual-Performance, and General Cognitive scales. The average reliabilities for these scales are 0.88, 0.84, and 0.93, respectively. Reliabilities for the Quantitative and Motor scales are lower but are still within minimally acceptable limits. Average reliabilities for these two scales are 0.81 and 0.79, respectively. No split-half reliability data are provided for the Memory Scale, since such a measure of reliability is generally considered inappropriate for the types of subtests of which this scale consists.

Test-retest reliability (one month) coefficients are reported for both the General Cognitive Scale and the other five scales. The coefficients for the General Cognitive Scale center around 0.90, while the average coefficient for the other five scales is 0.81. The internal consistency reliability data for the Verbal, Perceptual-Performance, and General Cognitive scales are encouraging. However, further research is needed. This work should focus on assessing the test-retest reliability of the MSCA over long periods of time. Evidence of long-term temporal stability would surely bolster confidence in the accuracy of its scores.

Validity and Educational Usefulness

The MSCA manual (McCarthy, 1972) reports several studies of the validity of the instrument. In one study, several MSCA scales were found to predict future school achievement in essentially all areas. These included the Perceptual-Performance, Quantitative, and General Cognitive scales.

Kaufman and Kaufman (1977) have reported the results of an extensive series of factorial validity studies on the MSCA. Although measured factors vary somewhat across ages, factors corresponding to each scale emerged in their analyses. Memory, motor, and verbal factors emerged at *all* ages. These data provide rather strong support for the factorial validity of the MSCA. That is, these data suggest that the MSCA is, in fact, a valid measure of several factors that might be categorized along the lines of verbal, motor, memory, etc. factors — factors that represent basic psychological processes that may affect learning.

Although there exists evidence that MSCA measures factors related to educational performance, there is no clear evidence that improvements in these areas result in incremental improvements in academic skills. While the MSCA appears to have some validity for use as a classification tool, its programming usefulness remains unassessed. Future research should assess the extent to which improvements in MSCA scales results in improvements in educational performance.

CONCLUSIONS

Instruments used to assess modality skills may, in some cases, have utility for classification and programming purposes. We, however, urge caution in their use for a number of reasons. First, some of these instruments lack sufficient technical adequacy to serve other than screening decisions. Second, we are not convinced that such instruments are actually required for the purpose of classifying children as learning disabled, despite a common assumption that they are (see pp. 59 – 61).

Perhaps more importantly, we question the use of modality assessment instruments for programming purposes. While modality skills may in fact be trainable, as suggested by investigators such as

Farb and Thorne (1978) and Kavale (1981), we are not persuaded that such training results in improved academic performance. Future evidence may change our minds, but we are currently skeptical, despite arguments supporting remedial training in modality skills advanced by Lund, Foster, and McCall-Perez (1978) and Minskoff (1975).

If assessment of modality skills has any utility for programming, we believe that this utility may involve matching children's modality strengths with instructional approaches compatible with those strengths. The rationale for this matching approach is the notion that a child can best learn material that is presented through his or her strongest learning channel (Ingram, 1980). Witkin, Moore, Goodenough, and Cox (1977) advocate this approach, and Reynolds (1981) cites data indicating its effectiveness in facilitating children's academic development. However, Bateman (1967) and Bruininks (1968) found that such matching failed to improve academic performance. Spache (1976) found such procedures to be effective with some children but not others. Hence, the efficacy data are inconclusive in relation to this programming strategy. Whether modality strengths should be considered in planning children's instructional programs has been discussed, both pro and con, by Barbe, Swassing, and Milone (1981), Kampwirth (1981), Kampwirth and Bates (1980), and Tarver and Dawson (1978).

In the final analysis, assessment results can only predict (and not guarantee) which instructional strategy will be most effective with a given child. Such predictions must be tested, and accepted or rejected, in the actual process of teaching that child. While modality assessment instruments may be helpful in making such predictions, we favor another approach. This approach is called *Direct Assessment* and involves actually experimenting with different instructional strategies and seeing how the child responds to each. Such experimentation specifically takes the form of presenting academic content through both visual and auditory channels and evaluating which type of presentation results in the most rapid learning. Since Direct Assessment allows for the simultaneous assessment of both modality skills and academic skills, we view it as a very efficient approach to assessment. The next chapter contains a more detailed description of Direct Assessment and of our reasons for preferring it to other approaches to modality assessment.

8

Assessment of Academic Functioning

IN THE PREVIOUS CHAPTER we examined a number of methods for assessing modality skills — factors that are frequently assumed to be integrally related to academic performance. In this chapter we will explore various techniques of assessing academic skills directly — that is, we will discuss individual measures of academic achievement, measures that assess a child's mastery of reading, writing, mathematics, and other skills taught in schools.

Three types of assessment of academic skills will be explored: psychometric measures of academic functioning, diagnostic tests of academic functioning, and informal assessment methods. Within each category, we will discuss several instruments or systems currently in use, attempting to provide a representative, rather than exhaustive, coverage of available instruments.

Our discussion of psychometric measures will focus on those instruments that utilize norms. These instruments, as a group, attempt to compare an individual child's level of achievement in a given area (for example, reading) to that of other children of similar age in the relevant normative group. Psychometric achievement measures, therefore, provide information about a child's relative standing in

George Fincher, a licensed psychological examiner in private practice, served as editorial consultant for this chapter.

some area of academic achievement. This approach is oriented toward the assessment of *inter*-individual differences, differences between a target child's achievement and that of others.

Diagnostic measures of achievement attempt to describe a child's absolute level of skill in various achievement areas. These tests focus not on a child's relative standing vis-à-vis a norm group but on what a child can and cannot do in terms of academic skills. In essence, these tests address the following questions:

- What *specific* academic skills has the child mastered?
- What *specific* academic skills has the child failed to master?

The basic orientation of diagnostic tests is toward the assessment of *intra*-individual differences, differences among a single child's competencies (for example, mastery as opposed to nonmastery) in many different academic skills. Although some diagnostic measures provide normative information, such data are clearly secondary in these tests to absolute descriptions of a child's academic strengths and weaknesses.

In recent years, researchers and practitioners alike have proposed various informal methods for assessing academic skills. These methods are almost invariably nonstandardized and "homemade." They frequently entail making detailed analyses of how a child goes about performing (or attempting to perform) a specific task and of the types of errors made during performance. Although some informal systems simply attempt to describe strengths and weaknesses in academic skills, most have the goal of task analysis — describing a child's performance vis-à-vis each component part of an academic task. We will explore the use of several such methods.

PURPOSES OF ASSESSING ACADEMIC FUNCTIONING

Before we engage in a detailed exploration of academic assessment technologies, we must address the question of why academic skills warrant individual assessment. As we have discussed in previous chapters, there are basically two reasons for performing any kind of psychoeducational assessment: *classification* and *programming.* In this section, we will focus on how the assessment of academic functioning relates to classification and programming issues.

The assessment of a child's academic skills is often essential for the purpose of classification. In order to classify a child as handicapped under the categories of Public Law (PL) 94-142, it is desirable and, in some cases, required that the examiner obtain data on academic achievement. The instruments discussed in this chapter provide a means of obtaining such data.

The criteria for classification of a child as learning disabled under PL 94-142 include the observation that the child's "achievement is not commensurate with age or ability levels." Quite clearly, before a child can be classified as learning disabled, the examiner must establish the existence of a deficit in an area of academic achievement. Psychometric achievement measures, through the use of norms, allow the examiner to determine whether a child's achievement in a given area is commensurate with age- or grade-level expectations.

The classification of a child as seriously emotionally disturbed under PL 94-142 requires that a child's emotional problems "adversely affect educational performance." Psychometric achievement measures provide one means of determining whether a child's academic performance has been so affected.

Psychometric achievement measures are clearly useful in the classification of learning disabled and emotionally disturbed children. In addition, many states have laws concerning handicapping conditions that include the categories of "learning problems" and "intellectual giftedness." In many cases, such state laws require that a child's academic performance be assessed as part of the overall assessment for classification in terms of either of these two categories.

Although the usefulness of psychometric measures in classification is clear, these types of measures have limited utility in programming. Psychometric achievement measures yield comparative statements about a child's academic skills vis-à-vis the skills of other children of similar age, but they do not tell the examiner the specific academic skills in which a child is deficient. For example, a psychometric measure may show that Johnny's skills in mathematics are equivalent to those of the average child in grade 3.2. If Johnny is currently in grade 6.2, these data would indicate a delay of approximately three years. The data do not, however, clearly specify the specific skill deficits in mathematics of which this delay is a function; they do not provide diagnostic information that lends itself to specific remediation and programming efforts. As many theorists and practitioners (Hallahan & Kauffman, 1976; Ingram, 1980) have pointed out, the absence of specific information about a child's academic deficits makes it very difficult, if not impossible, to design effective remedial programs.

Diagnostic tests of academic functioning have been developed primarily for the purpose of complementing the information obtained from psychometric measures. As indicated previously, psychometric measures focus on *inter*-individual differences, while diagnostic measures focus on *intra*-individual differences. As such, diagnostic tests provide information about a single child's strengths and weaknesses on specific skills that, although of limited utility for classification purposes, can be directly translated into remedial programming (Hallahan & Kauffman, 1976). The same is basically true of informal measures of academic functioning, since they, too, focus on the specific strengths and weaknesses of a single child.

Psychometric and diagnostic achievement measures have complementary functions in the assessment process. Psychometric measures have primary utility in classification, while diagnostic measures have primary utility in the design of remedial programs. In the remainder of this chapter we will explore, in detail, some examples of both types of measures.

PSYCHOMETRIC TESTS

Two of the most commonly used psychometric methods of assessing achievement are the Peabody Individual Achievement Test and the Wide Range Achievement Test. Both instruments purport to measure several different areas of academic skill, and both utilize norms for interpretaton — hence, their psychometric orientation.

Peabody Individual Achievement Test (PIAT)

The PIAT (Dunn & Markwardt, 1970) was originally standardized on a sample of 2889 children in kindergarten through 12th grade. With the exception of kindergarten, slightly more than 100 boys and 100 girls were included at each grade level. An attempt was made to approximate the black/white, geographical region, and occupational distributions found in the 1967 U.S. Census.

The PIAT yields achievement scores in five different areas of academic functioning: mathematics, reading recognition, reading comprehension, spelling, and general information. Raw scores for each area can be converted into any of four types of derived scores, including grade equivalents, age equivalents, percentile ranks, and standard scores.

As a norm-based measure, the primary purpose of the PIAT is to allow the examiner to compare a child's level of academic achievement to that of other children of the same age or grade level. The PIAT is therefore useful primarily in classification.

Reliability

Dunn and Markwardt (1970) have reported the results of a test-retest reliability study of the PIAT. This study involved samples of 50 to 75 students in kindergarten, 1st, 3rd, 5th, 8th, and 12th grade. The PIAT was administered to these students twice, at intervals of approximately one month.

Test-retest reliability coefficients ranged from a low of 0.42 for the spelling subtests with kindergarten students to a high of 0.94 for the reading recognition subtest with third graders. Median reliability coefficients for grade levels and subtest areas are shown in Table 8-1. The data in Table 8-1 suggest that in terms of median reliability across subtests the PIAT meets minimum reliability standards for children in grades 1, 5, and 8. However, the only subtest with an acceptable median reliability coefficient (measured across grade levels) is Reading Recognition.

On the basis of the above study, the following subtests could be described as exhibiting acceptable temporal stability at the indicated grade levels: Mathematics, grades 1 and 12; Reading Recognition, grades 1, 3, 5, 8, and 12; and General Information, grades 5 and 8.

Several additional studies have examined the test-retest, split-half, and Kuder-Richardson 20 reliability of the PIAT. LaManna and Ysseldyke (1973), using 58 first-grade students, obtained test-retest results similar to those reported in the PIAT manual (Dunn & Markwardt, 1970). These authors also examined the Kuder-Richardson 20 reliability of the PIAT and obtained coefficients ranging from 0.89 to 0.90.

Using 30 Mexican-American and 30 Anglo-American students (all ranging in age from 6 to 16 years), Dean (1977) examined the split-half reliability of the PIAT. For the Mexican-American group, reliabilities ranged from 0.75 to 0.90, with a mean of 0.81. For the Anglo group, reliabilities ranged from 0.73 to 0.92, with a mean of 0.82.

Table 8-1   Median Reliability Coefficients of the PIAT

Grade Level	Reliability	Subtest	Reliability
K	0.74	Mathematics	0.74
1	0.80	Reading Recognition	0.89
3	0.77	Reading Comprehension	0.64
5	0.80	Spelling	0.65
8	0.80	General Information	0.76
12	0.79		

Modified from Dunn & Markwardt, 1970.

Validity

Validity of a test, of course, must be evaluated in terms of the proposed uses of the test (Anastasi, 1976). Dunn and Markwardt (1970) assert that the PIAT is useful as a screening instrument for assessing students' gross strengths and weaknesses. However, the PIAT appears to be in wide use as a measure of achievement in the specific subtest areas (Reynolds, 1979).

In the absence of predictive validity studies, Dunn and Markwardt (1970) report two studies of the concurrent validity of this measure. In the first reported study, the authors correlated PIAT scores with Peabody Picture Vocabulary (PPVT) scores of children in kindergarten and grades 1, 3, 5, 8, and 12. Moderate correlations were obtained between the PIAT and the PPVT at all grade levels. The median correlation was 0.57. Assuming that the PPVT does, in fact, measure educationally significant factors, the reported results provide some evidence of the concurrent validity of the PIAT.

In the second study reported by the PIAT authors, Sitlington (1970) compared PIAT and Wide Range Achievement Test (WRAT) scores of 45 educable mentally retarded students. The correlation between PIAT and WRAT mathematics scores was 0.58. PIAT and WRAT reading recognition scores exhibited a correlation of 0.95, while spelling scores exhibited a correlation of 0.85. PIAT reading comprehension and WRAT reading recognition scores exhibited a correlation of 0.90. To the extent that the WRAT provides measures of academic achievement, these results provide further evidence of the concurrent validity of the PIAT.

In a recent investigation, Reynolds (1979) examined the factorial validity of the PIAT. In other words, this researcher assessed the degree to which the PIAT measures separate and distinct factors, such as are implied by the existence of different subtests.

Reynolds' study involved 1093 students in grades 1, 3, 5, 8, and 12. Interestingly, the results indicated that only two factors account for most of the variance in PIAT scores. In other words, instead of measuring five separate factors, as suggested by the existence of five separate subtests, the PIAT, in reality, appears to measure only two.

At grades 1, 3, and 5, the two PIAT factors include what Reynold's calls Verbal Comprehension/Reasoning Skills, and Acquired Factual Knowledge. The Verbal Comprehension/Reasoning Skills factor includes the following subtests: Reading Recognition, Reading Comprehension, and Spelling. The Acquired Factual Knowledge factor includes the mathematics and general Information subtests.

At grades 8 and 12, the two PIAT factors obtained by Reynolds include Verbal Comprehension/Reasoning Skills, and Word Recognition. The former factor includes the subtests for mathematics, reading comprehension, and general information. The latter includes the reading recognition and spelling subtests.

Content validity is also important for measures of achievement (see Chapter 1, and Anastasi, 1976). Content validity refers to the extent to which a test adequately samples the domain being assessed. In the case of the PIAT, this involves the extent to which the test adequately samples items from the areas of mathematics, reading, spelling, and general information. In the PIAT manual (Dunn & Markwardt, 1970), the authors contend that content validity was "built into" the PIAT through the manner in which items were selected. The authors' description of the item selection does, in fact, provide a strong argument for the content validity of the PIAT.

Educational Usefulness

As we have mentioned, the authors of the PIAT describe the instrument primarily as a screening tool, while it is widely used as an evaluative/diagnostic instrument. Two factors indicate that its use should be mainly for screening. The first of these involves its less than optimal test-retest reliability coefficients, which suggest that overall the PIAT is not sufficiently stable for use in making major decisions about individuals.

The second factor is the PIAT's factorial structure. An instrument measuring only two broad factors cannot be expected to provide meaningful information about differential performance on five factors. The results of Reynolds' (1979) factor analysis of the PIAT strongly suggest that it should be used cautiously, in classification and not, as is common, as a measure of five areas of academic performance.

As a screening measure, the PIAT might be used in the initial steps of the classification process. That is, a child might be assessed with the PIAT to determine whether she or he exhibits deficits in general achievement. If so, the child can be further assessed to determine whether a given classification category is appropriate. Likewise, a child might be initially screened with the PIAT to determine whether subsequent diagnostic assessment is necessary.

Wide Range Achievement Test (WRAT)

The 1978 edition of the WRAT (Jastak & Jastak, 1978) represents a revision of the original 1965 version of the test (Jastak, Bijou, & Jastak, 1965). The 1978 WRAT was standardized on approximately 15,000 subjects, representing equal proportions of males and females. As with the original WRAT, the 1978 WRAT is actually two tests. One (level 1) purports to assess mathematics, reading, and spelling achievement in persons 5 to 11 years, 11 months of age. Level 2 purports to measure these same achievement domains in persons 12 to 64 years of age.

Raw scores on the WRAT may be converted into three different types of scores: grade ratings (which are essentially grade equivalent scores), percentiles, and standard scores (deviation scores). A table provided in the manual (Jastak & Jastak, 1978) also allows for the conversion of standard scores into percentiles, stanines, scaled scores, T-scores, and normal curve equivalents.

Like the PIAT, the WRAT is a normative, psychometric instrument that allows the examiner to compare a target child's achievement with that of a comparable group. This, of course, suggests that the WRAT is primarily useful in classification.

Reliability

Jastak and Jastak (1978) present the results of several reliability studies in the WRAT manual. In the first reported investigation, split-half reliabilities were computed for 2800 subjects. At level 1 (ages 5 – 11, 11 months), reliability coefficients were 0.98, 0.96, and 0.94 for reading, spelling, and mathematics respectively. At level 2 (ages 12 – 64) the coefficients were 0.98, 0.97, and 0.94 for reading, spelling, and mathematics respectively. Clearly, the results indicate adequate internal consistency for the WRAT.

The WRAT authors also present a study of the correlations between levels 1 and 2 when they are administered simultaneously. Although the two levels of the WRAT do not represent true alternate forms, since they are intended for different ages, it could be argued that correlations between these two forms represent a measure of the content stability of the WRAT. In other words, correlations between the two levels could be viewed as evidence of alternate-form reliability of the measure. The correlations between WRAT levels 1 and 2 for reading (across ages) ranged from 0.88 to 0.94, with an average of 0.91. For spelling, the correlations ranged from 0.88 to 0.94, with an average of 0.91. For mathematics, the correlations ranged from 0.79 to 0.89, with an average of 0.85. The results indicate adequate reliability across both subtest areas and age ranges.

Jastak and Jastak report an investigation of the test-retest reliability of the original WRAT, conducted by DeLong (1962). In this investigation, DeLong administered the WRAT to 77 retarded adolescents five times within a three-week period. He found that with approximately 95 percent of the subjects, the variance from administration to administration was less than 10 percent. This result seems particularly encouraging in light of the extreme practice effects possible with five administrations over a three-week period.

Validity

In a rather extensive study involving 641 individuals, Jastak and Jastak (1978) compared the WRAT scores of "deprived" (socioeconomically), nondeprived, and retarded groups. The results very clearly indicated that all three WRAT subtests could discriminate among the various groups of individuals.

To assess the concurrent validity of the WRAT reading subtest, Wagner and McCloy (1962) compared WRAT reading performance to performance on the Woody-Snagren Silent Reading Test and the New Stanford Reading Test. Correlations between scores on the WRAT and the two criterion tests ranged from 0.74 to 0.80.

An evaluation of the concurrent validity of the WRAT mathematics subtest was conducted by Murphy (Jastak & Jastak, 1978). This evaluation involved a comparison of scores from the WRAT mathematics subtest and the New Stanford Arithmetic Computation Test. Murphy also compared WRAT mathematics scores and mathematics grades. For students in grade 5, the correlation between WRAT mathematics scores and mathematics grades was 0.64. The correlation between WRAT and Stanford mathematics scores was 0.59. For students in grade 6, the correlation between mathematics grades and WRAT scores was 0.56, while the correlation between WRAT and Stanford mathematics scores was 0.35. Particularly for students in grade 5, these results provide evidence of the concurrent validity of the WRAT mathematics subtest.

Perhaps the most comprehensive validity study reported in the WRAT manual is that conducted by the U.S. Public Health Service. In this investigation, WRAT reading and mathematics scores were correlated with scores on the widely used Stanford Achievement Test for children in grades 1 through 9. For children in grades 10 through 12, WRAT scores were correlated with scores on the equally well-known and used Metropolitan Achievement Test. Although a detailed description of this major study is beyond the scope of this book, the general results should be noted. Throughout all grade levels, moderate to high correlations were obtained between Stanford and WRAT mathematics scores, and Stanford and WRAT reading scores. Also, for students in pre–high school grades, moderate to high correlations were obtained between WRAT scores and Stanford scores in the areas of social studies, science, and study skills. Quite clearly, the results of this study attest to the concurrent validity of the WRAT as a measure of important dimensions of school achievement.

Although the authors of the WRAT do not describe the results of traditional factorial validity studies (Anastasi, 1976), they do present correlations among the WRAT subtests. These data allow for an esti-mate of the extent to which the WRAT measures three separate fac-tors (mathematics, reading, and spelling) as suggested by the sub-test names. At every age range, from age 5 to adult, each WRAT subtest exhibits very high correlations with the other two subtests. These correlations range from 0.64 to 0.93, with the vast majority of correlations clustering in the 0.71 to 0.89 range. What this means is that like the PIAT, the WRAT does not appear to be measuring a num-ber of separate and distinct factors. Each subtest, as indicated by high subtest intercorrelations, is apparently measuring something that is also heavily represented in each of the other subtests.

Educational Usefulness

In the WRAT manual, Jastak and Jastak (1978) provide an ex-tensive discussion of the diagnostic use of WRAT results. We, how-ever, have some reservations about the diagnostic usefulness of the WRAT. Our reservations are based primarily on two characteristics of the test.

The first is the fact that the item content is somewhat restricted. The reading subtest, for example, consists of a number of words that the examinee simply reads and then pronounces. No attempt is made to assess aspects of the extremely important domain of reading com-prehension. Also, the WRAT authors provide no evidence that the specific letter-sound associations measured tap all or even most of those that are crucially important in the development of reading skills (Hallahan & Kauffman, 1976). Likewise, the arithmetic subtest taps only a few items from the major aspects of mathematics perfor-mance. It is very hard to believe that the WRAT can generate any meaningful generalizations about specific skill deficits in the areas of reading or mathematics.

The second characteristic that proscribes the WRAT's use as a diagnostic instrument is the very high level of intercorrelation among the subtests. These data suggest that instead of serving as a diagnostic instrument, the WRAT is best used as a gross screening instrument for overall achievement; it appears to measure global achievement rather than several distinct achievement factors or skills.

The data on the reliability and validity of the WRAT suggest that it can be useful in classification. It appears to have sufficient reliabil-ity and validity to serve as an effective screen capable of indicating either the presence of a global achievement deficit or the need for further diagnostic assessment of specific academic skills.

Both the WRAT and the PIAT appear to have some usefulness for screening or classification purposes. In terms of internal consistency, these measures are similar. However, the WRAT appears to be psychometrically superior in terms of temporal stability (that is, test-retest reliability). Both tests appear adequate in terms of concurrent validity, as measures of overall achievement.

DIAGNOSTIC TESTS

In this section, we will focus on two examples of diagnostic or criterion-referenced tests. Criterion-referenced tests attempt to provide information about what specific skills an individual child can and cannot perform (see Chapter 1, and Anastasi, 1976). A child's performance on a criterion-referenced test is evaluated not against the performance of other children but aganist the test tasks themselves: the child either can or cannot perform task x. No attention is paid to how proficient a child is in performing task x in comparison with other children.

Reliability and Validity

Criterion-referenced tests present children with various examples of specific academic tasks and measure mastery or nonmastery of the tasks. This approach of directly measuring mastery or nonmastery of a task or skill has led to controversy regarding the extent to which traditional psychometric concepts, such as reliability and validity, apply to criterion-referenced tests (Carpenter & Carpenter, 1980; Hambleton, Swaminathan, Algina, & Coulson, 1978). Before we further explore this issue, it will probably be helpful for us to take a closer look at what a criterion-referenced test really is.

As Anastasi (1976) has pointed out, criterion-referenced tests should generally exhibit the following characteristics:

- The test specifies detailed instructional objectives (for example, the student will be able to say the sounds for individual letters when visually presented with each letter).
- The test provides adequate coverage of each objective with appropriate items. (In the example just cited, appropriate coverage would be provided through the presentation of letters A through Z.)
- The test provides at least a moderate range of difficulty across items. (In the example, the letters A through Z provide the full range of difficulty for the stated objective.)

In other words, criterion-referenced tests are essentially statements of educational objectives, with a built-in means of assessing mastery of these objectives. The most crucial psychometric property of such tests involves content validity, the extent to which each objective is sufficiently covered with representative items.

As Carpenter and Carpenter (1980) have pointed out, psychometric properties are typically not stated in the manuals of criterion-referenced tests. They suggest that traditional methods for assessing the psychometric properties of these tests are sometimes inappropriate and that statistical methods for assessing the reliability and validity of these tests are still in the exploratory stages.

The points above have been raised for several years by a number of theorists and practitioners. Carver (1974), for example, in a seminal article on the radical differences between psychometric and criterion-referenced (or "edumetric") tests, pointed out that psychometric methods are often inappropriate for the measurement of progress or change. Such methods are designed for assessing differences among individuals, not differences in the same person's performance at different points in time. Criterion-referenced tests, on the other hand, are designed explicitly for the purpose of measuring changes — changes indicated by students' progress toward educational objectives. While Carver strongly argued that this difference in the functions of criterion-referenced and psychometric tests makes it illogical to evaluate the former in terms of methods designed explicitly for the latter, it should be recalled from Chapter 1 that Anastasi (1976) and Salvia and Ysseldyke (1978) have proposed that some traditional methods of evaluating reliability and validity can be applied to criterion-referenced tests.

Given the arguments of Carpenter and Carpenter, and of Carver, and the current lack of concensus about methods of judging the reliability and validity of criterion-referenced tests, we will make the following working assumptions about these tests.

- Since criterion-referenced tests, in general, directly assess a student's mastery of specific skills, the stability of such tests is as much a function of the stability of a student's skill as it is of the reliability of the test itself.
- Since criterion-referenced tests directly assess mastery of specific skills, the primary validity issue involved in such tests is the representativeness and range of the items used to assess mastery on a given skill or task.

What these two assumptions mean, practically, is that until there exists a more complete analysis resulting in scientific consensus regarding necessary technical adequacy characteristics of criterion-referenced tests, we will advocate the position that direct measures of academic behavior — the ultimate "criterion" — are *reliable* to the extent that the measured behavior is stable and *valid* to the extent that sufficient samples of the behavior to be measured are tapped. We will, therefore, confine our discussion of the reliability and validity of the criterion-referenced tests reviewed in this chapter to issues regarding content validity. Let us turn to a detailed examination of two of the most common criterion-referenced tests in use today: the Criterion Tests of Basic Skills, and the Brigance Diagnostic Inventory of Basic Skills.

Criterion Tests of Basic Skills (CTBS)

The CTBS (Lundell, Evans, & Brown, 1976) is actually two separate criterion-referenced tests, one for reading and one for mathematics. Both tests provide explicit materials and directions concerning a large number of distinct educational objectives. Students' performances on each of these objectives are classified according to three categories of mastery or nonmastery:

- *Mastery level:* A student correctly responds to 90 to 100 percent of items for an objective. Performance at this level suggests that the student has mastered the objective in question and needs no subsequent instruction on that objective.
- *Instructional level:* The student responds correctly to 50 to 89 percent of items for an objective. Performance at this level suggests that the student is currently ready (that is, has the necessary prerequisite skills) to benefit from instruction on the objective.
- *Frustration level:* The student correctly responds to 0 to 49 percent of items for an objective. Performance at this level suggests that the student has probably not mastered the prerequisite skills for this objective.

On both the reading and mathematics portions of the CTBS the objectives are arranged in what appear to be valid cumulative learning sequences. That is, the objectives are arranged so that the skills associated with each objective become progressively more complex and build upon one another. This arrangement facilitates the diagnosis of where a student is in terms of the skills necessary to perform any basic academic skill involving reading or mathematics.

Criterion Test of Basic Skills – Reading (CTBS-R)

The reading portion of the CTBS presents a wide range of items relating to 19 different reading objectives. These objectives involve 6 skill areas: letter recognition, letter sounding, blending and sequencing, special sounds, sight word reading, and letter writing. (For a complete list of the subtests and types of items in CTBS-R, see Table 8-2.)

Table 8-2   CTBS-R Subtests and Items

Letter Recognition	*Special Sounds*
Lower-Case Letters (26 items)	Consonant Blends (20 items)
Capital Letters (26 items)	Consonant Digraphs (6 items)
Letter Discrimination (12 items)	Vowel Digraphs (5 items)
Letter Sounding	Controlling *R* (5 items)
Vowels (visual-vocal) (5 items)	Final *E* (5 items)
Consonants (visual-vocal) (21 items)	Diphthongs (4 item)
Vowels (auditory-vocal) (5 items)	
Consonants (auditory-vocal) (21 items)	*Sight Word Reading* (220 items)
Blending and Sequencing	
Two-Letter Blending (10 items)	*Letter Writing (optional)*
Three-Letter Blending (10 items)	Lower-Case Letters (26 items)
Letter Sequencing (6 items)	Capital Letters (26 items)

In terms of content validity, it appears that the CTBS-R does, in fact, tap most of the basic skills involved in elementary oral reading. It does not, however, provide a measure of reading comprehension. The CTBS-R has adequate content validity for use as a measure of basic reading skills involving phonics but not necessarily of all reading skills.

Criterion Test of Basic Skills – Arithmetic (CTBS-A)

The arithmetic portion of the CTBS provides a test for mastery of 26 different mathematics objectives. These objectives involve 11 skill areas: correspondence (counting), numbers and numerals, addition, subtraction, multiplication, division, money measurement, telling time, symbol operation, fractions, and decimals and percentages. (For a complete list of the subtests and types of items in CTBS-A, see Table 8-3.) As the table shows, the CTBS-A provides tests for the mastery of a wide range of basic mathematics objectives, adequate, we believe, to demonstrate the content validity of the CTBS-A.

Educational Usefulness

The CTBS has been designed to serve as a diagnostic assessment tool. The fact that it provides measures of mastery or nonmastery of objectives allows the examiner to pinpoint those specific mathematics and reading skills in which a child is deficient. Once skill deficits are determined through the CTBS, the examiner can then use this information to develop a remediation program linked directly to areas of weakness. In fact, the CTBS manual (Lundell et al., 1976) provides a number of specific remediation strategies for each skill area that can be adapted for use in the individualized educational program (IEP) of any child. The CTBS is therefore quite useful for programming.

Table 8-3   CTBS-A Subtests and Items

Correspondence: Counting (20 items)

Numbers and Numerals
  Sequencing Numbers (6 items)
  Sequencing Numerals (12 items)
  Reading Numerals (10 items)
  Printing Numerals (10 items)

Addition
  One-Digit Numbers (5 items)
  Two- and Three-Digit Numbers: No
    Regrouping (5 items)
  Two- and Three-Digit Numbers:
    Regrouping (5 items)

Subtraction
  One-Digit Numbers (5 items)
  Two- and Three-Digit Numbers: No
    Regrouping (5 items)
  Two- and Three-Digit Numbers:
    Regrouping (5 items)

Multiplication
  One-Digit Numbers (5 items)
  One- and Two-Digit Combinations (5
    items)

Division
  One-Digit Division (5 items)
  Two-Digit Division (5 items)

Money Measurement
  Currency Recognition (6 items)
  Cent Value (6 items)

Telling Time
  Hour and Half Hour (5 items)
  Five-Minute Intervals (5 items)

Symbols: Symbol Operation (7 items)

Fractions
  Identifying Fractions (5 items)
  Improper Fractions: Mixed Numbers
    (5 items)
  Addition and Subtraction (5 items)

Decimals and Percents
  Decimals to Percents and Vice Versa
    (5 items)
  Placing the Decimal (5 items)
  Conversion among Fractions,
    Decimals, and Percents (5 items)

As a classification instrument, the CTBS is of little or no use. Since CTBS results provide only a description of what tasks a child can and cannot perform, they cannot be used directly to provide an indication of the severity of achievement problems. That is, CTBS results do not directly tell the examiner where a child stands in relation to other children of similar age.

Brigance Diagnostic Inventory of Basic Skills (BDIBS)

Like the CTBS, the BDIBS (Brigance, 1977) is a criterion-referenced measure of a number of basic academic skills. Brigance tests are grouped into four basic skill areas: (general academic) readiness; reading; language arts; and mathematics. Within each of these four areas are a number of subtests. A complete list of BDIBS subtests is given in Table 8-4. Quite clearly, the BDIBS provides for the assessment of a child's mastery of an extremely wide array of educational objectives. One advantage the BDIBS appears to have over other commonly used criterion-referenced tests (such as the CTBS) is its provision of a measure of reading comprehension and a measure of basic academic readiness skills.

Table 8-4 BDIBS Subtests

READINESS
Color Recognition
Visual Discrimination
Visual-Motor Skills
Visual Memory
Body Image
Gross Motor Coordination
Identification of Body Parts
Directional/Positional Skills
Fine Motor Skills
Verbal Fluency
Verbal Directions
Articulation of Sounds
Personal Data Response
Sentence Memory
Counting
Alphabet
Numeral Recognition
Number Comprehension
Recognition of Lower-Case Letters
Recognition of Upper-Case Letters
Writing Name
Numbers in Sequence
Lower-Case Letters by Dictation
Upper-Case Letters by Dictation

READING

Word Recognition
Word Recognition Grade-Level Test
Basic Sight Vocabulary
Direction Words (recognition)
Abbreviations (recognition)
Contractions
Common Signs (recognition)

Reading
Oral Reading Level
Reading Comprehension Level
Oral Reading Rate

Word Analysis
Auditory Discrimination
Initial Consonant Sounds Auditorily
Initial Consonant Sounds Visually
Substitution of Initial Consonant
   Sounds
Ending Sounds Auditorily
Vowels

Short-Vowel Sounds
Long-Vowel Sounds
Initial Clusters Auditorily
Initial Clusters Visually
Substitution of Initial Cluster
   Sounds
Digraphs and Diphthongs
Phonetic Irregularities
Common Endings of Rhyming
   Words

Vocabulary
Context Clues
Classification
Analogies
Antonyms
Homonyms

LANGUAGE ARTS

Handwriting
Writing Cursive Letters, Lower-Case
Writing Cursive Letters, Upper-Case
Personal Data in Writing

Grammar Mechanics
Capitalization
Punctuation
Parts of Speech

Spelling
Spelling Dictation Grade Placement
   Test
Spelling: Initial Consonants
Spelling: Initial Clusters
Spelling: Suffixes
Spelling: Prefixes

Reference Skills
Alphabetical Order
Dictionary Use
Reference Books: Index
Reference Skills: Encyclopedia
Parts of a Book: Location
Parts of a Book: Purpose
Outlining
Graphs
Maps

(continued)

205

Table 8-4 (continued)

MATHEMATICS

Mathematics Grade Level Test

Numbers
  Rote Counting
  Counting Objects
  Sets
  Numerals in Sequential Order
  Number Words
  Ordinal Numbers
  Recognition of Numerals
  Dictation of Numerals
  Counting
  Roman Numerals
  Fractional Numerals
  Fractional Parts
  Decimals

Operations
  Addition Combinations
  Addition of Whole Numbers
  Subtraction Combinations
  Subtraction of Whole Numbers
  Multiplication Combinations
  Multiplication of Whole Numbers
  Division Combinations
  Division of Whole Numbers
  Addition of Fractions
  Subtraction of Fractions
  Conversion of Fractions
  Multiplication of Fractions
  Division of Fractions
  Addition of Decimals
  Subtraction of Decimals

Multiplication of Decimals
Division of Decimals

Measurement
  Recognition of Money
  Value of Coins
  Relationship of Coins
  Making Change
  Telling Time
  Relationship of Time Units
  Conversion of Time Units
  Future Time
  Past Time
  Days, Months, Seasons
  Relationship of Calendar Units
  Use of Calendar
  Location of Special Events on
    Calendar
  Measurement with Ruler
  Relationships of Linear Units
  Conversion of Linear Units
  Relationships of Liquid Units
  Conversion of Liquid Units
  Relationships of Weight Units
  Conversion of Weight Units
  Thermometer

Geometry
  Square
  Rectangle
  Triangle
  Circle
  Cube
  Rectangular Prism
  Triangular Prism
  Cylinder

Like the CTBS, the BDIBS can be used as a means of diagnosing a child's specific academic strengths and weaknesses. As such, its primary usefulness lies in programming.

The presence of grade-level tests on the BDIBS *appears* to make the test useful in classification. However, on close inspection, it becomes apparent that the calibration of grade-level scores is far too gross for classification purposes. That is, the grade-level scores do not allow for a precise measurement of the extent of a child's deficit in academic achievement areas.

In choosing between the CTBS or BDIBS, three factors should be considered. These include (1) the amount of time one can spend in assessment (the BDIBS is the more detailed and time-consuming of the two tests); (2) the level of skill-area coverage required (the BDIBS covers a wider range of skill areas than does the CTBS); and (3) how great a need one has for an instrument that provides clear instructions for programmed remediation. We have found the CTBS manual to be quite useful in generating remediation suggestions that are closely tied to test results.

INFORMAL MEASURES

A number of theorists and practitioners have proposed the use of informal or homemade criterion-referenced tests. These procedures usually involve nonstandardized ways of either assessing a child's mastery or nonmastery of a skill or of pinpointing the exact nature of a child's difficulty on a particular skill. Most informal methods are based, at least in part, on the use of task analysis (Hallahan & Kauffman, 1976). Such methods almost invariably utilize actual classroom tasks and materials in the assessment process.

Swanson (1978) has developed an informal assessment procedure that attempts to answer three basic questions:

• What exactly do you want the child to do?
• What specific tasks are required of the child?
• What exactly does the child do when presented with each task?

Swanson's system provides the examiner with a rather detailed checklist for answering these questions. The checklist covers a wide range of areas, including cognitive and perceptual skills, modality preferences, attention skills, instructional objectives, and task analysis procedures. The stated purpose of this system is to provide highly individualized information for the development and refinement of a child's IEP.

Dickinson (1980) has developed a system for performing a highly specific analysis of children's achievement problems and generating educationally relevant remedial strategies. This system is called Direct Assessment and combines behavior analysis and task analysis principles. There are four steps in the Direct Assessment system:

Pinpointing the problem. In this step, the examiner uses the child's classroom materials and tasks to determine the specific responses with which the child is having difficulty. For example, rather than merely indicating that the child has trouble with vowel sounds, the step would generate a list of the specific vowel sounds the child has not mastered.

Determining if the (correct) response is in the child's behavioral repertoire. In this step, the examiner ascertains whether the child has ever performed the problematic task correctly. If not, the necessary response must be taught. If, however, the child sometimes (but not always) performs correctly, it is necessary to determine what events "set the occasion for," or increase the probability of, the correct response. An example of what might occur in this step is that of a child who has trouble with numeral reversals. The examiner will determine whether the child ever reproduces numerals correctly.

Determining what sets the occasion for the correct response. If the child sometimes performs the problematic task correctly, then the examiner searches for the specific events that foster the correct response so as to eventually strengthen the control of these events. In other words, the examiner determines how the learning situation can be structured so as to ensure correct performance. Following the previous example, one might find that a child makes all numerals correctly when and only when she or he covertly verbalizes rules for appropriately reproducing numerals. The examiner might then train the student to make such verbalizations more frequently.

Performing a task analysis. If, during the second step, it is determined that the correct response to a task is not in the child's behavioral repertoire, a task analysis is performed; that is, the problematic task is broken down into the basic skills or subskills needed to perform the task. Then the examiner determines which of these necessary skills are and are not in the child's repertoire. Those skills not in the child's repertoire represent the point at which instruction should start. For example, suppose a child did not possess numeral-writing skills. This step would generate a description of all relevant subskills, and the child would be evaluated to determine which subskills instruction should initially focus on (for example, holding the pencil appropriately, starting the first stroke on the line.)

Dickinson's (1980) Direct Assessment system appears to possess great potential for the diagnosis of educational problems. The primary strength of the system lies in its ability to specifically pinpoint the exact nature of a child's academic difficulties and generate remedial strategies focusing most directly on these difficulties.

As indicated, the child's academic difficulty may stem not from his or her inability to perform the required operation but from a failure on the part of the child or the learning environment to structure the task so that the correct response occurs. When the use of Direct Assessment reveals this to be the case, then remediation of the difficulty involves teaching the child or the teacher to modify the conditions under which the operation is performed so as to increase the likelihood of the child's successful performance. This strategy, more generally referred to as conditions analysis in Chapter 11, can, when appropriate, be successfully applied to a wide range of academic and behavioral problems.

As also indicated, however, the child may never perform a particular operation correctly. When the use of Direct Assessment reveals this to be the case, then the child's skills must be increased through specific training procedures. Direct Assessment can be quite usefully employed to determine the exact skills that need to be trained. This strategy, more generally referred to as skills analysis in Chapter 11, can also, when appropriate, be successfully applied to a wide range of academic and behavioral problems.

Direct Assessment can also involve an examination of the instructional procedures that might be most effective in teaching the child the specific skills he or she needs to master. At this point in the analysis, one could briefly begin teaching the child these skills, alternating instructional strategies and seeing which the child seems most responsive to. This step (illustrated in Chapter 12) would then lead to predictions about the instructional strategy most likely to be effective in further efforts to teach these skills.

As noted in Chapter 7, such predictions can also be generated from the child's performance on formal modality assessment measures. We, however, favor the use of Direct Assessment for this purpose, since predictions generated by this approach come from actual attempts to teach the child specific skills. Nevertheless, such predictions (regardless of their origin) must be tested in subsequent efforts to teach the child, and no procedure for generating predictions is always accurate. Further research and practice will be required to determine best procedures and the degree to which they can be practically applied.

A final strength of the Direct Assessment system is that it could be argued that the system also assesses and results in the remediation of perceptual skills. That is, the system assesses perceptual skills indirectly, to the extent that such skills are involved in specific academic performance.

It will be recalled from previous chapters that the definition of "specific learning disability" found in the regulations implementing PL 94-142 imply (but do not appear to actually require) the use of formal measures of psychoeducational processing (or modality) skills, and that we are somewhat uncomfortable with this implication. As we suggested in Chapter 7, there are serious questions about whether some formal measures of such skills possess adequate reliability and validity for classification purposes, and there are equally serious questions about whether the training of such skills results in improvements in academic achievement. Direct Assessment, however, is sensitive to the presence of psychoeducational processing skill deficits, and remediation following such assessment will automatically build in training of both prerequisite perceptual skills and specific academic behaviors.

For example, suppose a child's numeral writing is characterized by reversals. It might be hypothesized that a directionality problem is responsible. Evaluation by the Direct Assessment system provides behavioral information that might result in remediation of the reversal problem. If this occurs, it could then be argued that the directionality problem — *as it affects a specific academic problem* — has also been remediated along with the specific academic deficit. On the basis, then, of several lines of reasoning, we advocate that the assessment of psychoeducational processing skills be conducted in the context of direct assessments of academic skills. We believe that such an approach will lead to appropriate programming. We also believe that this approach can also be defended, if need be, for the classification of children as learning disabled.

CONCLUSIONS

Our general conclusion concerning methods for assessing academic skills is that psychometric instruments such as the WRAT and PIAT are useful primarily for classification. They are generally of limited value for diagnosis and programming. On the other hand, diagnostic systems such as the BDIBS and CTBS have utility in diagnosis and programming but are of little or no value in classification. The reason for this difference lies in the fact that psychometric measures compare children to each other, while diagnositc measures evaluate each child's acquisition of specific skills.

Informal assessment systems such as Dickinson's Direct Assessment are designed to provide information that leads directly to effective remediation, and Dickinson's system functions effectively for this purpose. We see significant potential in the use of such approaches to isolate specific academic skill problems and develop meaningful and effective remediation programs. And, perhaps one of the most appealing features of the Direct Assessment system is that it provides a conceptual framework that allows each assessment practitioner to develop his or her own "homemade" tests that can be adapted to almost any imaginable assessment problem.

Assessment of Social/Emotional Functioning

ALTHOUGH VARIOUS METHODS EXIST for conceptualizing social/emotional behavior problems in children, extensive empirical research during the past decade has clearly demonstrated that effective treatment stems most often from assessment approaches that focus on specific problematic behaviors (Marholin, 1978; Ross, 1980). Furthermore, specific problem behaviors are currently viewed in terms of two basic categories: deficit behaviors and excess behaviors (Hersen & Bellack, 1976). *Deficit behaviors* refer to behaviors that occur at an excessively low rate and are problematic because of their low rate. For example, if a child's rate of social approach behavior in play settings is so low as to interfere with appropriate social behavior, the child may be described as having a deficit in social approach behavior. *Excess behaviors*, on the other hand, refer to behaviors that are problematic because they occur at an excessively high rate. An example would include a rate of fighting behavior that is so high as to interfere with the development of friendships with peers.

On the basis of current research and practices that rely heavily on the concepts of behavioral specificity and of deficit and excess behaviors we propose the following formal operational definition of social/emotional behavior problems: *social/emotional behavior problems are characterized by the presence of specific rates of overt (externally observable) or covert (directly observable only by the subject) behaviors that interfere with appropriate social or educational functioning.* This definition includes (but is not limited to) such problems as excessive physical or verbal aggressive behavior toward peers or adults, low rates of social interaction, low rates of compliance with adult instructions, excessive disruptive behaviors, excessive anxiety resulting in avoidance behavior, and excessive episodes of depression.

PURPOSES OF SOCIAL/EMOTIONAL ASSESSMENT

Methods for assessing social/emotional problems are needed for several reasons. The first of these is the inclusion in Public Law (PL) 94-142 of the handicapping category of *emotionally disturbed*. Some states label this category *behaviorally disordered*, which the present authors find both more accurate and less stigmatizing. In order to receive special education services, children with behavior disorders must be classifiable under either category, and the classification process must, of course, involve systematic procedures.

In addition to the requirements of the behavior disorder category, measures of social/emotional adjustment are also mandated by PL 94-142 in the classification of a child as learning disabled. Specifically, a learning disabled classification *cannot* be made if the child's learning problems are primarily the result of emotional disturbance (behavior disorder), among other factors. Therefore, in order for a learning disabled classification to be made, a child's social/emotional functioning must be assessed in order to rule out a social/emotional basis for the child's learning problems.

A third factor that emphasizes the importance of social/emotional assessment in psychoeducational settings is the relatively large number of school-aged children who exhibit serious social/emotional problems. Glidewell (1967) has provided data based on teacher reports that indicate that approximately 30 percent of all children aged 5 through 13 present some psychological problems. His data further indicate that approximately 9 percent of all children in this age group are in need of immediate intervention. This is very similar to the National Institute of Mental Health's estimate of a 10 to 12 percent prevalence rate of moderate to severe emotional problems in school-aged children (Engel, 1972). Although exact estimates appear to vary (Ross, 1980), most professional psychologists would agree that there are large numbers of children in our society who are currently having serious difficulties in coping and who are in need of assessment and intervention (Blau, 1979). Since the school system is the only agency with which practically all children interact on a long-term basis, school personnel have a unique vantage point for identifying those children who are in need of social/emotional intervention. It is, therefore, crucial that the psychoeducational assessment practitioner have well-developed skills for conducting assessments of social/emotional functioning.

GOALS OF ASSESSMENT

In order to fully address the objectives of classification and programming, assessment must accomplish four goals. These include (1) specification of the precise nature of the problem, if a problem in fact exists; (2) determination of the severity of the problem; (3) description of the child's treatment needs; and (4) description of specific treatment objectives.

Problem Specification

Target Behaviors. In order to accurately analyze a referred social/emotional behavior problem, it is necessary that the problem first be conceptualized in terms of the specific behaviors (target behaviors) that constitute the problem (Dickinson, 1978; Kazdin, 1980). Frequently, a child's problem is described by mediators (teachers, parents) in ambiguous terms. They may say, for example, "Johnny's problem is that he has no respect for authority." This statement provides little clear information about Johnny's problem except that Johnny has difficulty getting along with authority figures. It does not tell us *what he does* when he has no respect for authority figures. If, in the course of further discussions with mediators, we find that Johnny frequently makes obscene gestures and statements to his teachers and parents, we then have a much clearer and more useful description of the problem. A description of a problem in terms of specific target behaviors allows the assessment specialist both to verify the existence of the problem and to perform further analyses of factors related to the problem.

Functional Analysis. Once a referred problem has been conceptualized in terms of target behaviors, a functional analysis may be performed to determine the environmental events that are integrally related to the occurrence of the problem behavior. A functional analysis involves an examination of the environmental events that precede and follow the problem behaviors (Dickinson, 1978; Kazdin, 1980). Events that precede the behavior are viewed as "setting events," or *antecedents*, that serve as cues for the behavior. Events that follow the behavior are viewed as *consequences* that can either strengthen or weaken the behavior. Of particular importance are consequent events that may serve as reinforcing events, functioning to maintain the rate of the behavior. Once antecedent and consequent events have been identified and reliably measured, a treatment program can be designed to change the target behavior(s) by modifying the antecedents and consequences (Kazdin, 1980).

It should be noted that the foregoing discussion of functional analysis assumes that the target behavior is present in the child's repertoire of behaviors. Suppose, however, that the target behavior involves a behavior deficit. A functional analysis of a behavior deficit would require that the specialist determine (1) what situations should serve as antecedents for the behavior (that is, under what circumstances the behavior should be occurring), and (2) what consequences could be used to maintain the target behavior. A determination of desired antecedents and consequences provides the basis for remediating a behavior deficit, since remediation can be accomplished through the provision of the desired antecedents and consequences in the context of successive approximation procedures (Kazdin, 1980).

The end result of problem specification should be a statement of which of a child's behaviors must be changed in a specific direction in order for that child to function most adaptively. In addition, the statement should include a description of environmental events that must be altered in order for such behavior changes to occur.

Determining Severity

As Ross (1980) has recently pointed out, there exists no absolute definition of what constitutes a behavior disorder. Certainly, we can categorize a given target behavior as either a deficit or excess behavior, and we can perform functional analyses in order to obtain the information necessary for modifying the behavior. But when is a given excess behavior excessive enough to warrant classification (as a handicapping condition) and treatment? When is a deficit behavior deficient enough to warrant classification and treatment? Since the assessment specialist must make decisions regarding both classification and treatment of children with social/emotional problems, the determination of the severity of a problem is an important undertaking.

There are basically two avenues for establishing criteria to use in judging the severity of problems: (1) the use of objective, statistical norms (of a national, regional, or local nature), and (2) the use of subjective, local norms. The use of statistical norms involves the administration of standardized instruments in order to compare the referred child's responses or a mediator's descriptions of his or her behavior to that of the norm group. One of the most common examples of such a procedure is the use of normative behavior checklists, which will be discussed in greater detail later in this chapter. A child's teacher may be asked to complete a checklist that includes a number of statements about children's behavior. The teacher may be instructed to identify those items that characterize the referred child's behavior. If, for example, on a particular checklist, the referred child receives significantly more affirmative responses on those items indicating behavior disorder than does the average child of the same age, the child could be classifiable as behaviorally disordered. Furthermore, on the basis of the child's statistical deviance the assessment specialist could predict the intensity of the treatment required to remediate the child's problems.

Objective statistical norms of a local nature have been utilized with behavioral observation data. For example, Melahn and O'Donnell (1978) observed a wide range of behaviors of 186 preschool children and computed average rates of each behavior of interest. Whenever a child was referred for social/emotional problems, these local norms provided an objective means of determining the relative severity of the child's problems. O'Donnell (1977) has argued that such behavioral norms allow a consultant or assessment specialist to determine (1) whether a referred problem actually exists; (2) whether intervention is necessary; and (3) what specific behaviors should be targeted for intervention.

Although statistical norms provide relatively objective criteria, their use has not been as wide as one might expect. Traditionally, school behavioral consultants have utilized subjective, local norms for the determination of severity (Halfacre & Welch, 1973; Tharp & Wetzel, 1969; Tomlinson, 1972). The norms in this case are not true statistical norms but represent subjective norms adhered to by mediators (for example, parents, teachers) in a child's environment. In other words, these norms are mediators' views of appropriate behaviors and rates of behaviors under certain conditions. The behavioral consultant typically allows mediators to determine (within ethical limits) the behaviors that will be observed and targeted for intervention, implicitly making the assumption that if a competent mediator views a behavior as highly problematic then it is probably severe enough to warrant observation and possibly intervention. Certainly, competent behavioral consultants discuss with mediators the relevance of various behaviors targeted for observation and intervention. However, the consultant's decision to observe (and possibly intervene upon) a particular behavior is usually quite subjective and based on both the consultant's and the mediator's subjective judgments of what constitutes a severe problem for a given behavior in a classroom or home situation.

Describing Needs

A handicapped child's needs must be specified for the purpose of programming, according to federal regulations. In the case of behaviorally disordered children, the description of the child's needs usually focuses on necessary intervention procedures and the setting(s) in which intervention should take place. The results of the psychoeducational assessment should clearly delineate the specific child behaviors and environmental events (for example, teacher or parent behaviors) that need to be changed in order for the child to function most adaptively. The specification of target behaviors and environmental events alone facilitates specification of appropriate intervention procedures, since a vast literature describing intervention procedures effective in the treatment of specific types of problems exists (for example, Gambrill, 1977; Kazdin, 1980; Marholin, 1978). In addition, an appropriate assessment will indicate what resources are available, and these data will assist in determining the setting in which intervention will take place.

The basic format and setting for intervention can be classified into three categories: (1) indirect intervention, (2) direct intervention, and (3) cross-setting intervention. The selection of a particular format depends upon both the availability of resources and the needs of the child. Indirect intervention involves consultation with the relevant mediator(s) about ways to facilitate the child's functioning. For example, a consultant may assist a teacher in designing, implementing, and evaluating a behavior change program for a behaviorally disordered child (Meyers, Parsons, & Martin, 1979). Direct intervention involves a specialist's working directly with the child, usually on a one-to-one basis (Workman & Dickinson, 1979, 1980). This can take place in an individual setting outside the classroom (for example, in the guidance office) or within the classroom itself. An example of the latter might involve a consultant's entering a child's classroom and directly prompting and reinforcing desired behaviors in the context of naturalistic classroom activities. Cross-setting intervention involves consulting with both parents and teachers in order to facilitate the child's functioning at school. For example, a child's parents may be asked to contingently reward a child when certain behaviors have occurred at school each day as indicated by a note from the classroom teacher (Gambrill, 1977).

Stating Treatment Objectives

In order for the effectiveness of a behavior change program to be evaluated, it is necessary that the objectives of treatment be stated in clear and measurable terms (Kazdin, 1980). The statement of objectives, which should be written directly into the individualized educational program (IEP), should specify (1) the behavior(s) to be changed, (2) the direction in which the behavior will be changed (that is, whether it will be increased or decreased), (3) the setting in which the behavior change will occur, (4) the degree of change desired, and (5) the time limit for attaining the objective. For example, this might represent an acceptable objective for a child with a severe deficit in social approach behaviors: "Within three months of the present date, Genevieve will increase her rate of interaction with other children on the playground from the present rate of 15 percent (of the time period in which she is observed) to 60 percent." Compare this objective with the following: "Genevieve will improve her social behavior on the playground." Obviously, the former objective allows for clear, unequivocal evaluation, whereas the latter objective merely states an ambiguous desire that is difficult to evaluate.

SPECIFIC TECHNIQUES

This section will focus on four primary methods of assessing social/emotional functioning. The methods include the use of behavior checklists, interviewing, behavioral observations, and projective techniques. Each method will be discussed in terms of its use in providing data that fit into one or more of the four assessment goals. No attempt will be made to catalog and describe all of the methods available. However, we do describe the general features and uses of each methodological category and discuss representative instruments within each category.

Behavior Checklists

Behavior checklists usually consist of lists of behaviors that mediators (or, in some cases, referred children themselves) are asked to evaluate. More specifically, mediators are instructed to indicate whether a particular behavioral characteristic is part of the referred child's behavioral repertoire. In the case of some checklists, the mediator may also be instructed to indicate the extent to which the child exhibits a particular behavior (for example, "seldom," "occasionally," "frequently").

Behavior checklists may be either norm-referenced or criterion-referenced. Our discussion will focus initially on the former type. Norm-referenced checklists allow for the comparison of the referred child's score (based, for example, on the number of behavior items checked) to the scores of the children in the normative sample, providing a measure of the child's relative standing on the factor being measured. As indicated previously in this chapter, normative checklist data provide one means of determining the severity of a child's behavior problems. For example, suppose that a particular checklist has an aggressive behavior scale with a mean of 10 and a standard deviation of 3. If a child receives a score of 17 on this scale, it could be concluded that the child's level of aggressive behavior as measured by this scale is greater than 2 standard deviations above the mean. (A more detailed treatment of basic statistical principles can be found in other texts such as Anastasi [1976] or Sax [1980]). It would follow that this child's level of aggressive behavior is greater than that of approximately 97 percent of the children in the norm group, a finding that relates rather clearly to judgments of the severity of the child's problem.

A rather large number of norm-referenced behavior checklists that can be used by the assessment specialist to assess a wide variety of behavior domains are commercially available. Walls, Werner, Bacon, and Zane (1977) have compiled an extensive catalog of such instruments (as well as criterion-referenced scales) that provides a brief description of each scale. The interested reader is referred to this compilation. Our purpose here, as indicated, is to describe several representative instruments that we believe to be of particular value to the assessment specialist.

Walker Problem Behavior Identification Checklist (WPBIC)

This instrument (Walker, 1970) is designed for use with elementary school children and was standardized on a sample of 534 children in the fourth, fifth, and sixth grades. It consists of 50 statements about children's observable classroom behaviors that were judged to interfere with successful academic performance. A referred student's classroom teacher (who has informally observed the student for at least two months) is asked to complete the checklist by indicating which of the behaviors (if any) are in the child's repertoire.

The 50 behavior statements in the WPBIC are grouped into five broad categories of behavior disorder, including acting out, withdrawal, distractibility, disturbed peer relations, and immaturity. A child receives a raw score on each of these scales, on the basis of the number of behavior statements characterizing his or her behavior and the weighting of each statement in terms of its influence in handicapping school performance. Raw scores are then converted to T-scores that are plotted on the profile chart. The profile chart is reproduced in Figure 9-1. The T-scores for each scale provide a means of judging the severity of a child's problems, since these scores can be viewed in terms of standard deviation units.

In terms of reliability and validity, the WPBIC meets minimal criteria of acceptability. The Kuder-Richardson split-half reliability coefficient reported in the manual is 0.98, indicating very high interitem consistency. Furthermore, validity data for contrasted groups are provided, indicating that WPBIC can clearly differentiate between behaviorally disordered and non–behaviorally disordered children (Walker, 1970). Perhaps the strongest evidence of the WPBIC's validity is represented by the instrument's factorial structure. Factor analytic studies conducted by Walker (1970) indicate that the behavior statement items cluster rather neatly into the five global behavior disorder categories.

Although the WPBIC should be strengthened by further research focusing on its temporal stability and ability to differentiate among children with various types of behavior disorder, it does appear to represent a means of improving upon the typically subjective judgment of severity of social/emotional problems. In addition, it can also serve as a starting point in the specification of a child's problem. Although the behavior statements are not objective and specific enough for detailed problem specification, they can provide the assessment specialist with hypotheses to explore in further detail, using the interview methods to be described shortly.

Burks' Behavior Rating Scales (BBRS)

The BBRS is designed for use with students in grades one through nine. (A preschool and kindergarten edition of the BBRS is also available [Burks, 1977]. This edition is structurally analogous to

Figure 9-1 (following page)   WPBIC profile chart. (From Walker, H. *Walker Problem Behavior Identification Checklist*. Los Angeles: Western Psychological Services, 1970. Copyright © 1970, 1976 by Western Psychological Services, 12031 Wilshire Boulevard, Los Angeles, California 90025. Reprinted by permission.)

Walker Problem Behavior Identification Checklist

Revised 1976

by Hill M. Walker, Ph.D.

Published by

WPS **WESTERN PSYCHOLOGICAL SERVICES**
PUBLISHERS AND DISTRIBUTORS
12031 WILSHIRE BOULEVARD
LOS ANGELES, CALIFORNIA 90025

A DIVISION OF MANSON WESTERN CORPORATION

Name: _____ School: _____

Address: _____ Grade: _____

Age: _____ Sex: M F   Date: _____ Classroom: _____

Rated By: _____ Position of Rater: _____

INSTRUCTIONS

Please read each statement carefully and respond by circling the number to the right of the statement if you have observed that behavioral item in the child's response pattern during the last two month period. If you have not observed the behavior described in the statement during this period, do not circle any numbers (in other words, make no marks whatsoever if the statement describes behavior which is NOT present).

Examples:

1. Has temper tantrums ....
2. Has no friends ....
3. Refers to himself as dumb, stupid, or incapable ....
4. Must have approval for tasks attempted or completed. ....

Scales

1	2	3	4	5
②	①	4	3	

Statements 1 and 4 are considered to be present while statements 2 and 3 are considered to be absent. Therefore, only the numbers to the right of items 1 and 4 are circled, and the numbers to the right of 2 and 3 are NOT circled.

Profile Analysis Chart (PAC)

	Scale 1		Scale 2		Scale 3		Scale 4		Scale 5		
	Acting-out		Withdrawal		Distractibility		Disturbed Peer Relations		Immaturity		
T-Score	Male	Female	Male	Female	Male	Female	Male	Female	Male	Female	T-Score
Over 110			20-26					7-11			—

the original.) The item-selection sample included 200 students from the Los Angeles County Schools, half of whom were placed in special education classes and half in regular classes. The checklist consists of 110 behavior statements that are indicative (to some degree) of behavior problems. These statements were selected on the basis of their ability to differentiate between the two groups of students in the standardization sample (Burks, 1977).

Each of the 110 behavior statements is rated by a child's teacher or parent on a 5-point scale. The five rating categories include (1) "You have not noticed this behavior at all"; (2) "You have noticed the behavior to a slight degree"; (3) "You have noticed this behavior to a considerable degree"; (4) "You have noticed this behavior to a large degree"; and (5) "You have noticed this behavior to a very large degree." The rater assigns a number (1–5) to each statement on the basis of these rating categories. The 110 statements are grouped into 19 behavior problem subscales (Table 9-1). The total raw score for each of the 19 subscales is the sum of the weighted ratings (1–5) for each statement in the scale. Raw scores are plotted on the profile sheet and fall into one of the following ranges: not significant (indicating that no serious problems exist in this area); significant (indicating the presence of social/emotional problems); and very significant (indicating the presence of very serious social/emotional problems). The manual provides a set of "norms," based on samples of 494 elementary school children and 60 seventh- and eighth-grade children from regular classrooms, which indicate the percentage of children falling into each range on each behavior disorder category. These data can be used to judge the severity of a referred child's problems relative to those children in the "norm" sample, by comparing the child's score on a given scale to that received by the majority of children in the "norm" group.

In terms of reliability and validity, the BBRS appears to be minimally acceptable at best. In a study reported in the manual, test-retest reliability coefficients for each behavior statement (using a 10-day interval) ranged from 0.60 to 0.83, with a mean of 0.71 (Burks, 1977). However, the ratings of only 2 out of 110 statements were significantly different (at $p < 0.05$) from test to retest. Burks describes research indicating that the BBRS can discriminate between referred and nonreferred students, representing evidence of contrasted-groups validity. Furthermore, Burks' factor analytic studies suggest that the scale can differentiate between children with different types of handicapping conditions (for example, educable mentally retarded, learning disabled, physically handicapped, and speech/hearing impaired) on the basis of differential problem category clusters among the four groups.

Table 9-1 Behavior Problem Subscales of the BBRS

Excessive Self-Blame	Poor Impulse Control
Excessive Anxiety	Poor Reality Contact
Excessive Withdrawal	Poor Sense of Identity
Excessive Dependency	Excessive Suffering
Poor Ego Strength	Poor Anger Control
Poor Physical Strength	Excessive Sense of Persecution
Poor Coordination	Excessive Aggressiveness
Poor Intellectuality	Excessive Resistance
Poor Academics	Poor Social Conformity
Poor Attention	

Although many of the 19 BBRS subscales describe highly subjective and ambiguous entities (such as "poor ego strength"), the scale itself does appear to provide an adequate means of estimating the severity of a child's behavior problems. As with the WPBIC, an inspection of BBRS behavior statements should also provide a starting point for more detailed problem specification. One note of caution is necessary, however. Burks (1977) suggests that a major purpose of the BBRS is to assist in differential diagnosis. In light of the absence of data indicating the subscales' abilities to differentiate among children with different types of behavior problems, the differential diagnostic use of the instrument should be confined to the differentiation between children with behavior disorders (regardless of type) and those with other handicapping conditions.

Personality Inventory for Children (PIC)

This instrument has the same format as the Minnesota Multiphasic Personality Inventory (MMPI; Hathaway & McKinley, 1951) but is designed for use with children aged 6 to 16. (A version of the PIC is available that is designed for use with children ranging in age from 3 to 5 years.) The PIC boasts a normative standardization sample of 2390 public school children — 100 males and 100 females at each age level from 5½ to 16½ years (Wirt, Lachnar, Klinedinst, & Seat, 1977). The PIC itself consists of 600 behavior statements to which the referred child's parent (preferably the mother) responds on a yes or no basis. These 600 statements are template-scored in such a manner as to yield raw scores on 16 major variables. (Scoring keys for 17 supplemental scales are also available.) These raw scores are converted to T-scores on the PIC profile, allowing for the normative comparison of a referred child to the normative sample. A sample PIC profile form is shown in Figure 9-2. The 16 major variables purportedly measured by the PIC form 4 validity and screening scales and 12 clinical scales. The validity scales, which screen the respondent, include the Lie Scale, a measure of the respondent's tendency toward

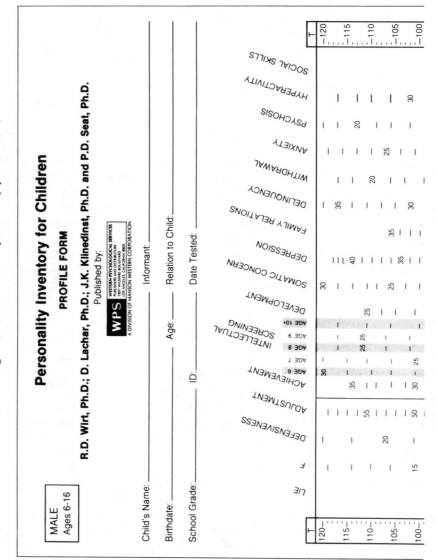

Figure 9-2 PIC profile forms for males and females. (From Wirt, R., Lachar, D., Klinedinst, J., & Seat, P. *Multidimensional description of child personality: A manual for the Personality Inventory for Children.* Los Angeles: Western Psychological Services, 1977. Copyright © 1977 by Western Psychological Services, 12031 Wilshire Blvd., Los Angeles, Calif. 90025. Reprinted by permission.)

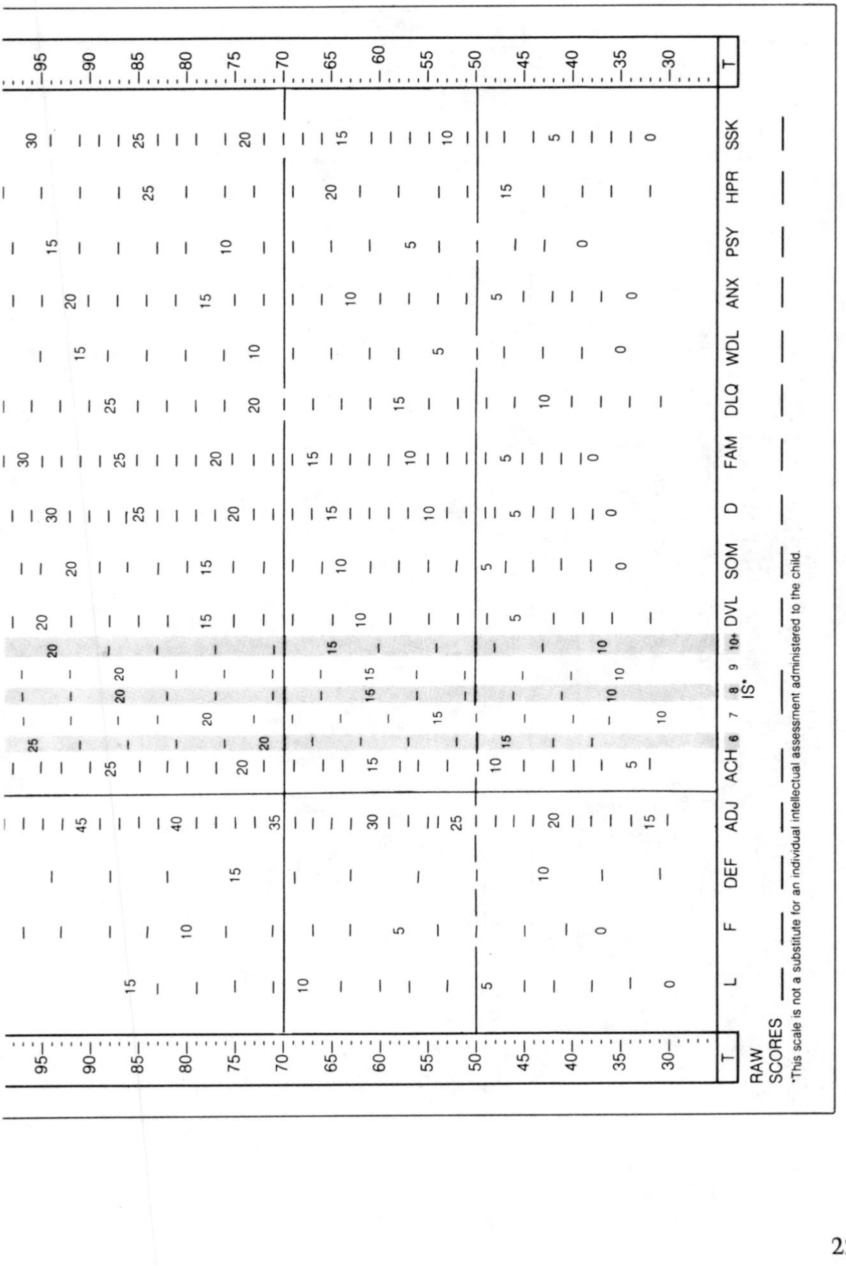
T
L
F
DEF
ADJ
ACH
IS*
DVL
SOM
D
FAM
DLQ
WDL
ANX
PSY
HPR
SSK
T
RAW SCORES

*This scale is not a substitute for an individual intellectual assessment administered to the child.

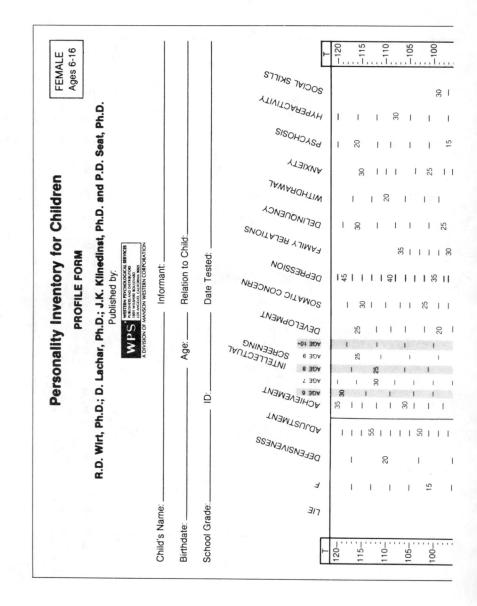

Personality Inventory for Children

PROFILE FORM

R.D. Wirt, Ph.D.; D. Lachar, Ph.D.; J.K. Klinedinst, Ph.D. and P.D. Seat, Ph.D.

Published by:

WPS | WESTERN PSYCHOLOGICAL SERVICES
PUBLISHERS AND DISTRIBUTORS
12031 WILSHIRE BOULEVARD
LOS ANGELES, CALIFORNIA 90025
A DIVISION OF MANSON WESTERN CORPORATION

FEMALE
Ages 6-16

Child's Name: _____

Informant: _____

Birthdate: _____ Age: _____ Relation to Child: _____

School Grade: _____ ID: _____ Date Tested: _____

T ... 95 90 85 80 75 70 65 60 55 50 45 40 35 30

SSK HPR PSY ANX WDL DLQ FAM D SOM DVL IS* ACH ADJ DEF F L

RAW SCORES

T 95 90 85 80 75 70 65 60 55 50 45 40 35 30

*This scale is not a substitute for an individual intellectual assessment administered to the child

protecting the child and family from close scrutiny; the F Scale, a measure of the respondent's tendency to exaggerate "symptoms" or respond to items randomly; and the Defensiveness Scale, a measure of the respondent's tendency to be defensive about the child's behavior. Elevations of these scales are indicative of an essentially uninterpretable profile. The Adjustment Scale is a screening scale designed to function as both a screening device for behavior problems and a general measure of poor psychological adjustment.

The 12 clinical scales assess the extent to which a wide range of possible child behavior problems are present. Although the factors measured by each scale are sometimes diverse and complex, it will be worthwhile to describe these factors briefly. The Achievement, Intellectual Screening, and Development scales provide global measures of difficulties in the areas of school achievement, cognitive skills, and physical development, respectively. The Somatic Concern Scale is a general measure of the extent to which a child exhibits symptoms of health problems that may have a functional basis. The Depression and Anxiety scales measure clusters of behavior associated with feelings of severe depression, and irrational fears and worries, respectively. The Withdrawal and Social Skills scales measure degree of social isolation and difficulties in interaction with peers, respectively. The Psychosis and Delinquency scales measure the extent and presence of psychotic behaviors, and the presence of rule-violating and noncompliant behavior, respectively. The Family Relations Scale provides a measure of the degree of conflict in the child's family. The Hyperactivity Scale measures the degree to which the child exhibits overactivity, distractibility, and difficulties in concentrating.

Reliability and validity data on the PIC were obtained during two decades of research and are simply too massive to discuss in detail in this text. Briefly, several test-retest reliability studies with varying retest intervals have provided a mean reliability coefficient of 0.86 (Wirt et al., 1977). The only scale with truly questionable reliability is the defensiveness scale. In terms of validity, it should be pointed out that many PIC scales were designed on the basis of the criterion-related validity of individual items (Darlington & Bishop, 1966). That is, the items were selected on the basis of their ability to distinguish between clinical groups. Exceptions to the procedure include the following scales: Lie, F. Development, Depression, Family Relations, Withdrawal, and Anxiety.

Although Wirt et al. (1977) describe several methods for interpreting PIC profiles (for example, linear scanning of the profile, examination of the unique configuration of profile scores), the most productive approach for the purposes described in this chapter is a linear scanning of the profile in order to determine which, if any, of the clinical scales are elevated to a T-score of 70 or above. Such a score indicates that the assessment specialist may attribute to the child the characteristics measured by that scale. In other words, the child probably has problems (in the area measured by the scale) that are severe in comparison to the normative sample. This linear scanning approach also allows the specialist to isolate those global areas within which it might be fruitful to inspect individual behavior statement items for the purpose of facilitating specification of the problem.

While the PIC represents an extremely well-constructed and potentially useful behavior checklist, several cautionary notes are in order. The first involves the fact that norms are available only for protocols completed by a child's parent. This negates the possibility of using PIC data obtained from a classroom teacher as a means of establishing normative severity estimates. The assessment practitioner could, however, ask the teacher to complete the PIC solely for the purpose of initial specification of the problem, ignoring normative considerations. Another possible limiting factor stemming from the required use of parental respondents involves a question of the accuracy of parental report. Lobitz and Johnson (1975) have provided data suggesting a frequently questionable relationship between parental reports of child behavior (obtained through checklists) and direct observations of child behavior. These data underscore the need to use the PIC and other behavior checklists only in the context of a total assessment package including direct observations and interviews. The data also suggest the need for further research focusing on the relationship between high and low PIC scores and observations of children's behavior.

Behavior Rating Profile (BRP)

This instrument is unique among behavior checklists in that it provides a normative evaluation of a child's overall adjustment from the perspective of teachers, parents, peers, and the child. Whereas the other checklists described in this chapter group behavior statements into various behavior disorder categories, the BRP groups statements into categories based on different environments in which a child functions. The instrument is intended for use with children in grades two through seven and is based on a standardization sample of 1326 students, 645 teachers, and 847 parents (Brown & Hammill, 1978).

The BRP is actually a compact set of four scales including student rating scales, teacher rating scales, parent rating scales, and sociograms. The student rating scales require the referred child to respond on a true false basis to 60 statements indicating the presence of behaviors common to home, classroom, and peer interaction situations. A separate raw score, indicating degree of adjustment (or absence of problems) is computed for each of these three situations. The teacher scales are completed by one, two, or three of the referred student's classroom teachers. Each scale consists of a list of 30 statements describing inappropriate classroom behavior that each teacher rates in terms of the degree to which a given statement characterizes the referred student ("very much like the student," "like the student," "not much like the student," "not at all like the student"). Raw scores, based on the degree to which the statements do not characterize the student, are computed for each teacher completing the scale. The parent scales are essentially identical to the teacher scales, except that the statements of inappropriate behavior focus on home rather than classroom situations. Raw scores can be computed for one or both parents.

The BRP sociogram is actually a peer nominating procedure rather than a behavior checklist or scale. All of the students in a referred child's classroom are presented with pairs of stimulus questions provided by the BRP manual (Brown & Hammill, 1978). These questions require the students to indicate the three students with whom they would most and least like to interact in some activity. These activities can include having lunch, working on a school project, working on school tasks, and playing at home after school, among others. Raw scores on the sociogram (for each selected activity) are based on the referred student's sociometric rank, as indicated by the relative number of peer acceptances and rejections the student receives.

Raw scores on the BRP scales and the sociogram are converted to scaled scores and plotted on the profile form. These scaled scores have a mean of 10 and a standard deviation of 3. An example of the BRP profile form is seen in Figure 9-3. According to the manual, scaled scores between 7 and 13 inclusive indicate a statistically normal level of adjustment. Scaled scores greater than 13 indicate a higher than average level of adjustment, while scores below 7 are indicative of adjustment problems that are serious, relative to the standards of the norm group.

The reliability and validity data provided by the BRP manual indicate that the instrument is sufficiently reliable and valid for general use (Brown & Hammill 1978). The average reported Kuder-Richardson reliability coefficient (across grade levels and BRP scales) is approximately 0.86 (ranging from 0.74 to 0.98). The Student

Scale: School for students in grades 6 and 7, and the Student Scale: Home for grades 2 and 3 are, however, of questionable reliability, with coefficients below 0.80. As no test-retest reliability data are currently available, future research is needed to address the temporal stability of the BRP.

Evidence of concurrent and contrasted groups validity are provided by Brown and Hammill (1978) in the form of high correlations with other behavior checklists, and data demonstrating the ability of the BRP to differentiate between "normal" and behaviorally disordered children. These data suggest that the BRP can be useful in obtaining normative estimates of the severity of children's behavior problems. Although most behavior checklists can be used to assist in the initial identification of problem behaviors (through an inspection of checklist items), the BRP provides the added advantage of an ecological categorization of problems. That is, not only can items be inspected to determine what behaviors, if any, may be problematic, but a child's various environments can be inspected and compared in terms of the presence of particular problems.

The psychometric purist may be somewhat disappointed by the absence of data demonstrating the ability of these normative behavior checklists to yield an accurate differential diagnosis of types of behavior disorders. Although we could clearly agree with such criticism, we should point out that we do not advocate the use of behavior checklists in differential diagnosis. We advocate only that norm-referenced behavior checklists be used to quantitatively supplement subjective clinical judgment, behavioral observations, and consensus norms in the determination of the severity of a child's behavior problems. We also suggest that behavior checklists can be useful in problem specification by providing the assessment specialist with clues about areas in need of further exploration.

Before concluding this section, we will briefly discuss the criterion-referenced behavior checklists mentioned earlier in this chapter. This type of checklist is, in most, cases, simply a list of specific child behaviors that a mediator identifies as being problematic owing to their presence or absence in the child's behavior repertoire (Gambrill, 1977). No attention is given to the normative significance of the mediator's description of the child's behavior, since, by definition, norms are not provided. Although formal criterion-referenced checklists are available (Walls et al., 1977) practitioners frequently develop "homemade" criterion-referenced behavior checklists consisting of behaviors of particular interest in their practice setting. The usefulness of this type of checklist lies exclusively in their use as an aid in initial problem specification.

Figure 9-3 BRP profile form. (From Behavior Rating Profile. © 1978 by Linda L. Brown and Donald D. Hammill. Reproduced by permission of the publisher, PRO-ED, 5431 Industrial Oaks Blvd., Austin, Tex. 78735.)

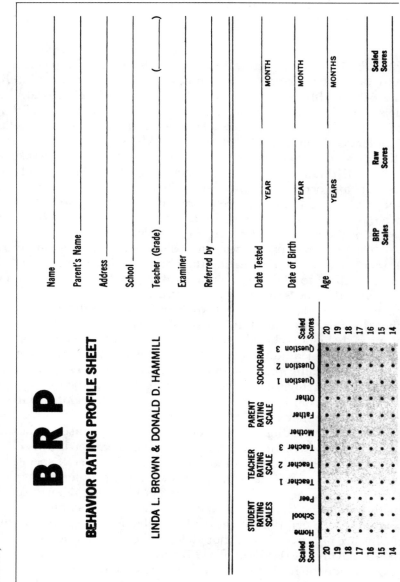

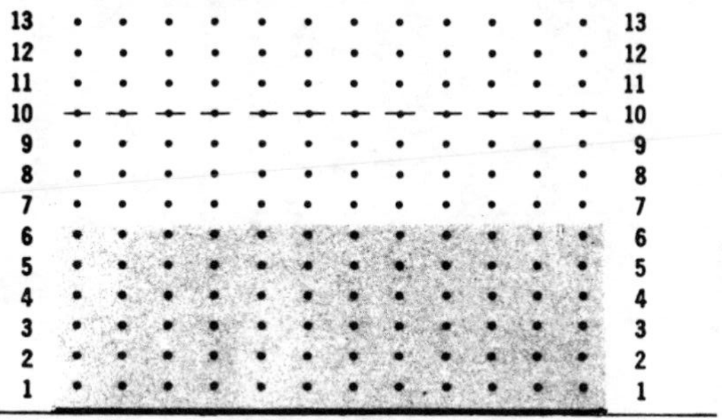

13
12
11
10
9
8
7
6
5
4
3
2
1

(Scaled Scores: Mean = 10, Standard deviation = 3)

COMMENTS:

Student Rating Scales

Home Scale

School Scale

Peer Scale

Teacher Rating Scale

Teacher # 1

Teacher # 2

Teacher # 3

Parent Rating Scale

Mother

Father

Other

Sociogram

Question # 1

Question # 2

Question # 3

233

A particularly important variation of criterion-referenced behavior checklists is the reinforcer checklist (Atkins & Williams, 1972; Cautela & Kastenbaum, 1967). These checklists consist of lists of potentially rewarding events that the student is asked to rate in terms of their desirability. Those events that are rated highly may be useful as contingent reinforcers in the modification of problem behaviors.

Behavioral Interviewing

Interviewing probably represents the most universal of assessment procedures (Marholin, 1978). It is the primary assessment tool used by practitioners of varying orientations for diagnosing a wide variety of problems. In the course of behavioral interviewing, the assessment specialist discusses the referred child's behavior with the classroom teacher, parent, or the child him- or herself in order to obtain a clear behavioral description of the child's problem(s). The behavioral interview also provides a primary means of determining antecedent and consequent events that are functionally related to the problem behaviors, and other factors that are important in the problem specification and treatment planning process (such as duration of the problem, types of interventions previously attempted, and severity).

A number of writers have proposed models or general guidelines for assessment interviews with teachers or parents (Bergan, 1977; Dickinson, 1978; Holland, 1970; Marholin & Bijou, 1978; Wahler & Cormier, 1970). Although these models vary slightly in terms of focus and question context, they yield a general interview strategy that includes six basic steps. These include (1) determining general areas of concern to the mediator; (2) obtaining a behavioral description of the problem; (3) obtaining a description of antecedent and consequent events; (4) determining the strength and duration of the problem behavior; (5) determining what interventions have been attempted in the past; and (6) determining resources available for resolving the problem.

Step 1.   In the first step, the interviewer attempts to elicit broad, general descriptors clarifying the problem(s) that have led to the referral of the child. Although questions usually relate to the referral problem, results of behavior checklists may prompt the interviewer to explore problems other than those initially presented (Marholin & Bijou, 1978). Examples of questions that the interviewer might use to elicit general descriptions of problems are:

- "What types of difficulties is _____ currently having?"
- "Describe _____'s problems."
- "The checklist you completed indicated that _____ is also having trouble in interacting with peers. Describe these problems."

Step 2. In the second step, behavioral description, the interviewer questions the mediator in such a manner as to elicit descriptions that pinpoint specific behaviors. The interviewer encourages the mediator to describe the problem in terms of discrete and observable behaviors, rather than vague, ambiguous generalities:

- "You indicated that _____ has trouble relating to peers. What, exactly, is she doing or not doing when she's having such trouble?"
- "When _____ is being disruptive in class, what is she doing? Is she talking out, getting out of her seat, or what?"
- "You said she fights with peers. What is she doing when she fights—is she hitting, calling names, or what?"
- "You indicated that _____'s problem is that she's defiant. Give me some examples of what she does when she's being defiant."

Step 3. Descriptions of antecedent and consequent events can take place once the problem has been described in terms of specific target behaviors. This is accomplished by the interviewer's questioning the mediator about what happens before and after the target behavior occurs. During this step the interviewer also isolates the specific environments (mathematics class, reading class, the lunchroom) in which the problem occurs. This is particularly important in light of data clearly indicating that most child problem behaviors occur in specific situations (Dickinson, 1978; Wahler, 1969). These data imply that the presence of a problem in one setting (for example, aggressive behavior in mathematics class) in no way indicates that the problem exists in other settings (recess, home, reading class). The setting(s) in which a problem occurs must be accurately determined in order to focus intervention strategies on only the relevant settings. To elicit descriptions of antecedent and consequent events as well as relevant settings the interviewer might say,

- "Describe what usually happens just before _____ begins to hit and scream at peers."
- "Describe what usually happens immediately after _____ hits and screams at peers." "What do the peers do?" "What do you do?"

- "Describe the usual sequence of events surrounding _____'s episodes of hitting and screaming at peers."
- "Where exactly do these episodes usually occur?" "Do they occur only in certain classes, on the playground, at lunch?"

Step 4.   In determining strength and duration of the problem behavior, the interviewer elicits descriptions of how frequently the target behavior occurs, how long each episode of the behavior lasts, and how long the child has exhibited the behavior. Currently, the strength of a child behavior disorder is measured in terms of its frequency per time unit and the length of time during which episodes of the behavior occur (Marholin & Bijou, 1978; Ross, 1980). Estimates of the strength of a target behavior, as well as data indicating its duration, can be used by the interviewer to make subjective judgments of the severity of the problem. As we have mentioned, optimal use of such data should include concurrent examination of the results of normative behavior checklists. To elicit information about the strength and duration of the problem, the interviewer might say,

- "How many times per day (on the average) would you say that _____ hits and kicks peers?"
- "Whenever _____ sobs and cries in class, how long would you say each episode usually lasts?"
- "When did _____ first start hitting and kicking peers?" "Do you know of any unusual events taking place in her life around that time?"
- "You indicated that _____ has been hitting peers since the beginning of the year. Have any of her previous teachers indicated that this occurred prior to this year? When?"

Step 5.   The next step in the interview is to determine what, if any, specific interventions have been attempted in the past. Obviously, if a child has been referred, any past intervention attempts directed toward the referral problem have been unsuccessful. The interviewer determines the nature of previous intervention attempts in order to avoid using ineffectual procedures again. For example, suppose that Samantha's teacher has attempted to decrease her hitting behavior by immediately and contingently placing her in a "time-out" area whenever she has hit someone. Samantha's teacher refers Samantha and reports that this procedure was ineffective. This report clearly indicates to the interviewer (who determines that the time-out procedure itself was used appropriately) that the teacher's time-out area does not, in reality, serve to remove Samantha from a reinforcing environment. The interviewer will then seek other procedures that have a higher probability of success. The interviewer wants to know not only what procedure has been attempted but also how the attempted procedure was implemented. Lack of an effect may be the result of either ineffectiveness of the procedure itself, owing, perhaps, to inappropriateness of selected "reinforcers" or "punishers" or inappropriate implementation (noncontingent presentation of reinforcers or punishers) (Kazdin, 1980). To elicit statements about previous intervention, the interviewer might say,

- "What exactly have you done to try to increase _____'s social approaches toward peers on the playground?"
- "Give me an example of how you used the procedure recommended by the consultant from the mental health center."
- "You say you punished _____ each time she refused to comply with your requests. Exactly how did you punish her? How soon after the act did you punish her?"
- "Did you praise _____ after each time she approached another child, or did you praise once in a while, whenever you could?"

Step 6.   In determining available resources, the interviewer attempts to isolate those persons and events in a child's environment that can be relied upon in the implementation of an intervention plan. This step is particularly crucial, since many intervention strategies involve the use of persons who are "natural" to the child's environment (such as teachers, parents, teacher aides) (Gambrill, 1977; Meyers, Parsons, & Martin, 1979). In regard to resource persons, the interviewer attempts to determine realistically who is available (in terms of time) and capable of becoming involved in a program to meet the child's needs. For example, who in the child's environment can monitor his or her behavior and contingently reinforce some particular behavior? Can the school counselor place the child in a social skills development group? In terms of resource events, the interviewer primarily attempts to isolate objects and events that are readily available and can be used as reinforcers or punishers to strengthen or weaken a target behavior. These data can, of course, be used in conjunction with information from reinforcer checklists. In order to isolate resource events, the interviewer questions the teacher or parent about objects with which the child likes to play, events the child seeks, and behaviors the child frequently engages in. Regarding the latter, research has indicated that a high-frequency behavior can be used contingently to positively reinforce a low-frequency behavior. This is known as the Premack Probability Principle (Gambrill, 1977;

Kazdin, 1980). In order to find out about available resources, the interviewer might ask,

- "Who in her school environment is _____ most affectionate toward? How responsive is she to that person's praise?"
- "What kinds of activities in the classroom does _____ most like to engage in?"
- "Our data indicate that _____ must initially be praised each time she approaches another child on the playground. We need someone toward whom _____ is responsive and who is willing to do this consistently. What are the possibilities?"

So far in our discussion, we have focused on six interviewing steps that provide information valuable to both classification and programming, particularly when used in the context of data from a normative behavior checklist and behavioral observation. These steps have focused entirely on interviews with mediators. As Ross (1980) has indicated, however, interviews with the referred child him- or herself can sometimes provide valuable information, depending on the age of the child. Such interviews can potentially focus on the same areas as interviews with adult mediators, including the child's perceptions of the problem, antecedent and consequent events, behavior strength and duration, and reinforcing persons and events. Interviews with the child regarding antecedent and consequent events can be particularly valuable in the identification of covert events (such as anxiety, or negative self-statements) that may be functionally related to overt behavior problems (Meichenbaum, 1977). In addition, interviews with the child, particularly when viewed in conjunction with any available standardized test data (screening tests of intelligence, for example), can yield an indication of the child's verbal/cognitive skills. Such indications can be used to ascertain what level of verbal and cognitive skill are appropriate for the child's behavior therapy (Workman & Dickinson, 1979, 1980).

Behavioral Observation

Clearly, the hallmark of effective behavioral assessment is the use of behavioral observation (Kazdin, 1980; Ross, 1980). These procedures involve the direct systematic observation of a referred child's behavior in the setting(s) in which problematic behaviors are occurring. For example, if a child's problems are reportedly occurring on the playground, observations would be taken on the playground, not in settings irrelevant to the problem. Furthermore, the child's behavior is observed on more than one occasion, over a period of time. Observations of behavior can be made by the assessment practitioner or by persons trained by the practitioner, including teachers, aides, parents, or volunteers (Ross, 1980).

Functions

Behavioral observation procedures serve a number of functions in relation to classification and programming. These functions include (1) objective verification of the existence of problem behaviors, as well as antecedents and consequences indentified in interviews with mediators; (2) assistance in the verification of estimations of the severity of the problem, based upon the observed strength (frequency) of the behavior; and (3) provision of a means for evaluating the effects of intervention procedures.

In regard to the latter function, several clarifications should be made. Systematic observations of a referred child's behavior are usually taken during a specific time each day, for 5 to 10 days prior to any intervention. This period is referred to as the *baseline period* (Kazdin, 1980; Williams & Anandam, 1973). The baseline period allows the assessment practitioner to examine an objective record of the child's target behavior(s), indicating the average rate of the behavior, as well as the extent of the behavior's temporal variability. Following the baseline period, intervention procedures designed to change a behavior can be implemented, while observations of the child's behavior continue. The rate of a given behavior during the baseline period can then be compared to the rate of the behavior during the intervention period, allowing for a direct evaluation of whether the behavior actually changed in the desired direction.

In addition to a simple comparison of baseline- and intervention-period rates of behavior, single-subject research designs are available that allow one to determine whether there is a functional relationship between the intervention procedure and changes in behavior. The most common examples of such designs include the "reversal" design and the "multiple baseline" design (Kazdin, 1980). In the reversal design, the intervention procedure is temporarily removed and then reinstated, in order to determine whether behavior rates coincide with the presence (or absence) of the intervention. In multiple baseline designs, intervention is implemented at different points in time in relation to various behaviors of a given child, in various settings, or with different children with the same target behaviors. The purpose of this temporal "staggering" of intervention across behaviors, settings, or children is to determine whether a behavior changes (that is, increases or decreases) when, and only when, intervention is implemented. Both reversal and multiple baseline designs allow the assessment specialist to determine whether observed changes in behavior are a function of the intervention or of other unrelated, extraneous factors. For a more detailed discussion of these and other single-subject designs, the interested reader is referred to Kazdin (1980) or Gambrill (1977).

Techniques

Static and Functional Observation.   Behavioral observation procedures fall into two broad categories: "static" and "functional" observations (Williams & Anandam, 1973). Static observations consist of observations only of the referred child's behavior. Functional observations entail the observation of both the child's behavior and antecedent and consequent events in the child's environment. A static observation, for example, may consist only of observations of a child's social approach behaviors on the playground, while a functional observation would also involve observing events that precede and follow each social approach behavior. Functional observation is required for initial assessment purposes, while the static approach is sufficient for evaluating the effect of intervention upon target behaviors.

Recording Systems.   After specific behaviors have been selected for observation (on the basis of interview and checklist data), a recording system must be selected upon which to base either static or functional observations. The most widely used recording systems include frequency recording, interval recording, and duration recording (Kazdin, 1980; Williams & Anandam, 1973).

In *frequency recording*, the observer continuously monitors and records (on an observation sheet or mechanical device) the number of times a target behavior or antecedent/consequent event occurs within a specified observation period. For example, suppose one is observing for 30 minutes each day during mathematics class, a child's behavior of talking out without permission. At the beginning of the 30-minute observation period one begins observing the child. Each time the child talks out without permission, one makes a mark on the recording sheet. At the end of the 30-minute period, the frequency of talking out is totaled and, for purposes of analysis, can be expressed in terms of the rate of the behavior per observation period or rate per minute (rate per minute is figured by dividing frequency of behavior by duration of observation in minutes). As subsequent observations are taken, the daily rates of behavior can be graphed (with number of instances on the ordinate and days on the abscissa), permitting visual inspection of trends in the data or of temporal relationships of a cyclical nature (Kazdin, 1980). If antecedent and consequent events (such as teacher or peer attention) are also recorded and graphed, the assessment specialist can inspect the data for possible relationships between the rates of these events and the target behavior.

Frequency recording is not appropriate for all target behaviors. As Williams and Anandam (1973) point out, this measurement system is most useful and efficient for discrete behaviors that are likely to occur at a moderately high rate (getting out of seat, talking out, hitting, and so forth). It is minimally useful with behaviors that occur infrequently but have long durations once they occur. Take, for example, crying. If one recorded the crying of a child with this method, one might find that the child cried only once during a 30-minute period, a rate of 0.03 per minute. Suppose, however, that that one crying incident occurred continuously for 20 minutes, or 67 percent of the observation period. The frequency system would obviously yield an inaccurate description of the child's behavior.

In *interval recording*, the observation period is divided into a number of equal time intervals. The observer observes and records the child's behavior only at specified intervals (for example, every 10 seconds, as indicated by a watch or tape recording device), rather than observing continuously as in frequency recording. The interval recording system, unlike the frequency system, can be used with an infinitely wide variety of behaviors. Two basic variations of this system are available (Williams & Anandam, 1973): on-the-count recording and full interval recording.

In *on-the-count recording*, the observer observes the child's behavior only at the beginning of each specified interval and then records the results of the observation during the remainder of the interval. More specifically, this procedure involves (1) looking at one's watch until a specific time period (such as 10 seconds) has elapsed; (2) observing the child for approximately 1 to 2 seconds in order to determine what behavior the child was engaging in at that moment or whether she or he was engaging in a particular behavior of interest; and (3) recording the results during the remaining portion of the interval. These three steps are continued throughout the observation period (Williams & Anandam, 1973). At the end of the observation period, the percentage of observation intervals during which a given behavior occurred is computed. The percentage occurrence for a given behavior is taken as a measure of the strength of that behavior during the observation period.

In *full interval recording*, the observer observes a child for the duration of a specified interval (such as 10 seconds) and then records the results during a subsequent interval (perhaps 5 seconds). For example, throughout an observation period an observer might be cued by a tape recording to begin observing a child, observe for a 10-second period, and then be cued to record for 5 seconds. During the 5-second recording period, the observer may either simply record whether a given single behavior occurred during the interval or may record all behaviors that occurred during the interval. (If all behaviors occurring were recorded, a coding system would be needed in order to allow for differentiation among behaviors occurring simultaneously.) Whether a single behavior or multitude of behaviors is observed and recorded depends entirely upon the type of data needed by the assessment practitioner. If only a single behavior is clearly indicated as a problem behavior by mediators, observations may focus only upon this single behavior. However, if a number of behaviors are indicated or if the specialist suspects problems other than those indicated, it would be wise to utilize measures of a broader range of behaviors.

Regardless of the number of behaviors observed and recorded, the initial analysis of full interval data consists of computing the percentage of the occurrence of each behavior. This is done by dividing the number of intervals during which a behavior occurred by the total number of intervals in the observation period. For example, if an observed child engaged in social interaction during 26 intervals and the total number of intervals during an observation was 120, the percentage of occurrence of social interaction behavior would be 26/120 x 100, or 22 percent. Such percentage data from both on-the-count and full interval recording can be graphed and analyzed in a manner analogous to that described for data from frequency recording.

Duration recording involves the measurement of the time period during which a behavior occurs (Ross, 1980; Williams & Anandam, 1973). The observer begins recording (usually with a stopwatch) upon initiation of a behavior and terminates recording whenever the behavior terminates. This procedure yields a total time duration for a behavior, which is computed as a percentage of the total observation period. For example, a child is observed during a 50-minute recess period. The child is observed crying for 15 minutes during one incident and 13 during another, yielding a total duration of 28 minutes. The child's crying behavior, therefore, occurs at a percentage rate of 28/50 × 100, or 56 percent of the observation period. Although this system can be used in measuring behaviors where duration is of primary concern, it is not without limitations. The most obvious limitation is that only one behavior can be observed during an observation.

Imagine the difficulty (and frustration) of attempting to simultaneously monitor and record the durations of three or four behaviors, each of which is being initiated and terminated at different points in time.

Comprehensive Observation Systems

Homemade Systems. It should be apparent from the previous discussion that an assessment practitioner can design his or her own observation system by selecting behaviors of interest, defining the behaviors (of course, in measurable terms), and selecting a recording system compatible with the behaviors to be observed. Although most observation systems used by practitioners are of such a homemade nature, several behavioral researchers have developed comprehensive systems for measuring a wide range of behaviors and environmental events in applied settings. For example, Williams and Anandam (1973) developed a system for use in the classroom focusing on task-relevant behaviors, time off task, social interaction, and various disruptive behaviors. In addition to the coding of these behavior categories, the observer also records the situation in which each behavior occurs (lecture, seatwork, small-group discussions). O'Leary, Kaufman, Kass, and Drabman (1970) developed a classroom observation system that focuses on nine behavior categories, including "out-of-chair," "modified out-of-chair," touching others' property, vocalization, playing, "orienting," noise making, aggression, and time off task.

Ecological Assessment of Child Problem Behavior. Perhaps the most comprehensive behavioral observation system has been developed by Wahler, House, and Stambaugh (1976). This system Ecological Assessment of Child Problem Behavior, is an ecologically oriented behavioral observation system that can be used in both school and home settings. A full interval recording system alternating 10 seconds of observation with 5 of recording is used to monitor 19 types of child behaviors and 6 types of environmental stimulus events. The categories included in this system are presented in Table 9-2. (The categories are not described here in sufficient detail for reliable scoring. The interested reader should consult Wahler et al. [1976].) Categories 1 through 6 describe antecedent and consequent events. The others (7 – 25) describe child behavior.

The Wahler et al. (1976) observation system represents an extremely useful tool for the assessment of social emotional behaviors, since it allows for the observation of a wide range of child behaviors

Table 9-2 Observational Categories in the Ecological Analysis
of Child Problem Behavior

1. Instruction, Nonaversive: direct instructions from an adult
2. Instruction, Aversive: same as no. 1, but instruction has aversive content
3. Social Attention, Adult, Nonaversive: adults make contact with child
4. Social Attention, Adult, Aversive: same as no. 3, but adult's contact is aversive
5. Social Attention, Child, Nonaversive: another child makes contact with the observed child
6. Social Attention, Child, Aversive: same as no. 5, but child's contact is aversive
7. Compliance: child complies with adult instructions
8. Opposition: child violates a rule or fails to comply with instructions
9. Aversive Opposition: same as no. 8, but child's behavior is aversive
10. Complaints: whining, crying, vocal protests
11. Sustained Schoolwork: full interval of teacher-assigned activity
12. Sustained Work: full interval of activity on nonacademic task
13. Sustained Attending: full interval of attending to people, objects, or activity
14. Social Approach, Adult: child makes contact with adult
15. Social Approach, Child: observed child makes contact with another child
16. Social Interaction, Adult: child interacts with adult
17. Social Interaction, Child: observed child interacts with another child
18. Sustained Toy Play: full interval of play with toys/objects
19. Self-Stimulation: body manipulation
20. Object Play: repetitive manipulation of object
21. Sustained Noninteraction: child fails to interact with objects or people for full interval
22. Self-Talk: verbalization not directed toward another
23. Mand, Adult: child directs command at adult
24. Mand, Child: observed child directs command at another child
25. Slash: behavior not scorable under any other category

as well as stimulus events. Further, observers trained in the use of the system are able to reliably record behaviors in terms of the coding categories. Inter-rater reliabilities are generally above 0.80, at least for the most frequently occurring categories (Wahler et al.). In addition to its use in problem verification, severity estimation, and evaluation of intervention effects, the provision of a means for reliable and simultaneous observation of a variety of behaviors allows for the investigation of "behavior covariation phenomena" (Wahler, 1975). Recent research (Kara & Wahler, 1977; Wahler, 1975) indicates that certain behaviors of an individual child may tend to "covary," or exhibit membership in the same response class. That is, behaviors may cluster, so that if one behavior is systematically changed, related behaviors (that is, those in the same response class) will also change, even though no systematic attempt is made to change them. Wahler (1975) has demonstrated correlational procedures that allow for the prediction of behavior covariation. Such prediction procedures provide for (1) the possibility of indirect behavioral intervention (for example, a readily changeable behavior might be modified in order to change a more resistive behavior in the same response class), and (2) the monitoring of possible side effects or unintended effects of behavioral intervention.

Reliability and Validity

As Salvia and Ysseldyke (1978) have implied, direct sequential observation procedures move toward resolving many of the reliability and validity problems associated with traditional single-administration psychometric instruments. Reasons for this involve the fact that (1) behavioral observations are taken frequently, thus directly measuring any temporal instability inherent in the data, and (2) such observations do not generally attempt to make generalizations to extremely different situations. Reliability and validity issues associated with behavioral observation do, however, warrant discussion.

Reliability. The type of reliability relevant to behavioral observation is inter-rater or interobserver agreement reliability (Kazdin, 1980; Kent & Foster, 1977). This refers to the extent of agreement between two independent observers (that is, those who do not see each other's recorded data) regarding the incidence of the behavior(s) being observed. Although several factors such as objectivity of behavior codes and number of categories would be expected to influence reliability (Kent & Foster), inter-rater reliability is usually not viewed as a constant characteristic of an observational system, as is the case with psychometric procedures. Rather, it is viewed as a characteristic of a particular observer using a particular system. That is, it is the observer who exhibits some degree of reliability when using a system, not the system itself.

It is generally agreed that a measure of inter-rater reliability should be obtained during observer training and then once during each condition of observation—that is, during baseline and intervention periods. Data are generally considered usable only if reliability coefficients greater than 0.85 (or 85 percent) are obtained. Reliability measurement is accomplished by having two observers (who are, of course, familiar with the observation categories) observe the child simultaneously.

Several methods are available for computing reliability coefficients on the basis of the data obtained by the two observers (Kazdin,

1980). When frequency data are used, reliability is computed by dividing the smaller frequency by the larger frequency and multiplying by 100. Likewise, when duration data are used, the smaller total duration is divided by the larger duration and multiplied by 100. The computation of reliability is slightly more complex with interval data. Two methods are generally used for analyzing such data, one considered liberal and one conservative (Wahler, 1975; Wildman, Erickson, & Kent, 1975). In the liberal method (also called "agreement reliability"), the number of intervals on which the two observers agree on the presence or absence of a behavior is divided by the total number of intervals (that is, sum of agreements plus disagreements) and multiplied by 100. In the conservative method (also called "occurrence reliability"), only those intervals on which either observer scores the presence of the behavior are used in reliability computation. In other words, the reliability coefficient is based only on agreements and disagreements on intervals where at least one observer scores an occurrence of the behavior.

Traditional reliability computation procedures (such as those described above) have been criticized because they do not take into account chance agreement between observers (Kent & Foster, 1977) Kent and Foster suggest several methods for remedying this problem, including (1) the computation of chance agreement against which the obtained reliability coefficient is compared, and (2) the use of the Kappa statistic (Cohen, 1960), which computes an agreement (liberal) reliability coefficient that is corrected for chance agreement. The interested reader should consult Kent and Foster for a more detailed discussion of these procedures.

Validity.   Direct observations of behavior have frequently been used as the criterion against which the validity of psychometric measures has been evaluated (Ross, 1980). This practice assumes that direct observations provide the ultimate measure of behavioral reality. Furthermore, it is assumed that if different observers agree that a behavior occurred at a given point in time, then the behavior must have actually occurred. In other words, the observations of the behavior are valid, on the basis of the consensus. From this line of reasoning, it follows that the higher the inter-rater agreement (reliability) for a given set of observations, the greater the degree of validity that can be attributed to the observations (Cone, 1977; Ross, 1980). Although the validity of observational data can be evaluated, to a large extent, in terms of obtained levels of inter-rater reliability, several other factors that can influence validity warrant brief discussion.

Observer bias refers to the tendency of an observer to commit systematic errors in rating children's behavior. This can involve an observer's underrating or overrating a student on a given behavior category in a direction dictated by the observer's expectations (Wildman, Erickson, & Kent, 1975). For example, if told that an attempt is being made to increase a student's social interaction behavior, the observer may expect an increase in this behavior and be more likely to rate the behavior as occurring than if no expectational set had been induced. Although there is conflicting evidence on the prevalence of observer bias (Kass & O'Leary, Note 8; Kent, O'Leary, Diament, & Deitz, 1973), Wildman et al. suggest that attempts can be made to minimize bias by avoiding the communication (to observers) of hypotheses regarding changes in the child's behavior. In those applied settings where this is not possible (as when a classroom teacher is both observing a child's behavior and implementing intervention), the number of reliability checks should be maximized, or the primary observer's data should be complemented with data periodically obtained from a less potentially biased source.

Observer drift refers to changes in reliability over time (Ross, 1980). In other words, following training, an observer may exhibit an acceptable inter-rater reliability, but the observer's inter-rater reliability may decrease as time passes. Given the relation between reliability and validity, such changes would probably influence validity in a negative manner. Kent, Kanowitz, O'Leary, and Cheiken (1977) suggest that one means of minimizing this threat to validity would be to increase the frequency of reliability checks. Periodic retraining of observers would also probably minimize drift.

Subject reactivity refers to changes in a child's behavior as a function of being observed. Nelson, Kapust, and Dorsey (1978) have provided methodologically sound evidence clearly suggesting that little if any reactivity occurs when children are observed in classroom situations. However, Lipinski and Nelson (1974) and Johnson and Lobitz (1974) present evidence indicating that home observation may result in substantial reactive effects on parent–child behavior patterns. Johnson and Lobitz suggest that reactivity in the home may be minimized through the use of long adaptational periods during which a family might adjust to the presence of an observer. These researchers also suggest that reactivity effects on validity may be assessed through the use of additional measures such as paper and pencil procedures (for example, behavior checklists).

Setting generality refers to the extent to which the results of observation in one situation (mathematics class in the morning) are generalizable to other situations (reading class after lunch). As Cone (1977) points out, validity becomes a potentially problematic issue in behavioral observation if results are assumed to have setting generality. For example, suppose we observe a child's fighting behavior in mathematics class and assume that the rate of fighting behavior there is similar to the rate in reading class. Given acceptable inter-rater reliability and the absence of observer bias and drift, the mathematics class observation can be viewed as a valid indicator of the child's behavior in mathematics class. But is the observation also a valid indicator of the child's behavior in reading class? This is an empirical question that would require data clearly demonstrating a strong relation between the child's behavior in the two settings. In the absence of such setting generality data, the assessment practitioner should make no attempt to generalize from one situation to another. If the practitioner needs information from both mathematics and reading situations, it would be wise to obtain observations in both settings, in order to avoid using observations that are valid for one setting but not for another.

Behavioral observations, we believe, provide the assessment practitioner with the most useful and accurate source of data on social/emotional functioning. Particularly when used in conjunction with behavior checklists and interviews, observational data allow the practitioner to diagnose, classify, and evaluate the treatment of behavior problems in a highly precise, empirical manner that simultaneously takes into account the richness and variety of human behavior.

Projective Techniques

Projective techniques generally involve asking the child to respond to relatively unstructured stimuli. In responding, the child is believed by some to structure the unstructured material in a manner that reflects some aspects of his or her psychological functioning. In other words, the child is believed to project his or her personality onto the instrument (Anastasi, 1976).

Rorschach Technique

The two most widely used projective techniques are the Rorschach Technique (Rapaport, Gill, & Schafer, 1968; Rorschach, 1942) and the Thematic Apperception Test (TAT) (Rapaport et al., 1968; Tomkins, 1947). The Rorschach Technique consists of a set of 10 inkblots that the examinee is asked to describe. In addition to eliciting a general description of each inkblot, the examiner questions the examinee about certain aspects of each inkblot to which responses were given. Although a number of scoring and interpretational systems have been developed for the Rorschach Technique (Anastasi, 1976), most systems include the categories of (1) location (the part of the inkblot to which the examinee responds); (2) determinants (form, color and movement features of a response); and (3) content (the presence of human figures, animal figures, anatomical parts and so forth). On the basis of the types of responses within each category, the examiner supposedly derives a global, psychodynamically based description of the examinee's personality.

Since the initial inception of the use of the Rorschach Technique, a number of different scoring systems have been developed. One of the primary problems of earlier systems was their extremely low level of inter-rater reliability (Zubin, Eron, & Schumer, 1965). That is, if two or more experienced raters examine a child's Rorschach responses, it is likely that the raters will derive radically different interpretations. This characteristic prompts the question of whether instruments such as the Rorschach Technique are, in fact, measuring the child's projections, or not.

Recent "innovations" in Rorschach scoring systems (Exner, 1974) claim to have moved toward improvements upon earlier systems by objectifying the scoring of some categories. However, the manuals for the Exner (1978) system fail to provide consistent inter-rater reliability data for all scoring categories. Several studies of test-retest reliability are reported, but such data reflect stability measures that would be considered inadequate by most standards. For example, Exner (1974) reports that for a seven-day retest interval with adult nonpatients, reliability coefficients ranged from 0.51 to 0.93, with a mean of 0.78. Assuming that Exner's system has improved inter-rater reliability through increased objectivity in scoring, the problem of inter-rater error variance on a number of scoring categories has been superceded by the problem of temporal instability.

As Anastasi (1976) has so emphatically pointed out, a test must be reliable before it can be valid. Clearly, the reliability problems of the Rorschach Technique have taken their toll on the instrument's concurrent and predictive validity. As early as the late 1950s, Elkins (1958) found that, contrary to clinical expectations, non–emotionally disturbed children exhibited significantly more Rorschach "danger signs" than did disturbed children. Other studies (for example, Draguns, Haley, & Phillips, 1967) have found essentially no significant relationship between children's Rorschach responses and the occurrence of problem behavior. Finally, Exner (1974) fails to provide validity evidence based on well-controlled and adequately designed investigations. These results call into serious question the use of the Rorschach with children for purposes of either classification or diagnosis.

Thematic Apperception Test (TAT)

The TAT consists of 19 pictures of vague black and white scenes involving people and 1 blank card. The examinee is asked to make up a story describing each scene, indicating what events led up to the scene, what is happening in the scene, and what is going to happen next (Tomkins, 1947). Interpretation of the TAT is highly subjective and involves determining the "hero" of each scene and the major "need themes" expressed in the examinee's descriptions.

Although the TAT is designed for use with individuals 4 years of age or older, Bellak (1975) developed a children's version, the Children's Apperception Test (CAT), for use with children between the ages of 3 and 10. The CAT consists of pictures of animal scenes that are designed to evoke descriptions related to common childhood problems (such as sibling rivalry or toilet training).

Jensen (1970) reports several studies of the reliability of the TAT. Interscorer reliability coefficients ranged from 0.54 to 0.91, with a mean of 0.77. Internal consistency (split-half) reliability coefficients had a mean of 0.13. Clearly, the TAT exhibits inadequate reliability, making its use highly questionable, at best.

Jensen (1970) also reviewed studies of the criterion validity of the TAT. He found that there existed no demonstrable relationship between TAT fantasy material and either behavioral "traits" or diagnostic classifications. What this means, simply, is that a person's descriptions of TAT scenes represent behaviors that are functionally unrelated to other "clinically significant" behaviors. These results suggest that the TAT is neither sufficiently reliable nor valid for use in classification or diagnosis. Children's responses to the CAT are interpreted in a manner analogous to that of the TAT, focusing on themes of needs and conflicts that the child projects onto the pictures. This suggests analogous validity problems.

Bender Visual-Motor Gestalt Test (BGT)

As indicated in Chapter 7, the BGT is primarily purported to measure perceptual-motor skills. However, it is also used as a projective technique (Koppitz, 1963, 1975). As a projective technique, the BGT is purported to yield, in the way that children copy the test drawings, several indicators of various emotional problems. These indicators include confused order of drawings, wavy lines, dashes substituted for circles, increasing size of figures, large figures, small figures, heavy lines, and fine lines. The presence of such factors supposedly suggests the possibility of various types of emotional problems.

The Koppitz manual for the BGT (1975) provides data regarding the reliability of the BGT emotional indicators. Two types of reliability information are needed, however: test-retest and inter-rater reliability. If BGT indicators are to be used in making meaningful predictions about a child's behavior, they should, at the least, exhibit (1) some degree of temporal stability and (2) consistency from one examiner to another. The absence of data with which to evaluate BGT emotional indicators on these two dimensions makes it impossible to recommend their use. Hopefully, future research will allow an evaluation of their reliability.

In terms of criterion-related validity, Koppitz (1975) cites several studies indicating that "emotionally disturbed" children exhibit BGT emotional indicators more often than do "nondisturbed" children. However, Trahan and Stricklin (1979) recently found no relationship between systematic teacher ratings of student behavior and either the total number of BGT indicators or any specific indicator. Gregary (1977) also failed to find a relationship between the Devereux Child Behavior Rating Scale, a behavior checklist designed to screen serious behavior problems, and specific BGT indicators. The results of these two studies present serious questions about the validity of BGT emotional indicators.

Projective Drawings

Methods using projective drawings include instruments such as the Draw-a-Person test (Urban, 1963) and the Human Figure Drawing Test (Koppitz, 1968). Such measures are used projectively in that the examiner interprets the individual's drawings in terms of what emotions, needs, and personality characteristics are "projected into" the drawings. In other words, the individual's drawings are viewed as reflections of his or her "psychological world," including perceptions, needs, conflicts, fears, and response predispositions.

Projective drawing techniques appear to be in relatively wide use with children. However, neither their reliability nor validity has been clearly established.

Myers (1978), using an "objective" scoring system for figure drawings, found that emotional indicators could be used to differentiate groups of emotionally disturbed and "adjusted" children, with disturbed children exhibiting a greater number of emotional indicators. McPhee and Wagner (1976), however, found that emotional indicators appeared significantly more often in the drawings of "normal" children than in those of seriously disturbed children. Pihl and Nimrod (1976) found that although emotional indicators could be consistently rated by two raters, the indicators were not significantly related to scores on the Children's Personality Questionnaire, a broad-based measure of children's emotional functioning.

Clearly, projective techniques do not have adequate reliability and validity for use in the classification or diagnosis of children's behavior disorders. However, Ellett and Bersoff (1976) have suggested that such techniques (used with nontraditional administration and interpretation—for instance, role playing) might, in some cases, be useful in the initial identification of problem behaviors. In other words, these techniques may be used as an innocuous means of stimulating a child's discussion of problem areas. It also seems possible that such instruments might be useful in generating tentative hypotheses about behavior that must be further assessed through more reliable and valid methods.

CONCLUSIONS

This chapter has focused on the assessment of social emotional functioning, a relatively neglected facet of psychoeducational assessment. The four techniques that we have described can be integrated in addressing the goals of social/emotional assessment. Problem specification, for example, can potentially involve all four techniques. Interviews allow the assessment practitioner to initially pinpoint the problem areas of concern to mediators. Behavior checklists and observations allow for both problem verification and the identification of problems, with observations sometimes calling attention to problems unknown to the mediator. Projectives may also be used for the latter purpose. Following the isolation of specific problem behaviors, functional observations and interviews both provide a means of determining antecedent and consequent events.

Determination of the severity of a child's problem can be done most objectively through the use of behavior checklists. Normative severity data can be complemented with more subjective judgments of severity based on interviews and observations. It is also possible to obtain objective, normative severity estimates from observational data, if local norms are established for observed rates of behaviors.

Determination of needs follows from clear problem specification and severity determination. Once a problem of given severity has been isolated, the assessment practitioner uses his or her knowledge of intervention procedures to determine what specific intervention has been empirically demonstrated to be most effective in treating that particular problem. This is essentially a literature review process wherein the practitioner attempts to match a problem with an empirically prescribed intervention. Integrally related to the determination of needs is the assessment of available resources. The practitioner uses interviews to identify capable and motivated persons who are available for intervention efforts; settings in which intervention can occur; and environmental events that are available for use in intervention (that is, reinforcers). Such efforts represent a "conditions analysis" of the problem—that is, an analysis of environmental variables influencing relevant behaviors.

Specification of intervention goals essentially means giving a clear description of what the child's behavior should be following successful intervention. The assessment practitioner must make judgments about such goals on the basis of the severity of the child's problem and the availability of resources for remediating the problem. In addition, a mediator's description of how a child should behave in a given situation also serves as a critical input for the goal specification process. Thus, the process requires data from three major sources: behavior checklists, interviews, and behavioral observations.

The primary classification system to which we have referred in this chapter is that mandated by PL 94-142. However, the assessment goals described in this chapter can be used to categorize children's social/emotional problems in the context of any classification system, including that provided by the *Diagnostic and Statistical Manual III* of the American Psychiatric Association (1980). In addition to classification, the assessment goals that we have stressed yield data that logically lead to effective intervention to help children (and not only those officially classifiable as handicapped) with social/emotional problems.

Assessment of Adaptive Behavior

THE MEASUREMENT of adaptive behavior is a relatively new area of psychoeducational assessment. The routine recommendation that adaptive behavior measures be included in assessments for certain disabilities is recent; as a result, the instruments available—and indeed the concept itself—are less well defined and validated than some more traditional assessment tools. Nonetheless, it has become important for psychoeducational assessment practitioners to be familiar with both concept and instruments.

Adaptive behavior reflects the extent to which a person meets personal and social demands for survival and independent functioning. The concept's origins are almost as old as those of IQ, and indeed some of the earliest concepts of intelligence sounded more like what would now be called adaptive behavior (Coulter & Morrow, 1978). The first formal measure of adaptive behavior was the Vineland Social Maturity Scale; the first version of this scale was published in 1935 (Doll), and revised editions have been issued periodically since that time; another revision is currently being prepared (Harrison, Note 9). The scale was originally developed because it was "increasingly evident that the ultimate goal of each individual is social competence, and that helping him to attain that goal is the purpose of schools and other agencies" (Doll, 1965, p. i). This demonstrates the initial focus for the concept of adaptive behavior as a concern with programming; the scale was designed to aid in educating children toward social competence.

Another early effort was initiated by the American Association on Mental Deficiency (AAMD). In 1959 the AAMD introduced the idea of adaptive behavior as a separate concept in working with the retarded; in 1961 the definition of mental retardation was expanded to include deficits in adaptive behavior (Heber, 1959, 1961).

In 1965 the AAMD, working with the Parsons State Hospital, an institution for the mentally retarded in Kansas, initiated a project that, among other goals, worked to develop an adaptive behavior scale. The purpose of this scale also was to aid in remediating inadequate social behaviors of retardates (Coulter & Morrow, 1978). Other early scales, such as the Cain-Levine Social Competency Scale (Cain, Levine, & Elzey, 1977), also focused specifically on training issues. All of these scales were conceptualized primarily as providing information for remediation of deficient social behaviors.

During the 1960s, the development of the concept of adaptive behavior received a great deal of impetus from a different direction. At that time an epidemiological study of mental retardation in one city in California was initiated (Mercer, 1979b). The study attempted to identify each retarded person in the community and examine such factors as how the person had initially been identified as retarded, what the prevalence rates were for various groups divided by age, sex, and other factors, who was providing services, and other demographic information. From this study came a number of findings with direct relevance to education and assessment:

- More than half of the persons identified as mentally retarded were initially labelled by the schools.
- The schools depended primarily on IQ data in making this judgment.
- The number of minority group children and the number of low socioeconomic status children labelled mentally retarded were higher than would be expected from their proportion in the population.
- Most children once labelled as retarded and placed in special classes stayed there — only 19 percent ever returned to the regular educational program.
- More than two-thirds of the children designated by the schools as retarded were perceived that way only by the schools. They were not perceived as retarded by their families or neighborhoods and were not served by any agency other than the schools.

These findings came at a time when concern with bias in education was growing and greatly strengthened the idea of a "nine-to-three" retardate, a child who functions normally outside the school setting but is labelled as retarded in the school.

As a result of Mercer's work and the increasing concern about bias in assessment, the purpose of assessing adaptive behavior moved from a primary emphasis on programming to one on classification, and newer scales reflect this shift. The assessment of adaptive behavior remains important for both purposes, and this chapter will discuss specific instruments within this dual framework.

CURRENT DEFINITIONS

There is no single generally accepted definition of adaptive behavior, and current definitions reflect the heterogeneous development of the concept. Some of the definitions currently in use are

- *Doll:* "A functional composite of human traits which subserves social usefulness as reflected in self-sufficiency and in service to others." (1953, p. 2)
- *Heber:* "The effectiveness with which the individual copes with the natural and social demands of his environment." (1961, p. 61)
- *AAMD:* "The effectiveness with which the individual meets the standards of personal independence and social responsibility expected of his age or cultural group." (Grossman, 1973, p. 11)
- *Mercer:* "Adaptive behavior is conceptualized as achieving an adaptive fit in social systems through the development of interpersonal ties and the acquisition of specific skills required to fulfill the task functions associated with particular roles." (1979, p. 93)

While each of these definitions has a somewhat different focus, certain elements are common to all of them. Most include the two elements specified in the AAMD definition—personal independence and social responsibility. Most either state or imply a developmental component—that expectations differ by age. Most scales include items that focus on self-help (e.g., dressing), language and communications skills (e.g., writing a letter), self-direction and responsibility (e.g., doing a chore reliably), and relationships with others (e.g., playing with other children). Thus some convergence in the views of adaptive behavior can be seen.

There are still concerns and unresolved questions, however. One of the most difficult to deal with derives from the relative nature of these definitions. Most deal, to a greater or lesser extent, with the behavior expected or demanded by society from an individual. However, the degree to which an individual meets these demands depends strongly on just what the demands are. The scales, if not the definitions, assume a sort of "standard society," imposing a standard set of demands, whereas in fact both the demands and the opportunity to meet them vary widely. The various scales available differ substantially on how they deal with this cultural relativity, depending on the model underlying the scale.

As indicated in Chapter 2, a more specific example of this issue is that of school as opposed to nonschool performance. School is one major cultural setting for students, and meeting its demands, including achievement demands, has been defined as one measure of adaptive behavior by at least one author (Mueller, 1974). More commonly, a number of instruments to measure adaptive behavior are designed specifically for completion by school personnel. However, as seen above, much of the impetus for measurement of adaptive behavior arose from concern about children who function well outside of school but not in the school setting. Thus, many professionals feel that adaptive behavior must be assessed outside of school, with information coming from a parent or someone else not directly involved with the school. This issue is especially important because some research has indicated that parents tend to rate their children more highly than do teachers on several of the most commonly used scales (Gutsch & Casse, 1970; Mealor & Richmond, 1980; Oakland, 1979; Wall & Paradise, 1981). It is unclear whether these differences reflect actual differences in children's behavior in the two different settings or bias on the part of either the parent or the teacher. The conflict remains unresolved and must be taken into account in making assessment choices and decisions.

Another related difficulty concerns how "effectiveness" is defined. Just as demands differ from subculture to subculture, acceptable standards of performance may differ also. The degree to which an adult is self-supporting rather than partially dependent on social agencies; the degree to which a 10-year-old assumes responsibility for his or her own clothing care and food preparation; the degree to which a wider "contribution to society" is important—all of these are components of adaptive behavior, and the actual expectations for each may differ widely from subculture to subculture.

All of these concerns make it difficult to arrive at a single accepted concept and definition of adaptive behavior. However, for assessment practitioners, the situation is not quite so bad. It is essential to bear in mind the kind of decision to be made on the basis of adaptive behavior data; this in turn gives guidance on the kind of error to be most concerned about and therefore the position to take regarding these issues. The model of adaptive behavior underlying the development and interpretation of most instruments can be readily specified and can serve as a guide to their use.

PURPOSES OF ASSESSING ADAPTIVE BEHAVIOR

The usual purposes of assessment—classification and programming—are very clearly reflected in the development of the concept of adaptive behavior, which originated in programming concerns but then broadened to include classification concerns. Programming decisions remain important, especially for more severely handicapped children, for whom the development of adaptive skills may be a major part, or even all, of their educational plan. For many children good training in specific adaptive behavior skills may mean the difference between a totally dependent life and some degree of independence. Programming decisions may also be important for less severely handicapped children who show deficits in this area, especially if these are greater than would be expected from their intellectual development. Scales must therefore be evaluated in terms of their usefulness for task analysis. Thus, for instance, they should show good content validity: the concepts included should be important to successful functioning as an adult. They should be well organized hierarchically, so that later skills build on earlier ones. They should have a good breadth of items in the most relevant age ranges; typically this need not include items covering normal or above normal behavior, since for a child with normal skills adaptive behavior would not be an educational goal. On the other hand, they may need very detailed items within the areas they do cover, to measure relatively fine changes in adaptive behavior. Norm data are relatively unimportant, since children's progress is measured only against their own previous level. In reaching a decision concerning adaptive behavior skills, we are more concerned that we not make a false negative decision; we do not want to decide that children have a skill if in fact they do not and therefore fail to teach it. The converse is less important; if a child has already mastered a skill, it will rapidly become apparent during execution of the educational program, and the focus of training can be moved to the next skill in the hierarchy.

For classification, the needs and concerns are quite different. Because of its roots in concerns about unfair placement, the use of adaptive behavior in classification decisions has played largely a preventive role; it is used to rule out mental retardation in some children who would otherwise be so designated on the basis of IQ but who function well outside of school. The focus is on being sure not to label children unless they definitely warrant it—a rule from the social-system model. The societal impact on adaptive behavior is explicitly recognized by many of the definitions presented earlier. For decisions made within the social system model, characteristics of the scale very different from those emphasized for programming become important. Among the most important are the characteristics of the norms available. Because adaptive behavior is a developmental concept, and therefore the expectations vary with age, a deficit, for classification purposes, is most appropriately defined as it is for IQ—with reference to an appropriate comparison group. Thus an ideal instrument, for classification purposes, will yield a reliable score interpreted with reference to a good set of norms. Means, standard deviations, and standard errors of measurement should be available by age groups. The instrument should span at least below average to average behaviors for each age covered; great detail in coverage of individual areas is not needed. A single overall score is adequate, although multiple scores may reveal a deficit in specific areas that might otherwise be hidden.

The degree to which multiple norms are important depends on concerns about the issue of cultural relativity raised above. Since one primary focus of classification is to prevent mislabeling of disadvantaged or socioculturally different children, multiple norms that allow the use of a pluralistic model might be useful. However, since to some extent everyone must conform to a "standard society," it can be argued that a single set of norms is appropriate, as long as the results are clearly interpreted in a social-system framework—that is, as adaptation to a standard culture, possibly different from the subculture from which the child comes. Ideally, however, the child should be given the benefit of the doubt in classification decisions, and a pluralistic framework should be applied in situations in which there is great variation between the expectations of the standard culture and the local subculture. As indicated later, research has not often shown great differences across groups in expectations for adaptive behavior. However, group-specific norms for adaptive behavior measures might be needed for locales in which great variation exists. Ideally, also, the parent or other community person should serve as the informant, both since research suggests that their scores tend to be higher than teachers' and since their view of the child provides a double check against the child's school behavior.

Some adaptive behavior scales have been developed specifically to meet one or the other of these needs, but the purpose of their development and the actual use to which they are best put are not necessarily congruent. The relevance of specific instruments for both purposes will be discussed below for several of the most commonly used scales.

SPECIFIC TECHNIQUES

Vineland Social Maturity Scale (VSMS)

The VSMS was the first adaptive behavior scale published, and it continues to be widely used. The original preliminary version was published in 1935 by Doll. In 1947 a revised edition was published, and in 1953 Doll published *Measurement of Social Competence: A Manual for the Vineland Social Maturity Scale*, a 664-page technical manual that presented extensive data about the development and characteristics of the scale. In 1965 a fourth edition was published.

The VSMS contains items that assess social competence from birth through age 30. Items are placed according to their "life age," the mean age norm for each item. Eight general areas are covered; however, these areas do not comprise separate subscales, since the coverage of areas differs widely by age. The scale yields a "social age" and a "social quotient." The eight areas covered are

- Self-help—general: Items in this area cover general skills such as gross mobility, toileting, and telling time. They range in life age from 0.25 to 7.28.
- Self-help—eating: These items cover the mechanics of eating; they range in life age from 0.55 to 9.03.
- Self-help—dressing: These items deal with dressing and bathing skills; they range in life age from 1.13 to 12.38.
- Locomotion: These items deal with directed movement, from crawling to going to distant towns. Life age range is 0.63 to 18.5.
- Occupation: These items deal with a person's ability to use his or her time productively, including a variety of play and work activities. They range in life age from 0.43 to 25+; half of all of the 25+ items in the scale are in this category.
- Communication: These items cover a variety of activities concerned with conveying and receiving information, including talking, reading, writing, using the telephone. They range in life age from 0.25 to 15.35.
- Self-direction: These items deal with taking responsibility for a variety of areas, including financial and health needs. They range from a life age of 5.83 to 25+.
- Socialization: These items cover relationships with other people, including general contributions to the community. They range from 0.30 to 25+ and include most of the rest of the 25+ items.

The VSMS is given in an interview format. The interviewer must determine whether the subject usually or typically performs the item being covered, not whether he or she can perform it. Typically, a third person serves as the informant. The informant must be very familiar with the person being assessed. Good administration of the VSMS requires good general interviewing skills and a detailed familiarity with the scale.

Items can be scored in a variety of ways. Usually an item is either passed (+, subject does it habitually), emergent (+ −, subject sometimes does it), or failed (−, subject does not do it). If the subject has no opportunity to carry out an activity but could if given the opportunity, it is scored as "passed, no opportunity" (+, No). Thus, for instance, a child living in an apartment in a busy city may have little opportunity to use skates, a bike, or other play vehicles; this would be scored " +, No" if he or she could use these if allowed. If, on the other hand, the child is not allowed or has no opportunity to carry out an activity because he or she cannot be trusted to do it or because of physical handicaps, it is scored as "failed, no opportunity" (−, No). Finally, an item may be scored as "no information" if the informant does not know whether it is habitually performed.

The VSMS was normed in 1935 on 620 Anglo subjects from Vineland, New Jersey. There were 10 males and 10 females at each age year from birth to 30. Children with known mental retardation or physical handicaps were excluded. The norm data were reanalyzed in 1965, and new life-age averages derived; a few items were replaced, and definitions for others were clarified; however, the changes were minor.

The reliability of the VSMS has generally been found to be good. Data presented in the manual (Doll, 1953) and in more recent studies (Mueller, 1974) have found both inter-rater and test-retest reliabilities above 0.9.

The validity of the VSMS has not been well determined. The overall areas covered match fairly well with most of the conceptions of adaptive behavior discussed above; however, the position of items is based on norms that are over 45 years old and may have altered substantially. Little concurrent validity information is available. Correlations between VSMS scores and overall ratings of subjects' social competence are reported in the manual; generally they range above 0.8.

The VSMS was developed for the purpose of programming, but it more nearly fits the purpose of classification. It covers a broad age range, including behavior that would be average or above average for the clientele of an assessment practitioner. It yields a single broad score, much more appropriate for classification purposes than for programming. Its items are too far apart on a hierarchy and have too little detail to be truly useful for programming decisions, although the eight subareas may be of some use for this. Its primary desirable features are that it can be given fairly quickly, within the overall format of a parent interview; that it has been used for a long time and has been generally accepted as appropriate for work with the retarded; that it has available detailed means and standard deviations by age, as well as extensive technical data on individual items; and that it is familiar to most assessment practitioners. Its biggest drawbacks are the age of the technical data and the non-representativeness of its norming sample. Recently, most research has focused on newer adaptive behavior measures. However, the VSMS continues to be used extensively.

A new version of the Vineland Scale is currently under development (Harrison, Note 9); it is intended for publication in 1983. It will contain five domains: communication, daily living skills, socialization, motor skills, and maladaptive behavior. There are three different forms planned. Two interview forms will yield standard scores for the five domains and total adaptive behavior. The longer interview form will also yield more detailed information for programming. The classroom checklist form will be designed for teacher completion and will also yield standard scores.

The interview forms of the new version, which will be known as the *Vineland Adaptive Behavior Scales*, will be appropriate for children from birth to age 19 and for low-functioning adults. The classroom version will be appropriate for children aged 3 to 13. Normative data will be based on a stratified national sample. Tables are also planned for children who are hearing impaired, visually impaired or emotionally disturbed and in residential settings.

Within the assessment models we have presented, the current Vineland Scale clearly reflects a social-system model. Some of the first items, especially in the self-help areas, do not have a heavy cultural component; the expectations for walking or eating skills, for instance, probably do not differ substantially among most subgroups. The later items, however, may differ substantially; items such as being left to care for oneself or enjoying books may have substantial cultural variation. Because of the age of the norm sample and its restriction to Anglos, VSMS scores must be interpreted with great care for disadvantaged or minority child. Nonetheless, it may be of value as an initial screening device. It serves particularly well for that function because of the wild range of its items. It may be the best choice for an older child, who may be outside the age range of most scales. The new version will need examination and research when it is available; it may prove to be a valuable addition to adaptive behavior measures.

AAMD Adaptive Behavior Scale (ABS)

As discussed earlier, the ABS grew out of a joint project of the American Association on Mental Deficiency (AAMD) and Parsons State Hospital in Kansas. Its initial focus was "to provide operational specifications for measuring and describing the adaptive behavior of mentally retarded individuals" (Nihira, 1978, p. 45); it was conceived of primarily as a programming tool.

The ABS has 24 domains, divided into two parts. The first 10 domains reflect adaptive behavior and were chosen to cover all of the behaviors that had previously been addressed by other scales and definitions. The remaining 14 domains reflect maladaptive behavior, intended to indicate various personality and behavior disorders. The 10 adaptive behavior domains are

- Independent Functioning: items in this domain reflect eating, dressing (including bathing, care of clothing, and general appearance), toilet use, travel, and general functioning.
- Physical Development: items in this domain measure sensory function and motor development.
- Economic Activity: items in this area deal with money handling, budgeting, and shopping skills.
- Language Development: items in this domain cover expression, comprehension, and social language development, including items that range from preverbal communication to letter writing and reading at the 9-year-old level.
- Numbers and Time: items in this domain deal with understanding of number usage in counting and simple arithmetic and of calendar and time usage and understanding.
- Domestic Activity: items in this domain cover house cleaning, table setting, food preparation, and other domestic activities.
- Vocational Activity: items in this domain cover the level of job the subject is capable of performing and the quality of job performance.
- Self-Direction: items in this domain deal with the amount of initiative and perseverence the subject shows in carrying out activities and in organizing leisure time.
- Responsibility: these items reflect care of personal belongings and degree of responsibility shown in carrying out assigned tasks.
- Socialization: these items cover a number of aspects of socialization, including awareness of and consideration for others, participation and group interaction with others, and selfishness.

The 14 subareas of part 2 cover any of the following behaviors:

Violent and Destructive Behavior; Antisocial Behavior; Rebellious Behavior; Untrustworthy Behavior; Withdrawal; Stereotyped Behavior and Odd Mannerisms; Inappropriate Interpersonal Habits; Unacceptable Vocal Habits; Unacceptable or Eccentric Habits; Self-Abusive Behavior; Hyperactive Tendencies; Sexually Aberrant Behavior; Psychological Disturbance; and Uses Medication.

The ABS is normally given in an interview format with an informant who knows the subject well; the form can also be given to a parent or other person to fill out directly. The questions about the individual items are presented directly; this differs from the Vineland Scale, where the interviewer makes a judgment about the item on the basis of a detailed description of the subject's behavior in the area. For part 2, an overall question about each domain is asked; detailed items are given only if the respondent indicates that there is a problem in a given area.

Raw scores are summed and subscale scores calculated. These can then be converted to "decile ranks," comparing performance in each subarea to the norm group. The ABS was normed on a group of approximately 4000 institutionalized subjects, ranging in age from 3 to 69 years. The mean IQs varied from a low of 28 for the 3-year-old group to a high of 45.8 for the 16- to 18-year-old group. Thus, the deciles are in comparison to a low-functioning, institutionalized mentally retarded population.

The manual (Nihira, Foster, Shellhaas, and Leland, 1975) presents inter-rater reliabilities by domain. For part 1, these range from a low of 0.71 for Self-Direction to a high of 0.92 for Independent Functioning. For part 2, the reliabilities are substantially lower, ranging from 0.37 for Unacceptable Vocal Habits to 0.77 for Uses Medication.

A number of validity studies have examined the factor structure of the ABS, generally showing three broad factors of personal self-sufficiency, community self-sufficiency, and personal-social responsibility (Nihira, 1978). Some correspondence between clinical ratings and ABS ratings is also presented. No data regarding concurrent validity with the Vineland Scale or other measures is available.

The ABS was developed primarily for programming purposes, and it fits those purposes fairly well. The items are detailed and provide sufficiently broad coverage to measure change. Although the norm sample is very restricted, the subscale norms do give some guidance in program planning, in that areas in which functioning is most retarded can be identified. However, there is little hierarchy to the items. Most items are not presented as sequenced, and for most the order in which skills need to be taught is simply not indicated. Thus the fit between this scale and the task analysis model is not good. The usefulness of this scale for programming ultimately rests primarily on the practitioner's judgment of the content validity of the items. The inter-rater reliability of part 2 is so low for most domains that care should be exercised in depending on the data for any purpose.

The ABS is inappropriate for classification purposes. The characteristics of the scale fit the medical model, since it has a low ceiling, truncated distribution, and negatively skewed distribution to measure degrees of deficit. Thus, for instance, the items on reading range from reading fewer than 10 words to reading at a 9-year-old level, for a scale whose norm group includes an adult population. However, the scale does not necessarily meet the medical-model assumption that sociocultural factors are not relevant to diagnosis or treatment, especially in part 2. This means that it is questionable to use the ABS for classification decisions within a medical-model framework, since relevant sociocultural factors are ignored. On the other hand, the ABS does not have the range, norms, or other technical characteristics to be considered an adequate measure within the social-system or pluralistic model. Its use is therefore best confined to programming decisions.

AAMD Adaptive Behavior Scale—Public School Version (ABS-PSV)

This measure (Lambert, Windmiller, Cole, & Figueroa, 1975) is a revision and renorming of the ABS to make it more suitable for use directly by school personnel. It covers most of the same items as the original ABS and is in the same format. Items that teachers indicated that they were very unlikely to observe were eliminated.

The impetus for the ABS-PSV grew out of the concerns arising over classification of the retarded. When these concerns first became a major issue, there were few available adaptive behavior scales of any kind. The ABS project had been under way for several years; however, the project had deliberately taken an institutional focus, and neither the norms nor in some cases the items themselves were suitable for use with a population actually in public schools. Therefore a revision to make the scale more suitable for public school use and a more comprehensive renorming were undertaken. These were designed to create a scale that could be used effectively in the classification of retarded and nonretarded children in the public schools, with the teacher serving as the informant.

Because teachers and other school personnel did not feel that they had enough information to rate these areas, the domains of Domestic Activity on part 1 and Self-Abusive Behavior on part 2 were deleted. The remainder of items and domains are the same as for the original ABS. Scoring also remains the same, although there are differences in interpretation.

This revised version of the ABS was then standardized on 2800 California school children, stratified by age, sex, and ethnic status. The sample was chosen to represent approximately equal numbers of children with no special education classification ("regular children") and children classified as educably mentally retarded, with smaller samples of children classified as trainably mentally retarded or educationally handicapped. Norms are presented as percentiles. Three sets of percentiles are available: by age and educational placement; by age, educational placement, and sex; and by age, educational placement, and ethnic status.

Internal consistency reliabilities derived from the standardization data average approximately 0.88 for both parts 1 and 2 of the scale. Additional inter-rater reliabilities beyond those for the ABS are not presented for the ABS-PSV.

Validation studies of the ABS-PSV have related primarily to the relationship of individual items and domains to classification status. For the standardization sample it was found that most items on part 1 and some items on part 2 were significantly related to classification. For children through age 11, there were strong relationships between all part 1 domains and classifications; for older children there were fewer relationships. Part 2 shows a less consistent pattern of relationships; there is a strong relationship between classification and scores for destructive behavior, inappropriate mannerisms, unacceptable vocal habits, and eccentric habits at all ages; there are almost no significant relationships for odd mannerisms and hyperactive tendencies. The remaining domains of part 2 show relationships that are significant for some age groups only (Lambert, Windmiller, Cole, & Figueroa, 1975).

Bailey and Richmond (1979) carried out a study comparing ABS-PSV part 1 scores for children defined as educably mentally retarded, slow learners, or average on the basis of IQ. They found that the average students scored significantly higher on five domains: Independent Functioning, Economic Activity, Language Development, Numbers and Time, and Socialization. No significant differences were found for the remaining domains. There were also no significant differences between the educably mentally retarded group and the slow learner group. On the Vocational Activity domain the average children obtained a mean score that was lower than that of the other two groups. The authors suggest that caution is needed in using some of the ABS-PSV domains, especially Vocational Activity.

All of these studies have used IQ as the definition of the groups being compared. Since much of the purpose of using the concept of adaptive behavior is to identify children who may score low on IQ tests even though they are capable of functioning well outside academic settings, a much more preferable method of validation would be to compare the functioning of these children with the actual functioning of children in other settings. However, such research does not yet exist.

In general, standardization results from the ABS-PSV show few differences by sex or ethnicity, although separate norms are provided by both these groupings. In part 1, scores show gradual improvement for older age groups; however, there was little relationship between age and score on part 2, suggesting that there is not a strong developmental component in what this measure terms "maladaptive behavior patterns."

The ABS-PSV has been presented by the authors as useful for both classification and programming decisions. For classification decisions it would fit primarily into a medical model, as does the ABS. Norm data from the PSV show few ethnic or sex differences, which adds justification to its use within this framework; nonetheless, adaptive behavior as a construct, as we have suggested, fits primarily within a social-system model, in which demands expectations may differ radically from culture to culture. The ABS-PSV fails to meet the properties of good measures for such a model primarily in having a very low ceiling and a focus on the identification of deficits only. In addition, validation studies for such a social-system measure would, as mentioned above, be more appropriately based on comparison to other similar instruments or other direct measures of adequate social functioning.

A more serious concern about the use of the ABS-PSV comes from its use of the teacher as informant. Although one substudy of the standardization examined teacher–parent ratings and did not find significant differences, other research with both this and other adaptive behavior scales suggests that parents do in fact tend to rate their children higher than teachers do. Within the context of a social-system model, it would be more inappropriate to risk labeling a child as below average than to risk the reverse. By using a teacher informant, however, the reverse may be happening.

For programming purposes, the same comments that apply to the original ABS hold. However, for programming for mildly handicapped children the ABS-PSV may be useful for only the youngest children, since the ceiling is fairly low.

Overall, then, although it is presented and discussed extensively as an instrument for classification purposes, the ABS-PSV has major drawbacks in serving this function. Its main advantages are that it is based on a good standardization sample with multiple norms and a broad base of items drawn from several areas. Its biggest disadvantages as a classification tool are the lack of adequate validation research, the low ceiling on most scales, and the somewhat restricted age range. In addition, some of the domains measured seem to be of questionable reliability and validity. The use of the teacher as an informant is a convenience, but, as mentioned earlier, may not be appropriate for adaptive behavior ratings used in classification decisions.

For programming purposes, the ABS-PSV, like the original ABS, provides detailed items and broad coverage, and for this purpose the use of a teacher as informant is not inappropriate. However, the lack of hierarchy in the items makes it difficult to structure a program based primarily on the ABS-PSV. The relatively low ceiling is not a problem in this area because most children who score near the ceiling do not need specific instruction in adaptive behavior. The maladaptive behaviors rated in part 2 may be useful in programming for children who are classified as behaviorally maladjusted or emotionally disturbed.

Adaptive Behavior Inventory for Children (ABIC)

The ABIC was initially published as part of the System of Multicultural Pluralistic Assessment (SOMPA), developed by Mercer following her work with the Riverside study (Mercer and Lewis, 1977). It is designed to measure overall adaptive behavior in children aged 5 through 11. It consists of 242 items divided into 6 adaptive behavior scales: Family, Community, Peer Relations, Nonacademic School Roles, Earner/Consumer, and Self-Maintenance. In addition to these 6 scales, some of the items form a veracity scale.

The ABIC is given in an interview with a parent or other caretaker who knows the child well. Because a large proportion of the items reflect behavior in the home and community, it is difficult for a teacher to complete it; an informant from the community is generally necessary. Unlike the instruments discussed so far, the ABIC has a very standardized presentation format. Items (questions about the child's behavior) are read to the informant word for word, and the respondent chooses one of the three responses (such as "sometimes," "never," or "often"; or "three or more times," "one or two times," or "never." The order of choices is varied so that a response set is not established). The ABIC is typically given as a part of a parent interview that also includes a health history and other information; the entire interview takes approximately an hour.

Items on the ABIC are scored 0, 1, or 2 points, depending on the response. Other possible responses include "no opportunity" and "don't know." "No opportunity" responses are scored as 0; "don't know" are scored as 1.

After scoring, the items for each scale are summed, and scaled scores are determined. In addition to the 6 adaptive behavior scales, 3 other measures can be examined. There are 24 "veracity" items altogether; these are items whose age placement in the scale is greater than 11 years. Thus, a child would not normally be expected to perform these actions. The manual indicates that if a child scores 2 on four or more of these items, the validity of the child's scores should be questioned.

The number of "no opportunity" responses allows an examination of whether the child's environment may be unduly restrictive. A score of 30 or more items answered with "no opportunity" is two standard deviations above normal for the standardization sample and suggests that the child's environment is so restrictive that the remainder of the scale may be invalid or very difficult to interpret.

Finally, a score of 9 or more "don't knows" is 2 standard deviations above the average and suggests that another informant more familiar with the child should be sought for the scale.

The ABIC was normed on a carefully stratified sample of children throughout California. A sample of 2085 children balanced by sex, age, and ethnic group was chosen randomly throughout the state. From this standardization sample the age level of each item was determined. The norms provide standard scores with a mean of 50 and a standard deviation of 15 for each subscale. In addition, raw score means and standard deviations are provided in the technical manual (Mercer, 1979b). The raw scores were analyzed by ethnic group during standardization; however, differences found were small, and therefore no separate norms by ethnicity are provided. Overall, the norm data available for the ABIC are based on a recent, carefully defined and selected sample and are presented in detail, making it the best normed of the current instruments available. However, norming on additional disadvantaged groups such as rural Appalachians would be desirable.

The technical manual for the SOMPA (Mercer, 1979b) presents split-half reliabilities for each scale of the ABIC. These range from 0.76 to 0.92, generally increasing with the age of the subjects. Split-half reliabilities for the overall score are all 0.96 or above. The SOMPA manual also presents the result of an inter-rater agreement study; it was found that the average difference in raw score points was between one and two points for each subtest. More recent research has found that for two scales (Peer Relations and Nonacademic

School Roles), however, the relationship between teacher ratings and mother ratings of the same child was low, with mothers consistently rating the child higher (Wall & Paradise, 1981). Thus there may be substantial inter-rater differences when the two raters see the child in quite different settings. The ABIC was not designed for use by school personnel, however, and teachers gave a higher proportion of "don't know" responses, indicating that the low inter-rater agreement may be due to the teacher's lack of familiarity with the subjects being rated.

The SOMPA manual does not present data regarding the concurrent validity of the ABIC. Other research supports the finding that there are not major differences by ethnic group overall, although some differences were found (Oakland, 1980; Oakland & Feigenbaum, 1980). This research also supports the arrangement of items into subscales, in that similar factor structures are found for different ethnic and socioeconomic status groups. This research also indicates that the correlations of ABIC scores with both IQ and achievement test scores are very low. A lack of relationship between IQ tests and the ABIC is consistent with the general construct of adaptive behavior. The lack of relationship between the ABIC and achievement tests, on the other hand, raises some concern about the usefulness of the ABIC in school decision making. This also may be more a function of the current conceptualization of adaptive behavior than of the ABIC alone.

The technical adequacy of the ABIC overall appears to be high, especially for a construct as complex as adaptive behavior. Additional research into its validity as a classification tool is needed; however, the norm data and other research carried out so far suggest that it is the best of the currently available adaptive behavior measures in technical quality.

The ABIC was designed from a social-system model, and it fits that model quite well. The explicit expectation that adaptive behavior is culturally determined underlies the scale; while few ethnic or cultural differences in overall scores were found for the population examined, the results are clearly intended to indicate adaptation to a specific set of cultural demands. The measure has the technical adequacy to serve as a classification tool within the social-system model. It reflects both below average and above average performance, with normal distributions. The manual suggests a cutoff point of approximately two standard deviations below the mean for considering the subject's adaptive behavior as below normal, consistent with the idea that it is a more serious mistake to label children below normal inappropriately than to label them normal inappropriately. Both standard deviations and standard errors are provided for each subscale, making it feasible for the user to determine the level of risk desired. The ABIC is also designed specifically for completion by a parent, which, as we have stressed, is generally preferable when classification decisions are being made.

The ABIC is less appropriate for programming. The items were designed to have good psychometric properties for classification decisions; they are not necessarily hierarchical in the sense that they form necessary sequences of instruction, although they are ordered by age. They provide overall broad scores, but not specific details on the skills that might make up an instructional program. The coverage of the scales differs by age, with some scales having more items for young children and others having more for older children. Because deviation-based scaled scores are provided for each subtest, a profile of subtest scores might give some help in programming, but this is not the main purpose of the ABIC.

In summary, the ABIC is a recently developed measure of adaptive behavior useful primarily for classification decisions. Its strongest points are its technical quality, the care that went into the norming, and the explicit use of an appropriate social-system model to design and interpret it. Among its disadvantages are the limited age range (5 – 11) it covers, the time it takes to do the interview, the lack of detailed information that this measure provides for programming purposes, and the lack of much validity data concerning the scale at this point.

Cain-Levine Social Competency Scale

The Cain-Levine Scale (Cain, Levine, & Elzey, 1977) is intended primarily as a measure of adaptive behavior for children at the trainable mentally retarded level. At this level of functioning, classification is seldom an issue; the Cain-Levine Scale is designed solely for programming. It consists of 44 items arranged into 4 scales: Self-Help, Initiative, Social Skills, and Communication. Self-help skills include skills such as dressing and feeding oneself and helping with simple chores. Initiative items measure the extent to which the subject actually initiates activities such as dressing, rather than waiting for someone else to take the initiative. Social skills include such items as playing with others and answering the telephone. Communication items range from use of any speech at all to delivering messages and telling simple stories. The Cain-Levine Scale is used in an interview format with an informant who knows the child well; this may be a parent, caretaker, or teacher. The items are not read directly; rather, each general area is introduced and the informant's answers gradually clarified.

Raw scores on the subscales and total raw score can be converted into percentiles within broad age categories, with approximately two-year intervals. The norm sample for the Cain-Levine Scale consisted of 414 retarded males and 302 retarded females in the state of California. The children aged 8 years and older were enrolled in public school programs; the younger children were nominated from a variety of sources. The range of IQ scores was 25 through 59, with means for the various age groups generally in the 40s. Thus the norm sample reflects low-functioning children, mostly within the trainable mentally retarded category.

Split-half reliability is in the range of 0.75 to 0.91; test-retest reliability over a three-week interval is generally above 0.90. Thus the test seems to have adequate reliability. No inter-rater reliabilities are reported.

The Cain-Levine items were chosen to reflect existing curricula for the trainable retarded; their major validation is thus content validity. The test scores correlated only slightly with IQ scores in the sample; they correlated somewhat more highly with chronological age. The items chosen reflect typical training goals; the possible responses within items appear to be well sequenced.

For classification purposes the Cain-Levine Scale is not generally very useful. The restricted nature of its norm population makes it difficult to interpret the score of a mildly handicapped child. The ceiling is low, making it difficult to distinguish between average, above average, and mildly below average children. The primary difficulty in classification of the retarded arises in classifying children whose IQ is in the range between 50 and 75; the skill range covered by the Cain-Levine Scale is too low to assist much in these decisions.

In terms of programming, the Cain-Levine Scale appears to be a useful instrument. Although no data are presented in the manual (Cain, Levine, & Elzey, 1977) regarding the hierarchical nature of the items, they are derived from curricula typically used, and they appear to provide good sequencing of skills and detailed responses allowing for the measure of small changes. The relevance of this measure for specific programs can be determined by an examination of the items, but in general it appears to be useful in programming for the trainable mentally retarded child or the young, more mildly handicapped child. It would not be useful for an older educable mentally retarded child, because of the low ceiling.

Children's Adaptive Behavior Scale (CABS)

The concept of adaptive behavior involves performance of specific roles and skills within the child's community, including the school community. However, it is difficult to directly assess this performance, since much of it takes place outside the observation of the assessment practitioner. Because it would be very difficult for the assessment practitioner to observe a child sufficiently to rate most adaptive behavior skills, all of the instruments so far discussed use an informant, someone who knows the child well. This carries risks of its own, in terms of possible rater error or bias, as noted above. The CABS was developed partially in response to this concern (Richmond & Kicklighter, 1980). This scale does not use an informant; rather, the child is directly presented with tasks that are representative of the adaptive behaviors being assessed. The scale is thus an examination of a selected sample of behavior, as is an IQ or achievement test.

The CABS is designed for children aged 5 through 10 and contains items reflecting skills for ages 3 through 12. Thus it has items appropriate for children both below and above average. It yields scores in the following five areas: language development, independent functioning, family role performance, economic-vocational activity, and socialization. It is administered in a standard format, much like any individual psychological examination. The child responds to questions in a variety of forms, including pointing to pictures, giving verbal responses, and, in some cases, writing responses.

The norm data available for the CABS are based on a sample of 250 mildly retarded children in South Carolina and Georgia public schools. Means and standard deviations are presented by age for each scale and for the total score. The manual (Richmond & Kicklighter, 1980) recommends that any school system using the CAB develop local norms for its use.

No reliability data are provided in the manual. Correlations between the CABS and the ABS-PSV are 0.42 for both parent and teacher informants when total scores are compared, suggesting some relationship but not a strong one. Correlations between the CABS total score and those from the Wechsler Intelligence Scale for Children — Revised are 0.57 for verbal IQ, 0.33 for performance IQ, and 0.51 for total IQ, suggesting that the scale is measuring skills more similar to IQ tests than to other adaptive behavior measures. An examination of individual items also suggests this; some of them strongly resemble items from specific IQ tests.

Overall, the CABS is based upon an interesting idea — that a better measure of adaptive behavior can be obtained directly from the child by a sample of behavior than from an informant. However, at present the validity of the scale is somewhat questionable. The fact that scores are moderately related to IQ, while not necessarily surprising, suggests extreme caution in using the scale for classification decisions, since scales are intended to provide a measure of functioning different from IQ tests. Although the manual suggests using CABS scores for programming, the items are not sufficiently detailed to

provide much programming information; the norm group is sufficiently weak to make using even the scores from the scales for a profile questionable. Thus, while the CABS is a step in a direction that
should probably be pursued further, it probably should be used at
present only to supplement information derived from other measures, at least until better evidence of its validity as a measure of
adaptive behavior, and not IQ, is obtained.

Other Techniques

A variety of other measures of adaptive behavior have been developed and are used primarily for programming in moderately to
severely handicapped populations. Among the instruments that are
widely used are the Balthazar Scales of Adaptive Behavior (Balthazar, 1973) and the Learning Accomplishment Profile (Sanford, 1974).
Both of these are either normed on moderately to severely retarded
populations or are designed for very young children, preschool-aged.
Thus they provide little information for the typical classification decisions faced by assessment practitioners; they are more commonly
used by teachers as a programming tool. For this purpose the detail
of their coverage in each area and the match between the curriculum
being used and the items of the test can be determined for a specific
setting; these probably provide the best information to use in choosing a scale. Because of their relative unimportance to the assessment
practitioner, the scales are not presented here in more detail.

CONCLUSIONS

The concept of adaptive behavior is an emerging one, with no
single established definition and with a number of unresolved issues.
Nonetheless, the measurement of adaptive behavior has become important to the assessment practitioner as a means of distinguishing
the mildly retarded child from the "nine-to-three" retardate, who
scores similarly on an IQ test but functions more normally outside
the school environment. The measurement of adaptive behavior may
also be important for programming purposes; the more seriously
handicapped a child is, the more likely it is that adaptive behavior
will be one area for programming to address.

Of the measures of adaptive behavior available, three have some
usefulness for classification: the Vineland Scale, the ABS-PSV, and
the ABIC. Each of these, as we have seen, has advantages and disadvantages. The VSMS covers a wide age range—birth to adulthood—
and thus provides appropriate scores for children throughout the

school years. As is appropriate for a measure that falls within a social-system framework, it has a high ceiling and allows the identification of children who have exceptionally high as well as exceptionally low levels of functioning. It can be given readily, in a comfortable format, to parents. A variety of technical data are provided for each item and the whole scale. However, the norm group and technical data are both very badly outdated, making their current representativeness open to question. Nonetheless, the VSMS may be the most appropriate measure to use in many school settings, especially for older children. The new version now being prepared will have better norms and may become the best available instrument.

The ABS-PSV is a modification of a scale developed primarily for programming purposes. It has a low ceiling, with detailed coverage of low-level skills but little ability to distinguish average from above average performance. The norms cover children aged 7 through 12, a rather restricted range for the public schools, and are provided only in terms of percentiles. All of these are weaknesses of the scale for classification purposes. In addition, some of the scales have questionable reliability. It is designed for completion by a teacher, rather than by a parent or community informant. However, it does provide detailed coverage of a number of scales, and the norm data are much more recent than those for the VSMS data.

The ABIC was developed specifically as a classification tool, and its technical qualities are higher than those of either of the previous scales. It is time-consuming to give and somewhat more formal in style than the previous two instruments, since each item must be read word for word to the informant. Its major limitation for classification purposes is the restricted age range: norms are provided for ages 5 through 11 only. A Spanish version is available, however, which may be very helpful in some settings.

For programming purposes, more instruments are available, primarily aimed at a population of trainable mentally retarded and below. The ABS, both the original version and the public school version, provide detailed items, but these items are not strongly ordered by difficulty, making it difficult to base a program sequence on them. Several scales, such as the Cain-Levine and the Balthazar scales, are widely used for programming purposes. The suitability of these scales for a specific assessment is best determined by examining the match between the content of the scale and the goals and curriculum of the relevant program.

Overall, then, there is no ideal instrument for measuring adaptive behavior throughout the school career, but there are several that can be used, as long as their limitations are borne in mind. No single instrument appears to be the best among those available.

Assessment of Environmental Influences on School Coping

IN THIS CHAPTER we will argue that environmental influences on the school coping behavior of children referred for psychoeducational assessment should be systematically considered in the assessment process. We believe that children's welfare requires that assessment of children with problems include an analysis of the skills and strategies they bring to school and also of the environmental conditions that affect their school performances.

Our belief is partially predicted on a preference for viewing human behavior in terms of what Wallace (1966) describes as a *response capability* model. From this perspective, behavior is viewed as resulting from an interaction of internal characteristics of people with environmental opportunities. Wallace contrasts the response capability model with what he calls the *response predisposition* model. In this model, behavior is seen as rather exclusively reflecting factors within the person. Bardon and Bennett (1974) suggest that viewing children's behaviors as mostly a reflection of their inner characteristics tends to limit consideration of how their performances might be enhanced, whereas the interactionist assumption embedded in the response capability model leads to a consideration of how environmental conditions might be altered to enhance performances.

Our preference for the response capability model can, we believe, be justified on several grounds. First, "it is not necessary to debate whether or not the environment affects behavior. There is ample evidence that for accurate prediction of individual behavior there must be information about the environment as well as the individual" (Murrell, 1973, p. 11). Second, this is the more optimistic model from which to view children's school problems, since the problems are viewed as potentially remediable, at least within limits set by children's genetic and organic capacities for growth, since changes can be made in the environment. Third, the regulations implementing Public Law (PL) 94-142 and other federal laws require that learning environments be adapted to be made more appropriate to the needs of handicapped children, with the goal of maintaining such children in the "least restrictive environment" possible. Fourth, analyses of how environmental influences affect child development may lead to valuable efforts to prevent problems from occurring in the first place. Catterall and Gazda (1978) suggest that some problems experienced by children in school originate from educational procedures, rather than from the children (p. 9). Hence, they propose that educators, as well as continuing programs to help children currently experiencing difficulties with academic or life-skill tasks, also try to establish programs for the purpose of preventing such problems from developing. They categorize interventions as either developmental (preventive) or remedial in nature and as having either an academic or a life-skills focus. In our view, this is the kind of comprehensive approach to children's school problems that is necessary for appropriate intervention.

In spite of the utility of systematically evaluating the impact of environmental influences on children's school performances, the history of psychoeducational assessment reflects a preponderant emphasis on assessing individual characteristics of children (Smith, Neisworth, & Greer, 1978). Fortunately, this disproportionate emphasis is beginning to shift toward a more balanced approach. The assessment techniques described in this chapter (as well as others not described) represent efforts to effect greater balance in assessment. Some of the techniques described in this chapter have been designed to assess school environments as they affect groups of children, while others have been designed to assess school environments as they affect individual children. Since home environments also affect children's school performances, techniques designed to assess the home environments of individual children are also discussed.

ENVIRONMENTAL FACTORS

Previous chapters have indicated the characteristics of children themselves that we believe most often warrant assessment—health factors, intellectual functioning, and so on. A comprehensive assessment of a child's school problems should include consideration of the following environmental factors: general school climate, curriculum, teachers, physical environment, and the home. Smith, Neisworth, & Greer (1978) stress the importance of assessing the environmental factors of curriculum, teachers, peers, and physical environment on children's performances in school. They suggest that such influences can enhance or impede children's accomplishments of school-required tasks. While Smith et al. do not mention general school climate as a factor worthy of assessment, we believe that this factor can have an indirect effect on how children perform in their classrooms. The same belief is reflected in a Phi Delta Kappa (undated) publication entitled *School Climate Improvement: A Challenge to the School Administrator*, which suggests that difficulties such as absenteeism, disciplinary problems, and underachievement may sometimes be the products of dysfunctional school climates. In a similar vein, Murrell (1973) proposes that such problems often result from a "bad fit" between the characteristics of the student body (or an individual student) served by a school and the school's requirements, policies, and procedures (all of which are aspects of the school climate). Murrell proposes a number of strategies that can be used to improve the fit between student characteristics and the climate of the school, which are briefly discussed later in this chapter.

Smith et al. (1978) omit any discussion of home influences. Their omission does not necessarily reflect a perception that home environmental factors are unimportant; their book is simply restricted to techniques appropriate to the assessment of the school environment. Our position is that the home environment influences the skills and strategies that children bring to school and hence should be understood through the assessment process. Murrell (1973) indicates that skills and strategies shaped at home sometimes interact negatively with the skills and strategies seen as important by schools. Children who fail to meet the school's expectations often experience difficulties in coping with required tasks, and Murrell refers to such difficulties as examples of poor "intersystem accommodation." He suggests that interventions designed to overcome these difficulties should involve efforts to bring schools and families into greater harmony in terms of the skills and strategies they are trying to instill in children. We concur, and are convinced that interventions will not be optimally successful unless they are directed toward this goal.

PURPOSES OF ENVIRONMENTAL ASSESSMENT

Systematic assessment of environmental influences on school coping behavior serves both classification and programming purposes. The regulations implementing PL 94-142 appear to require that children not be classified as handicapped unless their school problems result primarily from their own inherent disabilities; in other words, their problems are not attributable primarily to environmental influences. Those children whose school problems primarily reflect environmental influences are not classifiable as handicapped under the law. Assessment of the influence of environmental factors is obviously necessary, therefore, for classification decisions that meet the requirements of the law. In addition, children whose school problems do result from environmental influences, while not classifiable as handicapped, are in need of intervention and should, in our view, receive intervention services from non–special education sources. For both of these reasons, classification judgments should reflect an understanding of how environmental influences may have acted to enhance or impede children's school performances.

Assessment of environmental influences on school coping behavior can improve the appropriateness of special education classification judgments. Classifying children as handicapped when their problems primarily reflect conditions external to themselves inappropriately shifts the responsibility for their school problems to the children. Children experiencing school problems should not be classified as handicapped when their problems stem primarily from frequent changes in schools, inappropriate placements in curricular programs, or poor school instruction. Nor should children be classified as handicapped when they are able to meet the demands of most schools or classrooms but are unable to meet the demands of the particular schools or classrooms in which they are placed. This was illustrated by the plight of some rural children of low socioeconomic status whom we observed in East Tennessee. These children live on the fringes of newly developed subdivisions serving upper middle class families. The schools in these subdivisions gear their instructional programs to fit the skills and strategies of children from the subdivision, and the general academic achievement levels in these schools far exceed national averages. In these schools, many of the rural children of low socioeconomic status are referred for psychoeducational assessment as possibly handicapped. While some of them are found to be handicapped, others initially perceived to be handicapped achieve at, or only slightly below, national averages. These latter children do not, in our view, warrant handicapping condition classifications, but it is sometimes difficult to alter their teachers' initial perceptions of them as handicapped. This is understandable, for two reasons. First, these children do seem quite deviant in their subdivision schools. Second, they also need assistance in finding satisfactory social and academic niches in their schools. Again, we advocate that these children receive assistance—but not from their school systems' special education programs.

Assessment of environmental influences is also useful for programming. Good programming has as its goal the optimal development of each child. Optimal personal development, in turn, requires that each child learn the academic and life skills appropriately required by schools (and society in general) and that the child also learn to exhibit those skills in a consistent manner. As indicated in previous chapters, techniques appropriate to a life-skills analysis of a child can assist in determining which skills the child lacks, and those skills should be directly trained. Techniques appropriate to an analysis of environmental conditions can assist in determining the conditions under which the child has failed to learn certain needed skills in a consistent manner. Such determinations can be of great assistance in developing an appropriate program for the child.

An environmental analysis is helpful for each child assessed, regardless of whether that child is ultimately served by a special education program or not. First, environmental conditions can act to enhance or impede a child's school performance. Second, we concur with Murrell's (1973) proposal that any intervention is as good (effective) as the analysis of the problem on which the intervention is based. Obviously, an incomplete analysis can lead to an intervention that is less successful than desired. Third, environmental assessment can certainly help to ensure that programming for handicapped children meets the requirements of the law. Each individualized educational program (IEP) developed for a handicapped child must include specifications of the educational and related services to be provided the child. These services typically represent instructional and supportive efforts not included in the school's regular program and hence represent alterations of that regular program. In addition, each IEP must specify the degree to which the child will participate in the regular program of the school, and this specification requires making a judgment about the settings (environmental conditions) most appropriate to the child's development of needed or consistently applied skills. Further, each child is to be placed in the regular school program to the maximal extent possible, and such placements often require some programmatic alterations to accommodate the child. Finally, as we have mentioned, children who cannot be classified as handicapped but who are experiencing problems at school should also be given an opportunity to benefit from intervention that may involve altering the child's environment.

Some additional comments are probably required for a full understanding of our position on the relation between assessment of environmental influences on school coping behavior and programming efforts. We agree with Murrell's (1973) contention that disabilities are of greatest practical significance when they interfere with satisfactory compliance with legitimate requirements of social systems (such as schools). Murrel argues that "pathology" is located neither within the person nor within the social system but at the point where the person's skills and strategies conflict with social-system requirements. Intervention should be designed to eliminate or reduce the "bad fit" between the person and the social system. Murrell proposes five general approaches appropriate to that goal.

Two of these approaches are focused on the person. The first involves helping the person meet social-system demands through interventions such as counseling and direct training. We believe that this approach is appropriate for a child experiencing difficulty in school when the school's requirements reflect important academic and life skills and when the child can reasonably be expected to master those skills. A second approach involves relocating the person into another social system (such as a different class). We view this approach as appropriate for a child experiencing difficulty in school when the school's requirements reflect important academic and life skills and when the child is viewed as seriously deficient in the skills and strategies necessary to meet these requirements. Placing a handicapped child in a special education class is an example of this approach. The purpose of such a change should be, whenever possible, to assist the child to develop the skills and strategies needed for a later partial or full integration into a regular classroom. It must be acknowledged, however, that some severely handicapped children will never develop the skills and strategies necessary for integration into a regular classroom. For them, long-term relocation to a special education class is appropriate.

Murrell's other three approaches represent efforts to create more accomodating social systems. His third approach involves modifying a social system's responses to the skills and strategies a person brings to that system. We see this approach as appropriate for a child experiencing difficulty in school when the school is able to maintain its appropriate requirements while simultaneously allowing the child to use her or his existing skills and strategies to meet these requirements. Murrell's fourth approach involves modifying a social system's structure. This approach is appropriate, we think, when significant numbers of children in a school are experiencing difficulties and the school cannot provide for a better fit between its students and its practices without a large-scale reorganization. Murrell's last approach involves the creation of new social systems. This approach is appropriate when children experiencing difficulties in school cannot be well served through modifications of either existing regular or alternative programs.

In summary, we believe that children experiencing difficulties in school should be targeted for intervention according to one or more of Murrell's five general approaches. Choosing one of these strategies, however, necessitates some important judgments. Do the school's requirements reflect important academic and life skills? Can the child be expected to master such skills? If not, what skills are appropriate to train? Can the school's responses to the child's skills and strategies be modified in the regular classroom or in a special education program? Is a whole new program needed for a group of children falling between the cracks of existing regular or alternative programs? What are the legal and ethical implications of these judgments? While all of these questions are important for the goal of appropriate programming, many involve systematic consideration of environmental influences on children's school performances.

ENVIRONMENTAL ASSESSMENT AND THE BASIC ASSESSMENT MODELS

From one point of view, it is inappropriate to discuss techniques used to assess environmental influences on school coping behavior in terms of the assessment models presented earlier in this book. These models have been developed to assist in the assessment of children themselves. Hence, they cannot be applied directly to the assessment of environments. Nevertheless, these models at least suggest how environments might be viewed in terms of the classification and programming functions of psychoeducational assessment.

Medical model measures are designed to determine whether children suffer from biological symptoms such as deficient visual or auditory acuity. When children are found to have such conditions, it is extremely important to incorporate this knowledge in programming efforts. For example, for a child with limited vision the assessment practitioner might try to ensure that magnification was provided, or that the child was seated near the front of the classroom, or that large-print books were available. Programs that fail to incorporate strategies appropriate to medical problems will not promote the goal of children's optimum development. In addition, children should not be classified under handicapping condition classifications such as mental retardation when their school difficulties actually reflect undetected medical problems.

Social-system measures are designed to detect whether children deviate significantly from social-system norms. Such measures assist in determinations of the nature and extent of children's difficulties, and such determinations are useful for both classification and programming purposes. More specifically, a classification of a child as mentally retarded, learning disabled, or seriously emotionally disturbed should reflect a judgment that the child deviates significantly from social-system norms. As previously suggested, however, an issue in classification involves whether a child's functioning should be compared to general (that is, national) or to particular social-system norms. Our position is that a child should be classified in reference to national social-system norms for academic and behavioral skills. Such skills are incorporated in the specific assessment domains of academic achievement, social/emotional functioning, and adaptive behavior; and norm-referenced measures within these domains tend to reflect national norms. We also believe that programming efforts should, whenever appropriate, incorporate interventions designed to bring children's academic and behavioral performances up to national social-system norms. While some children will never be able to exhibit skills at this level, other children who can exceed these levels should be assisted to do so. Our stance on these matters was partially illustrated in our discussion of the difficulties of rural children of low socioeconomic status from East Tennessee who were attending schools in affluent subdivisions. We did not concur with some of the teachers' perceptions of these children as handicapped when the children had achievement test scores near national averages. In our view, some of the teachers were applying an overly narrow social-system perspective to these children's performances rather than the more general social-system perspective we deemed appropriate. While we did not favor the classification of such children as handicapped, we did advocate programming designed to help them find more comfortable academic and social niches in these schools. In essence, what we are advocating is that school environments be assessed in terms of whether or not they are applying appropriate social-system perspectives in their classification and programming activities.

Pluralistic model measures are designed to detect whether children deviate significantly from what is normal for their subcultural peers. We have previously suggested that pluralistic norms may be specifically applied to some children's performances on intelligence tests when making classification decisions relative to the mental retardation and learning disability categories. We have also indicated that the use of pluralistic norms is not generally seen to be a legal or ethical requirement. Our stance on the use of pluralistic norms is embedded in the controversy over the degree to which schools should accept, and perhaps even encourage, cultural differences among children. We have already indicated our belief that children should not be classified as handicapped when their school difficulties primarily reflect conditions external to themselves. Such conditions would include home and neighborhood training in languages other than English and in intellectual skills and strategies different from those usually taught in middle class homes and neighborhoods. For programming purposes, we believe that schools should initially accept such differences by adapting instruction to children's "entering skills." We also believe that schools should attempt to teach respect for different subcultural traditions. At the same time, schools should attempt to train all children in the skills and strategies necessary for later success in mainstream American culture. That is why we favor the use of national social-system norms in the specific assessment domains of academic achievement, social/emotional functioning, and adaptive behavior. Such norms, in our view, are the appropriate ones to apply in classification decisions and are usually appropriate in setting programming goals. Again, we are advocating that school environments be assessed in terms of whether or not they are appropriately applying a pluralistic perspective in their classification and programming activities. We have already indicated our view of the appropriate application of a pluralistic perspective.

Measures compatible with the task analysis model are designed to detect children's failures in mastering prerequisite academic and behavioral skills incorporated in various skill hierarchies. Detection of such failures is quite useful in planning for remedial programming. The relevance of this model for assessment of environmental factors lies in the need to use task-analytic measures appropriate to the particular skills the school is trying to teach. Hence the instructional goals and methods that are given priority in the school must be well understood. Children's skills can be task-analyzed in terms of these high-priority goals, and analysis of environmental conditions can identify the instructional methods and conditions most appropriate to the development and consistent use of skills.

Measures compatible with the psychoeducational process model are designed to detect children's difficulties in various modality skills such as visual and auditory perception and short-term memory. Since we believe that formal measures of these skills have not, to date, been conclusively shown to be usefully related to effective programming, we have suggested in Chapter 7 that their use be deemphasized in psychoeducational assessment. Since such measures are implied (though probably not actually required) in classifying children as learning disabled, we have proposed that deficits in modality skills may be detected in the task and conditions analyses undertaken in Dickinson's (1978, 1980) Direct Assessment approach. Any modality skills deficits detected by this approach can be used, if needed, to help justify the assignment of the learning disability classification. In addition, such deficits can be addressed in programming efforts, either by attempts to overcome them through direct training of academic skills or by attempts to train academic skills that involve "working around" modality skill deficits. The relevance of the psychoeducational process model for assessment of environmental influences lies in the need to assess the degree to which schools are programming in terms of this model and the ways in which this model is used. Regardless of the instructional models being implemented, attention needs to be given to the effectiveness of remedial methods. Critical analyses of current instructional methods and searches for more effective methods should be an ongoing process.

TECHNICAL ADEQUACY OF ENVIRONMENTAL ASSESSMENT TECHNIQUES

The technical adequacy of techniques designed to assess environmental influences on school coping will be addressed later in this chapter, as we discuss each technique, but a few general comments are in order. As we have already remarked, such techniques are of relatively recent origin. Further, since some of them focus on environmental influences on individual children, while others focus on influences on groups of children, for purposes of individual assessment the group-focused techniques must be adapted to the assessment of the individual child. In addition, some of the techniques have been systematically "packaged" by their creators, while others involve general procedures that can be tailored to the requirements of specific assessment situations. Some of the techniques yield data that are relatively subjective in nature, while others yield more objective data. Finally, while none of the assessment techniques discussed in this chapter have formal norms, some of the techniques can be discussed in terms of their reliabilities and validities. Our discussion of each technique includes reliability and validity data when such data are available. When reliability and validity data are unavailable, this will be noted. It is unfortunate that no data on the reliability and validity of some of the techniques used for assessment of the environment are available. We strongly advocate that greater research attention be given to the technical adequacy of environmental assessment techniques. For now, however, the importance of this assessment domain requires the use of available techniques, with due consideration given to their known or suspected limitations.

OBSTACLES TO ENVIRONMENTAL ASSESSMENT

A number of situational factors act to constrain the assessment of environmental influences on school coping behavior. One of these, frequently mentioned before, is the time pressure under which many assessment practitioners function. When there are large numbers of children to be assessed and limited numbers of practitioners available, short-term efficiency considerations may predominate, dictating the assessment of each child in the shortest time possible while still meeting the "letter of the law." As we have argued previously, assessment efficiency should not be judged from this perspective but instead from the perspective of the long-term efficiency that can be expected from thorough problem analyses.

A second factor often constraining environmental assessment is the absence of a response capability view, within a school or community, of children's functioning. Some school personnel and some parents tend to view children's school problems in terms of the response predisposition model. Practitioners who encounter these attitudes can try to explain the point of view involved in the response capability model to school personnel and parents. Practitioners can also point to those sections of the regulations implementing PL 94-142 that require modifications of the instructional arrangements (in both special education and regular classrooms) appropriate to the needs of handicapped children. Assessment practitioners attempting to provide such explanations will need to use available sources of influence. Meyers, Parsons, and Martin (1979) describe the expert and referent power of psychological consultants as legitimate sources of influence. These authors further describe how these sources of influence may be used in consultation activities. Kauffman and Vicente (1972) provide a humorous but telling description of how the kind of consultation we are advocating should *not* be done.

A third factor often constraining environmental assessment is the fact that some school personnel and parents perceive assessment of their influence on the child as threatening. No one wishes to be blamed for a child's school difficulties, and efforts to assess environmental influences are sometimes seen as directed toward assigning blame to teachers or parents. Assessment practitioners can counteract such a threatened feeling by adopting a helpful, rather than a judgmental, demeanor, and by striving to focus attention consistently on the problems and needs of the child toward a goal of comprehensive intervention. In addition, intervention responsibilities need to be cooperatively negotiated, and an overall spirit of teamwork must be developed among those providing intervention services. In general, what we are stressing here is that consultation subsequent to assessment is a necessary role for assessment practitioners, and that effective consultation requires well-developed interpersonal skills, clear conceptions of classification and programming goals, and understanding of the school's programs and procedures. Although it is sometimes difficult to influence schools to base intervention efforts on thorough assessments, including an evaluation of both school and home environments, and to react nondefensively, the gains for children are worth the effort involved.

SPECIFIC TECHNIQUES

While formal assessments of environmental influences should be done whenever possible, circumstances sometimes prevent this. Even when formal assessments are not possible, however, careful consideration of the available data on environmental influences can still be incorporated into classification and programming activities. Assessment practitioners should, at a minimum, consider whatever informally acquired data are available on a child's home and school environment.

General School Climate

Earlier in this chapter, we suggested that a school's general climate has indirect effects on a child's performance in one or more of its classrooms. Aspects of the school's climate include general curricular requirements, policies, and procedures. Normative pressures within each school bring classroom climates more or less into line with the general climate. At the same time, each classroom will, to some degree, have its own unique climate.

Since the general school climate will partially dictate the climates of all the classrooms, an understanding of a school's general climate becomes important. In addition to perhaps affecting a child's performance, the general climate may support or impede certain types of interventions for a child experiencing difficulty in a particular classroom. Such influences on programming need to be understood and perhaps overcome in efforts to provide effective programs for individual children. Moreover, if significant numbers of children are experiencing difficulty in a school, that school's general climate may need to be systematically examined by the entire school staff, with the goal of developing a more effective program.

CFK Ltd. School Climate Profile

The CFK Ltd. School Climate Profile has been developed to provide a general description of a school's climate as perceived by administrators, teachers, support staff members, students, and parents. This survey of school climate factors is contained in a document entitled *School Climate Improvement: A Challenge to the School Administrator* (Phi Delta Kappa, undated). No reliability, validity, or normative data are presented for this survey instrument. The lack of technical adequacy data is somewhat understandable because the instrument was designed to assess perceptions of what the school's climate currently is and what it ought to be. Intervention plans to improve a school's climate are to be developed on the basis of survey results that indicate discrepancies between "what is" and "what should be" or perceived differences in the existing school climate across role groups.

This survey instrument is to be administered to members of the school's various role groups, and results are to be summarized for each group in terms of scores on each item for what is and what should be. Each of the 130 items contained in the instrument falls under one of four climate determinants. Within each climate determinant are a number of subcategories, and each subcategory contains five positively worded items. The four climate determinants and the subcategories under each are shown in Table 11-1.

While assessment practitioners may not often have access to

Table 11-1   Climate Determinants and Subcategories in the CFK Ltd.
School Climate Profile

General School Climate
Respect
Trust
High Morale
Opportunity for Input
Continuous Academic and Social
Growth
Cohesiveness
School Renewal
Caring

Program Determinants
Active Learning
Individualized Performance
Expectations
Varied Learning Environments
Flexible Curriculum and
Extracurricular Activities
Support and Structure Appropriate to
Learners' Maturity
Rules Cooperatively Determined
Varied Reward Systems

Process Determinants
Problem Solving Ability
Improvement of School Goals
Identifying and Working with
Conflicts
Effective Communications
Involvement in Decision Making
Autonomy with Accountability
Effective Teaching-Learning
Strategies
Ability to Plan for the Future

Material Determinants
Adequate Resources
Supportive and Efficient Logistical
System
Suitability of School Plant

such data on perceptions of a school's climate, they will informally develop their own perceptions of these aspects of a school's climate as they gain increasing experience in a school. In addition, some of the specific items in the CFK Ltd. School Climate Profile shown in Table 11-2 can be quite usefully considered in the process of assessing an individual child. Considering the variables addressed by these items as they affect a child being assessed should lead to a more complete understanding of that child's school learning environment. Responses to some of the items may suggest aspects of the child's school environment that may be impeding her or his progress, while responses to other items may indicate aspects of the environment that are actually or potentially supportive. Responses to still other items may be of assistance in understanding how flexibly the school may respond to proposed interventions and what types of interventions may be favored by the school. As we have said, such aspects of the school environment must be considered in developing and sometimes even "selling" interventions for individual children. Even when assessment practitioners must covertly consider school environmental influences, the items listed in Table 11-2 can suggest some aspects of that environment worthy of consideration.

Table 11-2   Selected Items from CFK Ltd. School Climate Profile

General School Climate

- High Morale, item 1: "This school makes students enthusiastic about learning."
- School Renewal, item 3: "When a student comes along who has special problems, this school works out a plan that helps that student."

Program Determinants

- Individualized Performances Exceptions, items 3–4: "The same homework assignment is not given to all students in the class." "All students are not held to the same standards."
- Flexible Curriculum and Extracurricular Activities, item 3: "Students are given alternative ways of meeting curriculum requirements."
- Support and Structure Appropriate to Learner's Maturity, item 2: "The needs of a few students for close supervision and high structure are met without making those students feel 'put down.'"
- Varied Reward Systems, item 2: "Students know the criteria used to evaluate their progress."

Process Determinants

- Problem Solving Ability, item 3: "People in this school do a good job of examining a lot of alternative solutions first, before deciding to try one."
- Identifying and Working with Conflict, item 3: "This school believes there may be several alternative solutions to most problems."
- Effective Communications, item 4: "Teachers are available to students who want help."
- Autonomy with Accountability, item 3: "Teachers or students can arrange to deviate from the prescribed program of the school."
- Effective Teaching-Learning Strategies, items 2 and 5: "When one teaching strategy does not seem to be working for a particular student, the teacher tries another; does not blame the student for the initial failure." "The school systematically encourages students to help other students with their learning activities."

Material Determinants

- Supportive and Efficient Logistical Systems, item 1: "Teachers and students are able to get the instructional materials they need at the time they are needed."

From Phi Delta Kappa. *School climate improvement: A challenge to the school administrator.* Denver: Charles F. Kettering, undated, pp. 54–68. With permission.

Curriculum

We indicated earlier that a skills analysis of a child experiencing school difficulties should incorporate measures appropriate to the skills the child is being asked to learn. An understanding of the curriculum the child is being taught is therefore prerequisite to a useful skills analysis of the child. In addition, an evaluation of the curriculum content, teaching methods, and instructional materials that the child is being exposed to can provide useful information for a conditions analysis of that child's school difficulties.

Curriculum, Methods, and Materials Assessment Checklist

Smith, Neisworth, and Geer (1978) have developed a list of 65 positively worded questions that can be used to evaluate the curriculum, methods, and materials being used in a classroom. They refer to this list of questions as a Curriculum, Methods, and Materials Assessment Checklist. Answering each question with a "yes," "no," or "undecided" response requires a thorough understanding of the curricular influences present in a classroom, and the list of questions is designed to allow teachers to evaluate their own instructional programs. Questions are grouped in terms of components and, in some cases, subdivisions within components. The three components and their subdivisions are

- Curriculum
- Instructional Methods: includes Learning Environment, Selecting Objectives, Teaching Methods, Consequating Methods, and Evaluating Instruction
- Materials: includes Commercial Materials, Teacher Materials, and Student Materials

Each component and subdivision within a component is evaluated in terms of the number of questions answered yes relative to the total number of questions in that component or subdivision. Smith et al. (1978) suggest that a low percentage of yes answers indicates a component or subdivision needing improvement. Norms are not provided, since teachers are to use the list of questions to determine their own priorities for instructional improvements. Reliability and validity data are also lacking. Nevertheless, the Checklist calls attention to a number of instructional considerations and, in that sense, can serve to focus the attention of teachers and assessment practicioners on important aspects of a child's instructional environment. The questions from the checklist that seem most relevant to a conditions anal-

Table 11-3   Selected Questions from Curriculum, Methods, and Materials
Assessment Checklist

Curriculum   ·   ·

- Question 13: "Are behavioral objectives for group lessons applicable for the range of children within the group?"

Instructional Methods

- Learning Environment, questions 14 – 17: "Are both homogeneous and heterogeneous grouping used to enhance learning through modeling?" "Are instructional groups small enough so that all children have adequate access to the teacher?" "Are modeling effects considered in planning seating arrangements?" "Are environmental prompts used to assist children in discriminating what behaviors are expected of them?"
- Selecting Objectives, question 24: "Are criterion measures realistic for individual children?"
- Teaching Methods, questions 28 – 29: "Does the teacher model behaviors that he/she wishes to teach the children?" "Is peer tutoring used to maximize learning?"
- Consequating Methods, questions 30 – 34: "Can teachers list rewards and punishments that are successful with individual students?" "Are consequences delivered consistently?" "Are consequences delivered quickly?" "Are consequation techniques experimentally determined for individual chil ren?"
- Evaluating Instruction, question 38: "Are learners initially located on instructional task ladders (curriculums)?"

Materials

- Commercial Materials, questions 48 – 49: "Are materials useful for the needs of the particular class?" "Are materials relevant to the curricular objectives?"
- Teacher Materials, question 52: "Are objectives task-analyzed?"
- Student Materials, question 65: "Are varied and effective learning methods used?"

From Smith, R., Neisworth, J., & Greer, J. *Evaluating educational environments.* Columbus, Ohio: Charles E. Merrill, 1978, pp. 73 – 79. With permission.

ysis are shown in Table 11-3. Consideration of these questions in relation to a child's school difficulties should lead to a better understanding of the curricular influences on the child's performance. Answers to some of the questions may suggest curricular conditions impeding the child's performance, while answers to other questions may suggest aspects of the curricular program that are actually or potentially supportive. Such information should be incorporated into planning for programming that will provide conditions conducive to the development and consistent use of important skills.

Teachers

For our purposes, the influence of teachers on children's school performance involves the ways in which teachers interact with their classes and with individual children within those classes. A number of assessment techniques have been designed to evaluate teachers' interactions with their classes. Examples of such techniques are Flanders' Interaction Analysis (Flanders, 1964) and sections of the Social Environment Assessment Checklist developed by Smith, Neisworth, and Greer (1978). A number of assessment devices have also been designed to evaluate a teacher's interactions with individual children within a class. Since this book addresses assessment techniques used in individual psychoeducational assessment, we will discuss only the latter. Our "rule of thumb" for assessing environmental influences on individual children is to use individually focused techniques when such techniques are available and to adapt more general techniques to a conditions analysis of a child's performance when individually focused techniques are not available.

We have chosen to discuss three individually focused assessment techniques: the Ecological Assessment of Child Problem Behavior, the Dyadic Interaction Analysis, and homemade teacher attention scales.

Ecological Assessment of Child Problem Behavior

As indicated in Chapter 9 (pp. 243 – 245), the Ecological Assessment of Child Problem Behavior (Wahler, House, & Stambaugh, 1976) represents a comprehensive behavioral observation system for evaluating the behavior of a child in both home and school settings. The system involves 19 child behavior categories and 6 categories of environmental stimulus events. Of the 6 types of stimulus events, 4 focus on teacher behaviors in the school (or parent behaviors in the home), while 2 focus on the behaviors of other children present in the observational setting. The 4 categories focusing on teacher behavior toward the target child are Instruction, Nonaversive; Instruction, Aversive; Social Attention, Adult, Nonaversive; and Social Attention, Adult, Aversive. Brief descriptions of these categories were presented in Chapter 9 (pp. 243 – 245).

Wahler et al. (1976) present inter-rater reliability data for these 4 categories. For observations done in schools, inter-rater reliabilities for Instruction, Nonaversive, and Social Attention, Adult, Nonaversive are mostly in the 0.80 to 0.90 range, with a few reliabilities in the high 0.70s. These data suggest adequate inter-rater reliabilities for these two categories for observers specifically trained in the use of this observational package. Inter-rater reliabilities for Instruction, Aversive and Social Attention, Adult, Aversive coded in the school setting range from 0.69 to 0.80 and from 0.54 to 0.82, respectively. These data suggest caution in the use of the latter two categories. Nevertheless, all four categories represent important aspects of a teacher's interactions with a child and should be considered in a conditions analysis of a child's school difficulties.

Wahler et al. (1976) present two kinds of information relative to the validity of both the child behavior and stimulus event categories. They suggest that the categories possess content validity because the categories were derived from extensive interviews with parents and teachers closely involved with problem children. Hence, the categories were chosen, in part, to adequately reflect "the concerns of those who were and would continue to be intimately associated with the problem child" (p. 3). The authors also suggest that the categories possess concurrent validity in the sense that frequency counts of children's behaviors derived from the system tend to correspond rather closely to teachers' and parents' narrative descriptions of behaviors. Four case descriptions are presented to illustrate this point, and some of these case descriptions show quite different patterns of behavior at home and school as initially reflected in parent and teacher reports.

We are relatively satisfied with the reliability and validity data presented in the Ecological Assessment of Child Problem Behavior. We join Wahler et al., however, in urging that this observational system not be used by untrained observers and that even trained observers periodically check their category codings against those of other trained observers. While Wahler et al. present no norms for their observation system, this omission is appropriate to the intended use of the system, which involves ascertaining the frequency of a child's desirable and undesirable behaviors in a particular setting and evaluating adult and peer social interactions that may be stimulating and maintaining the child's undesirable behaviors.

Information about social interactions that serve to stimulate or maintain either desirable or undesirable behaviors is important to a conditions analysis of a child's school difficulties. Under the Ecological Assessment system, the collection of such information involves several steps. First, information about the child's problem behaviors is collected during an interview with the referral source. The child is then observed, using all the stimulus event categories and the specific child behavior categories relevant to the referral problem. Within each recording interval, stimulus events are marked as antecedent to or subsequent to those features of the child's behavior being coded. While no specific length of time is required for use of this system, Wahler et al. point to the need for sufficient time to permit valid conclusions to be drawn about the relations between antecedent and consequent events and a child's behaviors. When a sufficient number of observational intervals have been coded, frequency counts of each child behavior category and of each stimulus event category may be made. Then charts of antecedent and consequent events may be constructed indicating how often certain of the child's behaviors were preceded by and followed by each of the stimulus events. These charts can be analyzed to show the conditions under which the child exhibits desirable or undesirable behaviors. For programming purposes, conditions antecedent to and subsequent to desirable behaviors can then be presented more frequently. Also, attempts can be made to reduce the frequency with which the child is presented with conditions surrounding his or her undesirable behaviors.

This process is illustrated by data recently collected by one of the authors. The target child was a third-grade boy referred for frequent noncompliance with teacher instructions. Charts of antecedent and consequent events indicated that this boy almost always complied with instructions given nonaversively but hardly ever complied with instructions given aversively. This was pointed out to his teacher, and it was suggested that nonaversive instructions be given him whenever possible. The charts also indicated that his teacher infrequently provided nonaversive attention following his desirable behaviors but frequently provided aversive attention following his undesirable behaviors. The aversive attention did not seem to be bringing his undesirable behaviors under better control and, in fact, may have actually been serving as a reinforcer for these behaviors. The teacher was advised of this and encouraged to provide more attention following the boy's desirable behaviors. She was also advised to intervene when the child's behavior was clearly unacceptable but to limit the social attention given his undesirable behaviors. Such data-based intervention suggestions, we believe, illustrate the value of a conditions analysis of teacher influences.

Dyadic Interaction Analysis

This assessment technique was developed by Brophy and Good (1970) as a research tool for a series of studies investigating behavioral expressions by teachers of differential expectations for school achievement from various students. As a result of this emphasis, Dyadic Interaction Analysis focuses more on teacher responses to children's academic performances than does Ecological Assessment of Child Problem Behavior. The more narrow focus of Dyadic Interaction Analysis can, however, be quite useful within the context of a specific conditions analysis of a teacher's responses to a child's academic problems.

In this assessment technique, an observer codes teacher interactions with a target child (or children). Each teacher–child interaction is coded, and the behaviors of each participant are coded in sequence. Coding of each specific behavior of each participant continues as long as the interaction continues but ceases when the teacher and the target child terminate each interaction. While no specific observation time is specified, observations need to be extensive enough to cover a number of interactions so as to provide data representative of the quantity and quality of the interactions.

Five types of interactions are coded. One type involves opportunities given to the child for public response. Such opportunities occur when a target child attempts to answer a question posed by a teacher. A second type of coded interaction involves reading turns in which the child reads orally to the teacher. A third type involves private, work-related contacts in which a teacher interacts with the child concerning academic work. A fourth type involves private, procedural interactions in which the teacher discusses nonacademic matters with the child. The fifth type involves behavioral evaluations in which the teacher praises or criticizes the child's behavior. Within these categories, those interactions initiated by the child are distinguished during coding from those initiated by the teacher.

Interactions involving public response opportunities are coded in terms of the type and difficulty of the questions asked the child. In addition, the qualities of the child's responses to questions (correct, partially correct, incorrect, or no response) are coded. Finally, teacher responses to the child's responses are also coded (as praising, criticizing, giving the answer, giving process feedback, calling on someone else, repeating the question, giving a clue, asking a new question, or failing to provide feedback). Teacher responses are also coded for private work-related contacts with the child.

Brophy and Good (1974) indicate that Dyadic Interaction Analysis can be used to assess both the quantity and the quality of a teacher's interactions with a child. Quantity is reflected in the number of teacher–child interactions across observation sessions, and this number can be analyzed in terms of child-initiated and teacher-initiated interactions. Quality is reflected in the types and difficulties of the questions asked the target child and in the teacher's reactions to the child's responses. Process feedback to assist the child in under-standing curricular content is seen as more helpful to the child than is simply providing the child with answers to incorrectly answered questions. The quality of the interactions is described in terms of per-centage scores. "For example, the percentage of times a student is praised for a correct answer is computed by dividing his total num-ber of correct answers into the number of those correct answers which were followed by teacher praise" (p. 92).

Brophy and Good suggest that Dyadic Interaction Analysis be conducted only by observers who have established inter-rater reli-abilities of at least 0.80 with observers trained in the use of the sys-tem. They also suggest that the content validity of the coding catego-ries is derived from empirical and anecdotal studies of the effects of teachers' expectations for individual students on the students. Norms for the system are not presented, but this omission is understandable in terms of the system's focus on individual child – teacher interac-tions. We are satisfied with the technical adequacy of the system for both research purposes and for use in conditions analysis with indi-vidual children.

Brophy and Good have used Dyadic Interaction Analysis to in-vestigate differences in the quantity and quality of teachers' interac-tions with children from whom they expected high and low academic achievement. They have found that some teachers initiate interac-tions more frequently with children from whom they expect high achievement, that these teachers tend to provide more assistance in mastering curriculum requirements to these children, and that they tend to praise the correct answers of these children more often (p. 110). They have also found, however, that these teachers are often unaware of their differential treatments of their students and, at least in one study, used feedback about their practices in efforts to modify their responses to individual students. The researchers describe a nine-step model for assisting teachers in providing more helpful re-sponses to individual children (pp. 292 – 295). This model again illus-trates the ways in which data-based analyses of teacher influences can be incorporated into suggestions for improving a child's learning environment.

Homemade Teacher Attention Scales

Less elaborate, more narrowly focused measures of teacher influ-ences can be accomplished through the construction and use of homemade teacher attention scales. Such scales are discussed by Smith, Neisworth, and Greer (1978) and involve recording when a teacher either reinforces, punishes, or ignores a child's appropriate behavior or inappropriate behavior. Before recording procedures are implemented, the teacher and the observer must carefully specify appropriate and inappropriate child behaviors and how teacher responses are to be coded. It would also be helpful for the observer to obtain an inter-rater reliability check before beginning official recording. If these steps are followed by a sufficient period of observation time, the observer can supply information to the teacher about how effectively the teacher is responding to appropriate and inappropriate child behaviors. Homemade teacher attention scales can, therefore, provide information useful to a conditions analysis of a child's school difficulties, since the information can be incorporated into the planning of remedial programming efforts.

Peers

Practically no serious theorist or practitioner questions the profound influence of peer behavior on students. In fact, most would agree with the contention that a child's academic behaviors must be viewed in the ecological context of peer behavior. We explore three methods for assessing peer influence on students: the use of sociometric techniques, behavioral observation systems, and questionnaires on classroom norms.

Sociometric Techniques

Sociometric techniques are peer nomination systems wherein members of a class are asked to list the names of other children with whom they prefer to interact (Biehler, 1954; Moreno, 1953). The listing of names allows for the determination of each student's social position or status within the group.

As the first step in the use of a sociometric technique, children are presented with statements about various activities they might do and are asked to nominate two to four other members of the class with whom they would like to participate in the activity. Activities can focus on either work or play. Examples of activity statements are shown in Figure 11-1. Once all students in a classroom have responded to an activity statement, the second step is to enter each student's name in a matrix like the one shown in Figure 11-2. If more than one activity statement is used (for example, one for play, one for work), a different matrix will be needed for each.

From the matrix one can readily determine the number of times each class member is chosen by peers for participation in a given activity. The frequency of choices for a student is held to reflect each

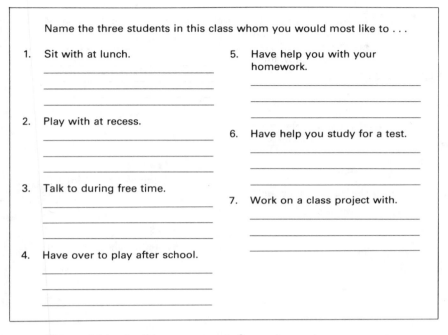

Figure 11-1   Activity statements for sociometric assessment.

student's status in the eyes of peers vis-à-vis that activity. Once choice frequencies are tabulated for each student in a class, one can begin analyzing the internal social structure of the class. One of the most common types of analysis involves the use of the following categories:

- Star: a child who receives the largest number (or, a large number) of choices or nominations by peers
- Isolate: a child who receives no choices from peers
- Neglectee: a child who receives relatively few choices
- Mutual choice: two or more children choose each other
- Sociometric clique: a number of children choose each other but give few choices to others outside their group
- Sociometric cleavage: lack of choices between two or more subgroups in the class (for example, males and females, Anglos and Chicanos, children of high socioeconomic status and those of low socioeconomic status)

To facilitate the determination of which children belong in each category practitioners frequently construct what is known as a socio-

Chosen	John	Mary	Jim	Susie	Ralph	George	Paul
Chooser							
John		1		2	3		
Mary			2	1			3
Jim				2	3	1	
Susie	2	3			1		
Ralph		3	2			1	
George	3	2					1
Paul				2	3	1	
Chosen as							
1st choice	0	1	0	1	1	3	1
2nd choice	0	1	2	4	0	0	0
3rd choice	0	1	2	0	3	0	1
Total	0	3	4	4	4	3	2

Figure 11-2   Matrix showing peer nomination.

gram. This is a diagram that allows for a visual representation of the social structure of the group. An example is seen in Figure 11-3. To complete the sociogram, each student's name is placed on the diagram in an appropriate area on the basis of the number of choices the child received. Notice that in our example, stars would be placed in the centermost concentric circle, while isolates would be placed in the outermost circle. All others would occupy less extreme positions. Once names are positioned appropriately on the sociogram, lines are drawn from one name to another to indicate choices with arrows pointing toward the chosen students. When the sociogram is complete, it is quite easy to visually determine the stars, isolates, neglectees, as well as the presence of cliques and cleavages.

Sociometric analyses have a number of potential uses. They can help to identify those students who might need some assistance in developing better social skills (isolates). They can help to identify stu-

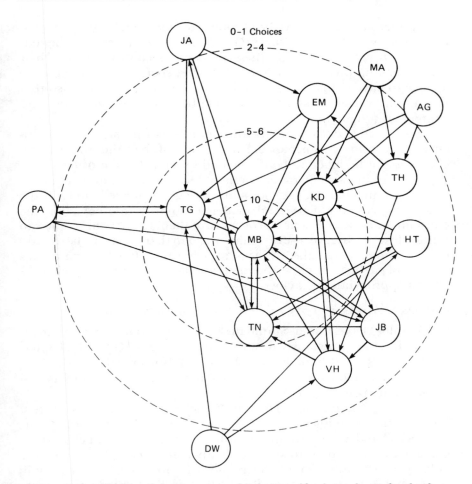

Figure 11-3 A sociogram. (Courtesy of John Bradford, Baylor School, Chattanooga, Tennessee.)

dents who can serve as effective role models for others; since chosen students hold status in the eyes of choosers, the chosen ones can be effective models for the choosers. Sociometric analyses can determine sources of environmental support for improving a student's behavior, since chosen students and mutual choices can be encouraged to socially reinforce the target student's appropriate behavior. By identifying a target student's mutual choices, sociometric analyses can also help to determine appropriate peer tutoring partners. Finally, this technique can help to identify souces of group conflict that reside in the group's sociometric cleavage.

Numerous studies have been conducted on the reliability and validity of sociometric procedures (Gronlund, 1959). In general, the reliability and validity data on these procedures contraindicates their use in making precise decisions. However, sociometric methods do appear to have potential as global measures of social status, so that they might be used in addition to direct behavioral observations and competent judgment.

Sociometric data can indicate a number of possible peer influences on a child's performance. For instance, if the child is an isolate, efforts might be made to teach the child social skills in order to improve his or her social status. Improved social status, in turn, might lead to greater liking of school and more concentrated effort. If the child's choices would be good models of appropriate behavior, the child might be seated near one or more of them to allow him or her to more closely observe their behaviors. Further, one of the child's choices might assist the child as a peer tutor. Finally, the child's choices of partners might be honored as one means for reinforcing the child's appropriate behaviors.

Ecological Assessment of Child Problem Behavior

Wahler, House, and Stambaugh's (1976) ecological assessment system has been previously discussed in some detail (see this chapter, pp. 293–295, and Chapter 9, pp. 243–245). However, further discussion is warranted here, since the system provides a means of assessing student–peer relations.

It should be recalled that the Wahler et al. observation system includes the stimulus categories of Social Attention Child, Nonaversive (SC+) and Social Attention Child, Aversive (SC−). Each of these categories can be used to systematically assess the influence of peer behavior on a child. Inter-rater reliabilities for the SC+ category in the school setting range from 0.82 to 0.91, indicating adequate reliability for this category. Inter-rater reliabilities for the SC− category in the school setting range from 0.62 to 0.82, indicating a need for some caution in the use of this category. Validity evidence for all the coding categories has been discussed previously.

The Social Attention Child category is scored for situations in which a peer (or peers) attend to, or verbally or physically interact with, a target child. If SC+ or SC− consistently precedes a given behavior—for example, disruptive/oppositional behavior—then it is suggested that peer attention might be prompting the behavior. On the other hand, if SC+ or SC− consistently follows the behavior, this suggests that peer attention might serve to reinforce or strengthen the behavior.

If observations indicate a strong functional relationship between peer attention and a student's inappropriate behavior, then steps can be taken to reduce inappropriate behavior by minimizing antecedent or consequential peer attention. On the other hand, if observations indicate a functional relationship between peer attention and an appropriate behavior, then steps can be taken to maintain or increase peer attention. Thus Wahler et al.'s Ecological Assessment of Child Problem Behaviors provides a mechanism for systematically assessing the impact of peer behavior on student behavior and developing interventions that take into account the influence of peer behavior.

The Wahler et al. system is an example of a standardized behavioral observation system. It should be noted that informal behavioral observation systems can be designed by practitioners for use in highly specific situations. For example, if highly specific information on different types of peer attention were needed, the practitioner could devise a system to make finer discriminations than those provided by the Ecological Assessment system. One might, for instance, include categories to tap a wide range of peer verbalization behaviors and physical contact behaviors. This would allow for the assessment of very specific types of functional relationships between peer and target child behaviors and for the development of more finely tuned interventions than are possible with the Ecological Assessment system. Again, types of peer attention to be recorded would need to be carefully specified, and inter-rater reliability checks would also be helpful.

Questionnaires on Classroom Norms

The Questionnaires on Classroom Norms (Fox, Luszki, & Schmuck, 1966) involve a set of two questionnaires designed to assess children's perceptions of how their classmates feel about various issues and the children's own feelings about these issues. As such, the Questionnaires on Classroom Norms (QCN) can provide measures of where a given child stands vis-à-vis peers on several aspects of classroom functioning. The two QCN questionnaires are shown in Figures 11-4 and 11-5.

Form A of the QCN (Figure 11-4) provides a measure of each child's perception of the values or norms of peers. Form B (Figure 11-5) provides a measure of each child's own feelings about important classroom issues. An analysis of the QCN involves the following steps:

Step 1: The results of form A are tabulated by listing the frequency of each response category for each item. The highest frequency responses reflect perceived classroom norms.

Step 2: The results of form B are tabulated, providing a composite of individual standards. The results of forms A and B are compared to determine the degree of congruence between perceptions of

Your number _____   Date _____
Class _____

How This Class Feels

School classes are quite different from one another in how pupils think and feel about school work, about one another, and about teachers. How do you think your classmates feel about the following things? Put a check (√) in one of the boxes under "How Many Feel This Way?" for each of the statements below. There are no right or wrong answers.

	How Many Feel This Way?				
	Almost All	Many	About Half	Some	Only a Few
1. It is good to take part as much as possible in classroom work.					
2. Asking the teacher for help is a good thing to do.					
3. It is good to help other pupils with their school-work except during tests.					
4. Schoolwork is more often "fun" than it is "not fun."					
5. Our teacher really understands how pupils feel.					

Figure 11-4   Form A, QCN questionnaire on class norms. (From *Diagnosing Classroom Learning Environments* by Robert Fox, Margaret B. Luszki, and Richard Schmuck. © 1966, Science Research Associates, Inc. Reprinted by permission of the publisher.)

norms and individual attitudes. Congruence indicates open communication among classmates, whereas discontinuity indicates limited communication and interaction.

Step 3: Each child's responses on form A are compared to the form A responses from the rest of the class. A large discrepancy suggests that a child is isolated from the class.

Step 4: Each child's responses on form A are compared with his or her responses on form B. A discrepancy suggests dissociation between the student and his or her peers, while congruence suggests compatibility.

Your number _____   Date _____
Class _____

How Do You Feel About These Things

Put a check (✓) in the box that tells how you feel about each of the statements below. There are no right or wrong answers.

	I agree almost always.	I agree more than I disagree.	I agree as often as I disagree.	I disagree more than I agree.	I disagree almost always.
1. It is good to take part as much as possible in classroom work.					
2. Asking the teacher for help is a good thing to do.					
3. It is good to help other pupils with their schoolwork except during tests.					
4. Schoolwork is more often "fun" than it is "not fun."					
5. Our teacher really understands how pupils feel.					

Figure 11-5 Form B, QCN questionnaire on personal norms. (From *Diagnosing Classroom Learning Environments* by Robert Fox, Margaret B. Luszki, and Richard Schmuck. © 1966, Science Research Associates, Inc. Reprinted by permission of the publisher.)

It seems that the QCN provides a reasonable way of assessing student–peer relations. Furthermore, it can be an extremely flexible measure, since items that might be especially appropriate for a particular situation can be substituted for those in forms A and B (Smith, Neisworth, & Greer, 1978).

In the case of a conditions analysis for an individual child experiencing school difficulties, the QCN can indicate incorrect understandings of peer norms. Individual or group discussions might assist the child (and perhaps other children) to better understand the normative framework from which her or his behavior will be evaluated. If analysis suggests lack of normative consensus, group discussions might lead to improved consensus and thereby make the social atmosphere of the classroom more predictable for all, including the child experiencing difficulties.

Physical Environment

Physical Environment Assessment Checklist

As Smith, Neisworth, and Greer (1978) have pointed out, a number of aspects of the physical classroom environment appear to affect student behaviors. These include illumination, seating patterns, furnishings layouts, temperature, noise, color, and crowding. Smith et al. have developed one of the few systems for assessing such factors. Their system is incorporated in a Physical Environment Assessment Checklist, which serves as a means of obtaining systematic information about physical aspects of classrooms.

Reliability, validity, and normative data are not presented in conjunction with the Physical Environment Assessment Checklist. Essentially, responses to the items on the checklist ("yes," "no," or "undecided") reflect the rater's best impressions. Nevertheless, such impressions may be usefully considered in performing a conditions analysis. The checklist is organized in terms of two major sections: School Environment and Classroom Environment. Classroom Environment is further subdivided into Physiological Effects (illumination, temperature, noise, color, and materials); Spatial Effects; Physical Effects; and Setting Effects.

While the Checklist is designed to assess physical environments for groups of children, several of the items under Spatial Effects can be usefully considered in a conditions analysis for a single child. These are items 25 through 27:

25. Are there special places that individual children can go: a) for isolation; b) for rest and quiet; c) to let off steam; d) to reward themselves; e) for private instruction; f) to work independently; g) to be disciplined privately?"
26. "Can children enter, leave, clean up, and dress, etc. without disturbing others?"
27. "Can children space themselves as they need or desire?"*

---

*From Smith, R., Neisworth, J., & Greer, J. *Evaluating educational environments.* Columbus, Ohio: Charles E. Merrill, 1978. With permission.

Consideration of these items may suggest ways in which the class-room environment can be physically modified to enhance the performance of a child or a group of children. In addition, existing features of the physical environment that have not been used as supports or prompts for improved performance can also be considered.

Home

Frequently, it becomes necessary to examine the relationship between children's home environments and a child's academic or social/emotional functioning in school. In this section, we will examine three methods for performing such an assessment. These methods include the use of the Family Environment Scale, parent interviews, and behavioral observations. Data gathered from such techniques can be used to judge the degree to which home and school influences are being directed toward similar goals. When there is evidence that school and home influences are pulling the child in opposite directions, interventions to improve accomodation between home and school demands are appropriate and often necessary.

Family Environment Scale (FES)

The FES (Moos, Insel, & Humphrey, 1974) is a questionnaire that purports to assess the social climate of all types of families. The scale can be completed by either children or adults and was normed on 1000 individuals in 285 families.

The FES yields 10 subscale scores that are grouped into the three major dimensions of Relationships, Personal Growth, and System Maintenance. The Relationship subscales assess aspects of the family's emotional functioning and include

- Cohesion: extent to which family members are helpful and supportive of each other
- Expressiveness: extent to which members are encouraged to express their feelings
- Conflict: extent to which anger and aggression characterize family interactions

The Personal Growth subscales assess the family's orientation toward various values. These subscales include

- Independence: extent to which members are encouraged to be self-sufficient and make their own decisions
- Achievement Orientation: extent to which various activities (such as school and work) are seen as competitive by the family members

- Intellectual Cultural Orientation: extent of family concern about political, intellectual, and cultural activities and events
- Active Recreational Orientation: extent of family interest in recreational and sporting events
- Moral-Religious Emphasis: extent of family interest in and discussion of religious issues

System Maintenance subscales measure a family's orientation in terms of structure and control of activities. Subscales include

- Organization: importance and clarity of family rules
- Control: extent to which a family is hierarchically organized

The FES manual provides relatively substantial data on the technical adequacy of the instrument (Moos et al., 1974). In terms of reliability, most internal consistency and test-retest coefficients for subscales range from approximately 0.70 to 0.86. This suggests that although the FES is relatively stable, future development is needed to increase the precision of subscale scores. In terms of validity, a number of studies indicate that FES scores can reliably differentiate between families with clinical problems and those not so characterized (Moos et al., 1974).

Clearly, the FES requires further research in regard to both reliability and validity. However, at this point, it does appear to represent a viable method for gathering global information about ways in which families relate to each other, and the basic values they hold. Data indicative of family values and practices that run counter to the legitimate skill and strategy concerns of schools may suggest a need to work toward improved accommodation between family and school. This will be the case particularly if a child's school difficulties seem to be linked to a lack of harmony between home and school requirements.

Interviewing was discussed in some detail in Chapter 9. The techniques discussed can be readily applied to interviews with families. Through interviewing parents, the interviewer can obtain important information about specific problematic behaviors of referred children and their antecedents and consequences. In addition, interviews can provide insight into family style by focusing on the rules of the family, the types of activities encouraged and discouraged, discipline and control methods utilized, and the expectations family members have for each other.

Ecological Assessment of Child Problem Behavior

Behavioral observations have also been discussed in detail in Chapter 9. It should be recalled that the Ecological Assessment of Child Problem Behavior (Wahler et al., 1976) has several categories through which family behaviors can be observed and analyzed. These include Instruction Adult, Nonaversive (IA+); Instruction Adult, Aversive (IA−); Social Attention Adult, Nonaversive (SA+); and Social Attention Adult, Aversive (SA −). The observer can use these categories to assess functional relationships between adult behaviors and child behaviors in the family, determining whether certain adult behaviors set the occasion for, reinforce, or punish certain child behaviors. In this context, it should be noted that inter-rater reliabilities for these categories coded in home settings are comparable to those obtained in school settings (presented on pp. 293 – 294).

Homemade Parent Attention Scales

As was the case with the use of observations in assessing peer influence in schools, it is possible to construct observation systems that focus more precisely on specific types of family influences. For example, instead of using the Ecological Assessment system's global SA + and SA − categories, one might devise a system that focuses on more specific types of adult attention (for example, various types of verbalizations, and physical contact). Such a system would allow for very precise statements of family environmental events and their relationship to a child's behavior. Of course, such statements are dependent on careful specifications of behaviors to be observed and attention to the adequacy of inter-rater reliabilities.

CONCLUSIONS

Environmental influences on children's school coping behaviors should be considered in the process of psychoeducational assessment. Assessment is a time-consuming process, and incorporating measures of environmental influences makes it even more time-consuming. The importance of this assessment domain however, dictates its tactful but vigorous defense. Assessment of environmental influences is necessary to ensure thorough problem analysis leading to optimally effective interventions. If, as we advocate, the assessment process is conducted as a team enterprise, parents, teachers, and others can assist by completing environmental influences checklists and by performing narrowly focused, highly structured behavioral observations. Wahler, House, and Stambaugh (1976) suggest procedures for enlisting the aid of parents and teachers in performing behavioral observations and for gaining congruence between observations by teachers or parents and those by assessment practitioners. We urge assessment practitioners to seek ways in which appropriate and cooperative assessment efforts can be implemented.

If assessment is to be followed by effective intervention, then assessment practitioners must possess skills in addition to those required by assessment activities. Participants in intervention planning must have clear conceptions of intervention goals, adequate understanding of the strengths and weaknesses of school programs, knowledge of various intervention strategies, and well-developed consulting skills. This point is well made by Mearig's (1974) comment that good intentions are not enough; one must also know *how* to help.

Part III

CONCLUSIONS

An Integrative Approach to Psychoeducational Assessment

THE CONTENTS OF THIS BOOK reflect our personal assumptions about the assessment process and our judgments about a number of assessment issues. We will be content if our discussion of the problems and issues involved in psychoeducational assessment today stimulates our readers to draw their own conclusions on these matters. Our readers must also make their own decisions about the assessment techniques they find most useful. Here it should be remembered that we have described what we believe to be representative assessment techniques. Our field is a very dynamic one, in constant change. While it is difficult to keep up with the number of changes and the pace of changes, best practice requires the effort. With these comments behind us, we now turn to a summary of some of our major points. These points can be conveniently grouped in terms of assumptions about the assessment process and judgments about assessment issues.

Many of our assumptions about the assessment process hinge on our choice of children being assessed as the appropriate clients of psychoeducational assessment practitioners. In choosing children as the appropriate clients, we are aware that other choices are possible. Trachtman (1979), for example, argues rather persuasively that parents represent the most appropriate choice as the primary client group. We agree with his points that parents are usually the persons finally responsible for children's welfare and that there are potential problems in designating children as clients. Perhaps the most serious of these problems involves the possible assumption that parents and

313

school personnel lack sufficient expertise to contribute much to the assessment process, which sometimes results in attempts by assessment practitioners to dictate strategies to parents and school personnel. This is not the kind of cooperative decision making relative to children's welfare that we have advocated. While we have suggested that assessment practitioners present their views clearly and attempt to use their legitimate sources of influence, we have also noted that they must be willing to have their views rejected. The checks and balances in cooperative decision making are, we believe, generally conducive to children's welfare, as long as parties to decisions have access to due process hearings and the judicial system as means of presenting grievances. While we are sympathetic to Trachtman's choice of parents as clients, we have been involved with some cases where parents were clearly not acting in their children's best interests. Hence, our choice is to view children as clients, while trying to avoid the pitfalls of this choice.

We also have some difficulty viewing schools as the appropriate clients of assessment practitioners. While we believe that most school administrators and teachers conscientiously attempt to help children experiencing school problems, the demands on school personnel often seem overwhelming in light of limited resources. Hence, it is often tempting to follow the path of least resistance in dealing with the problems presented by a child. Assessment practitioners can assist in finding strategies that do meet the needs of the child, are legally and ethically appropriate, and yet are practical enough to be implemented by the school. Such efforts, however, require truly cooperative decision making, with parties to the process having access to grievance procedures when the process does not work effectively. The process will not work effectively unless there is consensus on several points: that efficient assessment requires appropriate classification followed by effective programming; that close attention must be paid to the social consequences of classification and programming decisions for individual children; and that continuing efforts must be made to improve assessment and programming activities. In essence, the process of helping children experiencing school problems will work, in a true sense, only when efforts are made to meet the spirit of legal and ethical guidelines, as well as their letter, and that can happen only if no party to the assessment process views it as an adversary process in which the goal is to triumph over others.

We have also made some judgments about a number of important issues in assessment. We have urged that children be given the benefit of the doubt in special education classification decisions. While this decision rule is compatible with social and legal trends, we are aware that our judgment can be questioned in terms of social consequences for children. For example, Lambert (1981) has summarized a number of studies on the efficacy of classes for children classified as educably mentally retarded and has concluded that it is difficult to judge whether the consequences of these classes are detrimental, beneficial, or neutral for these children. While indicating that more definitive research is needed to judge this issue, she suggests that such children may be no worse off (and possibly better off) in such classes than in regular classes. She supports this point by citing studies that compare academic achievement, peer acceptance, self-concept, and post–high school adjustment of such children following their placement in either special education or regular classes.

We have not argued, however, that such children be left to sink or swim in regular classes. Instead, we have consistently suggested that children found ineligible for special education placement should receive needed assistance in their regular classrooms, not from special education programs but from programs developed especially for these children. Our position may be understood partly in terms of MacMillan and Meyers' (1980) contention that the *Larry P.* v. *Riles* decision inappropriately focused on the issue of test bias in classification of children as mentally retarded. They think that this decision failed to address the fact that large numbers of racial minority and cultural minority children are referred for assessment because of their past school failures. They suggest that the court's decision could more productively have "advanced the cause of adequately funded and implemented compensatory-type education for such learners" (p. 138). We agree, particularly in view of Reschly's (1979) statement that issues of test bias may never be satisfactorily resolved (p. 217).

While we believe that children ineligible for special education placements should be provided needed services, we are aware that it may be difficult, in practice, to convince school systems to provide such non–special education services. Teachers and other school personnel may tend to see referred children as handicapped even when assessment information suggests otherwise and view special education services as appropriate to the needs of such children. Such a tendency is suggested by the results of a recent study conducted by Algozzine and Ysseldyke (1981). In this study, 51 percent of the respondents (regular teachers, special education teachers, school psychologists, school administrators, and other support-services personnel such as school nurses and social workers) judged referred children as eligible for a special education classification in spite of the fact that all assessment results for each child were within the normal range. Sixty percent viewed part-time resource class placement as appropriate (but less than 10 percent viewed full-time exclusion from a regular classroom as appropriate). Algozzine and Ysseldyke suggest that these results may represent a reaction to "the ills of regular education" and the adoption of a "better safe than sorry" attitude to special education services (p. 243). In contrast, we favor giving greater attention to the needs of children as they attempt to function in regular classrooms, with efforts directed toward remediating "the ills of regular education." We also favor the development of more non–special education services, such as compensatory education programs.

In addition to our concern about possible tendencies to overuse special education services for children experiencing school problems, we are also concerned that the current economic and political climate may lead to a lessened commitment to assisting such children. If our fears are realized, and compensatory education programs are not adequately funded, then many children will fall between the cracks in service-delivery systems, while other children may receive services that may be at least somewhat inappropriate for them.

In regard to assessment techniques, we favor a deemphasis in the use of measures of psychoeducational processing skills and in the use of projective techniques. To ensure that children who might be classified as mentally retarded are fairly evaluated, we urge that adaptive behavior be assessed in children's home and neighborhood settings. In addition, we think that measures appropriate to a task-analytic approach to children's academic and behavioral problems are most likely to yield information useful to programming. Finally, we advocate assessment of the influence of environment on children's school performances, to help ensure that programming adequately reflects an understanding of conditions that impede or facilitate good school performance.

THE BRANCHING ASSESSMENT SYSTEM

Having built these foundations, we have learned to express our assumptions and judgments in practice through our branching assessment system, briefly described in Chapter 1.

This system is intended both to streamline the assessment process and to provide adequate information for classification and programming decisions (see Chapter 1, pp. 35 – 38). It should be understood that this system is designed for the assessment of children judged likely to be eligible for special education services. Less formal assessment procedures should be utilized for children seen (on

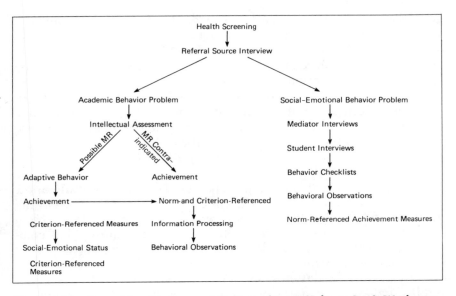

Figure 12-1   Branching Assessment System. (From Helton, G., & Workman, E. Considerations in assessing the mildly handicapped. In T. Miller & E. Davis (Eds.), *The mildly handicapped student.* New York: Grune & Stratton, 1982. With permission.)

the basis of referral information) as unlikely to be eligible for special education.

The branching assessment system is shown schematically in Figure 12-1. Following health screening and an interview with the referral source, a child is "branched," or channelled, into assessment procedures that our analysis of assessment issues has shown are specifically relevant to the problem(s) for which the child is referred. If health screening indicates no problems, the assessment practitioner first determines from the interview whether the child's difficulties involve academic and/or social/emotional behavior problems. While written information is usually available on a referred child, a referral-source interview promotes the goal of increasing the practitioner's chances of initially entering the appropriate branch of the system. The interview should involve examination of cumulative folder data and samples of the child's schoolwork.

If the interview with the referral agent suggests social/emotional problems, the child is branched into the appropriate component of the system. Assessment would then consist of detailed interviews with mediators (adults in the child's life), interviews with the student, the use of behavior checklists, behavioral observation, and the administration of norm-referenced achievement tests. These procedures would allow the practitioner to determine whether the child is classifiable under the emotional disturbance category and to develop appropriate intervention strategies.

If interviews with the referral agent suggest an academic problem, the practitioner's first step would be to determine whether a classification of mental retardation is plausible. An intelligence measure would be administered for this purpose. If classification of mental retardation is contraindicated, the child is further branched into procedures involving the assessment of achievement, modality skills (if needed), and social emotional/behavior. This branch would allow for determination of whether the child can be classified as learning disabled and the development of a remedial program. Classifying a child as learning disabled, as we have stressed, requires that emotional problems be ruled out as a primary causative factor in the child's school problems.

If mental retardation does appear possible on the basis of the intellectual assessment, the practitioner would then assess the child's adaptive behavior. If the results of the adaptive behavior assessment also indicated mental retardation, the examiner would assess academic achievement (using criterion-referenced measures) and social/ emotional behavior. Assessment in both domains should assist in making programming decisions. If, on the other hand, the adaptive behavior assessment contraindicated mental retardation, the child would be branched back into procedures used to assess the appropriateness of the learning disabilities classification.

In the cases presented below, we illustrate the use of our branching assessment system. Each case is presented as a psychoeducational report and is then discussed in terms of various important assessment issues. The case reports also illustrate the use of a number of assessment techniques, data integration, and report writing. These reports include data derived from some assessment techniques that we have said are probably not essential to the assessment process. We include them primarily for the purpose of illustrating their possible uses.

PSYCHOEDUCATIONAL ASSESSMENT REPORT: CASE 1

Name: Johnny (fictitious)
Sex: Male
Age: 10 years, 1 month
Grade: 4.4 (fourth month in fourth grade)

Reason for Referral

Johnny was referred because of suspected learning disorders, suspected skill deficits in basic reading and mathematics skills, and behavior problems in the classroom. According to teacher reports, Johnny frequently has tantrums when asked to complete assignments and frequently daydreams and stares out the window.

Assessment Procedures

- Hearing and vision screening
- Wechsler Intelligence Scale for Children—Revised (WISC-R)
- Visual-Aural Digit Span Test (VADST)
- Wide Range Achievement Test (WRAT)
- Criterion Tests of Basic Skills (CTBS; administered by the resource teacher)
- Teacher and parent interviews
- Behavioral observations
- Record review
- Burks' Behavior Rating Scales (BBRS)

Assessment Results

On the WISC-R, Johnny received a Verbal Scale IQ score that was within the borderline range. This indicates that his current ability to learn language-oriented tasks is delayed as compared to his age. It could be said that he is "at risk" in terms of his ability to learn such tasks. He received a Performance Scale IQ score that was within the average range. This indicates that Johnny's ability to learn non-language-oriented performance tasks is within the range expected for his age. The contrast between his Verbal Scale and Performance Scale IQs indicates that he is stronger in perceptual organization skills than in verbal comprehension skills. Johnny's Full Scale IQ score places him within the low-average range. This indicates that his current level of overall intellectual functioning is slightly delayed as compared to the level expected for his age.

The results of the VADST indicated that Johnny's weakest learning channel is the auditory-oral channel (remembering what he hears and responding to such information orally). Johnny's performance on the written components of the VADST contraindicates motoric problems. These results are compatible with his performance on the WISC-R, indicating better skills in responding to materials presented in a visual perceptual mode.

On the WRAT, Johnny received a reading standard score of 55. This indicates a severe delay in basic word recognition skills, as compared to the level expected for his age. The CTBS reading test indicated several areas of serious deficits. These deficits included (1) letter-sounding skills for the vowels *e*, *i*, and *u*, and (2) letter-sounding skills for the consonants *t*, *n*, *g*, *b*, *d*, *f*, *r*, *l*, and *y*.

Also on the WRAT, Johnny received a mathematics standard score of 62.

This indicates that his basic mathematics skills are also severely delayed. The CTBS mathematics test indicated that Johnny has skill deficits involving (1) adding three-digit numbers without regrouping, (2) adding two- and three-digit numbers with regrouping, (3) subtracting two- and three-digit numbers without regrouping, and (4) subtracting two- and three-digit numbers with regrouping. The behavioral analysis of Johnny's mathematics skills indicated that his major problem involved his failure to verbalize the procedural rules to himself when he attempts to solve addition and subtraction problems with two digits. In other words, when presented with the problem of the type stated above, Johnny responds to the item impulsively, rather than sequentially working through the problem. Whenever Johnny was very clearly instructed to verbalize softly the procedural rules for solving several problems, his error rate decreased dramatically.

Behavioral observation of Johnny's behavior in the classroom indicated that (1) he has an extremely low rate of on-task/attending behavior and a relatively high rate of noncompliance and tantrumming behaviors when presented with tasks. These behaviors appear to stem from Johnny's low entering-skill levels and a high level of frustration when presented with tasks that he has difficulty solving. Both the low rate of on-task behaviors, as well as oppositional and tantrumming responses to the presentation of such tasks, appear to function as ways that Johnny can avoid dealing with the tasks and therefore avoid becoming more and more frustrated.

The interview with Johnny's mother indicated that the family falls within the average range of socioeconomic functioning. Their income level is slightly above the U.S. median, and the family appears to practice a relatively standard middle class life-style. These impressions contraindicate environmental or economic deprivation as possible causes for Johnny's difficulties. However, his mother also indicated that she sometimes "gives in" when Johnny has a tantrum in order to "keep the peace" in the family.

The results of the BBRS (administered to Johnny's teacher) indicated moderate levels of depression and self-blame, as well as a moderate rate of negative/punitive self-statements (poor self-concept). Interviews with Johnny, his teacher, and his mother suggested that "depressive" episodes are almost always preceded by negative feedback for his school performance. This information, particularly when viewed along with the moderate BBRS scores, suggests that emotional disturbance is not a *cause* of Johnny's current academic problems. In fact, his depression, self blame, and so on, are most likely *effects* of his academic problems.

Diagnostic Summary

The results of this assessment indicate that Johnny is currently eligible for special education services under the learning disability category. There is a severe discrepancy between expected achievement (estimated on the basis of his WISC-R scores) and actual achievement (as reflected by his WRAT performance). His basic problem appears to involve difficulty in the area of verbal comprehension skills, including auditory memory functioning. The results of the hearing screening performed on Johnny prior to this assessment would contraindicate a hearing loss as the basis of his difficulties. In addition, vision screening suggests no visual acuity problems. Interview and questionnaire data contraindicate environmental, cultural, and emotional problems as causes of Johnny's learning problems.

Recommendations

1: Johnny should be provided with resource services on a daily basis in both reading and mathematics.

2: When working on mathematical problems, Johnny should be provided with a visual cue chart that clearly demonstrates the specific sequential steps involved in adding and subtracting problems with two and three digits. Such a chart should be directly in front of him on his desk. While working mathematical problems, Johnny should be periodically instructed to softly verbalize the steps involved in each problem-solution process. His teacher should monitor this periodically in order to ensure that he is following through on this procedure. The school psychologist could provide consultation to assist in the implementation of this procedure.

3: Johnny's work in reading should focus, at this point, on those specific skill deficits cited above. When comprehension reading tasks are involved in his reading program, he should be exposed only to low skill/high interest stories that maximize the use of visual cues (pictures). A highly structured reading program would be most beneficial to Johnny, particularly one that provides immediate feedback as he is learning new reading skills. The Distar Reading Program would be an optimal program for Johnny's learning style and is available at his school.

4: The present examiner has held a conference with Johnny's mother, and he and his parents are currently being referred to Child and Family Services for counseling. His counseling should focus on decreasing his depressive and negative self-evaluative statements and increasing his level of frustration tolerance. Counseling for his parents should focus on increasing their skills in managing his tantrumming behavior so that this behavior will not be reinforced at home. The school psychologist will provide consultation to his Child and Family Service counselor regarding the development of such counseling programs. It should, however, again be noted that counseling should be directed toward specific problematic behaviors and that Johnny is not seen as a primarily emotionally disturbed child.

5: Johnny's classroom teacher should consistently verbally praise him whenever he (1) complies with instructions within 30 seconds of their presentation and (2) works on a task for more than 3 to 4 sustained minutes. The school psychologist will provide consultation in the development of this intervention program.

6: Johnny's progress in the above program should be carefully monitored. The school psychologist could contact his teachers and parents periodically for this purpose and assist in modifying aspects of the program as needed.

The assessment procedures used in this case were selected to assess the problems initially isolated by the referral-source interview. The primary problems involved reading and mathematics performance. Classroom behavior was identified as a secondary problem. Since the intellectual assessment contraindicated mental retardation, adaptive behavior was not assessed. The student was thus branched into assessment procedures involving achievement (WRAT and CTBS), modality skills (VADST), and behavioral observations. The BBRS was also administered to the child's teacher to assess the general severity of classroom behavior problems.

Personnel other than the assessment specialist were utilized in two ways in this case as required by the guidelines for assessing learning disabled students contained in the regulations implementing PL 94-142. First, they were extensively involved in the assessment process. The child's classroom teacher completed the BBRS and was also interviewed, and the resource teacher administered the CTBS. This approach served to maximize the information obtained and minimize the assessment practitioner's time expenditure. These (and other) personnel were also utilized in the programming process: the resource teacher was involved in recommendations 1, 2, and 3; the classroom teacher was utilized in recommendation 5; and community agency personnel were involved in recommendation 4.

The major assessment decisions in this case involved the child's classification as learning disabled and the recommendation of several specific programming strategies. The learning disabilities classification was justified on the basis of discrepancies between actual and expected academic achievement in the absence of health factor problems, primary emotional disturbance, or cultural differences or economic disadvantage. Johnny's WRAT scores, while reported as subtest scores, suggest a general delay in educational skill development. In addition, Johnny showed clear deficiencies in verbal comprehension (including short-term auditory memory) skills. The justification of the various programming recommendations lies in the fact that each is directly tied to a deficit or a performance style characteristic observed during the assessment. Recommendation 4, counseling for Johnny and his parents, is not seen as a related service under PL 94-142 (since the suggested program is expected to lead both to academic progress and a decrease in school tantrums) but was recommended to his parents as helpful largely to Johnny's home adjustment. The recommendation should also improve intersystem accommodation between home and school, but such improvement was not seen as important enough to justify the school's paying for counseling as a related service.

It should be noted that the assessment practitioner (a school psychologist) suggested his own involvement in recommendations to be incorporated into the child's individualized educational program (IEP), specifically recommendations 2, 4, 5, and 6. One way to legitimize consultation by the assessment practitioner is to make specific written recommendations that involve consultation. Furthermore, it has been our experience that the assessment practitioner who follows this approach eventually takes on the role of assessment practitioner and consultant. As we have indicated in other chapters, we view consultation as a necessary role for assessment practitioners.

Finally, it should also be noted that the programming recommendations made in this case incorporated instructional conditions seen as conducive to the child's acquisition and utilization of needed skills. Specifically, a visual cue chart for arithmetic operations and instructions to the child to softly verbalize computational rules were recommended as helpful to his acquisition of math skills. Low skill/high interest reading stories and the Distar Reading Program were recommended in terms of his need to acquire better reading skills. Teacher praise for compliance with instructions and sustained schoolwork was recommended as an aid to his acquisition of more productive work habits.

PSYCHOEDUCATIONAL ASSESSMENT REPORT: CASE 2

Name: Tommy (fictitious)
Sex: male
Age: 6 years, 10 months
Grade: 1.9 (ninth month of first grade)

Reason for Referral

Tommy was referred for a periodic psychoeducational reassessment. He has been receiving special services since kindergarten under the special education category of emotional disturbance. His teachers requested that a re-evaluation be performed owing to suspected deterioration in his emotional condition since his previous assessment and serious delays in reading performance. The purpose of this assessment was to provide information that can be used in the further development of an IEP designed to meet Tommy's needs.

Assessment Procedures

- Hearing and vision screening
- Extensive record review
- Wechsler Intelligence Scale for Children—Revised (WISC-R)

- Wide Range Achievement Test (WRAT; administered by the resource teacher)
- Teacher and parent interviews
- Direct Behavioral Assessment of Reading Skills
- Burks' Behavior Rating Scales (BBRS)
- Psychological interview with Tommy
- Projective drawings
- Behavioral observations

Assessment Results

Previous psychoeducational assessment performed on Tommy two years ago found that on the Wechsler Preschool and Primary Scale of Intelligence (WPPSI) he received Verbal, Performance, and Full Scale IQ scores that were within the average range. During the present assessment, Tommy achieved a WISC-R Verbal Scale IQ score that was within the low-average range and a Performance Scale IQ score that was within the average range.

His overall style of performance on the WISC-R indicated that Tommy is easily frustrated, quickly gives up on tasks, and frequently refuses to cooperate on those tasks that he perceives as difficult. This was particularly evident on the vocabulary subtest, where he refused to try to even guess at words that he thought he did not know. Throughout the WISC-R, Tommy exhibited high evaluation anxiety as indicated by overt negative self-statements. This most likely results from an intense fear of failure. He would frequently refuse to respond to tasks, as indicated above, and this most likely serves to allow him to avoid being evaluated in task situations.

On the WRAT, Tommy received a mathematics standard score of 98. Also on the WRAT, Tommy received a reading standard score of 93. These scores suggest that Tommy's academic skills are not seriously delayed at this time.

Interviews with Tommy's teachers indicated that he consistently refuses to attempt even relatively easy tasks in classroom situations. He also is reported to verbalize fears regarding going out onto the playground to play, and once he gets onto the playground, behavioral observations indicated that he interacts at an extremely low rate with other children. His teachers pointed out, however, that Tommy truly excels in art and music and appears to have substantial talent and potential in these areas.

Tommy's mother indicated in an interview that Tommy's two older brothers are perceived as outstanding students. She also reported that while she and her husband hold high standards for their own efforts and tend to be self-critical of their efforts, they try very hard not to be critical of Tommy or compare him to his brothers. However, she acknowledged that Tommy may impose pressure on himself by virtue of being in a family of high achievers.

The Direct Behavioral Assessment of Reading Skills indicated that Tommy is weak or deficient in the following phonics skills (each letter was presented, and he was asked to make the sound for that letter): b, c, d, f, h, i, j, l, m, n, q, r, s, u, v, x, and y. It was noted that Tommy can more readily learn and retain a given phonics skill when he is taught by using combinations of a receptive and expressive format. For example, in teaching the skill for the letter-sound association involving the letter *b*, Tommy was presented with the letters *b*, *d*, *c*, and *e*. He was then asked to point to the one that makes the sound for *b*. After several trials using this procedure, he was then present-ed with each of the letters again and asked to make the sound that is associat-ed with the letter. He quickly learned the letter-sound association for *b* and retained this skill from the beginning to the end of a two-hour assessment period.

The results of the BBRS completed by his teacher *and* mother indicated that Tommy had significantly high scores in several areas that indicate rela-tively intense behavior pathology. These included (1) excessive self-blame, (2) excessive anxiety, (3) excessive dependency, and (4) poor attention skills. His highest scores occurred on the excessive self-blame and excessive anxiety scales.

During the administration of the projective drawings, Tommy exhibited an extremely high rate of erasures and frequently "drew over" aspects of the pictures that he had already drawn. These are possibly indications of exces-sively high self-evaluation standards. He appears to expect perfection of him-self and appears to give up if his standards of perfection are not reached. This is clearly in line with other results in this assessment indicating a low level of frustration tolerance. It should be noted that while he was drawing, he would make derogatory statements toward himself if he did make an error or have to erase.

Vision screening indicated no visual acuity problems. Also, hearing screening revealed no auditory acuity problems.

Diagnostic Summary

The results of this assessment indicate that Tommy continues to be eligi-ble for special education services under the emotional disturbance category. He is currently experiencing intense evaluation anxiety, and this anxiety is suppressing his performance in the classroom. Essentially this suppression process involves Tommy's perceiving himself as being evaluated, becoming anxious over the prospect of being negatively evaluated, and refusing to at-tempt tasks in order to avoid being evaluated and, therefore, avoid anxiety.

Recommendations

1: Tommy should be allowed to work with the resource teacher on a regular basis for further development of his reading skills. The skills deficits cited above should be focused on, and a receptive and expressive teaching format (as described) should be used extensively prior to training in the ex-pression of letter-sound associations. Such training should assist in improv-ing Tommy's skills and confidence. While Tommy's development of academic skills do not appear seriously delayed at this time, his failure to attempt work is problematic and requires attention.

2: Tommy should be seen for 10 to 12 cognitive behavior therapy ses-sions by the school psychologist. These sessions should focus on (1) increasing the frequency with which Tommy praises himself for attempting to complete tasks, (2) decreasing the frequency with which Tommy verbally punishes himself for not attaining his standards of perfection, and (3) teaching Tommy to relax in anxiety-provoking situations through the use of progressive muscle relaxation and desensitization hierarchies involving evaluation situations.

3: Tommy should be reassessed at the end of the next school year.

4: It would be helpful if Tommy were allowed to work in a small-group setting with the school counselor in order to focus on his areas of strength and learn to acknowledge these areas and praise himself for his strengths.

5: The regular classroom teacher should frequently praise Tommy for appropriate performance of tasks. The use of verbal criticism should be minimized.

6: Tommy's parents should attempt to provide specific and accurate praise of Tommy's accomplishments. They should also try to model less self-critical behavior and instead model acceptance of their achievements when they have exerted their best efforts.

The assessment techniques utilized in Tommy's case were selected to assess both academic and social emotional problems. Behavioral observations and teacher conferences, interviews with the child and his parents, and projective drawings were used to generate data regarding the nature of the child's social/emotional problems. (The BBRS was utilized as a global means of estimating the normative severity of such problems.) It should be noted that the child's behavior during the projective drawings was of more interest than what was drawn. The WISC-R, WRAT, and Direct Assessment procedures were used to assess the nature and extent of the child's academic problems.

As in case 1, case 2 involved the utilization of the resource teacher and the regular classroom teacher in both assessment and programming. The regular teacher took part in interviews and completed the BBRS. The resource teacher took part in interviews, administered the WRAT, and assisted in reviewing the child's work records. The regular classroom teacher was involved in recommendation 5, while the resource teacher was involved in recommendation 1. The school counselor was also recommended as an additional resource for assisting the child (recommendation 4), and suggestions to the parents were made (recommendation 6). Recommendations 2 and 4 were seen as needed related services in terms of the regulations implementing PL 94-142.

Tommy's classification as emotionally disturbed was reaffirmed by this reassessment on the basis of teacher reports of rather extreme task-avoidance behavior, behavioral observations of excessively low rates of social interaction, and observations of behaviors suggesting very high rates of self-criticism. Also, the BBRS indicated that the child's behavior problems are rather serious, from a normative-statistical standpoint. Recommendations 2, 4, 5, and 6 were based on these findings regarding social/emotional behavior problems. Recommendation 1 was based on data indicating specific academic behavior deficits and an informal analysis of the conditions under which the child appears to learn most effectively.

As in case 1, the assessment practitioner suggested that her services be included in the child's remedial program (recommendation 2). Specifically, she recommended a series of behavior therapy sessions designed to remediate anxiety problems found through the assessment.

Again, the recommendations in Tommy's case incorporated instructional conditions potentially conducive to his acquisition and utilization of needed skills. The receptive and expressive teaching format to be used during remedial reading training, the sessions with the school counselor, and the teacher's and parents' roles in praising the child's efforts represent efforts to provide appropriate environmental conditions for optimal learning.

Finally, this child's reassessment followed his original assessment by two years, and this report recommends a third assessment at the end of the next school year. Such frequent assessment represents a commitment to the child's welfare and illustrates the point that reassessment is required by the regulations implementing PL 94-142 at least once every three years but more frequently if needed.

PSYCHOEDUCATIONAL ASSESSMENT REPORT: CASE 3

Name: Susie (fictitious)
Sex: Female
Age: 9 years, 4 months
Grade: 1.9 (ninth month in first grade)

Reason for Referral

Susie was referred for a periodic psychoeducational reassessment. Her current classification is mentally retarded, and she is receiving all her academic instruction in a resource setting. Interviews with her resource teacher indicate that Susie is seriously delayed in both basic mathematics and basic reading skills. The interview also revealed, however, that Susie was mainstreamed in nonacademic activities shortly after her initial assessment and that her social skills have resulted in her successful participation in these activities.

Assessment Procedures

- Hearing and vision screening
- Wechsler Intelligence Scale for Children—Revised (WISC-R)
- Vineland Social Maturity Scale (VSMS)
- Direct Behavioral Assessment of Mathematics Skills
- Direct Behavioral Assessment of Reading Skills
- Behavioral observations
- Record review
- Teacher interviews
- Wide Range Achievement Test (WRAT)

Assessment Results

On the WISC-R, Susie achieved Verbal and Performance IQ scores that were within the educable mentally retarded range. Her Full Scale IQ score of 60 suggests the possibility of mental retardation.

On the VSMS (administered to her mother in the home setting), Susie received a social quotient of 89. This rather clearly contraindicates comprehensive mental retardation, even in light of her low scores on the WISC-R. It should be noted that her previous assessment did not include a measure of adaptive behavior such as the VSMS. It should also be noted that information gathered during the home visit indicates lower socioeconomic status for Susie's family and conscientious parenting on the part of parents with very limited formal educations.

The WRAT results indicate that Susie's mathematics standard score was 46, while her reading standard score was 56. These data indicate that Susie's reading and mathematics skills are seriously delayed when viewed in the context of her current age and the fact that this is her third year in "first grade."

The Direct Assessment of Mathematics Skills indicates that (1) Susie has not yet mastered basic correspondence skills and (2) she has not yet mastered concepts of smaller versus larger. These two skills are prerequisite to the further development of this child's mathematics skills. It was noted, during this assessment, that Susie was able to begin learning these skills when concrete visual referents were used to teach the concepts. For example, when pictures were associated with numerals, Susie began to learn basic number discriminations.

The Direct Assessment of Reading Skills indicated deficits in letter-sound associations for the following letters: b, c, e, g, i, j, k, v, w, y, and z. It was discovered, however, that Susie's error rate decreased when a receptive format was used to teach these letters (for example, if she were asked to "point to the letter that sounds like _____"). She can probably learn letter-sound association skills if a receptive teaching format is alternated, trial by trial, with a traditional expressive format.

Behavioral observations confirm that Susie's classroom behavior (as compared to that of her chronological age peers) is not characterized by any serious problems. She does not engage in excessive disruptive behavior, follows overall directions well, and appears to have only slightly delayed social skills. In addition, hearing and vision screening indicate no problems in either area.

Conclusions

On the basis of this assessment, Susie is no longer classifiable as mentally retarded, since her adaptive behavior is within generally normal limits. Her serious academic behavior deficits, however, warrant continued remedial efforts. Since Susie does not appear to be classifiable under any special education category, such efforts probably must come from non–special education sources.

Recommendations

1: Susie should receive remedial services on a daily basis for both reading and mathematics. Remedial efforts should focus on the skill deficits cited above. The school psychologist could provide consultation in the development of a program appropriate to her skill deficits and to the conditions under which these deficits might be improved.

2: The school psychologist has determined that Susie is eligible for an after-school tutoring program at the neighborhood Girls' Club and could consult with staff at the club relative to Susie's participation in that program.

3: A group meeting to plan and coordinate in- and out-of-school services to Susie should be convened. This group, in particular, should consider Susie's eligibility for her school's compensatory education program.

The assessment techniques utilized in Susie's case were selected primarily to assess the appropriateness of her continued classification as mentally retarded. This is particularly true of the WISC-R and VSMS. The WRAT and Direct Assessment procedures were used to assess the extent and specific nature of the child's academic deficits. Behavioral observations were included to assess the need for behavioral intervention in the classroom.

This case exemplifies some of the issues involved in the classification of children. Mental retardation, although suggested by the WISC-R, was clearly contraindicated by the VSMS. The VSMS utilizes information obtained from parents, and care was taken in its administration to ensure that Susie's adaptive behavior skills were not being overestimated. The results of the VSMS and their contraindication of mental retardation branched the child into another sector of our assessment system. The procedures used in that sector indicated the degree of delay in the child's academic skills and clearly delineated the specific skills in which she was deficient. This branching did not result in Susie's classification as learning disabled, since it was believed that economic disadvantage could not be ruled out as a primary cause of her achievement deficits. In addition, other school and neighborhood sources of assistance were seen as available and appropriate relative to Susie's needs.

While Susie was subsequently served by a compensatory education program and an after-school tutoring program, some children such as Susie are ineligible for either special education or compensatory education programs. Such children often receive no special services and illustrate the need for more comprehensive service-delivery systems. In the present, such children present very difficult decisions, but efforts to meet their needs in appropriate ways should always be undertaken.

CONCLUSIONS

The branching assessment system provides comprehensive information for *both* classification and programming. It streamlines the assessment process, avoiding the wasting of time, while also making it possible to meet both the letter and—perhaps of greater importance—the spirit of current legal and ethical guidelines. Other systems designed to accomplish these goals are described in Reschly (1979) and Tucker (1977). Readers will wish to examine alternative systems before adopting or modifying a particular system for their own purposes.

The cases that we have described clearly show, we believe, how the system can streamline the assessment process yet provide meaningful information for classification and programming. Furthermore, the system serves to individualize the assessment process by utilizing only these techniques that relate directly to the problem for which a child is referred.

Some may ask how a system that uses so many different assessment procedures (as seen in the cases) can be described as "streamlining." The truth is that in all three cases, resource and regular teachers were used extensively in the assessment process. This approach, combined with the fact that the system mandates only the use of procedures related to the referral problem, allows the practitioner to obtain maximal information in a relatively short period of time.

One of the most important features of the three cases presented is the fact that they clearly show how the assessment practitioner can suggest his or her inclusion in the child's remedial program. Whether this involves a recommendation for consultation with the teacher or individual therapy with the child, this process definitely expands the role of the assessment practitioner into that of psychoeducational consultant and serves to logically tie the assessment process to intervention. And that, after all, is the ultimate reason for assessment—intervention in the lives of children in order to improve their ability to function effectively and, we hope, more happily.

References

Algozzine, B., & Ysseldyke, J. Special education services for normal children: Better safe than sorry? *Exceptional Children*, 1981, *48*, 238–243.

American Psychiatric Association, Task Force on Nomenclature and Statistics. *Diagnostic and statistical manual of mental disorders (DSM-III)* (3rd ed.). Washington, D.C.: American Psychiatric Association, 1980.

American Psychological Association. Ethical principles for psychologists. *American Psychologist*, 1981, *36*, 633–638.

American Psychological Association, Division of School Psychology. Guidelines to work conditions for school psychologists. In *Position papers on school psychology*. Washington, D.C.: American Psychological Association, undated.

American Psychological Association, Division of School Psychology. Test protocols in relation to sole possession records. In *Position papers on school psychology*. Washington, D.C.: American Psychological Association, undated.

American Psychological Association, American Educational Research Association, and National Council on Measurement in Education. *Standards for educational and psychological tests*. Washington, D.C.: American Psychological Association, 1974.

Anastasi, A. *Psychological testing* (4th ed.) New York: Macmillan, 1976.

Atkins, J., & Williams, R. The utility of self-report in determining reinforcement priorities of primary school children. *Journal of Educational Research*, 1972, *65*, 324–328.

Bailey, B., & Richmond, B. Adaptive behavior of retarded, slow-learner, and average intelligence children. *Journal of School Psychology*, 1979, *17*, 260–263.

Balthazar, E. *Balthazar Scales of Adaptive Behavior*. Palo Alto, Calif.: Consulting Psychologists Press, 1973.

Barbe, W., Swassing, R., and Milone, M. Teaching to modality strengths: Don't give up yet! *Academic Therapy*, 1981, *16*, 262–266.

Bardon, J., & Bennett, V. *School psychology.* Englewood Cliffs, N.J.: Prentice-Hall, 1974.

Bateman, B. The efficacy of an auditory and a visual method of first grade reading instruction with auditory and visual learners. *Curriculum Bulletin* (School of Education, University of Oregon), 1967, *23*, 6–14.

Becker, J., & Sabatino, D. Reliability of individual tests of perception administered utilizing group techniques. *Journal of Clinical Psychology*, 1971, *27*, 86–88.

Bellack, A., & Hersen, M. *Behavior modification: An introductory textbook.* New York: Oxford University Press, 1977.

Bellak, L. *The TAT, CAT, and SAT in clinical use* (3rd ed.). New York: Grune & Stratton, 1975.

Bender, L. *A Visual-Motor Gestalt Test and its clinical uses.* Research Monograph No. 3. New York: American Orthopsychiatric Association, 1938.

Bergan, J. *Behavioral consultation.* Columbus, Ohio: Charles E. Merrill, 1977.

Bersoff, D. Professional ethics and legal responsibilities: On the horns of a dilemma. *Journal of School Psychology*, 1975, *13*, 359–376.

Bersoff, D. P. v. Riles: Legal perspectives. *School Psychology Review*, 1980, *9*, 112–122.

Bersoff, D., & Miller, T. Ethical and legal issues of behavioral assessment. In D. Sabatino & T. Miller (Eds.), *Describing learner characteristics of handicapped children and youth.* New York: Grune & Stratton, 1979.

Biehler, R. Companion choice behavior in the kindergarten. *Child Development*, 1954, *25*, 45–50.

Binet, A., & Henri, V. La Psychologie individuelle. *L'Année psychologique*, 1895, *2*, 411–465.

Binet, A., & Simon, T. Méthodes nouvelles pour le diagnostic du niveau intéllectual des anormaux. *L'Année psychologique*, 1905, *11*, 191–244.

Binet, A., & Simon, T. Le Développement de l'intelligence chez les enfants. *L'Année psychologique*, 1908, *14*, 1–94.

Blau, T. Diagnosis of disturbed children. *American Psychologist*, 1979, *34*, 969–972.

Boyd, L., & Randle, K. Factor analysis of the *Frostig Developmental Test of Visual Perception. Journal of Learning Disabilities*, 1970, *3*, 253–255.

Brigance, A. *Brigance Diagnostic Inventory of Basic Skills.* Woburn, Mass.: Curriculum Associates, 1977.

Brophy J., & Good, T. Brophy-Good system (teacher-child dyadic interaction). In A. Simon & E. Boyer (Eds.), *Mirrors for behavior: An anthology of observational instruments continued, 1970 supplement* (Vol. A). Philadelphia: Research for Better Schools, 1970.

Brophy, J., & Good, T. *Teacher-student relationships: Causes and consequences.* New York: Holt, Rinehart, & Winston, 1974.

Brown, L., & Hamill, D. *Behavior Rating Profile: An ecological approach to behavioral assessment.* Austin, Tex.: PRO-ED, 1978.

Bruininks, R. Relationship of auditory and visual perceptual strengths to methods of teaching word recognition among disadvantaged Negro boys. *Institute on Mental Retardation and Intellectual Development Behavioral Science Monograph*, 1968, *12*.

Bruininks, R. *Bruininks-Oseretsky Test of Motor Proficiency*. Circle Pines, Minn.: American Guidance Service, 1978.

Budoff, M., & Friedman, M. "Learning potential" as an assessment approach to the adolescent mentally retarded. *Journal of Consulting Psychology*, 1964, *28*, 433–439.

Burgemeister, B., Blum, L., & Lorge, I. *Columbia Mental Maturity Scale*. New York: Harcourt, Brace, Jovanovich, 1972.

Burks, H. *Burks' Behavior Rating Scales*. Los Angeles: Western Psychological Services, 1977.

Buss, W. What procedural due process means to a school psychologist: A dialogue. *Journal of School Psychology*, 1975, *13*, 298–310.

Cain, L., Levine, S., & Elzey, F. *Manual for the Cain-Levine Social Competency Scale*. Palo Alto, Calif.: Consulting Psychologists Press, 1977.

Carlberg, C., & Kavale, K. The efficacy of special vs. regular class placement for exceptional children: A meta-analysis. *Journal of Special Education*, 1980, *14*, 295–309.

Carpenter, D., & Carpenter, S. Reliability and validity of the *Criterion Test of Basic Skills*. *Diagnostique*, 1980, *6*, 16–23.

Carter, D., Spero, A., & Walsh, J. A comparison of the Visual Aural Digit Span and the Bender Gestalt as discriminators of low achievement in the primary grades. *Psychology in the Schools*, 1978, *15*, 194–198.

Carver, R. Two dimensions of tests: Psychometric and edumetric. *American Psychologist*, 1974, *29*, 512–517.

Catterall, C., & Gazda, G. *Strategies for helping students*. Springfield, Ill.: Charles C Thomas, 1978.

Cautela, J., & Kastenbaum, R. A reinforcement survey schedule for use in therapy, training, and research. *Psychological Reports*, 1967, *20*, 1115–1130.

CEC joins New Mexico suit. *CEC Update*, 1981, *12*(5), 5.

Cegelka, W. Competencies of persons responsible for the classification of mentally retarded individuals. *Exceptional Children*, 1978, *45*, 26–31.

Church, M. Does visual-perception training help beginning readers? *Reading Teacher*, 1974, *27*, 361–364.

Cleary, T. Test bias: Prediction of grades of negro and white students in integrated colleges. *Journal of Educational Measurement*, 1968, *5*, 115–124.

Cohen, J. Coefficient of agreement for nominal scales. *Educational and Psychological Measurement*, 1960, *20*, 37–46.

Cohen, J., & De Young, H. The role of litigation in the improvement of programming for the handicapped. In L. Mann & D. Sabatino (Eds.), *The first review of special education* (Vol. 2). Philadelphia: JSE Press, 1973.

Cone, J. The relevance of reliability and validity for behavioral assessment. *Behavior Therapy*, 1977, *8*, 411–426.

Coulter, W. Mattie T. and the prescience of individual plans for all. *NASP Communique*, 1979, *8*(1), 6–7.

Coulter, W. Adaptive behavior and professional disfavor: Controversies and trends for school psychologists. *School Psychology Review*, 1980, *9*, 67 – 74. (a)

Coulter, W. Chicago judge sets a different "PASE" with current issues. *NASP Communique*, 1980, *9*(2), 2. (b)

Coulter, W., & Morrow, H. A contemporary conception of adaptive behavior within the scope of psychological assessment. In W. Coulter & H. Morrow (Eds.), *Adaptive behavior: Concepts and measurements*. New York: Grune & Stratton, 1978.

Coulter, W., & Morrow, H. (Eds.). *Adaptive behavior: Concepts and measurements*. New York: Grune & Stratton, 1978.

Cruickshank, W. Foreword. In D. Sabatino & T. Miller (Eds.), *Describing learner characteristics of handicapped children and youth*. New York: Grune & Stratton, 1979.

Darlington, R. Another look at "culture fairness." *Journal of Educational Measurement*, 1971, *8*, 71 – 82.

Darlington, R., & Bishop, C. Increasing test validity by considering interim correlations. *Journal of Applied Psychology*, 1966, *50*, 322 – 330.

Davidson, R. Mediation and ability in paired associate learning. *Journal of Educational Psychology*, 1964, *55*, 241 – 246.

Davis, W. *Educator's resource guide to special education*. Boston: Allyn & Bacon, 1980.

Dean, R. Internal consistency of the PIAT with Mexican-American children. *Psychology in the Schools*, 1977, *14*, 167 – 168.

Dean, R. Factor structure of the WISC-R with Anglos and Mexican-Americans. *Journal of School Psychology*, 1980, *18*, 234 – 239.

Dean, R. Cerebral dominance and childhood learning disorders: Theoretical perspectives. *School Psychology Review*, 1981, *10*, 373 – 380.

DeAvila, E., & Havassy, B. Piagetian alternative to IQ: Mexican-American study. In N. Hobbs (Ed.), *Issues in the classification of children* (Vol. 2). San Francisco: Jossey-Bass, 1975.

DeLong, A. The limits of accuracy of test scores of emr individuals. *Journal of the Association for Research in Growth Relationships*, 1962, *3*, 26 – 44.

Dickinson, D. Direct assessment of behavioral and emotional problems. *Psychology in the Schools*, 1978, *15*, 472 – 477.

Dickinson, D. The direct assessment: An alternative to psychometric testing. *Journal of Learning Disabilities*, 1980, *13*, 472 – 479.

Doll, E. A genetic scale of social maturity. *American Journal of Orthopsychiatry*, 1935, *5*, 180 – 188.

Doll, E. *Measurement of social competence: A manual for the Vineland Social Maturity Scale*. Circle Pines, Minn.: American Guidance Service, 1953.

Doll, E. *Vineland Social Maturity Scale*. Circle Pines, Minn.: American Guidance Service, 1965.

Draguns, J., Haley, E., & Phillips, L. Studies of Rorschach content: A review of the research literature. Pt. 1: Traditional content categories. *Journal of Projective Techniques and Personality Assessment*, 1967, *31*, 3 – 32.

Duffey, J., Salvia, J., Tucker, J., & Ysseldyke, J. Nonbiased assessment: A need for operationalism. *Exceptional Children*, 1981, *47*, 427 – 434.

Dunn, L., & Dunn, J. *Peabody Picture Vocabulary Test — Revised*. Circle Pines, Minn.: American Guidance Service, 1981.

Dunn, L., & Markwardt, F. *Peabody Individual Achievement Test Manual*. Circle Pines, Minn.: American Guidance Service, 1970.

Editor. Editor's note. *Exceptional children*, 1981, *47*, 492 – 493.

Elkind, D. Piagetian and psychometric conceptions of intelligence. *Harvard Educational Review*, 1969, *39*, 171 – 189.

Elkins, E. The diagnostic validity of the Ames "danger signals." *Journal of Consulting Psychology*, 1958, *22*, 281 – 287.

Ellett, C., & Bersoff, D. An integrated approach to the psychosituational assessment of behavior. *Professional Psychology*, 1976, *7*, 485 – 494.

Englehardt, W. The validity of the Frostig Developmental Test of Visual Perception. *Zeitschrift fur Entwicklungspychologie und Pädagogische Psychologie*, 1975, *7*, 100 – 112.

Engel, M. *Psychopathology in childhood: Social, diagnostic, and therapeutic aspects*. New York: Harcourt, Brace, Jovanovich, 1972.

Evans, J., & Nelson, R. Assessment of child behavior problems. In Ciminero, A., Calhoun, K., and Adams, H. (Eds.), *Handbook of Behavioral Assessment*. New York: Wiley, 1977.

Exner, J., Jr. *The Rorschach: A comprehensive system* (Vol. 1). New York: Wiley, 1974.

Fagan, T. The dilemma of clientage. *NASP Communique*, 1980, *9*(3), 1.

Farb, J., & Throne, J. Improving the generalized mnemonic performance of a Down's syndrome child. *Journal of Applied Behavior Analysis*, 1978, *11*, 413 – 419.

Federal Register. Privacy rights of parents and students. Regulations implementing Family Rights and Privacy Act of 1974. June 17, 1976, pp. 24670 – 24675.

Federal Register. Nondiscrimination on basis of handicap. Regulations implementing Section 504 of the Rehabilitation Act of 1973. May 4, 1977, pp. 22676 – 22702.

Federal Register. Education of handicapped children. Regulations Implementing Education for All Handicapped Children Act of 1975. August 23, 1977, pp. 42474 – 42518.

Federal Register. Procedures for evaluating specific learning disabilities. December 29, 1977, pp. 65082 – 65085.

Federal Register. Reference to autistic children under the definition of handicapped children. January 16, 1981, pp. 3865 – 3866.

Federal Register. Assistance to states for the education of handicapped children. January 13, 1982, pp. 1861 – 1862.

Federal Register. Nondiscrimination on the basis of handicap in programs and activities receiving or benefitting from federal financial assistance. January 13, 1982, pp. 1858 – 1859.

Feuerstein, R. *The dynamic assessment of retarded performers: The learning potential assessment device, theory, instruments, and techniques*. Baltimore: University Park Press, 1979.

Flanders, N. *Interaction analysis in the classroom: A manual for observers*. Ann Arbor: University of Michigan School of Education, 1964.

Flygare, T. Disciplining special education students. *Phi Delta Kappan*, 1981, *62*, 670–671.

Fox, R., Luszki, M., & Schmuck, R. *Diagnosing classroom learning environments*. Chicago: Science Research Associates, 1966.

Frith, G. "Advocate" vs. "professional employee": A question of priorities for special educators. *Exceptional Children*, 1981, *47*, 486–492.

Frostig, M., LeFever, W., & Whittlesey, J. *Frostig Developmental Test of Visual Perception*. Palo Alto, Calif.: Consulting Psychologists Press, 1966.

Frostig, M., Maslow, P., LeFever, D., & Whittlesey, J. *The Marianne Frostig Developmental Test of Visual Perception: 1963 standardization*. Palo Alto, Calif.: Consulting Psychologists Press, 1964.

Gaddes, W. *Learning disabilities and brain function: A neuropsychological approach*. New York: Springer-Verlag, 1980.

Gambrill, E. *Behavior modification: Handbook of assessment, intervention, and evaluation*. San Francisco: Jossey-Bass, 1977.

Gerken, K. Performance of Mexican-American children on intelligence tests. *Exceptional Children*, 1978, *44*, 438–443.

Gerken, K. Assessment of high-risk preschoolers and children and adolescents with low-incident handicapping conditions. In G. Phye & D. Reschly (Eds.), *School psychology: Perspectives and issues*. New York: Academic Press, 1979.

Glidewell, J. The prevalence of maladjustment in elementary schools. Mimeographed report prepared for the Joint Commission on Mental Health of Children. December, 1967.

Goddard, H. A measuring scale of intelligence. *Training School*, 1910, *6*, 146–155.

Goodman, L., & Hammill, D. The effectiveness of Kephart-Getman activities in developing perceptual-motor and cognitive skills. *Focus on Exceptional Children*, 1973, *4*, 1–9.

Gregary, M. Emotional indicators on the Bender Gestalt and the Devereaux Child Behavior Rating Scale. *Psychology in the Schools*, 1977, *14*, 433–437.

Gronlund, N. *Sociometry in the classroom*. New York: Harper & Brothers, 1959.

Grossman, H. (Ed.). *Manual on terminology and classification in mental retardation*. Washington, D.C.: American Association on Mental Deficiency, 1973.

Grow, R. Junior high norms for the Bender Gestalt. *Journal of School Psychology*, 1980, *18*, 395–398.

Guilford, J. *The nature of human intelligence*. New York: McGraw-Hill, 1967.

Gutsch, K., & Casse, R. A comparison of mothers' and teachers' perceptions of normal and retarded preschool and adolescent children. *Southern Journal of Educational Research*, 1970, *4*, 1–17.

Halfacre, J., & Welch, F. Teacher consultation model: An operant approach. *Psychology in the Schools*, 1973, *10*, 494–497.

Hallahan, D., & Cruickshank, W. *Psychoeducational foundations of learning disabilities*. Englewood Cliffs, N.J.: Prentice-Hall, 1973.

Hallahan, D., & Kauffman, J. *Introduction to learning disabilities: A psycho-behavioral approach.* Englewood Cliffs, N.J.: Prentice-Hall, 1976.

Hallahan, D., & Kauffman, J. *Exceptional children: Introduction to special education.* Englewood Cliffs, N.J.: Prentice-Hall, 1978.

Hambleton, R., Swaminathan, H., Algina, J., & Coulson, D. Criterion referenced testing and measurement: A review of technical issues and developments. *Review of Educational Research,* 1978, *48*, 1 – 47.

Hammill, D. Training visual perceptual processes. *Journal of Learning Disabilities,* 1972, *5*, 552 – 559.

Hammill, D., & Larsen, S. The effectiveness of psycholinguistic training. *Exceptional Children,* 1974, *41*, 5 – 14.

Hammill, D., & Larsen, S. The effectiveness of psycholinguistic training: A reaffirmation of position. *Exceptional Children,* 1978, *44*, 402 – 417.

Hathaway, S., & McKinley, J. *The Minnesota Multiphasic Personality Inventory Manual* (Rev. ed.). New York: Psychological Corporation, 1951.

Heber, R. A manual on terminology and classification in mental retardation. *American Journal of Mental Deficiency,* 1959, *64*.

Heber, R. A manual on terminology and classification in mental retardation. *American Journal of Mental Deficiency,* 1961, *66*.

Helton, G., & Workman, E. Considerations in assessing the mildly handicapped. In T. Miller & E. Davis (Eds.), *The mildly handicapped student.* New York: Grune & Stratton, 1982.

Hersen, M., & Bellack, A. (Eds.). *Behavioral assessment: A practical handbook.* Elmsford, N.Y.: Pergamon Press, 1976.

High Court refuses to hear appeals of Florida schools, New Jersey parents. *Phi Delta Kappan,* 1982, *63*, 363.

Hildman, L. The Mattie T. Case in Mississippi. *NASP Communique,* 1979, *8*(1), 6.

Hobbs, N. *The futures of children.* San Francisco: Jossey-Bass, 1975.

Hobbs, N. An ecologically oriented, service based system for the classification of handicapped children. In S. Salzinger, J. Antrobus, & J. Glick (Eds.), *The ecosystem of the "sick" child.* New York: Academic Press, 1980.

Holland, C. An interview guide for behavioral counseling with parents. *Behavior Therapy,* 1970, *1*, 70 – 79.

Hutt, M. *The Hutt adaptation of the Bender-Gestalt Test* (3rd ed.). New York: Grune & Stratton, 1977.

Hynd, G., & Obrzut, J. (Eds.). *Neuropsychological assessment and the school-age child: Issues and procedures.* New York: Grune & Stratton, 1981.

Ingram, C. *Fundamentals of educational assessment.* New York: D. Van Nostrand, 1980.

Jastak, J., Bijou, S., & Jastak, S. *Wide Range Achievement Test.* Los Angeles: Western Psychological Services, 1965.

Jastak, J., & Jastak, S. *Wide Range Achievement Test manual of instructions.* Los Angeles: Western Psychological Services, 1978.

Jensen, A. Review of *Thematic Apperception Test.* In O. K. Buros (Ed.), *Personality tests and reviews.* Highland Park, N.J.: Gryphon Press, 1970.

Johnson, S., & Lobitz, G. Parental manipulation of child behavior in home observations. *Journal of Applied Behavior Analysis,* 1974, *7*, 23 – 32.

Kampwirth, T. Not just another fish story: A response to Barbe, Swassing, and Milone. *Academic Therapy*, 1981, *16*, 267 – 269.

Kampwirth, T., & Bates, M. Modality preference and teaching method: A review of research. *Academic Therapy*, 1980, *15*, 597 – 605.

Kara, A., & Wahler, R. Organizational features of a young child's behaviors. *Journal of Experimental Child Psychology*, 1977, *24*, 24 – 39.

Kaufman, A. Factor analysis of the WISC-R at eleven age levels between 6½ and 16½ years. *Journal of Consulting and Clinical Psychology*, 1975, *43*, 135 – 147.

Kaufman, A. *Intelligent testing with the WISC-R*. New York: Wiley-Interscience, 1979.

Kaufman, A. & Kaufman, N. *Clinical evaluation of young children with the McCarthy Scales*. New York: Grune & Stratton, 1977.

Kauffman, J., & Vicente, A. Bringing in the sheaves: Observations on harvesting behavioral change in the field. *Journal of School Psychology*, 1972, *10*, 263 – 268.

Kavale, K. Functions of the Illinois Test of Psycholinguistic Abilities (ITPA): Are they trainable? *Exceptional Children*, 1981, *47*, 496 – 513.

Kazdin, A. *Behavior modification in applied settings*. (Rev. ed.). Homewood, Ill.: Dorsey Press, 1980.

Kent, R., & Foster, S. Direct observational procedures: methodological issues in naturalistic settings. In A. Ciminero, K. Calhoun, & H. Adams (Eds.), *Handbook of behavioral assessment*. New York: Wiley, 1977.

Kent, R., Kanowitz, J., O'Leary, K., & Cheiken, M. Observer reliability as a function of circumstances of assessment. *Journal of Applied Behavior Analysis*, 1977, *10*, 317 – 324.

Kent, R., O'Leary, K., Diament, C., & Dietz, S. Expectation biases in observational evaluation of therapeutic change. *Journal of Consulting and Clinical Psychology*, 1973, *81*, 46 – 50.

Kirk, S., McCarthy, J., & Kirk, W. *Illinois Test of Psycholinguistic Abilities*. Urbana: University of Illinois Press, 1968.

Koppitz, E. *The Bender Gestalt Test for Young Children*. New York: Grune & Stratton, 1963.

Koppitz, E., *Human Figure Drawing Test*. New York: Grune & Stratton, 1968.

Koppitz, E. Bender Gestalt Test, Visual Aural Digit Span Test and reading achievement. *Journal of Learning Disabilities*, 1975, *8*, 154 – 157. (a)

Koppitz, E. *The Bender Gestalt Test for Young Children* (Vol. 2). New York: Grune & Stratton, 1975. (b)

Koppitz, E. The Visual Aural Digit Span Test performance of boys with emotional and learning problems. *Journal of Clinical Psychology*, 1975, *8*, 154 – 157. (c)

Koppitz, E. *The Visual Aural Digit Span Test*. New York: Grune & Stratton, 1977.

Kratochwill, T. The movement of psychological extras into ability assessment. *Journal of Special Education*, 1977, *11*, 299 – 311.

LaManna, J., & Ysseldyke, J. Reliability of the Peabody Individual Achievement Test with first-grade children. *Psychology in the Schools*, 1973, *10*, 437 – 439.

Lambert, N. Psychological evidence in Larry P. v. Wilson Riles: An evaluation by a witness for the defense. *American Psychologist*, 1981, *36*, 937 – 952.

Lambert, N., Windmiller, M., Cole, L., & Figueroa, R. *Manual for the Public School Version of the AAMD Adaptive Behavior Scale.* Washington, D.C.: American Association on Mental Deficiency, 1975.

Laosa, L. Non-biased assessment of children's abilities: Historical antecedents and current issues. In T. Oakland (Ed.), *Psychological and educational assessment of minority children.* New York: Brunner/Mazel, 1977.

Leonard, J. 180 day barrier: Issues and concerns. *Exceptional Children*, 1981, *47*, 246 – 253.

Levine, E. Psychological evaluation of the deaf client. In B. Bolton (Ed.), *Handbook of measurement and evaluation in rehabilitation.* Springfield, Ill.: Charles C Thomas, 1976.

Lezak, M. *Neuropsychological assessment.* New York: Oxford University Press, 1976.

Lipinski, D., & Nelson, R. Problems in the use of naturalistic observation as a means of behavioral assessment. *Behavior Therapy*, 1974, *5*, 341 – 351.

Lobitz, G., & Johnson, S. Normal versus deviant children: A multimethod comparison. *Journal of Abnormal Child Psychology*, 1975, *3*, 353 – 374.

Lund, K., Foster, G., & McCall-Perez, F. The effectiveness of psycholinguistic training: A reevaluation. *Exceptional Children*, 1978, *44*, 310 – 321.

Lundell, K., Evans, J., & Brown, W. *Criterion Test of Basic Skills.* San Rafael, Calif.: Academic Therapy Publications, 1976.

MacMillan, D., & Meyers, C. Larry P: An educational interpretation. *School Psychology Review*, 1980, *9*, 136 – 148.

Makuch, G. Year-round special education and related services: A state director's perspective. *Exceptional Children*, 1981, *47*, 272 – 275.

Marholin, D. (Ed.). *Child behavior therapy.* New York: Gardner Press, 1978.

Marholin, D., & Bijou, S. Behavioral assessment: Listen when the data speak. In D. Marholin (Ed.), *Child behavior therapy.* New York: Gardner Press, 1978.

Martin, R. *Educating handicapped children: The legal mandate.* Champaign, Ill.: Research Press, 1979.

Martin, R. Ethics column. *The School Psychologist*, 1981, *35*, 3 – 4.

McCarthy, D. *Manual for the McCarthy Scales of Children's Abilities.* New York: Psychological Corporation, 1972.

McPhee, J., & Wagner, K. *Kinetic Family Drawings (KED)* styles and emotionally disturbed childhood behaviors. *Journal of Personality Assessment*, 1976, *40*, 487 – 491.

Mealor, D., & Richmond, B. Adaptive behavior: Teachers and parents disagree. *Exceptional Children*, 1980, *46*, 386 – 389.

Mearig, J. On becoming a child advocate in school psychology. *Journal of School Psychology*, 1974, *12*, 121 – 129.

Meeker, M. *The structure of intellect.* Columbus, Ohio: Charles E. Merrill, 1969.

Meeker, M. Individualized curriculum based on intelligence test patterns. In R. Coop & K. White (Eds.), *Psychological concepts in the classroom*. New York: Harper & Row, 1973.

Meeker M. *Learning to solve problems: A structure of intellect convergent production source book*. El Segundo, Calif.: SOI Institute, 1979.

Meeker, M., & Meeker, R. *S.O.I. Learning Abilities Test Examiner's Manual*. El Segundo, Calif.: SOI Institute, 1979.

Meichenbaum, D. *Cognitive-behavior modification: An integrative approach*. New York: Plenum Press, 1977.

Melahn, C., & O'Donnell, C. Norm based behavioral consulting. *Behavior Modification*, 1978, 2, 309–338.

Mercer, J. In defense of racially and culturally nondiscriminatory assessment. *School Psychology Digest*, 1979, 8, 80–115. (a)

Mercer, J. *Technical manual: System of multicultural pluralistic assessment*. New York: Psychological Corporation, 1979. (b)

Mercer, J., & Lewis, J. *SOMPA Parent Interview Manual*. New York: Psychological Corporation, 1977.

Mercer, J., & Ysseldyke, J. Designing diagnostic-intervention programs. In T. Oakland (Ed.), *Psychological and educational assessment of minority children*. New York: Bruner/Mazel, 1977.

Messick, S. Test validity and the ethics of assessment. *American Psychologist*, 1980, 35, 1012–1027.

Meyers, C., Sundstrom, P., & Yoshida, R. The school psychologist and assessment in special education. *School Psychology Monographs*, 1974, 2. (1)

Meyers, J., Parsons, R., & Martin, R. *Mental health consultation in the schools*. San Francisco: Jossey-Bass, 1979.

Miller, S. Career education: Lifelong planning for the handicapped. In D. Sabatino & T. Miller (Eds.), *Describing learner characteristics of handicapped children and youth*. New York: Grune & Stratton, 1979.

Miller, T. A review of the psychometric approach to measurement. In D. Sabatino & T. Miller (Eds.), *Describing learner characteristics of handicapped children and youth*. New York: Grune & Stratton, 1979.

Minskoff, E. Research on psycholinguistic training: Critique and guidelines. *Exceptional Children*, 1975, 42, 136–144.

Monroe, V. Roles and status of school psychology. In G. Phye & D. Reschly (Eds.), *School psychology: Perspectives and issues*. New York: Academic Press, 1979.

Moreno, J. *Who shall survive?* New York: Beacon House, 1953.

Moos, R., Insel, P., & Humphrey, B. *Preliminary manual for the Family Environment Scale, the Work Environment Scale, and the Group Environment Scale*. Palo Alto, Calif.: Consulting Psychologists Press, 1974.

Mueller, M. Mental retardation. In M. Wisland (Ed.), *Psychoeducational diagnosis of exceptional children*. Springfield, Ill.: Charles C Thomas, 1974.

Murray, H. *Uses of the Thematic Apperception Technique*. New York: Basic Books, 1965.

Murrell, S. *Community psychology and social systems: A conceptual framework and intervention guide*. New York: Behavior Publications, 1973.

Myers, D. Toward an objective evaluation procedure of the Kinetic Family Drawing (KFD). *Journal of Personality Assessment*, 1978, *42*, 358–365.

National Association of School Psychologists. Principles for Professional Ethics. *Membership Directory*. Washington, D.C.: National Association of School Psychologists, 1978. (a).

National Association of School Psychologists. Procedures for Handling Complaints of Alleged Violations of Ethical Principles. *Membership Directory*. Washington, D.C.: National Association of School Psychologists, 1978. (b)

National Association of State Directors of Special Education. *Functions of the placement committee in special education*. Washington, D.C.: NASDSE, 1976.

Nelson, R., Kapust, J., & Dorsey, B. Minimal reactivity of overt classroom observations on student and teacher behaviors. *Behavior Therapy*, 1978, *9*, 695–702.

Nihira, K. Factorial descriptions of the AAMD Adaptive Behavior Scale. In W. Coulter & H. Morrow (Eds.), *Adaptive behavior: Concepts and measurements*. New York: Grune & Stratton, 1978.

Nihira, K., Foster, R., Shellhaas, M., & Leland, H. *AAMD Adaptive Behavior Scale, 1974 Version*. Washington, D.C.: American Association on Mental Deficiency, 1975.

Nunnally, J. *Psychometric theory*. New York: McGraw-Hill, 1967.

Oakland, T. Research on the Adaptive Behavior Inventory for Children and the estimated learning potential. *School Psychology Digest*, 1979, *8*, 63–70.

Oakland, T. An evaluation of the ABIC, pluralistic norms, and estimated learning potential. *Journal of School Psychology*, 1980, *18*, 3–11.

Oakland, T., & Feigenbaum, D. Comparisons of the psychometric characteristics of the Adaptive Behavior Inventory for Children for different subgroups of children. *Journal of School Psychology*, 1980, 18, 307–316.

Oakland, T., & Goldwater, D. Assessment and interventions for mildly retarded and learning disabled children. In G. Phye & D. Reschly (Eds.), *School psychology: Perspectives and issues*. New York: Academic Press, 1979.

Oakland, T., & Laosa, L. Professional, legislative, and judicial influences on psychoeducational assessment practices in schools. In T. Oakland (Ed.), *Psychological and educational assessment of minority children*. New York: Bruner/Mazel, 1977.

Oakland, T. & Matuszek, P. Using tests in nondiscriminatory assessment. In T. Oakland (Ed.), *Psychological and educational assessment of minority children*. New York: Bruner/Mazel, 1977.

Obrzut, J. Neuropsychological assessment in the schools. *School Psychology Review*, 1981, *10*, 331–342.

O'Donnell, C. Behavior modification in community settings. In H. Hersen, R. Eisler, & P. Miller (Eds.), *Progress in behavior modification* (Vol. 4). New York: Academic Press, 1977.

O'Leary, D. The assessment of psychopathology in children. In H. Quay & J. Werry (Eds.), *Psychopathological disorders of childhood*. New York: Wiley, 1972.

O'Leary, K., Kaufman, K., Kass, R., & Drabman, R. The effects of loud and soft reprimands on the behavior of disruptive children. *Exceptional Children*, 1970, *37*, 145–155.

Paraskevopoulous, J. & Kirk, S. *The development and psychometric characteristics of the revised ITPA*. Urbana: University of Illinois Press, 1969.

Patton, P. A model for developing vocational objectives in the IEP. *Exceptional Children*, 1981, *47*, 618–623.

Peterson, J. *Early conceptions and tests of intelligence*. New York: World Book Company, 1925.

Phi Delta Kappa. *School climate improvement: A challenge to the school administrator*. Denver: Charles F. Kettering, undated.

Piaget, J. *The psychology of intelligence*. New York: Harcourt, Brace, 1950.

Pihl, R., & Nimrod, G. The reliability and validity of the Draw a Person in IQ and personality assessment. *Journal of Clinical Psychology*, 1976, *32*, 470–472.

Prasse, D. Supreme Court rules on the commitment of minors. *NASP Communique*, 1979, *8*(1), 3; 5.

Prasse, D. Editorial comment: The Larry P. decision. *School Psychology Review*, 1980, *9*, 111. (a)

Prasse, D. PASE v. Hannon. *NASP Communique*, 1980, *9*(3), 3. (b)

Prasse, D. Armstrong v. Kline: Defining appropriate programming. *NASP Communique*, 1981, *9*(7), 3. (a)

Prasse, D. Professional standards versus system procedure. *NASP Communique*, 1981, *9*(6), 3. (b)

Ramage, J. Dateline: Washington. *NASP Communique*, 1982, *10*(6), 6.

Rapoport, D., Gill, M., & Schafer, R. *Diagnostic psychological testing*. New York: International Universities Press, 1968.

Raven, J. *Guide to using the colored progressive matrices*. London: H. K. Lewis, 1965.

Reagan again proposes cutting special education. *CEC Update*, 1982, *13*(6), 1.

Reitan, R., & Davidson, L. *Clinical neuropsychology: Current status and applications*. Washington, D.C.: Winston, 1974.

Reschly, D. Nonbiased assessment. In G. Phye & D. Reschly (Eds.), *School psychology: Perspectives and issues*. New York: Academic Press, 1979.

Reschly, D. Psychological evidence in the *Larry P.* opinion: A case of right problem – wrong solution. *School Psychology Review*, 1980, *9*, 123–135.

Reschly, D., & Reschly, J. Validity of WISC-R factor scores in predicting achievement and attention for four socio-cultural groups. *Journal of School Psychology*, 1979, *17*, 355–361.

Reynolds, C. Factor structure of the Peabody Individual Achievement Test at five grade levels between grades 1 and 12. *Journal of School Psychology*, 1979, *17*, 270–274.

Reynolds, C. Neuropsychological assessment and the habilitation of learning: Considerations in the search for the aptitude x treatment interaction. *School Psychology Review*, 1981, *10*, 343 – 349.

Richmond B., & Kicklighter, R. *Children's Adaptive Behavior Scale*. Atlanta: Humanics Limited, 1980.

Rights of retarded rejected. *APA Monitor*, 1981, *12*(6 – 7), 13.

Rorschach, H. *Psychodiagnostics*. Berne, Switz.: Verlaz Hans Huber, 1942.

Rosner, J. *Test of Auditory Analysis Skills*. San Rafael, Calif.: Academic Therapy Publications, 1975.

Ross, A. *Learning disabilities: The unrealized potential*. New York: McGraw-Hill, 1977.

Ross, A. *Psychological disorders of children: A behavioral approach to theory, research and therapy* (2nd ed.). New York: McGraw-Hill, 1980.

Ross, S., De Young, H., & Cohen, J. Confrontation: Special education and the law. *Exceptional Children*, 1971, *4*, 5 – 12.

Sabatino, D., Ysseldyke, J., & Woolston, J. Diagnostic-prescriptive perceptual training with mentally retarded children. *American Journal of Mental Deficiency*, 1973, *78*, 7 – 14.

Salvia, J., & Ysseldyke, J. *Assessment in special and remedial education*. Boston: Houghton-Mifflin, 1978.

Sandoval, J., & Haapanen, R. A critical commentary on neuropsychology in the schools: Are we ready? *School Psychology Review*, 1981, *10*, 381 – 388.

Sattler, J. Analysis of functions of the 1960 Stanford-Binet Intelligence Scale, form L-M. *Journal of Clinical Psychology*, 1965, *21*, 173 – 179.

Sattler, J. *Assessment of children's intelligence*. Philadelphia: Saunders, 1974.

Sattler, J. *Assessment of children's intelligence and special abilities*. Boston: Allyn & Bacon, 1982.

Sax, G. *Principles of educational and psychological measurement and evaluation* (2nd ed.). Belmont, Calif.: Wadsworth, 1980.

Sewell, T. Intelligence and learning tasks as predictors of scholastic achievement in black and white first-grade children. *Journal of School Psychology*, 1979, *17*, 325 – 332.

Shaffer, M. President's message. *The School Psychologist*, 1981, *36*(2), 2.

Shumar, L. The relationship of the Visual Aural Digit Span Test to reading achievement for lower elementary school children. Unpublished masters thesis, University of Akron, 1976.

Sitlington, P. Validity of the Peabody Individual Achievement Test with educable mentally retarded adolescents. Unpublished masters thesis, University of Hawaii, 1970.

Slosson, R. *Slosson Intelligence Test for Children and Adults*. New York: Slosson Educational Publications, 1963.

Smith, R., Neisworth, J., & Greer, J. *Evaluating educational environments*. Columbus, Ohio: Charles E. Merrill, 1978.

Spache, G. *Diagnosing and correcting reading disabilities*. Boston: Allyn & Bacon, 1976.

Spearman, C. *The abilities of man*. New York: MacMillan, 1927.

Stern, W. *The psychological methods of testing intelligence.* Baltimore: Warwick & York, 1914.

Stodden, R., & Ianacone, R. Career/vocational assessment of the special needs individual: A conceptual model. *Exceptional Children,* 1981, *47,* 600–609.

Stotland, J., & Mancuso, E. U.S. Court of Appeals decision regarding Armstrong v. Kline: The 180 day rule. *Exceptional Children,* 1981, *47,* 266–270.

Supreme Court refuses to hear *Battle. CEC Update,* 1981, *13*(2), 5.

Swanson, H. Functional analysis Q sheet for LD children. *Academic Therapy,* 1978, *14,* 209–217.

Tarver, S., & Dawson, M. Modality preference and the teaching of reading: A review. *Journal of Learning Disabilities,* 1978, *11,* 17–29.

Tennessee State Board of Education. *Rules, regulations, and minimum standards, 1979–1980.* Nashville, Tenn.: Tennessee State Board of Education, 1979.

Terman, L. *The measurement of intelligence.* Boston: Houghton-Mifflin, 1916.

Terman, L. & Merrill, M. *Stanford-Binet Intelligence Scale, manual for the third revision, form L-M, 1972 norms edition.* Boston: Houghton-Mifflin, 1973.

Tharp, R., & Wetzel, R. *Behavior modification in the natural environment.* New York: Academic Press, 1969.

The 1983 education budget. *Education Week,* 1982, *1*(21), 8.

Thomason, J. Up front with the president. *CEC Update,* 1981, *13*(1), 2.

Thompson, G. The relationship between the VADS Test and selected measures of reading. Unpublished masters thesis, University of Akron, 1976.

Title I coalition lobbies against further cuts. *Education Week,* 1982, *1*(26), 10.

Tomkins, S. *The Thematic Apperception Test.* New York: Grune & Stratton, 1947.

Tomlinson, J. Implementing behavior modification programs with limited consultation time. *Journal of School Psychology,* 1972, *5,* 64–78.

Trachtman, G. The clouded crystal ball: Is there a school psychology in our future? *Psychology in the Schools,* 1979, *16,* 378–388.

Trahan, D., & Stricklin, A. Bender-Gestalt emotional indicators and acting out behavior in young children. *Journal of Personality Assessment,* 1979, *43,* 365–375.

Tucker, J. Operationalizing the diagnostic-intervention process. In T. Oakland (Ed.), *Psychological and educational assessment of minority children.* New York: Bruner/Mazel, 1977.

Turnbull, H. The past and future impact of court decisions in special education. *Phi Delta Kappan,* 1978, *59,* 523–527.

Tymitz-Wolf, B. Guidelines for assessing IEP goals and objectives. *Teaching Exceptional Children,* 1982, *14,* 198–202.

Urban, W. *Draw-a-Person.* Los Angeles: Western Psychological Services, 1963.

Valett, R. A clinical profile for the Stanford-Binet. *Journal of School Psychology*, 1964, *2*, 49–54.

Vance, H. Instructional strategies with the ITPA. *Academic Therapy*, 1976, *11*, 223–231.

Waddell, D. The Stanford-Binet: An evaluation of the technical data available since the 1972 restandardization. *Journal of School Psychology*, 1980, *18*, 203–209.

Wagner, R., & McCloy, F. *Two validity studies of the Wide Range Achievement Reading Test.* Richmond, Va.: Academy of Science, 1962.

Wahler, R. Setting generality: Some specific and general effects of child behavior therapy. *Journal of Applied Behavior Analysis*, 1969, *2*, 239–246.

Wahler, R. Some structural aspects of deviant child behavior. *Journal of Applied Behavior Analysis*, 1975, *8*, 27–42.

Wahler, R., & Cormier, W. The ecological interview: A first step in outpatient child behavior therapy. *Journal of Behavior Therapy and Experimental Psychiatry*, 1970, *1*, 279–289.

Wahler, R., House, A., & Stambaugh, E. *Ecological assessment of child problem behavior: A clinical package for home, school, and institutional settings.* New York: Pergamon Press, 1976.

Walker, H. *Walker Problem Behavior Identification Checklist.* Los Angeles: Western Psychological Services, 1970.

Wall, S., & Paradise, L. A comparison of parent and teacher reports of selected adaptive behaviors of children. *Journal of School Psychology*, 1981, *19*, 73–77.

Wallace, G., & Larsen, S. *Educational assessment of learning problems: Testing for teaching.* Boston: Allyn & Bacon, 1978.

Wallace, J. An abilities conception of personality: Some implications for personality measurement. *American Psychologist*, 1966, *21*, 132–137.

Walls, R., Werner, T., Bacon, A., & Zane, T. Behavior checklists. In J. Cone & R. Hawkins (Eds.), *Behavioral assessment: New directions in clinical psychology.* New York: Bruner/Mazel, 1977.

Weatherly, R., & Lipsky, M. Street-level bureaucrats and institutional innovations: Implementing special education reform. *Harvard Educational Review*, 1977, *47*, 171–197.

Wechsler, D. *Manual for the Wechsler Adult Intelligence Scale.* New York: Psychological Corporation, 1955.

Wechsler, D. *The measurement and appraisal of adult intelligence* (4th ed.). Baltimore: Williams & Wilkins, 1958.

Wechsler, D. *Manual for the Wechsler Preschool and Primary Scale of Intelligence.* New York: Psychological Corporation, 1967.

Wechsler, D. *Manual for the Wechsler Intelligence Scale for Children—Revised.* New York: Psychological Corporation, 1974.

Wechsler, D. *Manual for the Wechsler Adult Intelligence Scale—Revised.* New York: Psychological Corporation, 1981.

Weincott, M., Garrett, B., & Todd, N. The influences of observer presence on classroom behavior. *Behavior Therapy*, in press.

Wepman, J. *Auditory Discrimination Test.* Chicago: Language Research Association, 1973.

White, E. Congress seeks more funds for E.D. *Education Week,* 1982, *1*(25), 8. (a)

White, E. President reportedly will seek block grants for handicapped and vocational education. *Education Week,* 1982, *1*(20), 1. (b)

Wildman, B., Erickson, M., & Kent, R. The effect of two training procedures on observer agreement and variability of behavior ratings. *Child Development,* 1975, *46,* 520–524.

Will reauthorization jeopardize the handicapped? *CEC Update,* 1982, *13*(4), 5.

Williams, R., & Anandam, K. *Cooperative classroom management.* Columbus, Ohio: Charles E. Merrill, 1973.

Williams, R., & Mitchell, H. What happened to ABPsi's moratorium on testing: A 1968 to 1977 reminder. *Journal of Black Psychology,* 1977, *4,* 25–42.

Wirt, R., Lachar, D., Klinedinst, J., & Seat, P. *Multidimensional description of child personality: A manual for the Personality Inventory for Children.* Los Angeles: Western Psychological Services, 1977.

Witkin, H., Moore, C., Goodenough, D., & Cox, P. Field-dependent and field-independent cognitive styles and their educational implications. *Review of Educational Research,* 1977, *47,* 1–64.

Woodcock, R. *Goldman-Fristoe-Woodcock Auditory Skills Test Battery technical manual.* Circle Pines, Minn.: American Guidance Service, 1976.

Workman, E., & Dickinson, D. The use of covert positive reinforcement in the treatment of a hyperactive child: An empirical case study. *Journal of School Psychology,* 1979, *17,* 67–73.

Workman, E., & Dickinson, D. The use of covert conditioning with children: Three empirical case studies. *Education and Treatment of Children,* 1980, *2,* 24–36.

Yoshida, R., MacMillan, D., & Meyers, E. The decertification of minority group EMR students in California: Student achievement and adjustment. In R. Jones (Ed.), *Mainstreaming and the minority child.* Reston, Va.: Council for Exceptional Children, 1976.

Ysseldyke, J. Issues in psychoeducational assessment. In G. Phye & D. Reschly (Eds.), *School psychology: Perspectives and issues.* New York: Academic Press, 1979.

Zigler, E., & Muenchow, S. Principles and social policy implications of a whole-child psychology. In S. Salzinger, J Antrobus, & J. Glick (Eds.), *The ecosystem of the "sick" child.* New York: Academic Press, 1980.

Zubin, J., Eron, L., & Schumer, F. *An experimental approach to projective techniques.* New York: Wiley, 1965.

Reference Notes

1. Office of Special Education and Rehabilitative Services. Briefing paper: Initial review of regulations under Part B of the Education of the Handicapped Act as amended. Washington, D.C.: U.S. Department of Education, September 1, 1981.
2. Bersoff, D. Legal issues in the practice of psychology. Workshop presented at the joint convention of the Kentucky Psychological Association, the Tennessee Psychological Association, and the Tennessee Association for Psychology in the Schools. Nashville, Tennessee, October 31, 1979.
3. Ramage, J., & Johnston, M. Government and professional relations report. National Association of School Psychologists, December, 1981.
4. Helton, G., & Kicklighter, R. Evaluating and responding to trends in school psychology. Paper presented at the joint convention of the Tennessee Psychological Association and the Tennessee Association for Psychology in the Schools. Memphis, Tennessee, October 17, 1980.
5. Roberts, L. Personal communication, July 8, 1981.
6. Miller, L. Personal communication, December 29, 1981.
7. Reschly, D. Comparisons of bias in assessment with conventional and pluralistic measures. Paper presented at the annual meeting of the Council for Exceptional Children, Kansas City, Missouri, 1978.
8. Kass, R., & O'Leary, K. The effects of experimental bias in field experimental settings. Paper presented at the Behavior Analysis in Education Symposium, University of Kansas, Lawrence, Kansas, April 9, 1970.
9. Harrison, P. Personal communication, May 17, 1982.

348

Suggested Readings

Note: The works listed here have not been cited in the text.

Chapter 1

Berke, J., & Moore, M. A developmental view of the current federal government role in elementary and secondary education. *Phi Delta Kappan,* 1982, *63,* 333–337.

Clark, D., & Amiot, M. The impact of the Reagan administration on federal education policy. *Phi Delta Kappan,* 1981, *63,* 258–262.

Glaser, R. The future of testing: A research agenda for cognitive psychology and psychometrics. *American Psychologist,* 1981, *36,* 923–936.

Glaser, R., & Bond, L. (Eds.). *Testing: Concepts, policy, practice, and research.* Special issue of *American Psychologist,* 1981, *36.*

Hanna, G., Bradley, F., & Holen, M. Estimating major sources of measurement error in individual intelligence scales: Taking our heads out of the sand. *Journal of School Psychology,* 1981, *19,* 370–376.

Hobbs, N. (Ed.). *Issues in the classification of children* (Vol. 1–2). San Francisco: Jossey-Bass, 1975.

Hohenshil, T., & Anderson, W. *School psychological services in secondary vocational education.* Blacksburg, Va.: Virginia Polytechnic Institute and State University, 1981.

Iannaccone, L. The Reagan presidency. *Journal of Learning Disabilities,* 1981, *14,* 55–59.

Lambert, N. (Ed.). *Special education assessment matrix.* Monterey, California: CTB/McGraw-Hill, 1981.

Maher, C. Time management training for providers of special services. *Exceptional Children,* 1982, *48,* 523–528.

Scarr, S. (Ed.). *Psychology and children: Current research and practice.* Special issue of *American Psychologist,* 1979, *34.*

Chapter 2

Bennett, R. Assessment of exceptional children: Guidelines for practice. *Diagnostique,* 1981, 7, 5 – 13.

Burgdorf, R., & Bersoff, D. *Equal educational opportunity for handicapped children.* Baltimore: P. H. Brookes, 1980.

Cross, L., & Goin, K. *Identifying handicapped children: A guide to casefinding, screening, diagnosis, assessment, and evaluation.* New York: Walker and Company, 1977.

Maher, C. Decision analysis: An approach for multidisciplinary teams in planning special service programs. *Journal of School Psychology,* 1981, *19,* 340 – 349.

Mopsik, S., & Agard, J. *An education handbook for parents of handicapped children.* Cambridge, Mass.: Alt Associates, 1980.

Reynolds, C. The fallacy of "two years below grade level for age" as a diagnostic criterion for reading disorders. *Journal of School Psychology,* 1981, *19,* 350 – 358.

Chapter 3

National Center for State Courts. *Student litigation: A compilation and analysis of civil cases involving students.* Williamsburg, Va.: National Center for State Courts.

Sattler, J. Intelligence tests on trial: An "interview" with Judges Robert F. Peckham and John E. Grady. *Journal of School Psychology,* 1981, *19,* 359 – 369.

Chapter 4

Mearig, J. *Working for children: Issues beyond professional guidelines.* San Francisco: Jossey-Bass, 1978.

Chapter 6

Reschly, D. (Ed.). SOMPA: A Symposium. *School Psychology Digest,* 1979, *8.*

Chapter 7

Mann, L. *On the trail of process.* New York: Grune & Stratton, 1979.

Chapter 8

Egner, A., & Cates, J. The Vermont consulting teacher program: Case presentation. In C. Parker (Ed.), *Psychological consultation: Helping teachers meet special needs.* Reston, Va.: Council for Exceptional Children, 1975.

Merkin, P., & Deno, S. *Data-based program modification.* Reston, Va.: Council for Exceptional Children, 1977.

Chapter 11

Gallagher, J. *Ecology of exceptional children*. San Francisco: Jossey-Bass, 1980.

Good, R., & Brophy, J. *Looking in classrooms* (2nd ed.). New York: Harper & Row, 1978.

Jackson, P. *Life in classrooms*. New York: Holt, Rinehart, & Winston, 1968.

Sarason, S. *The culture of the school and the problem of change* (2nd edition). Boston: Allyn and Bacon, 1982.

Index